Public Opinion in the Middle East

INDIANA SERIES IN MIDDLE EAST STUDIES

Mark Tessler, *general editor*

Public Opinion in the Middle East

Survey Research and the Political Orientations of Ordinary Citizens

MARK TESSLER

Indiana University Press
Bloomington and Indianapolis

This book is a publication of
Indiana University Press
601 North Morton Street
Bloomington, Indiana 47404-3797 USA

iupress.indiana.edu

Telephone orders	800-842-6796
Fax orders	812-855-7931
Orders by e-mail	iuporder@indiana.edu

♾ The paper used in this publication meets the minimum requirements of the American National Standard for Information Sciences—Permanence of Paper for Printed Library Materials, ANSI Z39.48-1992.

Manufactured in the United States of America

Library of Congress Cataloging-in-Publication Data

Tessler, Mark A.
    Public opinion in the Middle East : survey research and the political orientations of ordinary citizens / Mark Tessler.
       p. cm. — (Indiana series in Middle East studies)
    Includes bibliographical references and index.
    ISBN 978-0-253-35631-4 (cloth : alk. paper) — ISBN 978-0-253-22315-9 (pbk. : alk. paper) 1. Public opinion—Middle East. 2. Public opinion—Arab countries. 3. Social surveys—Middle East. 4. Social surveys—Arab countries. I. Title.
    HN656.Z9P88   2011
    306.20956'090511—dc22

                        2010045633

1 2 3 4 5   16 15 14 13 12 11

To Pat
and to my coauthors and all the students and colleagues whose
collaboration has helped to make this research possible

CONTENTS

ACKNOWLEDGMENTS

Full bibliographic citations and reprint information for all the articles in this volume are given below. Copyright information is included when requested by the publisher. Each coauthor has also given permission to reprint.

Mark Tessler and Patricia Freeman, "Regime Orientation and Participant Citizenship in Developing Countries: Hypotheses and a Test with Longitudinal Data from Tunisia," *Western Political Quarterly* 34 (December 1981): 479–98. Reprinted by permission of SAGE/SOCIETY.

Mark Tessler, "The Origins of Popular Support for Islamist Movements: A Political Economy Analysis," in John Entelis, ed., *Islam, Democracy, and the State in North Africa* (Bloomington: Indiana University Press, 1997).

Mark Tessler, "Islam and Democracy in the Middle East: The Impact of Religious Orientations on Attitudes toward Democracy in Four Arab Countries," *Comparative Politics* 34 (April 2002): 337–54. Reprinted by permission of City University of New York.

Mark Tessler, Carrie Konold, and Megan Reif, "Political Generations in Developing Countries: Evidence and Insights from Algeria," *Public Opinion Quarterly* 68 (summer 2004): 184–216. Reprinted by permission of Oxford University Press.

Amaney Jamal and Mark Tessler, "The Democracy Barometers: Attitudes in the Arab World," *Journal of Democracy* 19 (January 2008): 97–110; reprinted as "The Arab Aspiration for Democracy," in Larry Diamond and Marc Platner, eds., *How People View Democracy* (Baltimore, Md.: The Johns Hopkins University Press, 2008). Copyright © 2008 National Endowment for Democracy and The Johns Hopkins University Press, and reprinted by permission of The Johns Hopkins University Press.

Mark Tessler and Ebru Altinoglu, "Political Culture in Turkey: Connections among Attitudes toward Democracy, the Military, and Islam," *Democratization* 11 (March 2004): 22–51. Reprinted by permission of Taylor & Francis UK http://www.informaworld.com.

Mark Tessler, "Assessing the Influence of Religious Predispositions on Citizen Orientations Related to Governance and Democracy: Findings from Survey Research in Three Dissimilar Arab Societies." *Taiwan Journal of Democracy* 1(January 2006): 1–12. Reprinted by permission of *Taiwan Journal of Democracy*

Mark Tessler and Eleanor Gao, "Democracy and the Political Culture Orientations of Ordinary Citizens: A Typology for the Arab World and Perhaps Beyond," *International Social Science Journal* (UNESCO) 192 (2009): 197–207. Reprinted by permission of Wiley-Blackwell.

Mark Tessler and Ina Warriner, "Gender, Feminism, and Attitudes toward International Conflict: Exploring Relationships with Survey Data from the Middle East," *World Politics* 49 (January 1997): 250–81. Copyright © 1997 Trustees of Princeton University. Reprinted by permission of Cambridge University Press.

Mark Tessler and Jodi Nachtwey, "Islam and Attitudes toward International Conflict: Evidence from Survey Research in the Arab World," *Journal of Conflict Resolution* 42 (October 1998): 619–36. Reprinted by permission of SAGE/SOCIETY.

Mark Tessler, Jodi Nachtwey, and Audra Grant, "Further Tests of the Women and Peace Hypothesis: Evidence from Cross-National Survey Research in the Middle East," *International Studies Quarterly* 43 (1999): 519–31; reprinted in *International Security and Conflict,* ed. Bruce Russett (Aldershot, England: Ashgate, 2008). Reprinted by permission of Wiley-Blackwell.

Jodi Nachtwey and Mark Tessler, "The Political Economy of Attitudes toward Peace among Palestinians and Israelis," *Journal of Conflict Resolution* (March 2002): 260–85. Reprinted by permission of SAGE/SOCIETY.

Mark Tessler and Michael D.H. Robbins, "What Leads Some Ordinary Men and Women in Arab Countries to Approve of Terrorist Acts against the United States: Evidence from Survey Research in Algeria and Jordan," *Journal of Conflict Resolution* 51 (April 2007): 305–28. Reprinted by permission of SAGE/SOCIETY.

INTRODUCTION:
PUBLIC OPINION RESEARCH IN THE
ARAB AND MUSLIM MIDDLE EAST

The Missing Dimension

Until recently, the investigation of individual attitudes, values, and behavior patterns was the "missing dimension" in political science research dealing with the Arab world.[1] Such research was not completely absent, but it was limited to a very small number of American and Arab political scientists. It was also limited with respect to the countries where systematic survey research could be conducted, the degree to which representative national samples could be drawn, and the extent to which sensitive questions about politics could be asked.[2]

There are complaints about this situation going back to the 1970s. A major review of the scholarship on Arab society, published in 1976, called attention to the absence of systematic research on political attitudes and behavior patterns. The author, I. William Zartman, stated that "the critical mass of research [in the field of political behavior] has been done outside the Middle East" and "data generation and analysis in the region remain to be done."[3] A similar assessment was offered a few years later by Malcolm Kerr, another leading student of Arab politics. Writing in the introduction to *Political Behavior in the Arab States,* Kerr stated that much more research in which the individual is the unit of analysis was needed "to bring a healthier perspective to our understanding of Arab politics . . . and so that we may see it less as a reflection of formal cultural norms or contemporary world ideological currents and more as [the behavior] of ordinary individuals."[4]

Political scientist Michael Hudson echoed these concerns in the mid-1990s. In his contribution to a 1995 volume, *Liberalization and Democratization in the Arab World,* Hudson observed that "compared to other regions, empirical survey work on the Arab world is meager." Like Kerr, Hudson also noted that this encourages a "reductionist" approach to inquiry, one in which grand generalizations are advanced in the mistaken belief that citizen orientations can be explained and predicted from a knowledge of the "essential" attributes of Islamic or Arabic culture.[5] William Quandt, another prominent student of Arab politics, also wrote about the danger of accounts, and the misconceptions and stereotypes to which they can lead, that are not based on systematic and objective empirical research. Writing about the extensive civil violence in

Algeria during the 1990s, Quandt noted that people, including some Arabs, often ask "Why does Algeria have this deep crisis," and then answer their own question with statements like "The Algerians are violent people; they live in mountains. That is the way they have always been." Emphasizing the problematic nature of such explanations, Quandt wrote: "It is too easy to explain any country's problems by 'that's the way they are.'"[6]

Essentialist explanations are problematic not only because they assert that people hold certain views *because* they are Arabs and Muslims, but also, and even more fundamentally, because they assume that there *are* "Arab" and "Muslim" orientations. Such analyses ignore the very significant differences between Arab countries. Equally important, they also ignore the significant individual-level variation that exists within Arab countries, as within all countries; important differences associated with age, education, class, gender, ethnicity, residence, and more are, in effect, defined out of existence by essentialist characterizations or are at least deemed to have so little explanatory power as to be unworthy of attention. The antidote to such flawed reasoning resides in rigorous survey research, which offers an objective, empirical basis for determining not only the views held by Arabs and Muslims, or any population, but also the degree to which these views vary across important and identifiable population categories.

Beyond contributing to misinformation, and perhaps to myths and stereotypes, the absence of valid and reliable survey data has limited the contribution of insights about the Arab world to the less descriptive and more theoretical research agenda of contemporary political science. For example, the initiation of democratic transitions in many developing and post-communist countries in the 1980s and 1990s brought increased interest in the political attitudes and values of ordinary citizens. But while important generalizable insights emerged from survey research in Latin America, Sub-Saharan Africa, East Asia, and Eastern Europe, little was known either about the extent to which patterns observed elsewhere apply to Arab countries or, equally important, about whether evidence from the Arab world might contribute to a refinement of explanatory models.

Writing in this connection in 1999, political scientist Lisa Anderson discussed some of the topics and issues with respect to which research on the Arab world might inform, as well as be informed by, approaches and theories within the discipline of political science. Among the examples she discussed are accounting for individual-level variance in support of Islamist political movements and in conceptions of national identity. Further, although she also complained, like others, that there was too little rigorous survey research, Anderson went on to observe that "the limited survey research done in the Arab world has had disproportionately high payoffs, as both transient attitude shifts and more profound changes in conceptions of national identity have been revealed and verified."[7]

Emerging Opportunities

This situation is now changing. This reflects, in part, the training that graduate students in political science with an interest in the Middle East today receive with increasing frequency. Tension between the analytical perspectives of area studies and disciplinary social science, once significant with respect to the Middle East, has not disappeared but is becoming much less pronounced.[8] The importance of giving students solid grounding in both perspectives is not new in principle, but there does seem to have been an important change in practice, with doctoral students at major universities acquiring, and being expected to acquire, not only the substantive knowledge and linguistic skills necessary for the study of Arab politics and society but also competence in relevant bodies of disciplinary theory and in social science research methods, including quantitative methods.

An even more significant factor accounts for the changing situation, however. The most important explanation for the dearth of survey research in the Arab world is not a lack of interest on the part of political scientists or an absence of the training necessary to carry out such research. Nor is it, as is sometimes alleged, that ordinary citizens in the Arab world are overly deferential to political authority and hence do not have clear and independent views on salient political issues. The explanation lies, first and foremost, in the undemocratic character of most Arab countries, which frequently has made survey research impossible, or at least very difficult, and thus has discouraged scholars and students with an interest in Arab politics from selecting topics that require this kind of research. As explained in 1987 by political scientist Iliya Harik, political attitude surveys are possible "only under conditions of political freedom," and the most important explanation for the paucity of such surveys in the Arab world is that the "political climate for this type of research does not exist."[9] Another prominent Arab social scientist, Saad Eddin Ibrahim, made the same point. Basing his conclusion on surveys carried out in the 1980s under the auspices of the Center for Arab Unity Studies, Ibrahim reported that "the Arab political environment is extremely hostile to scientific field research and deeply suspicious of the motives of serious and objective inquiry."[10]

Harik and Ibrahim offered these observations in the 1980s, but the situation has changed significantly since that time. The Arab world still lags behind other world regions with respect to freedom and civil liberties. But there has been notable progress in some countries, and at present there are perhaps nine or ten in which it is possible to carry out systematic and objective political attitude surveys. Moreover, and equally important, the field is not being left to American or other foreign social scientists. There are a growing number of Arab scholars with the interest, training, and institutional support needed to carry out political attitude research, and these scholars are making important contributions. A good example is *Revisiting the Arab Street: Research from Within*, published in 2005 by the Center for Strategic Studies at the University of Jordan.[11] This volume presents findings from political attitude surveys in five Arab countries. Another important example is the work of the Ramallah-based Center for Policy and Survey Research, which has carried out more than one hundred polls among Palestinians in the West Bank and Gaza Strip since 1993.

Scholars in the Arab world frequently collaborate with their American counterparts, provide guidance to American doctoral students, and participate in training programs in the U.S. and elsewhere. For example, during the last five years the University of Michigan has brought more than 50 social scientists from seven different Arab countries to Ann Arbor for intensive summer programs in social science research methods. During the same period, Michigan faculty and graduate students have conducted survey research training workshops in eight Arab countries. More than 250 Arab scholars, analysts, and graduate students have participated in these workshops.

Also worthy of note is the extension to six Arab countries of the World Values Survey (WVS). The WVS is a global network of social scientists who have been surveying the social, cultural, and political orientations of ordinary men and women at five-year intervals since 1990.[12] Hundreds of scholarly articles and policy papers have been written using WVS data; and during the fourth wave of surveys, in 2005–2006, the WVS questionnaire was administered to national samples in more than eighty societies. The WVS was not carried out in a single Arab country during the first two waves of surveys. Since then, however, beginning with the third wave in 2000, the WVS has been conducted at least once, and in most cases twice, in Egypt, Morocco, Jordan, Algeria, Iraq, and Saudi Arabia, as well as Turkey and Iran, two non-Arab Muslim-majority countries in the Middle East. Moreover, several of the WVS directors, in collaboration with Arab and Muslim partners, have added to the standard survey instrument a number of questions pertaining to religion and other topics that increase the relevance of the WVS to Arab and Muslim publics.

Finally, the establishment of the Arab Barometer should be noted. The Barometer is a cross-national and collaborative project involving original survey research in a number of Arab countries.[13] The surveys focus on issues of governance and include a wide range of items pertaining to political conceptions and preferences, as well as to attitudes about Islam, the status of women, and international relations. The first wave of the Arab Barometer, carried out between 2006 and 2009, involved face-to-face interviews with large and nationally representative samples of ordinary men and women in Morocco, Algeria, Palestine, Jordan, Lebanon, Kuwait, Yemen and Bahrain. The data from these surveys have been placed in the public domain and may be obtained for secondary analysis from either the Arab Barometer website or the Inter-University Consortium for Political and Social Research at the University of Michigan. The second wave of the Arab Barometer, which at the time of this writing is scheduled to begin shortly, will include surveys in ten or more Arab countries.

The Arab Barometer represents an important evolution of the trends noted above. Its particular significance lies in three areas. First, it is a truly collaborative project, representing a partnership between American and Arab scholars but also, and equally important, between social scientists from all parts of the Arab world. The project was originally organized by Mark Tessler and Amaney Jamal, both of whom are American, but it has been governed from the beginning by a steering committee composed primarily of Arab scholars. The committee met in both the Arab world and the U.S. to design the interview schedule and make decisions about methodological and administrative issues. The University of Jordan's Center for Strategic Studies provided administrative support during the first wave and will continue to do so during the second wave.

Second, the Arab Barometer is genuinely comparative in two important ways. On the one hand, the administration of the same survey instrument in countries across the Arab world makes it possible to identify any normative trends or determinants of variance that are broadly applicable to the region, as well as any that are conditional on particular country-level attributes and experiences. Upon completion of the second wave, it will be possible to undertake analyses addressed to the description and explanation of variance over time as well as space, making temporal events another important category of determinants. Thus, even though less than half the Arab countries are being surveyed, the Arab Barometer represents a breakthrough in the kind of questions about Arab political attitudes and values that can be investigated.

In addition, the Arab Barometer is a member of the Global Barometer Survey project, a federation of five multi-country regional barometers that investigate public attitudes toward important and policy-relevant political, social, and economic issues.[14] Other members are the regional barometers of Latin America, Sub-Saharan Africa, Asia, and Eurasia. Roughly one-quarter of the items on the Arab Barometer interview schedule are also used by the other barometers, which makes possible the direct comparison of patterns observed in the Arab world and those observed in other world regions. This, in turn, encourages and facilitates the incorporation of insights about Arab publics into broader theoretical inquiries concerned with assessing generalizability and identifying conditionalities.[15]

Third, the objectives of the Arab Barometer, like several of the other regional barometers, are practical as well as scholarly. With respect to the latter, the goal is to shed light on the nature, locus, and determinants of citizen orientations relating to governance in general and democracy in particular. As noted earlier, survey research in other world regions has shown the importance for good governance and progress toward democracy of the political orientations held by ordinary men and women. But the Arab Barometer also seeks to make a more direct contribution. Through outreach and dissemination activities in which survey findings are presented, including press releases, media appearances, and public presentations, it attempts to give visibility and legitimacy to the expression of popular sentiments. The goal in this connection is to inform policy makers and other leaders, or at least to make it more difficult for officials to ignore or misrepresent the views of the people they claim to serve, and also to encourage ordinary citizens to reflect on the issues affecting their society and become more politically informed and engaged.

Four Decades of Public Opinion Research in the Middle East

These trends, past and present, describe the environment in which the research reported in this collection of articles was carried out. The early studies, beginning with a survey in Tunisia in 1966–67, were conducted in a restricted number of countries, and they also are based on smaller stratified quota samples rather than probability-based samples. The later articles use data from surveys in additional countries, are in most cases based on larger probability samples, and are frequently the result of projects involving collaboration with local scholars. Notably, two of the countries in which it was possible to conduct political attitude research during the earlier period, Tunisia and Egypt, have become more restrictive in recent years, making political research in these countries far more difficult at the present time. Some of the later surveys use data from the World Values Survey and the Arab Barometer, as well as data from cross-national surveys conducted by the author with funding from the National Science Foundation and the United States Institute of Peace.

Some of the research reports in this volume address disciplinary concerns, with specific hypotheses presented and tested; others examine issues that at a particular time have been central preoccupations in the Arab and

Muslim Middle East; and still others address both disciplinary concerns and issues with a prominent place on the region's political agenda. Examples of the former are articles that use data from Arab countries to investigate propositions from the social science literature on political generations and to test the hypothesis that women are more predisposed than men to favor peaceful means for the resolution of international conflicts. Examples of articles that focus on issues of particular importance in the Middle East are those that investigate attitudes toward political Islam and toward the Israeli-Palestinian conflict. The articles with roughly equal relevance for both the discipline and the region deal with democratization, political culture, and terrorism. In each case, the goal of the research is to identify the extent, locus, and determinants of relevant political attitudes and values.

Read in chronological order, the articles provide an overview of the Arab world's political evolution during the last three or four decades. With respect to domestic politics, the dominant political and ideological formula during the 1960s and much of the 1970s was based on Arab socialism, paternalistic modernization, sometimes including a secular orientation, and the mobilization strategy of the regimes in Egypt and a number of other Arab countries. Led by Gamal Abdul Nasser, and with leaders in Tunisia, Algeria, Syria, Iraq, and the Palestinian resistance movement on the same ideological page, despite important differences between them, this radical and modernist vision was championed by young people and many others in much of the Arab world.

By the 1980s, if not earlier, Arab publics had lost confidence in this political formula, and most of the political leaders who embraced it had either disappeared, lost influence, or abandoned their previous policies. Islamist movements became important political actors during this period, attracting adherents and placing on the Arab world's agenda the proposition that Islam is the solution to the region's problems.

Finally, the view that the Arab world needs to democratize had gained currency by the mid-1990s. Although an understanding of what constitutes genuine democracy is sometimes limited, and though support for democracy is not always accompanied by the embrace of democratic values, support has been growing for the view that an absence of mechanisms for holding governments accountable is a prominent reason for the region's political and other problems. With democracy and governance under the banner of Islam having emerged as the most influential political formulae in the region, questions about the relationship between the two visions, and about whether democracy and Islam are compatible, have inevitably arisen.

All these trends and the issues associated with them are investigated in the present collection of articles. Relevant attitudes, values, and behavior patterns are identified and measured, and analyses are then undertaken to shed light on the factors that lead different people to different views. Many of the essays, though not all, also provide a significant amount of substantive information about politics and society in the countries where the data were collected.

To a lesser extent, the evolution of regional and international issues is also reflected in this collection. Some articles investigate attitudes toward the Israeli-Palestinian conflict with data from surveys conducted before Israel and the Palestine Liberation Organization (PLO) signed a Declaration of Principles in 1993. Others use data from surveys conducted after the declaration was signed and a peace process had been established. The last piece in the collection deals with attitudes toward international terrorism, which became a dominant issue after the September 11, 2001, attacks by al-Qaeda on the United States and subsequent terrorist attacks in a number of European and Arab countries.

All the articles, including those based on data collected when opportunities for survey research in the Arab world were more limited, pay serious attention to issues of methodology. When probability samples were not possible, stratified quota samples were constructed in order to ensure that all relevant population categories were surveyed and to increase representativeness more generally. Measurement issues are addressed in all the surveys. Unidimensional and multidimensional scaling have frequently been employed to select items and construct indexes so as to ensure reliability and increase confidence in validity when measuring normative orientations. Laying a foundation for causal inference has been another concern. This is addressed most frequently through standard multivariate statistical analysis, which does not prove that relationships are causal but does significantly strengthen the case for inferring causality. Other techniques have been used in some cases, as in the construction of matched samples to assess the impact of regime change over time.

Another concern is the description and explanation of variance both within and across societies. With respect to the former, some studies disaggregate the data in order to determine whether patterns are different or similar across important population categories in the same country. Regarding the latter, some also compare findings from different countries, frequently employing the logic of either a "most similar systems" or a "most different systems" research design in order to assess generalizability or, alternatively, to generate hypotheses about the country-level attributes and experiences that account for cross-country differences.

A final point to note about these research reports is that most are coauthored. With one exception, my coauthors were doctoral students at the time the articles were written, and in almost all cases they played an important role in completing the analysis and preparing the article for publication. This should be noted not only so that these individuals are recognized as genuine coauthors, rather than as research assistants whose contributions were valuable but nonetheless limited, but also to demonstrate the value of collaboration between faculty and graduate students and the role this collaboration can play in graduate programs that attach importance to both regional and disciplinary expertise.

PART 1

Domestic Politics

Regime Orientation and Participant Citizenship in Developing Countries: Hypotheses and a Test with Longitudinal Data from Tunisia (1981)

Mark Tessler and Patricia K. Freeman

The concept of political culture has received much attention in recent years. Introduced by Gabriel Almond more than two decades ago, political culture is conceptualized as the summary value of citizens' orientations toward the political system and is important because it provides a link between the individual and the political system.[1] Accordingly, political culture is also an essential component of the broader construct of political development.[2] Social scientists do not always define political development in a consistent fashion, but there nevertheless is wide agreement that appropriate individual attitudes and values are essential for a society to develop politically. This view is found in early general studies of politics,[3] the literature on democratic political systems,[4] and studies of developing countries.[5] Relevant individual orientations include political interest and information, participation in civic affairs, identification with the national community and its political institutions, and the absence of political alienation. Following Inkeles, this collection of civic political orientations may be referred to as "participant citizenship."

Though not independent of other aspects of political development, participant citizenship is a central ingredient in the quest for political modernization, making it critical for students of nation-building to understand the conditions under which it does and does not come into existence. Yet there have been relatively few systematic and empirical studies aimed at discovering the determinants of participant citizenship in developing countries. Moreover, most of the studies which have been carried out are set in a "modernization" framework, inquiring about the effect on individual political orientations of life-style variables associated with social mobilization. Dissatisfaction with available knowledge about the determinants of participant citizenship in developing countries derives from (1) unresolved ambiguities associated with the results of modernization studies focusing on political attitude change and (2) a failure to investigate such questions from a broader perspective, wherein the principal theoretical problem is to account for variance on the dependent variable, political culture or participant citizenship, rather than to assess the impact on political orientations of a particular independent variable, such as level of social mobilization.

Findings from a number of studies suggest that positive and participatory political orientations tend to emerge as a result of urban residence, education, media consumption and other similar aspects of the process of individual-level change usually referred to as social mobilization.[6] The methodology of these studies is generally convincing and their findings are consistent with the results of studies carried out in developed polities. But other research suggests that civic orientations may not be absent among persons with little exposure to standard modernization-related stimuli,[7] that traditional life-styles and institutions can also be used to foster "modern" political orientations,[8] that social mobilization is sometimes associated with the maintenance or even the strengthening of traditional political values,[9] that social mobilization also sometimes produces political alienation or conflict,[10] and that the relationship between social mobilization and political attitudes is not the same for all dimensions of participant citizenship.[11]

The possibility of turning these contradictory findings to theoretical advantage lies in identifying the conditions under which comparable social change stimuli bear different relationships to the same political orientations, in discovering, in other words, specification variables in the relationship between social mobilization and political attitude change. Some of this work has already been done. For example, it has been convincingly argued that social mobilization is less likely to produce participant citizenship and more likely to produce political dissatisfaction and conflict to the extent that the society in which it occurs is either culturally heterogeneous[12] or lacking in well-developed political institutions.[13] On the other hand, few studies have rigorously tested hypotheses about the specification effects of these system-level properties, and many other political system attributes that may affect the relationship between social mobilization and participant citizenship have not even been the object of inquiries aimed at hypothesis formation. Among the attributes that may be relevant are ideological orientation, development strategy, institutional structure and regime effectiveness.

It is also probable that the relationship between social mobilization and political attitude change varies within systems, as a function of individual demographic characteristics. One possibility is sex-linked differences. While Inkeles has hypothesized that the causes and consequences of modernization are "broadly similar" for men and women,[14] others argue that social change has a differential impact upon the sexes, tending to generate more negative social and political attitudes among women than men.[15] Similar questions may be raised about differences associated with age, ethnicity, residence, political status and other personal attributes. As with system-level properties, however, inquiries about the locus of dissimilar relationships between social mobilization and political orientations in developing countries have been restricted to a few broadly defined conceptual categories, and empirical investigations that systematically test hypotheses incorporating specification variables are extremely rare.

Even more essential than discovering relevant specification variables is the need to broaden the range of independent variables whose role in the formation of individual political attitudes is examined and, in particular, to investigate the impact of government institutions and policies established for the explicit purpose of inculcating civic political orientations among the populace. The theoretical significance of such work derives from an expansion of the conceptual categories in which causes of participant citizenship are sought and from the fact that attention is focused on agents of political attitude change deemed important by Third World leaders themselves. Practical significance resides in the evaluation of specific political education programs and strategies and in the provision of more complete information to policy makers concerned with nation-building.

An approach to the study of participant citizenship in developing nations which includes these and other independent variables may be described as a "socialization" approach. As mentioned earlier, it is characterized by a focused attempt to account for variance on the dependent variable, rather than to assess the consequences of any particular independent variable. In addition, it recognizes that in developing as well as developed countries government institutions and programs are major instruments of political socialization, shaping and transmitting the national political culture. The utility of this approach to the study of political culture in developing nations has been argued before.[16] But, despite calls for research, few studies in developing nations have investigated the origins of participant citizenship or other political cultural orientations from this perspective, and there is as yet no coherent body of theory linking political attitude formation to the character or behavior of the government.

The preceding discussion has identified gaps in the study of participant citizenship and other political cultural orientations in developing nations and suggested some avenues for conceptual and empirical work in this area. The remainder of this paper is devoted to the development and testing of specific hypotheses with two objectives in mind. The first goal is to support general arguments about the need to examine specification effects in the relationship between social mobilization and participant citizenship and to consider government institutions and programs as independent variables in the study of political attitude change. The second goal is to make a specific contribution to the development of a body of theory accounting for variance with respect to participant citizenship in developing countries. The major concept organizing the discussion and analysis to follow is regime orientation, which will be linked as both an independent and a specification variable to participant citizenship.

Regime Orientation

Third World regimes giving heavy emphasis to planned programs of political education and resocialization are often referred to as mobilization regimes.[17] These regimes are usually characterized by centralized political structures, the foundation of which is a single mass-oriented political party supported by auxiliary organizations devoted to workers, youth, women and the like. Such regimes also usually possess an explicit and revolutionary ideology, what Apter calls a "consummatory" ideology in contradistinction to a more secular political philosophy. The function of this ideology is to define the nation's political culture and to guide those responsible for achieving its inculcation. Finally, mobilization regimes are noted for their efforts to foster political participation. Unlike Western societies, where political involvement is essentially voluntary, there is pressure upon citizens to take part in political life, the object being to assure involvement in institutions and programs charged with the dissemination of political values. Though sometimes at pains to disassociate themselves from international communism, mobilization regimes in the Third World usually adopt the political style of those socialist and communist countries where a national program stressing continuous political participation has been successful in creating a participant political culture obedient to regime directives.[18] Mobilization regimes are also frequently described as "radical," "revolutionary" and "transformation-oriented."[19]

Many African and Asian nations were led by mobilization regimes in the years following their independence. Among the best examples are Tanzania, Ghana, Tunisia, Guinea and Egypt. The leaders of these countries articulated in countless speeches the need to change popular political attitudes.[20] They also established national institutions and programs designed to foster modern and participant political orientations among their citizens, whom they regarded as largely parochial and apathetic in political outlook. Mayfield notes of Nasser's Egypt, for example, that "since the government is committed to the creation of a whole new set of attitudes, values and behavior norms, the Arab Socialist Union has been strengthened and reorganized to provide a mechanism for the initiation and maintenance of these new patterns of political culture."[21] Further, Mayfield describes not only the work of the party (ASU) in this regard, he discusses public information campaigns in the press, youth camps devoted to political indoctrination, and other similar programs of political socialization. The Egyptian situation is typical of mobilization regimes in this regard.

Other Third World regimes have opted for more laissez-faire strategies of development. Such regimes are usually described as "instrumental," "accommodationist," "pluralist" or "moderate" in orientation. Differences between radical and moderate states include dissimilar perspectives on foreign policy issues, and this has sometimes led Western analysts to discuss regime orientation from the viewpoint of international relations. But strategies of domestic development also sharply differentiate these regimes. Not all mobilization regimes have the ability to carry out their programs effectively. Also, political centralization and single-party rule are not uncommon in states without a mobilization orientation. Nevertheless, there are clear and potentially significant differences between radical and moderate states with respect to domestic policy. In the areas of concern to this paper, these differences center on the presence or absence of a revolutionary ideology and the extent to which existing institutional capacity is devoted to social engineering and the transformation of political culture.

The argument that differences in regime orientation may be of practical consequence comes from diverse sources. For example, Kwame Nkrumah, former President of Ghana, once confidently proposed that the relative merits of Ghana's mobilization orientation be assessed by comparing the country's progress after ten years of independence to that of Ivory Coast, Ghana's conservative neighbor to the West.[22] A more scholarly evaluation of the potential importance of regime orientation is to be found in the conclusions of a Social Science Research Council conference on "The Relevance of China's Development Experience for Other Developing Countries." Most participants agreed that China has accomplished more than most other Third World countries and that this is due primarily to the country's revolutionary social and political system.[23] A similar view is advanced by Myrdal. Basing his work primarily on India, Myrdal argues that development requires changes which can be accomplished only by an authoritarian and revolutionary political system,[24] although it should also be noted that not all students of India concur in this judgment.[25] These statements and studies are concerned principally with the relationship between the character of the political system and economic development. But they also call attention to a need to think systematically about the relevance of regime orientation and other political system attributes for political development, including political cultural change.

Regime orientation not only differs from country to country, it also differs over time within countries. In many Third World countries, a revolutionary ideology stressing political transformation has waned or even disappeared in recent years and national institutions charged with shaping political culture have either been allowed to atrophy or turned to other objectives.[26] Egypt, Ghana, Tunisia, Algeria and Indonesia are among the best examples of this. At the same time, there are also instances of movement in the opposite direction. In Libya, Zaire and Ethiopia, for example, a concern for articulating national values and for creating the political machinery to inculcate these values among the populace has expanded in the last decade. Thus, the concept of regime orientation calls attention to longitudinal as well as cross-sectional variation.

This discussion of regime orientation may now be tied to our earlier inquiry about participant citizenship. In an attempt to provide specific information about the determinants of participant citizenship in developing countries, and to illustrate more generally the importance of studying the impact of the political system on political culture, a number of hypotheses may be formulated and tested. These hypotheses consider participant citizenship as the dependent variable and posit regime orientation as either an independent or a specification variable. In formulating specific hypotheses, we have been guided by two broad and widely accepted propositions from the literature on political socialization in developed countries. The first is that the greater the exposure to agents of socialization teaching the same values, the greater the likelihood those values will be accepted. This proposition requires us to inquire about the relationship between official political education programs and other agents of socialization and to recognize the existence of intra-societal variations in socialization experiences. The second proposition is that values being taught are accepted most readily when they are compatible with an individual's perception of reality and with his own self-interest. In this connection, it is necessary to recognize that regimes are judged by what they do as well as by what they say and to ask whether citizens find particular messages believable and desirable. We may briefly elaborate on each of these considerations.

There is little congruence among agents of socialization in developing nations. State institutions seek to inculcate a national and participant political culture but socialization within the family often teaches localistic norms. Religious, ethnic and other associations may also reinforce parochial political orientations.[27] In view of this, it seems reasonable to propose that participant citizenship is generated to a greater degree in mobilization regimes. The political education programs found in these regimes are a significant counterweight to traditional agents of socialization. Also, many parochial associations are suppressed or co-opted in mobilization regimes, whereas in other regimes they tend to have greater autonomy and an important role in political communication and recruitment.

It is probable too that the impact of regime orientations on participant citizenship varies from one population category to another. On the one hand, it is possible that differences between persons residing in mobilization regimes and those in non-mobilization regimes are substantial among individuals with high levels of social mobilization but more limited among individuals with low levels of social mobilization. For one thing, individuals who are high in social mobilization are more likely than others to be involved in political activities,[28] and thus more exposed to any official political education programs that exist. In addition, since social mobilization involves extended schooling, exposure to communications media and other experiences that introduce new values, these persons may also be more receptive than others to new political norms proposed by the regime. For the same reason, regime-related differences in participant citizenship may also be greater among urban residents than among peasants or village dwellers of comparable socioeconomic status. On the other hand, since individuals high in social mobilization and residents of urban areas are more likely than others to have life-styles that produce participant citizenship, no matter what the character of the regime by which they are governed, differences associated with regime orientation may be greatest among individuals low in social mobilization and persons who do not inhabit urban centers. Only among such individuals are variations in regime orientation synonymous with the presence or absence of a strong counterweight to agents of socialization teaching parochial political values.

Efforts to inculcate participant citizenship are most likely to be successful in regimes perceived as effective and dedicated to the national welfare. Conversely, positive political values are unlikely to be accepted by citizens whose experience teaches them that the government is corrupt or inept. This point had been stressed by students of political socialization in Western countries[29] and there is evidence from developing countries of a relationship between system responsiveness and political support.[30] It may be argued as a general proposition that a tendency toward socialism and the redistribution of wealth, attributes usually associated with mobilization regimes, is more likely than a capitalistic development strategy to generate interest in politics and to inspire political trust and support. But perceptions of political reality vary and are influenced by individual self-interest. Indeed some studies suggest that positive political attitudes develop primarily in response to rewards and incentives.[31]

It seems obvious that persons with limited resources and opportunities are more likely than others to judge themselves favored by revolutionary development strategies. In addition, to the extent the traditional authority system has not brought prosperity or personal satisfaction to these individuals, they may welcome a new political hierarchy giving opportunities for patronage and social mobility. Thus mobilization regimes may be viewed most favorably by persons low in social mobilization and regime-related differences in participant citizenship may accordingly be greatest among such individuals. Again, however, the opposite can be argued. Persons high in social mobilization are undoubtedly aware that their skills and social position give them a significant advantage in utilizing and even controlling available political machinery, and thus they may see themselves as most advantaged in mobilization regimes. In another type of system, there would be fewer opportunities for political participation and mobility and many political institutions would be under the control of traditional elites.

Specific hypotheses may be derived from this discussion, some of which are mutually exclusive:

> *Hypothesis 1.* Levels of participant citizenship are higher in regimes with a mobilization orientation than in regimes with a pluralist orientation.
>
> Rationale: Exposure to agents of socialization teaching positive, participant and national political values is greater in mobilization regimes and such regimes are more likely than others to be viewed by individual citizens as contributing to their personal welfare.
>
> *Hypothesis 2a.* Differences in participant citizenship between persons living under mobilization regimes and those living under non-mobilization regimes are greater among individuals with high levels of social mobilization than among individuals with low levels of social mobilization.
>
> Rationale: Participation in the political institutions and programs of a mobilization regime is greatest among individuals high in social mobilization, making planned programs of political education most salient for these persons and giving them the greatest opportunity to utilize political institutions for personal advancement.
>
> *Hypothesis 2b.* Differences in participant citizenship between persons living under mobilization regimes and those living

under non-mobilization regimes are greater among individuals with low levels of social mobilization than among individuals with high levels of social mobilization.

Rationale: The relative importance of official programs of political education is greatest among those individuals who would otherwise be exposed little to national political norms. Individuals low in social mobilization are also more disadvantaged by the status quo than others and more dependent upon regime-directed political change to improve their situation.

Hypothesis 3a. Differences in participant citizenship between persons living under mobilization regimes and those living under non-mobilization regimes are greater among urban residents than among comparable residents of non-urban areas.

Rationale: Urban life introduces new cultural and economic values, making urban residents more receptive than others to the revolutionary political values being taught by mobilization regimes.

Hypothesis 3b: Differences in participant citizenship between persons living under mobilization regimes and those living under non-mobilization regimes are greater among residents of non-urban areas than among comparable residents of urban areas.

Rationale: Localistic and parochial values are stronger outside urban centers and hence the presence or absence of official programs of political education is of greater relative importance.

Hypotheses 2a and 2b also give rise to the general proposition that social mobilization is not related to participant citizenship in the same fashion in mobilization and non-mobilization regimes. Specifically:

Hypothesis 4a. The relationship between social mobilization and participant citizenship is more positive in mobilization regimes than in other regimes.

Hypothesis 4b. The relationship between social mobilization and participant citizenship is more negative in mobilization regimes than in other regimes.

Regime orientation is both an independent variable and a specification variable in the preceding hypotheses, the other non-dependent variables being social mobilization and residence. An independent relationship between regime orientation and participant citizenship is proposed, as are variations in this relationship specified by level of social mobilization and place of residence. In addition, differences in the relationship between social mobilization and participant citizenship specified by regime orientation are posited. Hypotheses 2a and 2b, 3a and 3b and 4a and 4b are of course mutually exclusive.

Methodology

The hypotheses proposed above will be tested with political attitude data collected in Tunisia at two points in time. Evidence from a single country can provide only a limited test of general propositions. Thus, additional investigation will be necessary to build confidence in any relationships discerned. Nevertheless, systematic data from a single country can provide a meaningful test of general hypotheses,[32] and Tunisia's recent history makes it a particularly appropriate setting for testing those set forth above. The character of the Tunisian regime changed in the late 1960s as a mobilization orientation was replaced by a laissez-faire political strategy. By comparing the political attitudes of Tunisians living under the two regimes, the impact of regime orientation on participant citizenship may be assessed.

Following independence in 1956, Tunisia was characterized by a high level of unplanned social change and the country was led by a regime firmly dedicated to political mobilization.[33] During this period urbanization increased dramatically, as did school enrollments at all levels. Major legal reforms were enacted and a public information campaign was launched in order to effect what the country's president, Habib Bourguiba, termed a national "psychological revolution." Regime objectives included women's emancipation and a reinterpretation of religious values. A national agricultural and commercial cooperative scheme was also initiated, its aim being to increase productivity and to distribute wealth more equitably. Finally, the Destourian Socialist Party (PSD) and its auxiliary organizations became effective instruments of mobilization and political education. Their local committees met regularly, involving the masses in political life and introducing new political values. Indeed, according to a leading student of the Arab world, more than any other Arab state Tunisia had "a durable political organization that articulated and implemented its ideology."[34]

In 1968 and 1969 the character of the Tunisian political system began to change and the regime lost most of its ideological zeal and institutional effectiveness.[35] The reasons for this need not be discussed at length here. Suffice it to say that struggles within the government and various external pressures resulted in the emergence of a new regime, one displaying little concern for the kind of planned political and cultural revolution that had previously been emphasized. This led one Tunisian scholar to conclude that the country was experiencing a "reactivation of tradition."[36] The experiment in cooperative socialism was also curtailed, with emphasis being placed instead on policies designed to maximize private investment and entrepreneurial activity. Finally, not only did the philosophy of the regime change, the institutional structure of the PSD was permitted to atrophy at the local level, making the party and its auxiliary organizations ineffective as vehicles for political education. Thus, in the view of another Tunisian scholar, the Tunisian elite lost its "dynamizing and liberating powers."[37]

Despite the change in regime orientation, social and economic change have remained intense in recent years and in some ways have even accelerated since 1969. Urbanization continues to grow, for example, and the important educational gains of the sixties have been maintained. Also, the economy has performed well of late, due in part to several good harvests and increasing revenues from tourism and petroleum. Thus, there is a substantial measure of comparability between Tunisia in the 1960s and the 1970s so far as aggregate social change is concerned, making it more reasonable to attribute any changes in popular political orientations to variations in regime orientation.

To determine whether there are political attitude differences associated with variations in regime orientation in Tunisia, we shall analyze survey data collected in that country in 1967 and 1973, the Tunisian regime having had a mobilization orientation in the first but not the second of these two years. Information about the 1967 survey is presented elsewhere in detail. Briefly, stratified quota samples of literate and regularly employed adults were drawn in Tunis and three smaller towns. Variables of sample stratification were education, income, and place of residence, and quotas were established to assure that all empirically existing combinations of these variables were included in the sample. Interviews were conducted with 283 persons. In 1973, a similar sample was selected, again using education and place of residence as variables of sample stratification and substituting occupational category for income to control for inflation between 1967 and 1973. Using the survey instrument employed in 1967, 349 persons were interviewed. Table 1.1 presents the distribution of respondents in each sample across categories of education, income, and place of residence. The table shows that respondents in each year are drawn from a wide range of social categories and, collectively, reflect much of the diversity of the Tunisian middle and working classes. They range from semiliterate agricultural workers in a remote oasis town to university-trained executives of national corporations in the capital.

The 1967 and 1973 samples are highly similar. But samples were not selected randomly and hence respondents may not be completely representative of the same population categories at different points in time. As a result, additional steps were taken to maximize comparability and to minimize

Table 1.1. Distribution of 1967 (N = 283) and 1973 (N = 349)
Respondents along Dimensions of Sample Stratification

	RESIDENTS OF TUNIS				RESIDENTS OF SMALLER TOWNS*			
Educational Level	University	High School	Intermediate	Primary	University	High School	Intermediate	Primary
1967 Sample								
Income per month:**								
<30 dinars	0	0	13	17	—	—	7	17
30–49 dinars	0	17	30	17	—	4	13	5
50–69 dinars	6	18	9	7	—	11	6	1
70–99 dinars	9	6	7	7	—	1	—	1
>100 dinars	23	18	13	0	—	—	—	—
1973 Sample								
Income per month:								
<30 dinars	1	6	10	20	—	—	4	12
30–49 dinars	3	8	40	24	—	—	12	14
50–69 dinars	5	10	35	12	—	1	7	1
70–99 dinars	21	10	20	7	—	2	4	5
>100 dinars	29	6	6	14	—	1	1	—

*In 1967 interviewing was done in Grombalia, Mahdia, and Nefta. In 1973 it was done in Nabeul, Ksar Hillal, and Houmt Souk. All six towns had a population of less than fifteen thousand when surveyed. In each year, one of the three towns selected was from, respectively, the northern part of the country near Tunis, the Sahel, and the southern part of the country.

**Only four income categories were employed when selecting respondents in 1967. The additional category is provided here to maximize descriptive information about the sample ultimately selected and to facilitate comparisons with the 1973 sample. Income data from the 1973 sample are similarly provided for descriptive purposes. As reported in the text, occupation rather than income was used in the actual construction of the sample, as a control for inflation between 1967 and 1973. On average, incomes were 25 percent higher in 1973 than in 1967.

extraneous variance and the possibility of multi-colinearity when making comparisons between 1967 and 1973. A subsample of pairs of matched respondents was selected by matching each respondent from the 1967 survey to an individual with similar characteristics from the 1973 survey, and respondents who could not be paired in this way were excluded from further analysis. To constitute a matched pair, respondents from the two samples had to be of the same sex and highly similar with respect to age, educational level, income (adjusted for inflation) and place of residence. In cases where a respondent from one year could be matched with equal accuracy to two or more respondents from the other year, selections were made on a random basis. Two hundred and eleven matched pairs were formed, and it should be noted that these respondents closely approximate the original samples in their distribution on variables of sample stratification. In the present analysis only 184 of these matched pairs will be employed, the eliminated cases being female respondents. Substantial differences have been found in the patterns of attitude change among women and men, and female respondents are thus being analyzed in a separate research report focusing on a slightly different set of theoretical issues.[38]

These longitudinal data are the basis of a quasi-experimental research design with which we shall test the hypotheses under investigation.[39] Measures of the dependent variable at Time 1 and Time 2 can be contrasted, there having occurred in the interim a change in the independent variable equivalent to an experimental stimulus. Obviously, not all extraneous variance is eliminated, forcing us to acknowledge limitations on internal as well as external validity and indicating again the need for replication. Nevertheless, many important factors are held constant. Social and cultural differences are controlled because comparisons involve the same society at two relatively close points in time. Also, as mentioned, aggregate levels of social mobilization are about the same in 1967 and 1973. This is particularly important given the possibility that social mobilization affects political attitudes. Finally, since comparisons are based on carefully matched subsets of respondents, extraneous variance associated with individual attributes and the related danger of the ecological fallacy are held to a minimum. Thus, in sum, it is reasonable to infer that a significant proportion of any variation in the political attitude and behavior patterns of individuals surveyed in 1967 and 1973 is due to the change in regime orientation that occurred during this period.

Participant citizenship is the dependent variable in the present study and attitudes relating to participant citizenship have been measured by five items included in an identical fashion on the 1967 and the 1973 survey instrument. These items, which are listed below, deal respectively with political participation, political information, political efficacy and political trust, basic dimensions of participant citizenship as defined earlier in this paper. Information on procedures used to design and administer the survey instrument has been presented in detail elsewhere and testifies to item validity and reliability and to the absence of interviewer bias and other forms of response set. Briefly, a large number of standard survey techniques were incorporated into the research methodology in an attempt to minimize problems of measurement, and extended ex-post-facto analysis, based principally but not exclusively on unidimensional and multidimensional scaling, was undertaken to evaluate measures and select the most satisfactory elements from a large battery of items.[40] In addition, an earlier analysis of political attitude data from the 1967 survey used two different tests of construct validity and found the items to be accurate measures.[41] Finally, it should be noted that the senior author had resided in Tunisia for several years prior to undertaking this research, that local social scientists contributed to the initial preparation of the survey instrument, that extensive pretesting was carried out to make sure that the content of items and responses was understood by both respondents and the researcher, and that interviewers took elaborate precautions to put respondents at ease and assure them of anonymity.[42] Thus, despite the many pitfalls of survey research in developing countries,[43] we are confident that the items are satisfactory measures of at least some key dimensions of participant citizenship in Tunisia. Following each item, given in parentheses, is the response code indicating a positive association with the concept.

1. *Political Participation:* What are the groups of which you are a member? Do you have any responsibilities in these groups? (An active member of at least one political group)

2. *Political Information:* Identify the following four individuals. (At least three out of four prominent political figures correctly identified)

3. *Political Efficacy:* Government and politics are often so complicated that persons like yourself cannot understand what is happening. (Disagree)

4. *Political Efficacy:* People like yourself have little ability to influence the affairs of government. (Disagree)

5. *Political Trust:* The government does not care much about people like yourself. (Disagree)

In addition to regime orientation, other non-dependent variables in our hypotheses are residence and level of social mobilization. Variation associated with residence is examined by comparing residents of Tunis to those of a series of small towns, all of which have fewer than 15,000 inhabitants. Level of social mobilization is operationalized in terms of education and income

Figure 1.1. Distribution of Education and Income Used to
Operationalize Level of Social Mobilization

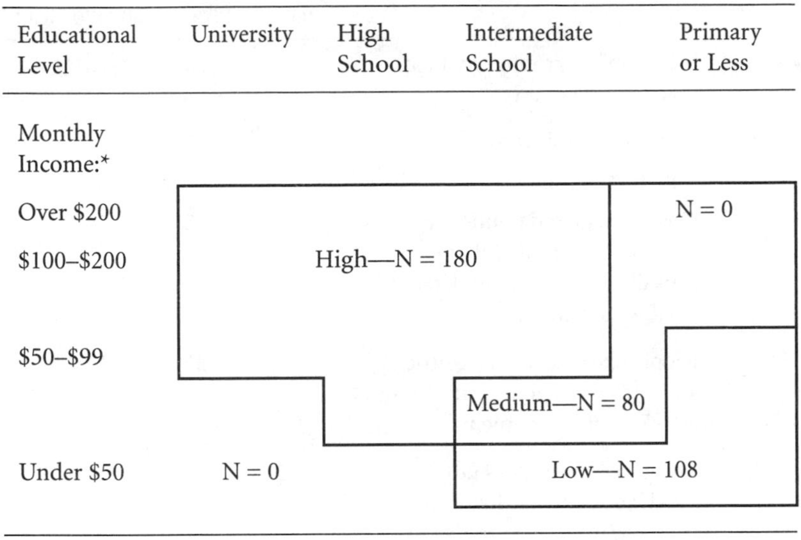

Educational Level	University	High School	Intermediate School	Primary or Less

Monthly
Income:*

Over $200   N = 0

$100–$200   High—N = 180

$50–$99

                                              Medium—N = 80

Under $50   N = 0   Low—N = 108

*Income of respondent from 1967 survey. In 1967, U.S.$1.00 equaled about .5 Tunisian dinars.

levels, the two variables being cross-tabulated and the resultant distribution trichotomized as shown in Figure 1.1. The validity of these indicators should be clear on their face, but it may also be noted that analysis of the 1967 data reveals that education and income taken in combination are associated with a large number of life-style variables, including foreign travel, media consumption and the like, and several psychological attributes, including personal and social efficacy.[44]

Findings

Hypothesis 1 proposes that levels of participant citizenship are higher in regimes with a mobilization orientation than in non-mobilization regimes. To test this hypothesis, the aggregated responses of matched pairs from the 1967 and the 1973 samples are compared in Table 1.2. The table gives the percentage of respondents answering each item in a fashion indicative of participant citizenship in each year and it shows the difference between the two figures for each item. As can be seen, levels of participant citizenship were higher in 1967, when the Tunisian regime was oriented toward political mobilization, than in 1973, when the regime had a more conservative

Table 1.2. Percentage of Matched Pairs Giving a Response
Indicating Participant Citizenship

ITEM		1967	1973	DIFFERENCE
1.	What are the groups of which you are a member?	19	1	−18***
2.	Identify the following individuals.	76	45	−31***
3.	Government and politics are often so complicated that persons like you cannot understand what is happening.	56	42	−14***
4.	People like yourself have little ability to influence the affairs and activities of government.	52	37	−15***
5.	The government does not care much about people like yourself.	63	38	−25***

***Statistically significant at the .01 level.*

political philosophy. The difference is statistically significant at the .01 level in every instance. Thus, on the basis of our data, Hypothesis 1 is confirmed.

Hypotheses 2a and 2b posit dissimilar relationships between participant citizenship and regime orientation as a function of level of social mobilization. One of these propositions argues that the relationship will be stronger among individuals with high levels of social mobilization and the other suggests that differences in participant citizenship associated with regime orientation are greater among persons low in social mobilization. The data presented in Table 1.3 may be used to test these hypotheses, and the table shows that for all five items differences associated with regime orientation vary as a function of social mobilization to a statistically significant degree. However, the direction of the difference is not the same in every instance. For the items pertaining to political participation and political information, it is among respondents high in social mobilization that differences between 1967 and 1973 are greatest. Thus Hypothesis 2a is confirmed in these two instances. For the remaining three items, pertaining to political efficacy and political trust, differences between 1967 and 1973 are greatest among respondents low in social mobilization. In these instances, Hypothesis 2b is thus confirmed. As mentioned, there are no instances when neither Hypothesis 2a nor Hypothesis 2b is confirmed.

Table 1.3. Difference between 1967 and 1973 in Percentage of Matched Pairs Classified by Level of Social Mobilization Giving a Response Indicating Participant Citizenship

ITEM		LEVEL OF SOCIAL MOBILIZATION		
		HIGH *(N = 180)*	*MEDIUM* *(N = 80)*	*LOW* *(N = 108)*
1.	What are the groups of which you are a member?	−27	−15	−7**
2.	Identify the following individuals.	−41	−32	−14***
3.	Government and politics are often so complicated that persons like yourself cannot understand what is happening.	−3	−12	−32**
4.	People like you have little ability to influence the affairs and activities of government.	+1	−25	−34**
5.	The government does not care much about people like yourself.	−12	−15	−52***

**Statistically significant at .02 level.
***Statistically significant at .01 level.

To make sense of the fact that both Hypothesis 2a and Hypothesis 2b are confirmed in specific instances, we may recall that differing dimensions of political culture and participant citizenship may relate to social mobilization in dissimilar ways.[45] The findings presented in Table 1.3 are another example of this, suggesting that specification effects associated with social mobilization may also vary according to the particular aspect of participant citizenship being examined. Moreover, there are conceptual similarities underlying the items lending support to hypotheses 2a and 2b respectively, suggesting the possibility of a theoretical formulation that subsumes both hypotheses and that posits dimension of participant citizenship as an additional specification variable. Our measures of political participation and political information are both behavioral items, relating to the performance of respondents and involving factual inquires about what they do and know so far as politics is concerned. We may characterize these items as pertaining to individual political involvement. Items focusing on political efficacy and trust, on the other hand, are more evaluative and pertain primarily to the regime rather than to respondents themselves. Naturally respondent competence *vis-à-vis* the regime is involved, but these items are distinct from those focusing on participation and information in that they call for an assessment of the regime. These items may be characterized as pertaining to regime evaluation. Thus, recalling from Hypothesis 1 that there is a positive association between participant citizenship and the presence of a mobilization orientation, we may restate our findings about hypotheses 2a and 2b in terms of the following more general theoretical formulation:

> Differences in political involvement associated with regime orientation are greatest among persons high in social mobilization and differences in regime evaluation associated with regime orientation are greatest among persons low in social mobilization.

These findings make conceptual as well as empirical sense since persons high in social mobilization are better prepared to take advantage of the increased opportunities for political participation available under a mobilization regime and since individuals low in social mobilization are more likely to favor government programs emphasizing political mobilization and resource redistribution.

Hypotheses 3a and 3b propose that differences in participant citizenship associated with regime orientation vary as a function of residence. Hypothesis 3a suggests that these differences are greatest among urban residents and Hypothesis 3b suggests that they are greatest among non-urban residents. These propositions are tested with data presented in Table 1.4, and the table offers clear evidence in support of Hypothesis 3b. On all five items, the percentage of individuals giving responses indicative of participant citizenship declined more from 1967 to 1973 among residents of smaller towns than among residents of the capital city of Tunis. Differences range from 10 percent to 29 percent and are statistically significant at the .01 or .02 level in four of the five cases.

The last two hypotheses, 4a and 4b, may be tested with data presented in Table 1.5. It will be recalled that these hypotheses propose variations in the relationship between social mobilization and participant citizenship as a function of regime orientation, and the table clearly shows the presence of specification effects associated with the latter variable. Two kinds of patterns may be noted. First, the data suggest that a strong relationship between social mobilization and participant citizenship is more likely to exist in mobilization regimes than in non-mobilization regimes. In the case at hand, the observed relationship between these variables is statistically significant in four out of five instances in 1967 and in only one out of five instances in

1973. Second, the direction of the relationship between social mobilization and participant citizenship varies according to the particular dimension of participant citizenship being considered, and it also varies, for each single dimension, as a function of regime orientation. In 1967, when Tunisia was governed by a mobilization regime, there was a positive association between participant citizenship and social mobilization for the behavioral items pertaining to individual political involvement. In the same year, items pertaining to regime evaluation involved a negative association between these variables in two out of three cases, there being no significant relationship at all in the third instance. In 1973, by contrast, when the Tunisian regime was not characterized by a mobilization orientation, neither of the items pertaining to political involvement was related to social mobilization in a meaningful way and the items pertaining to regime evaluation were positively associated with social mobilization. In the latter instance, the observed relationship was statistically significant in one case and close to the minimum level of statistical significance in the other two cases. The following general formulation summarizes these findings:

> Personal political involvement is positively related to social mobilization in regimes with a mobilization orientation and it is unrelated to social mobilization in regimes without such an orientation; regime evaluation is negatively related to social mobilization in regimes with a mobilization orientation and it is positively related to social mobilization in regimes without such an orientation.

For the reasons stated with respect to Hypotheses 2a and 2b, these findings again make conceptual as well as empirical sense.

Discussion and Conclusion

These findings and their significance may be discussed from three points of view. The first is concerned with gaps in our general knowledge about the determinants of participant citizenship and other dimensions of political culture in developing countries. The second concerns the role of government institutions and policies in the formation of political attitudes in developing countries. The third focuses on socialization processes and the reasons that individuals respond as they do to particular political stimuli.

Studies in developing countries have examined the impact of social mobilization on participant citizenship but have not produced an accepted body of theory linking the two concepts. The present study argues that this is primarily because the relationship between social mobilization and participant citizenship can only be properly understood in the context of a conceptual framework that incorporates additional specification variables.

Table 1.4. Difference between 1967 and 1973 in
Percentage of Matched Pairs Classified by Residence
Giving a Response Indicating Participant Citizenship

ITEM		RESIDENCE	
		URBAN (N = 130)	NON-URBAN (N = 58)
1.	What are the groups of which you are a member?	−2	−28**
2.	Identify the following individuals.	−18	−28
3.	Government and politics are often so complicated that persons like yourself cannot understand what is happening.	−17	−37*
4.	People like yourself have little ability to influence the affairs and activities of government.	−21	−50**
5.	The government does not care much about people like yourself.	−28	−54**

Note: Given that few non-urban residents have high levels of social mobilization, only respondents with low and medium levels of social mobilization are included in the analysis. All urban residents are from Tunis. Non-urban residents are from three small towns.

**Statistically significant at .01 level.*

Statistically significant at .02 level.

We earlier contended that such variables include personal attributes, such as sex, age, and political status, and system-level properties, such as regime orientation and cultural pluralism. We have also examined some possible relationships with data from Tunisia and found that (1) different dimensions of participant citizenship bear dissimilar relationships to social mobilization and (2) regime orientation in turn affects the way that social mobilization relates to these dimensions. These findings support our conviction that formulating and testing hypotheses which account for variations in the relationship between social mobilization and participant citizenship is an important avenue for future research.

The absence of information about how the character and performance of the political system affect political culture has been lamented by a number of scholars concerned with developing countries. The present study has responded to their calls for research in this area and has investigated the

Table 1.5. Percentage of Matched Pairs Classified by
Level of Social Mobilization Giving a Response
Indicating Participant Citizenship in 1967 and in 1973

ITEM			LEVEL OF SOCIAL MOBILIZATION		
			HIGH (N = 180)	MEDIUM (N = 80)	LOW (N = 108)
1.	What are the groups of which you are a member?	1967 1973	27 0	15 0	9* 2
2.	Identify the following individuals.	1967 1973	89 48	66 34	62*** 48
3.	Government and politics are often so complicated that persons like yourself cannot understand what is happening.	1967 1973	56 53	52 40	60 28***
4.	People like yourself have little ability to influence the affairs and activities of government.	1967 1973	41 42	63 38	63** 29
5.	The government does not care much about people like yourself.	1967 1973	55 43	53 38	84*** 32

***Statistically significant at the .01 level.*
**Statistically significant. at the .02 level.*
Statistically significant. at the .05 level.

impact of one important political system attribute on a salient dimension of political culture. Moreover, it has shown that the former does affect the latter, demonstrating the utility of the kind of research that has been urged.

Finally, our findings suggest that under different conditions political system variables bear dissimilar relationships to the same political orientations. In the present instance, the impact of regime orientation on participant citizenship was found to vary as a function of individual levels of social mobilization, which are more or less synonymous with class, and as a function of residence patterns. These latter findings suggest that to account for political cultural variations in developing countries it is necessary not only to consider political system attributes as independent variables but also, as in the case of social mobilization, to develop propositions specifying in conceptual terms the locus of particular bivariate relationships.

The preceding discussion highlights some general parameters of a conceptual framework for investigating determinants of political culture in developing nations. This framework requires looking at both individual- and system-level properties and examining each as specification as well as independent variables. It also requires investigating dissimilar relationships between these variables and individual dimensions and subdimensions of political culture.

The findings reported in this paper not only suggest avenues for future research, they also constitute a specific contribution to the development of bodies of theory concerned with the consequences of regime orientation and the determinants of participant citizenship in Third World countries. In the first connection, we have found in Tunisia that the presence of a mobilization orientation is associated with increased participant citizenship generally, particularly among residents of non-urban areas, and with especially large increases in (a) political participation and political knowledge among individuals high in social mobilization and (b) political efficacy and political trust among persons low in social mobilization. Thus, to the extent these findings are generalizable, mobilization regimes will tend to have, in comparison to non-mobilization regimes, more civic political orientations, smaller political cultural differences between urban and non-urban areas, greater differences in political involvement associated with individual levels of social mobilization, and smaller differences in regime evaluation associated with individual social mobilization. It is beyond the scope of this paper to speculate about the broader implications of these differences in the nature and distribution of political orientations. Nevertheless, given that regime orientation appears to affect at least some important dimensions of political culture, and since political culture in turn influences the overall character and performance of the political system, a country's decision to pursue one or another development strategy is not an academic decision of interest only to intellectuals and ideologues. It rather represents the initiation of a series of political stimuli that significantly affect politics and social life.

Our findings also contribute to the development of theory linking participant citizenship in developing countries to attributes of a political system and to experiences and circumstances of individual citizens. Participant citizenship tends to increase when a national regime stresses and provides opportunities for individual political involvement, when it works actively to inculcate civic political values among the populace, and when it is viewed as standing for a relatively egalitarian distribution of resources. This collection of regime policies and programs, constituting what we have referred to as a mobilization orientation, is particularly critical among citizens who do not reside in urban centers, probably because in these areas regime orientation tends to be synonymous with the presence or absence of agents of socialization teaching non-traditional political orientations. It is also particularly critical for two subdimensions of participant citizenship, political efficacy and trust, among persons low in social mobilization. This is probably because these individuals are similarly less exposed than others to experiences that weaken traditional political values and also because they stand to gain more than others from the redistribution of wealth that regime policies portend. Finally, a mobilization orientation is especially critical for two other subdimensions of participant citizenship, political participation and political information, among persons high in social mobilization. The reason for this is probably that these individuals are more qualified and motivated than others to take advantage of the expanded opportunities for political involvement that exist in mobilization regimes.

Participant citizenship also tends to be strongly related to social mobilization, reminding us that individual- as well as system-level variables are important determinants of political culture. Social mobilization increases political participation and political information in mobilization regimes, where, as mentioned, opportunities for political involvement are greater and where the government more actively disseminates information about itself. Social mobilization also increases political efficacy and political trust, but only in non-mobilization regimes. This is probably because the middle class and elite view themselves as most advantaged by government policies in such regimes. In mobilization regimes, on the other hand, social mobilization is negatively associated with political efficacy and political trust, probably because those who are disadvantaged see themselves as benefiting most from the government's political philosophy. These observations by no means provide a complete basis for explaining and predicting variations in the locus and extent of participant citizenship in developing countries. But they do make a partial and, we hope, significant contribution toward answering the more general questions about determinants of participant citizenship that have been raised.

We conclude with a word about the logic underlying our hypotheses, which will bring us back to our concern with directions for future research. Two kinds of reasons have been advanced for the relationships considered in this study, both being derived from socialization research. First, our hypotheses reflect an assumption that the greater the exposure to agents of socialization teaching the same values, the greater the likelihood that these values will be accepted. Second, our hypotheses also assume that values being taught will be accepted most readily when they are believable and compatible with an individual's self-interest. Having found evidence for hypotheses based on these assumptions, we would conclude that each will probably be helpful in developing additional propositions.

It would be useful to assess the relative importance of these two assumptions as they apply to the study of participant citizenship in developing countries. Unfortunately, however, this is beyond the capability of the present study. Even where competing hypotheses were advanced, findings in favor of one or another do not resolve the matter. For example, a mobilization orientation increases political efficacy and trust disproportionately among persons low in social mobilization. But is this because such individuals are otherwise relatively unexposed to agents of socialization teaching national and civic political values, is it because they are more favored in regimes with a mobilization orientation than in other regimes, or do both explanations apply with equal force? Nevertheless, while additional research is needed to answer such questions, our own investigation does suggest that these assumptions can shed light on the question of why particular stimuli produce variations in political culture in developing nations, and for this reason they will be useful points of departure for deducing from the kind of broad conceptual framework previously set forth additional testable propositions.

CHAPTER 2

The Origins of Popular Support for Islamist Movements: A Political Economy Analysis (1997)

Mark Tessler

This chapter addresses the reasons there has been growing popular support for Islamist movements in many countries of the Middle East. It argues that the origins of this support are to be found primarily in the political and economic circumstances of these countries rather than in the religious and cultural traditions of their inhabitants. The analysis stands in opposition to the assessments offered by Islamist leaders themselves, who usually insist that popular support for their movements derives principally from the religious faith of the Arab masses.

The central thesis of this political economy analysis is reflected in the following statement of a young Algerian, who was asked in June 1990 why he had supported the Islamic Salvation Front (FIS) in the local and regional elections being held at that time: "In this country, if you are a young man ... you have only four choices: you can remain unemployed and celibate because there are no jobs and no apartments to live in; you can work in the black market and risk being arrested; you can try to emigrate to France to sweep the streets of Paris or Marseilles; or you can join the FIS and vote for Islam."[1]

In developing the argument that support for Islamist movements derives primarily from economic and political circumstances, this chapter will devote most of its attention to Algeria, Tunisia, and Morocco, although some information about the other Arab countries will be presented as well. The chapter will also present original public opinion data from Egypt, and comparative data from Kuwait, in order to shed additional light on the nature and determinants of relevant popular attitudes. These data are presented in the text and discussed more fully in the appendix to this chapter.

The Immediate Causes of Popular Discontent

As suggested by the young Algerian quoted above, the government in Algiers has for some time been unable to create jobs on the scale needed to accommodate the country's expanding population. While more than three hundred thousand young men and women seek entry into the labor force each year, job creation lags, having declined by one-third in 1991 alone, according to a report published the following year. As a result, according to the same study, "one of the few ways out for many is to eke out a living as a small-time black market entrepreneur." These *trabendistes,* as they are called, fly between Algiers and Spanish coastal cities "loaded down with recorded tapes, jeans, auto parts, and anything else scarce and portable enough to make the trip worthwhile."[2]

The situation is similar in other North African countries. In Morocco, for example, a household survey carried out in December 1984 by the semi-official *Le Matin du Sahara* reported that urban unemployment stood at 18.4 percent, with 44.9 percent of those having jobs working as unskilled or semi-skilled laborers, and with many of these workers employed only on an irregular basis. These figures were also cited by an economic report published in 1987, which stated that they underline the severity of the urban employment problem, particularly among the young, and concluded that "it is unlikely these proportions have altered much since 1984."[3] Further, the pattern has remained about the same or, if anything, has worsened since the mid-1980s.[4] Urban unemployment is in the 20–25 percent range, and among urban young men under the age of thirty, especially those with limited schooling, estimates regularly range as high as 40 percent. Writing of Morocco in 1994, a knowledgeable analyst thus reports that "underemployment is endemic and millions are dependent on the huge informal sector for their income."[5]

Well-educated North Africans are increasingly affected, too, as the situation continues to deteriorate or at least fails to improve. Indeed, unemployed Moroccan university graduates formed an association in 1992, the Association des Diplômés Chômeurs, in an effort to call attention to their plight. A recent doctoral thesis dealing with the attitudes of young Moroccans reports in this connection that "education increasingly leads to unemployment" and that many young men and women "attach little importance to their diplomas." Indicative of this view are the bitter comments of a number of informants who insisted that "a diploma has absolutely no value in Morocco" and that "after graduation it will be a nightmare."[6]

Education is a second area where demands are unmet and expectations unfulfilled. Even though schooling no longer carries a guarantee of secure employment, millions of young North Africans seek an education in the hope of achieving a better life, and a large proportion of these are disappointed *before* completing their studies. Educational opportunities have expanded dramatically at the primary school level, but this has not been matched by comparable growth at higher levels, requiring many young men and women to drop out after only six or eight years. The previously mentioned *Matin du Sahara* investigation reported, for example, that 79.3 percent of the active urban population was either illiterate or had received only a primary school education. As late as 1986, only one-third of Moroccan youth between the ages of twelve and eighteen were attending school, and in Tunisia the figure was only 39 percent. With even high school and university graduates having difficulty finding suitable jobs, the prospects are particularly dim for those with only primary schooling.

Writing in 1988, an Algerian scholar reported in this connection that "in spite of democratization, the new educational system turned out to be highly selective,"[7] and he presented statistics from the late 1970s to illustrate his point. He noted that for every one hundred pupils enrolled in primary school, twenty dropped out before the sixth year and another forty failed to pass the examination for a primary education certificate, which meant they were not allowed to stay in school. Of the remaining forty, only eighteen were admitted to high school, of whom sixteen were subsequently candidates for the *baccalaureate* examination. And with a pass rate of 25 percent for 1978–79, this meant that "only 4 pupils out of 100 would have a chance to go to the university."

Inadequate housing is yet another source of discontent. A study in Algiers in the mid-1980s documented the problem and offered striking illustrations.[8] For example, "colonial houses in the center of town have been converted into groups of dwellings of one or two rooms, each rented to a whole family and connected to a central court." An entire family may have as little as eighteen square meters, and five or more families may share a court with one water tap and one toilet. In addition:

> Shared houses are not found only in the colonial center of town. . . . The low income houses, planned for one family, had two rooms, a small kitchen, a toilet and a court. Most of them now have electricity but still no private water tap. The rural exodus filled them up quickly, however, and soon there were two families in each house, one in each room. More immigrants came, more children were born . . . the [two-room] houses now often contain four families.

A more recent study indicates that the situation has become even worse during the 1990s. The author concludes that "the housing problem in Algeria has become quasi-insoluble," adding that "in spite of ambitious plans, never achieved, the lack [of adequate housing] has not ceased to become more serious."[9]

The demographic pressures contributing to these problems are well known. The population of many Arab countries is growing by as much as 3 percent a year and in some cases even more. Moreover, this not only increases the aggregate demand for goods and services, but it also gives rise to an increasingly skewed age distribution and makes it particularly difficult to meet the needs of young people. In the early and mid-1980s, for example, over 50 percent of North Africa's population was under the age of twenty, over 60 percent was under twenty-five, and almost 70 percent was under thirty. More recently, some decline in fertility has begun to reduce the proportion of the population under the age of fifteen. This is having little effect in the short run, however, as the fifteen to twenty-four age group, which includes most entrants into the labor force, continues to swell.[10] In addition, a continuing exodus from the countryside has intensified the pressure in urban areas. In Morocco, for example, the urban population grew by 61 percent during the 1970s and early 1980s, in contrast to only 17 percent growth in rural areas. Two-thirds of all Moroccans now live in cities, whereas only one-fifth did so in 1965. In Tunisia, the rate of population growth in the capital was more than twice the national average from the mid-1960s to the mid-1980s, and the rate was higher still in many regional urban centers, such as Gafsa and Gabes.

All of this means, as noted, that the supply of jobs, education, and housing has been unable to keep pace with demand and, as a result, a steadily increasing number of individuals finds it impossible to fulfill aspirations for social mobility and a better life. According to an Algerian newspaper editor, quoted in 1991, "Out of the entire population of this country, there are barely one million persons with a civilized cycle of life, in the sense that they have good jobs, collect a reasonable salary, deal with banks and sometimes take vacations. The rest of the country lives at subsistence levels or below."[11]

While these problems and pressures affect huge numbers of individuals and almost all sectors of society, they are most pronounced among the young and in the cities. They also appear to be most intense among those who have received some but not extensive schooling, and particularly among men in this category.[12] Unable to compete for the jobs that are available, often because their education is limited, legions of unemployed young men in the cities while away their days on street corners or in coffeehouses, becoming ever more disillusioned and embittered. In Algeria, where the problem is presently most intense, they are sometimes called "homeboys" (*houmistes*), boys from the neighborhood, or "wall boys," (*hittistes*), unemployed youth who have nothing to do and so "hang out," leaning against the walls that line many city streets.[13] Characterizing the situation more generally, a colloquium on cities and social movements in the Maghrib and the Middle East held several years ago in Paris concluded that the urban areas of North Africa are "accumulating a mass whose transition is blocked" and which increasingly lives at a level "below that of normal city life."[14]

Expressions of Public Anger in the 1980s

The serious unrest that occurred in Tunisia, Algeria, and Morocco, as well as in a number of other Arab countries during the 1980s, may be understood against the background of the difficult living conditions affecting large segments of the population. A Moroccan economist referred in this context to the "population/jobs problem," which he characterized as a "time bomb that is ticking away."[15] Similarly, a series of *Jeune Afrique* articles on Algeria and Tunisia, written about the same time, described the situation as "explosive."[16]

And indeed there were explosions in North Africa during the 1980s. In June 1981, tensions associated with economic and political grievances exploded in the form of violent riots in Casablanca, Morocco. The immediate cause of the disturbances was a reduction in food subsidies, which the government enacted in response to pressure from foreign creditors; but the scope and intensity of the rioting revealed the depth of public anger. As thousands of young men from the city's sprawling slums poured into the streets, roaming mobs attacked banks, auto dealerships, and other businesses and public buildings identified with elite privilege or government authority. In subduing the rioters, police sometimes fired into the crowd, and at least two hundred protesters were killed. Some estimates place the number much higher.

The rioting that broke out in Morocco in January 1984 made it clear that these disturbances were not an aberration. A rise in the price of basic commodities subsidized by the government was announced, and again the burden fell most heavily on the working class and the poor. In response, violent protests occurred in many parts of the country and rioting lasted for more than a week, leaving Morocco badly shaken when order was finally restored.

The first disturbances took place in Marrakesh, where students and unemployed youth from poorer neighborhoods took to the streets; these protests were then followed by demonstrations in Agadir, Safi, and Kasbah-Tadla in the south and in Rabat and Meknès in the central part of the country. Disturbances of greater intensity thereafter developed in the north, the most neglected and underdeveloped region of Morocco. In Nador, for example, there were attacks on banks and the agency of the national airline, Royal Air Maroc, indicating anger at the government and special bitterness at institutions symbolizing elite privilege. In Al Hoceima, another northern city, protesting students were joined by fishermen, sailors, port workers, and many others, including women. Moroccan security forces used considerable

violence in quelling the riots in these and other northern cities. Press reports
spoke of 150 to 200 deaths, or in some cases even more, as well as hundreds
injured and approximately nine thousand arrested.[17]

January 1984 also was a time of unrest in Tunisia, and the country's
experience was broadly similar to that of Morocco. Rioting actually began at
the end of 1983, triggered by the government's December 29 announcement
of a rise in the price of semolina. In response to this action, which served as a
catalyst and released pent-up frustration produced by underlying economic
and social problems, protests and demonstrations took place in the oases of
the south, some of the nation's poorest and most neglected communities.

New Year's Day brought a new wave of rioting in Tunisia, with disturbances in major towns of the south, including Kasserine, Gafsa, Mitlaoui,
and Gabes, and by January 3 there was also rioting in Tunis, Sfax (the country's second-largest city), and other urban centers. In the capital, thousands
of students, workers, and unemployed young men from the city's slums
roamed the streets, shouting antigovernment slogans and attacking symbols of authority and wealth. Thousands more shouted encouragement from
open windows and rooftops. Protesters attacked cars and buses, tore up street
signs, looted and set fire to shops, and, in some areas, attacked public buildings. They also fought police and military units, which had brought in tanks,
armored personnel carriers, and even helicopters to repulse the rioters. Order
was not restored until January 5, by which time the country had witnessed a
week of unrest and security forces had killed over 150 persons.[18]

Algeria, too, experienced serious unrest during this period. In April 1985,
for example, following rumors that homes being built for the poor would be
allocated instead to government bureaucrats, there were riots in the Algiers
casbah that brought police units into the streets. Disturbances continued for
several days. There were also clashes between police and youthful members
of militant Islamic groups, including a violent confrontation in October 1985
that resulted in the death of five policemen. Fall 1986 brought additional
and more widespread disturbances. In November, student demonstrations
in Constantine ignited three days of rioting, in which four protesters died
and many more were wounded. Further, the Constantine riots were followed almost immediately by disturbances in other cities, including Setif,
where the Air France office was attacked, as well as in Batna, Annaba, Skikda,
and Oran.

In October 1988, Algeria was shaken by the most intense rioting since it
became independent in 1962, experiencing its own equivalent of the January
disturbances in Tunisia and Morocco.[19] In Algiers, Oran, Constantine, and
several other cities, thousands of young people took to the streets to vent
their anger over worsening economic and social conditions. There was con-

siderable property damage during the three days of rioting, with protesters setting fire to government buildings in several parts of Algiers. There were also lethal clashes between protesters and government security forces charged with putting an end to the disturbances. Estimates of the number of casualties varied widely, but it is generally agreed that at least five hundred of the protesters were killed and many more wounded. After order was restored, the government imposed a state of emergency on the capital and nearby areas.

People's Understanding of their Predicament

To the extent one can judge, it does not appear that ordinary Arab men and women see their problems solely, or even primarily, as the unavoidable result of shortages created by population growth and other demographic pressures. Rather, many seem to regard their problems as grounded in existing patterns of political economy, and they accordingly attribute much of the responsibility for their plight to the political regimes by which they are governed. Complaints thus go beyond the fact that masses of people live in impoverished conditions and that for much of the population, especially the young, the prospects for an improved standard of living are not growing brighter and may even be declining.

Ordinary citizens in North Africa also complain about a large and growing gap between rich and poor. In their view, the burdens of underdevelopment are not shared equitably and, despite economic difficulties, there are islands of affluence and elite privilege that often involve luxury and excess. Moreover, these complaints are compounded by a widespread belief that membership in the country's elite is determined in most instances not by ability, dedication, or service to society but by personal and political connections, the result being a system where patronage and clientelism predominate in decisions about public policy and resource allocation. Thus, although many live in conditions of distress, there is also a consumer class that is believed to support its privileged lifestyle with resources that should be used for national development.

Scholarly observers confirm the accuracy of at least some of these popular perceptions. For example, a 1988 study of economic reform in Morocco noted that the structural adjustment policies being pursued by the government were hurting the poorest categories of the population while benefiting others, and it then concluded that only "a very different kind of structural reform—involving a substantial redistribution of resources and a genuine democratization of Moroccan politics . . . [would] be sufficient to change the situation of the poorest social groups in Morocco."[20] Moreover, and significantly, a study published in 1994 concluded that the situation had changed little: "Below the strata of the richest Moroccans, all social classes are [still] waiting to feel the benefits of reform."[21] Even the World Bank and the European Commission, the study added, "readily concede the need for a more equitable distribution of resources."

As far as privileged access is concerned, a number of investigations report not only the limited magnitude but also the highly skewed distribution of opportunities for educational and professional advancement. A study conducted in Algeria, for example, reported that the chances for entering a university are 30 times greater for the son of an agricultural manager than for the son of a farm laborer, and that those for the son of a technocrat or businessman are 285 times greater.[22] Noting that students at Algerian universities constitute a select group drawn from the most favored sectors of society, an American scholar described them as

> the 1 to 3 percent of Algerians who are destined, because of their family and personal connections, acquired wealth and influence, type and level of education, multilingual fluency, and technical-scientific accreditation, to assume the top- and secondary-level positions in each of the principal institutional components of the technocratic system: government, party, military, bureaucracy.[23]

Other studies come to similar conclusions with respect to Tunisia and Morocco. Reporting on the Tunisian case, for example, one analyst observes that "university students and skilled cadres come predominantly from middle- and upper-middle-class social strata."[24] A recent account of the situation in Morocco notes that there is privilege not only in access to higher education but to post-university employment as well. "Morocco remains a very closed, very proprietary system," this analysis concludes, noting that "even college graduates without necessary family connections cannot get jobs."[25]

In addition, there are also accounts of the indulgence and conspicuous consumption that characterize some segments of the elite. Describing the sources of popular discontent in Algeria, for example, a political scientist of Algerian origin writes that "in the midst of [the present] economic and managerial crisis, a few people succeeded in not only increasing their wealth but also displaying it in the form of late-model cars, new villa construction and new businesses," which in turn, understandably, "exacerbated the frustration of the masses" and "made them potentially rebellious against a state of affairs they neither liked nor understood."[26]

Other observers also make these points, citing examples not only from North Africa but from elsewhere in the Arab world. In writing about the origins of popular discontent in Jordan, for example, one scholar notes that, at the level of the masses, "many people were not willing to tighten their belts to pay for an economic crisis which they felt was the result of widespread corruption," and that, among the elite, "a system of cronyism is pervasive," with opportunities for enrichment channeled by insiders to their friends and with top positions always going to the "same old faces, families and clans."[27]

Indignation over the gap between rich and poor, over privileged access to opportunities for economic advancement, and over the perceived misuse of available national resources was readily apparent in the rioting that shook North Africa during the 1980s. In the Tunisian disturbances of January 1984, for example, knowledgeable local observers described the mood of demonstrators as one of "rage," or even "hatred." This was most apparent in the attacks on shops selling luxury goods and the incursions into fashionable elite neighborhoods. Also, in at least one instance, Mercedes and other luxury cars were set on fire by roaming bands, while less expensive models were damaged little if at all. Anger was thus directed not only at the government but also at the consumption-oriented middle and upper classes, population categories perceived to be prospering at a time when the circumstances of the masses were deteriorating and the regime was asking the poor to tighten their belts even more.[28] Similar sentiments were observed in Morocco during the disturbances of January 1984. In Nador, for example, some protesters carried pink parasols to express their disdain for royal pomp and their indignation at the excesses of the king and the elite.

The way that many understand their predicament is also illustrated by a conversation that took place during the Tunisian riots of January 1984.[29] A Tunisian professional told of a discussion a few days earlier with several young men who worked in menial and low-paying jobs at the institution where he himself held a senior position. Upon learning that there had been riots in the residential quarter where he lived, the workers expressed the hope that he had not personally sustained any losses; for while he was indeed quite wealthy by their modest standards, they believed he was entitled to the rewards of his labors. He had gone to school for many years, and he now worked long hours in a position that contributed directly to the welfare of the nation.

The problem, the workers added, was that the same could not be said for most members of the nation's privileged classes. The young workers expressed their belief that the majority of Tunisia's elite prospered because of personal and political connections, gaining preferential access to, and then spending frivolously, resources that should be invested in the country's future. Moreover, most of these individuals were said to offer the country little in return, preferring to spend their wealth on imported luxury goods and only rarely investing in ventures that either created employment or increased economic productivity. In recalling this conversation, the Tunisian professional stated that he had told his interlocutors that their view of a corrupt and parasitic elite was exaggerated and oversimplified. In fact, however, he added privately that the analysis was not as wide of the mark as he would have wished.

There is clearly a political as well as a socioeconomic dimension to these complaints. As the frequent eruption of popular unrest makes evident, citizens throughout North Africa are deeply dissatisfied with the political systems by which they are governed. They are angered by an inability to hold their leaders accountable or to press for political change. Those who are more politically conscious complain that there are few legitimate mechanisms by which the populace can articulate grievances in a way that will have a meaningful impact on the political process, and none whatsoever by which it can remove senior political leaders whose performance is unsatisfactory. They note that the political openings of the late 1980s were timid and halting, with the partial exception of Algeria, and that progress toward democratization in Algeria ceased in the early 1990s.

More generally, political opposition is tolerated, if at all, only to the extent that it does not threaten the established political order. Dissident political activity is vigorously suppressed in this environment, with serious human rights violations in the treatment of radical opponents and strict limits imposed even on opposition movements which accept the rules of the game. As described in a 1988 study of political control in Morocco, "the government ensures that the behavior [of even loyal opposition parties] conforms to the major decisions taken by the Palace." The leaders of these parties are closely monitored by Moroccan authorities, who do not hesitate to limit their action or even to arrest them "if there is doubt about the nature of their activities."[30]

A number of analysts advance similar conclusions about the political judgments reflected in popular discontent. One observer writes of Algeria, for example, that people are no longer impressed by tales of their leaders' struggle for independence: "They want to know, as one student bitterly stated . . . why more than half of them are jobless 'while we earn billions per year from natural gas, and [the former head of the ruling party] lives like a king.'"[31] Discussing the Constantine riots of 1986, another author makes the same point: the young protesters constitute a generation raised on "state corruption, social problems and political abuse." The overall cause of political alienation, he concludes, is a "system of power, patronage and privilege that entrenched interests in the party, government and the economy are unwilling to sacrifice in the name of some larger good."[32] And again, writing more recently about the failure of Algeria's short-lived experiment in democratization, a scholarly analysis concludes that public anger has been fueled not only by an inadequate national development strategy but by the insistence of government and military hard-liners on total economic, political, and ideological control.[33]

A few public opinion surveys also document the depth and breadth of political alienation.[34] In the case of Morocco, for example, a recent account summarizes four important survey research projects and reports that "while the state is feared, it is also often resented, if not hated . . . [and is] widely recognized as not representative of the people. This produces two main reactions, either complete apathy or at least passivity (sometimes viewed as acceptance), or alienation and activism in some anti-establishment form or medium."[35] Thus, in sum, evidence from a variety of sources supports the thesis that political discontent is widespread in North Africa and is in the first instance a response to systems of governance considered unresponsive at best and frequently exploitative.

Government officials often contend that complaints about regime performance are unreasonable and exaggerated. They assert that demands for rapid progress are unrealistic, with many citizens, and especially the young, failing to appreciate that development goals can only be achieved over the long haul. Many of these officials also insist that much has been accomplished, sometimes suggesting that complaints are the result not of government failures but, rather, of aspirations fostered by successful development efforts, most notably in the field of education. They sometimes argue as well that there has been progress toward the construction of democratic political systems, even though here, too, they call for patience.

Whatever the accuracy of these rebuttals, they rarely strike a responsive chord among the disillusioned and alienated segments of North Africa's citizenry, presumably because so many find confirmation in their own lives of the charge that something fundamental is amiss in the nation as a whole. They reason, logically though perhaps somewhat simplistically, that if the government were allocating resources wisely and in accordance with the true interests of the populace, they, their families, and so many of their friends would not be confronted with stagnation or even a decline in their modest standards of living. But their leaders do not give highest priority to the welfare of the masses, these critics continue. They instead preside over a political and economic system that is dedicated to the preservation of elite privilege and which accordingly distributes resources and opportunities on the basis of personal relationships.

This situation is often characterized as the problem of the "Arab regimes" or as the "crisis of leadership and legitimacy" in North Africa and other parts of the Arab world. As expressed by a scholar of Egyptian origin, there is a "severe, multi-dimensional, and protracted crisis faced by many regimes in

the Muslim [and Arab] world. This crisis has been evidenced by a decline of
state legitimacy and has resulted in 'state exhaustion.'"[36] The same point is
stressed by a Moroccan analyst, who describes the problem as one of "azma-
tology," from *azmah,* the Arabic word for crises.[37]

Lessons from the Crisis in the Gulf

Students, professionals, and other politically conscious Arabs frequently
speak of a tacit alliance between domestic, regional, and even international
political interests committed to maintaining the status quo. Those deemed
responsible for their predicament, therefore, include not only the leaders and
privileged elements within their own countries but also both the political
regimes and classes throughout the Middle East that stand in opposition to
change and the foreign powers (including the United States) that are believed
to be working to preserve existing patterns of political economy.

These sentiments were readily visible in North Africa during the Gulf
crisis of 1990–91, confirming that the deep discontent felt by many ordinary
citizens extends into the present decade and offering additional insights into
the nature of popular attitudes. Iraq invaded Kuwait in August 1990, and
shortly thereafter the United States took the lead in establishing an international military coalition that threatened to go to war against Iraq unless the
country's leader, Saddam Hussein, withdrew his forces from Kuwait. The U.S.-
led coalition attacked in January 1991 and quickly scored a decisive victory.
Yet in many Arab countries, including all three states of the Maghrib, there
was substantial popular sympathy for Saddam Hussein and broad opposition to the United States and its coalition partners.[38] Moreover, a number of
analysts have pointed out that such sentiments were expressed most clearly
and forcefully in Arab states characterized by a measure of political openness
and by relative freedom of expression—in those states, in other words, where
public opinion could be most readily discerned.[39]

In Tunisia, for example, there were demonstrations in support of Iraq
and expressions of militant opposition to the actions of the U.S.-led coalition.
While public protests were for the most part limited in scope, both Tunisian
and foreign observers agree that there was a very strong pro-Iraq and anti-
U.S. undercurrent among the public at large.[40] Popular attitudes were similar in Algeria, where there were also massive public protests. Hundreds of
thousands marched in Algiers and other cities following the attack on Iraqi
forces in January 1991, and in Constantine there were attacks on the French
consulate and the office of Air France. As a result, the governments of both
Tunisia and Algeria, in response to public pressure, condemned the Iraqi
invasion of Kuwait but reserved their sharpest denunciations for the United
States and its allies.

Pro-Saddam and anti-Western sentiments were no less present in Morocco, even though the country's leader, King Hassan II, had sent troops to Saudi Arabia as part of the international force put in place under UN auspices. Indeed, the expressions of support for Iraq coming from Morocco were among the most intense in the Arab world. In December 1990, street demonstrations and unrest in Fes, Tangiers, and several other cities, although only partly in response to developments in the Gulf, produced violent clashes with police. At least 5 protesters were killed and 127 injured, with opponents of the government putting the figures significantly higher. Much larger, although nonviolent, protests took place in February 1991, following the attack on Iraq by the U.S.-led coalition. A crowd that some observers estimated at three hundred thousand took to the streets of Rabat to demand the withdrawal from Saudi Arabia of all allied forces, including those from Morocco. Marchers burned American, British, French, and Israeli flags. Many carried copies of the Quran, and some displayed portraits of Saddam Hussein.

The Moroccan government responded by quietly distancing itself from the coalition and adopting a posture of undeclared but effective neutrality in the fighting in the Gulf. Moreover, the United States displayed an understanding of the situation facing the Moroccan king and did not complicate Hassan's position by pressing for active Moroccan participation in the anti-Iraq campaign. But although the monarch's action, and U.S. understanding, were sufficient to keep domestic protests from getting out of hand, support for Saddam Hussein among the Moroccan public remained strong almost three years after the crisis. A poll conducted late in 1993, for example, found that 55 percent of the urban respondents in a nationally representative sample had a very favorable view of the Iraqi leader, and 25 percent had a favorable view.[41]

It is doubtful that many North Africans actually approved of the Iraqi invasion of Kuwait. Most would probably agree that Iraq should have used political means to defend its interests rather than attack a brother Arab country and divide the Arab world. It is also unlikely that many Tunisians, Algerians, or Moroccans would wish to live under Saddam's rule; the authoritarian and brutal character of the Baath regime in Iraq is well known, even in the Maghrib. Nor would most consider Saddam a credible champion of Arab independence, since for many years he was a willing client of the former Soviet Union. Finally, Saddam's use of Islamic symbols appeared cynical and hypocritical to many North Africans, particularly since the Iraqi leader is well known as a secular nationalist who in fact claimed to be defending the Arab world against militant Islam during his country's eight-year war with Iran.

Thus, the outpouring of public anger in North Africa in 1990 and 1991 was not produced by a high regard for Saddam Hussein or by support for his actions in Kuwait. Rather, as in a number of other Arab countries, the Gulf crisis served as a proxy for a very different set of grievances and gave citizens of the Maghrib an occasion to express once again the discontent that had produced disturbances during the preceding decade. More specifically, there is intense opposition to the economic and political status quo and a profound desire for change, and Saddam Hussein, whether justified or not, was regarded by many North Africans as a champion of the desired transformation.

Kuwait, the United States, and allied Arab regimes, by contrast, were seen by many ordinary men and women as defenders of the established order, as cynical political actors who claimed to want a new world order but in reality were using force to ensure that change did not take place. In this popular view, Saudi Arabia, Kuwait, and other oil-rich Gulf states constitute national islands of privilege and represent a replication within the Middle Eastern regional system of the very pattern of political economy that exists within their own country and is at the root of their frustration and anger. A handful of privileged Arab states, like the rulers and associated elites within most Arab countries, are believed to be dedicated to the preservation of a political and economic order that provides benefits for the few and is indifferent or even hostile to the well-being of the majority.

These themes were repeatedly stressed at a colloquium on the Gulf crisis held in Tunis in March 1991, shortly after the conclusion of the fighting in Iraq. Academics and other intellectuals from Morocco, Algeria, Egypt, and several other Arab countries joined Tunisian colleagues for two days of discussion; and frequently articulated was the view that the war divided the Arab world's rich and poor and at its core was a confrontation between supporters and opponents of change.[42] According to one participant, while the Arab world suffers from poverty, inequality, and social injustice, the war in the Gulf was fought and won by "les gros consommateurs mondiaux"—that is to say, by a coalition of Western and Arab governments with an interest in defending the established world order.[43] Many others spoke of the imperialist alliance that defeated Iraq, and while the United States, and to a lesser extent France, were frequent targets of criticism, so also were privileged and indulgent Arab regimes that were accused of defending the status quo and, consequently, of joining the anti-Iraq coalition. Similar assessments of the coalition's motives, emphasizing a defense not of Kuwaiti sovereignty but of existing political and economic relationships, were advanced by analysts in other parts of the Arab world as well.[44]

Such judgments are relevant for an understanding of popular as well as intellectual opinion, as demonstrated, for example, by a recent study of the attitudes of young Moroccans, and also of the popular slogans and jokes that circulated in Morocco during the crisis in the Gulf.[45] Saddam was represented as a man of action among those who saw themselves as powerless and marginalized, whereas there was little sympathy for Kuwait, which was judged to be arrogant and selfish. "Unshared wealth was the central theme of discourse," the study reported,[46] although there was also concern for Palestinian rights and the removal of non-Muslim forces from the territory of Saudi Arabia. Thus, the members of the anti-Iraq coalition, which included Saudi Arabia and "bad Arabs," as well as foreign elements, were "associated with negative values" and were regarded as "the enemies of the people." In the view of many young Moroccans, "the sole motivation of the sultans of the Gulf, of Mubarak and even of Asad was to remain in power and protect their personal interests . . . to defend themselves against their own people, whom they fear."[47]

A final indication of the continuing anger felt by many young North Africans is provided by the riots that broke out in Fez, Morocco, in February 1994. Protests by university students, many associated with Islamic movements, led to clashes with police, and these were followed by riots in which the students were joined by hundreds of young men from nearby Meknès and other towns. There were also violent clashes between Islamist and leftist students. At least seven people were killed as a result of the disturbances, with several dozen arrested and police anti-riot squads occupying the Fez campus before order was restored.[48]

The Meaning of Support for Islamist Movements

In searching for an alternative to an unacceptable status quo, many North Africans and other Arabs are turning to Islamist political movements. The current Islamic revival actually began during the 1970s. New Muslim associations and study groups emerged, and there was also a sharp increase in such expressions of personal piety as mosque attendance and public prayer. Another indication of this development was a boom in the sale of cassettes dealing with Islamic themes, which, according to a journalistic investigation in Tunisia, were at the time estimated to be selling thousands of copies every month.[49] A study by a Tunisian scholar reported a few years later that militant Muslim groups were having particular success in attracting the young, including the relatively well educated, and that high schools and university campuses were accordingly serving as centers of activity and recruitment.[50]

The origins of this Islamic resurgence are diverse. They are rooted to a significant degree in the enduring religious attachments of ordinary Muslims, but they have been shaped to an equal or even greater extent by events that were transforming the political landscape of the Arab world. Of particular importance was the Arab-Israeli war of June 1967, which brought

the Arabs a crushing defeat and thus cast doubt on the development ideologies of the states, particularly Egypt and Syria, that had led in the struggle
against Israel. In the wake of the Arabs' defeat in the 1947–48 war for Israeli
independence, traditional and feudalistic regimes had been swept away in
Egypt, Syria, and elsewhere, to be replaced by governments which promised
that a political formula based on socialism and some mix of pan-Arabism
and secular nationalism would enable their countries to prosper.

Moreover, such revolutionary thinking assumed a dominant position
in Arab political discourse during the late 1950s and early 1960s. It was
championed by intellectuals and students, to the point that Islamic political
movements were in fact having difficulty attracting followers among these
categories of the population. To the extent one can judge, there was also
broad popular support for the Arab world's revolutionary leaders, most
prominently for Gamal Abdul Nasser but also, in North Africa, for the socialist regimes in Tunisia and later Algeria. These regimes enjoyed a high degree
of legitimacy during the early and mid-1960s—despite their indifference or
even hostility to political movements advocating greater respect for Islamic
prescriptions in the formulation of public policy.

But this situation began to change after June 1967. With revolutionary
regimes in Egypt and Syria defeated even more decisively than had been
their feudalistic predecessors, there was suddenly a new logic and credibility
to the Islamist argument that progress could be achieved only if the Arabs
were guided by an indigenous political formula, namely, that provided by
Islam. Some Muslim thinkers asserted that the defeat was punishment for the
Arabs' flirtation with foreign ideologies, for a turning away from the faith.
More common, however, and almost certainly more persuasive to thoughtful
Muslims, was the assertion, summarized in a major study of Arab political
thought during this period, that Islam "could do what no imported doctrine could hope to do—mobilize the believers, instill discipline, and inspire
people to make sacrifices and, if necessary, to die."[51] Significantly, both radical and conservative Islamic thinkers also emphasized the importance of
Israel's identification with Judaism, arguing that Israel was strong precisely
because it accepted and embraced its association with an ancient religion.
The implication, made explicit by Islamic theoreticians, was that Muslims
should exhibit the same religious zeal and, as had the Israelis, reject the secu-
larist fallacy of a contradiction between religion and modernity.[52]

In addition to shedding light on the origins of the Islamic resurgence in
the Arab world, including North Africa, the June war and its consequences
call attention to the instrumental character of the case being advanced in the
name of Islam. This remains the situation at present, with Muslim groups
presenting themselves as vehicles for the expression of political discontent

and campaigning for change under the banner, "Islam is the Solution." Further, there is evidence that those who respond positively to this message desire not only that their political community be strong enough to meet external challenges but also, and equally, that it be governed by a regime that is able and willing to deal effectively with domestic political and economic problems—hence the salience of a "solution." In Tunisia, for example, an empirical study based on surveys carried out in the late 1960s and early 1970s found that the Islamic revival in that country was being fueled, in substantial measure, by political and economic grievances and by a desire for political change.[53] Several studies carried out in Tunisia during the 1980s reached similar conclusions and in fact documented an acceleration of this trend.[54]

Moving closer to the present, it thus appears that popular support for Islamist movements, including votes cast for candidates associated with these movements in Algeria (FIS) and Tunisia (an-Nahdah), does not necessarily reflect a desire for religious fulfillment or mean that most North Africans genuinely favor governance in accordance with Islamic law in order to give existential meaning to their political community. Rather, many and perhaps most are motivated by more temporal considerations. As one knowledgeable analyst wrote of Tunisia in 1988: "The impact of the Islamist movement on Tunisia's political agenda in the years ahead will depend largely on how the country's political and economic problems are resolved. . . . [The growth of this movement is] only a symptom of a deeper malaise within Tunisian society."[55] Research carried out in Morocco offered a similar assessment, concluding that radical groups, particularly those with an Islamic ideology, will be able to attract support only so long as "the problems of social disadvantage and deprivation and of political marginalization" remain unaddressed and become increasingly severe.[56]

Writing of Algeria, where the Islamist movement has been strongest, many observers also emphasize the instrumental character of the FIS's appeal. According to a journalistic investigation carried out in 1992, for example, the Islamist movement has gained ground by winning converts "among victims of the corruption and inequality evidenced by the [gap between the] comfortable life of the old political leadership and the appalling housing and other conditions in which most other citizens live."[57] And again, advancing a more generalized conclusion, two American scholars of Algerian origin argue that "economic deprivation, social exclusion, and political underrepresentation [have] encouraged the development of Islamist movements not only in Algeria but also in many other Muslim countries."[58]

Thus, what many North Africans and other Arabs appear to want is meaningful political change and, above all, responsive and accountable government, rather than Islamic solutions per se. For a variety of reasons,

Islamist movements have been well positioned to capitalize on discontent with the status quo. They offer effective vehicles for registering political dissatisfaction, and they have answers to the problems of their societies which, on the surface at least, appear coherent and plausible. But other mechanisms of political change and alternative visions of the future, to the extent they are available, might also be championed by those who have given their votes to Islamist candidates. Indeed, this is precisely the reason that Saddam Hussein received considerable support during the crisis in the Gulf, despite the Iraqi leader's history of opposition to radical Islam.

This underlying concern for an alternative to the political and economic status quo was forcefully articulated during the Gulf crisis by a journalist in Jordan, who wrote of an "essential message reverberating throughout the Arab world" and who castigated the United States and other Western powers for failing to understand the content of this message: There are everywhere "signs of a profound desire for change—for democracy and human rights, for social equity, for regional economic integration, for accountability of public officials, for morality in public life, for the fair application of international law and U.N. resolutions, and for a new regional order characterized by honesty, dignity, justice and stability."[59] The problem, he wrote in another article, is the pervasiveness of "autocratic rulers and non-accountable power elites [that] pursue whimsical, wasteful and regressive policies," and it is this situation that "will be challenged by the will of the Arab people."[60]

Describing the situation in the Arab world more generally, another analyst reports that the "demand for human rights, participation and democracy comes from across the political spectrum. . . . The call for democracy is the subject of meetings, conferences and academic studies."[61] And still another scholar, a political scientist from the United Arab Emirates, makes explicit the relationship between these calls for political change and support for Islamist groups: "As long as Arab governments resist political participation and refuse to tolerate different political opinions, the strength of Islam as an alternative political ideology will continue to grow."[62]

Empirical evidence based on survey research in the Middle East also points to the conclusion that support for Islamist movements does not necessarily reflect a belief that existing political systems should be replaced by patterns of governance based on Muslim legal codes. In particular, this evidence indicates that considerations unrelated to the faith and religious attachments of ordinary Muslims are producing much of the support for contemporary Islamist groups. An original public opinion survey conducted in Egypt and Kuwait in 1988 found only a weak relationship between a scale measuring support for political Islam and contemporary Islamist groups, on the one hand, and, on the other, a scale measuring personal piety and attitudes toward the social salience of Islam. Surprisingly, perhaps, more than half of those with higher ratings on the scale measuring piety and social salience, and over 70 percent of the Egyptians with such ratings, expressed less favorable attitudes toward political aspects of Islam. Conversely, one-third of those who expressed greater support for Islamist political movements had lower ratings on the scale measuring religious piety and social salience. Moreover, this was the case in both Egypt and Kuwait, suggesting that the pattern may apply broadly throughout the Arab world. More information about the research on which these findings are based is presented in the appendix to this chapter.

These findings are consistent with the conclusions of several other recent studies that have sought to explicate the relationship between Islamic attachments in general and support for political Islam in particular. For example, an American scholar who has conducted fieldwork in Morocco insists upon distinguishing between traditional religious beliefs on the one hand and the ideology of Islamist political movements on the other, arguing that the latter "is not how most Muslims understand their religion" and that "a politicized conception of Islam differs radically from how Islam is normally understood by ordinary Muslims."[63] A similar point is made by a scholar from the United Arab Emirates, who conducted additional survey research in his own country and concluded that the "ideology and socio-political programs of religious groups are too political to appeal to traditional mainstream Muslims."[64]

Other findings from the 1988 survey in Egypt and Kuwait lend additional support to this thesis. For example, again in both Egypt and Kuwait, those expressing greater support for Islamist movements but having lower personal piety and social salience ratings are disproportionately likely to disagree with the statement that "Western values have led to moral erosion in my society." Further, in Egypt, younger individuals and men are over-represented among those who support Islamist groups but are not personally pious. Younger men constitute the most volatile sector of society and the demographic category among which political and economic grievances appear to be most intense. All this suggests, once again, that it is the search for an alternative to the political and economic status quo, rather than an attraction to the specific content of Islamist slogans, that has produced much of the support that Muslim political groups currently enjoy.

Why Islamist Movements Are Filling the Void

Although non-Islamic challenges to the status quo would in theory find support among the discontented social classes of North Africa and other parts of the Arab world, it is in fact the case that large numbers of ordinary citizens are concluding that they can best work for political change by giving their support to militant Muslim movements. And in large part this is because of the organizational and ideological advantages that Islamic groups enjoy.

For one thing, in the undemocratic environment that until recently prevailed in most Arab countries, and that still prevails in many instances, mosques and other religious establishments offer opportunities to recruit and organize followers that are unavailable to more secular movements. Indeed, this is precisely the role that Islamic institutions played during the pre-independence period, when nationalist movements in North Africa and elsewhere were seeking to build mass organizations capable of challenging colonial domination. In Morocco, for example, the nationalist movement was built on a foundation established at the Qarawiyin Mosque University in Fez. In Tunisia, where the resistance movement was in fact led by men who had received a Western-style education and whose normative orientations were largely secular, nationalists held clandestine meetings in mosques and *zawiyyas* [religious lodges] and urged followers to pray five times a day for the martyrs of the revolution.

Analogous developments took place in the late 1960s and throughout the 1970s, a period marked by authoritarianism in North Africa and elsewhere in the Arab world. For example, a journalistic investigation conducted in Tunisia reported in 1979 on the crystallization of a political tendency that characterized its platform as the "revival of Islam."[65] It had begun with the formation of the Association for the Protection of the Quran, a group that in 1970 gained legal status as a "cultural" organization and then established an important center in the theology faculty of the University of Tunis. Over the course of the decade, however, while the political climate of the country was becoming more repressive,[66] this tendency developed and organized itself into a "parallel society with its own laws and rules." French was not spoken, for example, and men and women did not shake hands. The "movement" held meetings devoted to the study and discussion of religious themes, and it organized theater groups and operated a bookstore and publishing house.

The Islamic "underground" opposition continued to grow and gain followers in the 1980s, with developments in Tunisia paralleled by those in other Arab countries. According to a recent study of Algeria, for example, "at first, through a network of independent mosques, the Islamists preached educational and mobilizational sermons. Later, they directly criticized governmental policies and proposed their own remedies. . . . Their activities began to spread to different cities, where they challenged the secular authorities," and by 1985 there were signs of a well-structured political organization.[67] It is against the background of these activities designed to build their movement during the first and middle part of the decade, when there was no legal political opposition, that the dramatic victories of the Islamic Salvation Front in the Algerian elections of 1990 and 1991 may be understood.

In some countries, Islamic groups have also built support through the provision of social services and through community assistance projects carried out under the banner of religion. The operation of clinics, schools, day care centers, and welfare distribution programs are among the most common of these activities. Also, in addition to these efforts aimed primarily at the urban poor, some Islamic groups have established publishing societies, investment companies, and even banks. Such efforts require a measure of organization that political authorities are usually required to tolerate, even though they may foster a belief that Islamic groups are more dedicated to helping ordinary men and women than are government officials.

The importance of these institutions and programs was stressed in a recent journalistic study of Jordan, which reported that the institutional network of the Muslim Brotherhood alone includes "some 20 Islamic clinics, one of Amman's largest hospitals, well over 40 Islamic schools, some 150 Quranic studies centers and other elements of what anti-fundamentalists call 'the infrastructure of an Islamic republic.'"[68] This is a very sizable operation in a country of only four million inhabitants.

A similar or even larger Islamist network exists in other countries, most notably in Egypt, but also in Algeria, Tunisia, among Palestinians, and elsewhere. As one scholar reports, groups associated with political Islam use socioeconomic institutions and programs, particularly those that target the poor, to "participate in the political process within the official parameters of permissible action while working to extract concessions from the state to allow the [Islamist] movement greater access to the masses and through them access to power."[69] According to another scholarly analysis, focusing on Algeria, Islamists gained followers when they "quickly assumed certain social welfare functions, on such occasions as the earthquake of Tipaza, west of Algiers, and opened 'Islamic souks,' whose prices were well below those of the regular distribution circuits."[70]

Under such circumstances, Islamic groups have the additional advantage possessed by all opposition groups: they are free to criticize but have no statutory responsibility for delivering services, which means they can derive significant political advantage by making even modest contributions. This advantage would disappear should Islamists come to power, however. Indeed, after the FIS gained control of a number of Algerian municipalities in the elections of June 1990, the party began to be criticized for serious shortcomings in the operation of local government and for failing to deliver on a number of promised improvements.[71] Similar complaints were heard in Jordan after leaders of the Muslim Brotherhood took control of several ministries following the November 1989 parliamentary elections.

Yet another factor working to the advantage of Islamist movements, and in some ways the most important, is the absence of alternative opposition parties with a credible platform. In particular, although Morocco is a partial exception, it is generally the case that North Africans and other Arabs no longer regard parties of the political left as suitable vehicles for the expression of opposition to existing regimes. This was evident in the Tunisian elections of April 1989, for example, where the leading socialist party received less than 4 percent of the vote and where the absence of any credible legal opposition contributed directly to the success of Islamist candidates who ran as independents.

This was also evident in Algeria, where leftist parties fared poorly in the election of June 1990, and about which one study concludes that gains made by the FIS reflect not only social and economic grievances but also, in combination, an "inability of the traditional secular opposition to channel popular demands."[72] Overall, the situation was summed up in the summer of 1991 by an Egyptian socialist, who told the author that his party was finding it increasingly difficult to counter the Islamists' appeal. "Islam may not be able to solve this country's problems," he stated, "but the Islamists at least have a credible slogan. They may be without a real solution, but we are without even the name of a solution."

Under these conditions, those who wish to register opposition to the government have little choice but to support Islamist movements, and it appears that in recent elections in Tunisia and Algeria, and presumably elsewhere, some voted for the candidates of these movements for precisely this reason. While it is impossible to determine the extent to which those who voted for the FIS or independents affiliated with an-Nahdah did so merely to express discontent, rather than because they genuinely consider Islam the solution to their country's problems, it is probable that the former explanation accounts for a significant proportion of the votes these parties' candidates received.

According to a recent scholarly account of the June 1990 elections in Algeria, for example, the results were much more of a defeat for the government than a victory for the FIS. The study reports that "the majority of the voters (between 55 and 82 percent depending on the parameters used) were not identifiable with the hard core of Islamist themes," and so concludes that "on evidence the 'rejection votes' very likely constituted a strong element in the old single party's defeat," rather than "sanction votes" indicating an identification with the FIS's ideology.[73] This assessment is also supported by the investigation of an American journalist, who was told by one of his informants that "I voted for the FIS out of revenge."[74]

Another recent example, coming from outside the Maghrib, is provided by an account of the March 1992 election for the Chamber of Commerce in Ramallah in the Israeli-occupied West Bank. Candidates associated with the Islamist HAMAS movement handily defeated those identified with secular nationalism and the PLO. According to press reports, Palestinians complained of PLO officials who live lavishly and whose bank accounts contain funds that should be spent in the occupied territories; it is for this reason, at least in part, that HAMAS was victorious in "a city with a large number of Christian Palestinians who normally would never vote for an Islamic fundamentalist."[75]

Although this analysis has stressed the instrumental considerations producing support for Islamist movements, the assertion that Islam is the solution strikes a responsive chord for other reasons as well. Islam is an indigenous belief system, familiar to almost all Arabs, even those who are Christian. It has shaped the Arabs' history, helps to define their collective national identity, and gives spiritual meaning to the lives of millions, even many who are not personally devout. Equally significant, by its very nature, as a culture and a legal system, as well as a religion, Islam presents Muslims with a complete and coherent blueprint for the construction of a just political community. All this makes it an attractive ideology to Arabs and other Muslims who are searching for an alternative political formula.

Nevertheless, growing popular support for activist Muslim movements cannot be explained exclusively, or even primarily, by Islam's familiarity and considerable normative appeal. On the one hand, as discussed earlier, available evidence suggests that there is only a weak association between the strength of personal religious attachments and the degree of support for Islamist groups and their political program. On the other, the salience of Islam as a religious faith and cultural system transcends historic swings in the strength of Islamist movements, suggesting once again that the present-day success of these groups is due primarily to recent political and economic developments rather than to the nature of Islam and its abiding importance in the lives of many ordinary Arabs. As one scholar argues in the case of Tunisia's an-Nahdah party, "feelings of dislocation and alienation among Tunisia's Muslims gradually turned the essentially apolitical group into an activist organization."[76]

If this assessment is correct, if it is indeed political economy rather than religion and culture that holds the key to a proper understanding of the current Islamic resurgence, then the popular anger producing support for the

FIS, an-Nahdah, and other Islamist movements will begin to dissipate if Arab governments display new vision and dedication in addressing the grievances of ordinary men and women. These regimes, with active encouragement and assistance from their external allies, will have to work with increased honesty and effectiveness on behalf of all their citizens, and this in turn will require greater respect for human rights, a more equitable distribution of those burdens of underdevelopment that cannot be avoided, and, above all, progress toward democratization and genuine government accountability.

APPENDIX:
Public Opinion Data from Egypt and Kuwait

Public opinion surveys carried out in Egypt and Kuwait in mid-1988 deal with issues of religion and politics and may accordingly shed additional light on the origins of popular support for Islamist movements.

Data from Egypt may provide clues about attitudes in North Africa and other Arab countries where much of the population lives in impoverished conditions, where there has been some movement toward democratization in recent years, and where Islamic-tendency movements made major gains during the 1980s. Comparisons between Egypt and Kuwait will be helpful in determining whether particular attitudes emerge in this kind of environment or, alternatively, whether the normative patterns observed apply more generally throughout the Arab world and thus are not dependent on economic and political conditions.

Stratified samples of adults were selected in Cairo and Kuwait. Each sample includes both men and women, and each is heterogeneous with respect to age, education, socioeconomic status, and neighborhood. Although better-educated individuals are somewhat overrepresented, the samples are generally representative of the active, adult, urban population. The distribution of each sample with respect to gender, age and education is presented in Table 2.1.

The surveys were carried out under the direction of Professor Jamal Al-Suwaidi of the United Arab Emirates University and the Emirates Center for Strategic Studies and Research. Interviews were conducted by teams of research assistants, or "intermediaries," who were selected on the basis of previous experience in survey research administration. Intermediaries were also given a four-day orientation, and the survey instrument was pretested in both countries.

The validity and reliability of survey items selected for subsequent analysis were evaluated through a technique known as factor analysis. Factor analysis identifies clusters of items that vary together, and which thus may be analyzed in combination since they reliably measure the same concept. In

Table 2.1. Distribution of Egyptian and Kuwaiti Respondents
along Dimensions of Sample Stratification

	TOTAL (N = 592)	EGYPTIANS (N = 292)	KUWAITIS (N = 300)
Gender			
Male	51%	52%	48%
Female	49	48	52
Age			
Under 30	62	55	67
30–39	29	32	27
40 and Over	9	13	6
Education			
Intermediate or Less	19	25	13
High School	28	27	28
Some Post-secondary	22	17	28
University	31	31	31

the present instance, factor analysis has been used to measure two distinct dimensions of attitudes toward Islam, personal-social and political, as well as attitudes toward domestic politics, toward the United States and the West, and toward the local application of Western norms.

Nine items dealing with Islam were selected for subsequent analysis, and through the use of factor analysis it was determined that these items constitute two distinct attitudinal clusters. One deals with personal and social aspects of religion, and the other with political aspects of Islam. All the items and the strength of their association with each cluster are shown in Table 2.2.

Two attitudinal scales have been formed by combining the items in each cluster: a five-item scale measuring personal piety and social salience, and a four-item scale measuring support for political Islam and contemporary Islamist groups. Further, the strength of the association between the two dimensions of Islamic attachments has been examined, and, as discussed in the text, attitudes toward personal-social and toward political aspects of Islam do not covary to the extent that might be expected. Specifically, more

1. Personal and Social Aspects of Islam

30. Would you support anyone in your family who wants to study in a religious institution?

32. How often do you refer to religious teachings when making important decisions about your life?

31. Do you support the application of Islamic law in social life?

15. Do you support the application of Islamic law to deal with civil and criminal matters?

36. How often do you read the Koran?

2. Political Aspects of Islam

38. Do you agree or disagree that religion and politics should be separate?

62. What do you think of the following statement: religious practice must be kept private and   must be separated from sociopolitical life?

72. Do you support current organized Islamic movements?

69. What do you think of the religious awakening now taking place in society?

ITEM	FACTOR 1 PERSONAL-SOCIAL	FACTOR 2 POLITICAL
30	**.72945**	.00157
32	**.68098**	.13009
31	**.67403**	.21164
15	**.66808**	.22825
36	**.55939**	.11639
38	.01436	**.80070**
62	.12740	**.76350**
72	.16159	**.61355**
69	.32806	**.53887**

than half of the most pious respondents do not express strong support for political Islam, and more than one-third of those who do strongly support political Islam have lower levels of personal piety. These findings are shown in Table 2.3, which cross-tabulates dichotomized ratings on the two attitudinal scales.

Taken together, the two dichotomized dimensions of attitudes toward Islam produce a four-category typology of religious attachments. Respondents may be (a) higher both on measures of personal piety and social salience and on measures of support for political Islam and contemporary Islamic groups; (b) higher on the former set of measures but lower on the latter; (c) lower on the former set of measures but higher on the latter; or (d) lower on both sets of measures. Table 2.3 shows that respondents are found in meaningful proportions in all four categories.

These four categories of religious attachments may be compared in order to determine whether any is more likely to be found in either Egypt or Kuwait, to determine whether any is associated with a particular set of demographic attributes, and to determine whether demographic correlates are similar or different among the two national samples.

As shown in Table 2.4, there are significant national differences for three of the four categories. Specifically, (a) Egyptians are underrepresented among respondents with higher ratings on both the personal-social and the political dimensions of Islam, (b) Egyptians are also underrepresented among respondents with lower ratings on the personal-social dimension but higher ratings on the political dimension, and (c) Egyptians are overrepresented among respondents with higher ratings on the personal-social dimension but lower ratings on the political dimension.

Table 2.4 also shows that support for political Islam and contemporary Islamic groups is lower in Egypt than in Kuwait. While it is possible that this is due to the differing cultural and religious traditions of the two countries, it is also possible that the difference is due, at least in part, to the more open and competitive political environment that existed in Egypt at the time the survey was conducted.

Table 2.5 presents summary information about demographic correlates of the four categories of Islamic attachments. It indicates, for both the Egyptian and Kuwaiti samples, whether any attributes associated with either gender, age, or education are overrepresented in each category, thus presenting a partial demographic profile of the kinds of individuals who are disproportionately likely to possess particular attitudes toward Islam.

An interesting finding is that in Egypt those with higher ratings on the personal-social but not the political dimension of Islam are disproportionately likely to be older men and those with higher ratings on the political

Table 2.3. Two-Dimensional Typology of Attachments to Islam

		PERSONAL PIETY AND SOCIAL SALIENCE OF ISLAM		
	Count Row Percent Col. Percent	Lower	Higher	**Row Total**
Support for Political Islam and Contemporary Islamic Groups	Higher	72 36.9% 24.0%	123 63.1% 47.3%	195 34.9%
	Lower	227 62.5% 76.0%	137 37.6% 52.7%	364 65.1%
	Column Total	299 53.4%	260 46.6%	559 100.0%

Table 2.4. Distribution of Egyptian and Kuwaiti Respondents
across Four Categories of Attachment to Islam

	COUNT ROW PERCENT COL. PERCENT	**EGYPT**	**KUWAIT**	**ROW TOTAL**
Personal-Social Political	Higher Higher	39 31.7% 14.3%	84 68.3% 29.4%	123 22.0%
Personal-Social Political	Higher Lower	98 71.5% 35.9%	39 28.5% 13.6%	137 24.5%
Personal-Social Political	Lower Higher	19 26.4% 7.0%	53 73.6% 18.5%	72 12.9%
Personal-Social Political	Lower Lower	117 51.5% 42.8%	110 48.5% 38.5%	227 40.6%
	Column Total	273 48.8%	286 51.2%	559 100.0%

Table 2.5. Demographic Correlates of
Four Categories of Attachment to Islam

		EGYPT	KUWAIT
Personal-Social	Higher	High school	
Political	Higher		
Personal-Social	Higher	Male, older	Intermediate
Political	Lower		school
Personal-Social	Lower	Male, younger	University
Political	Higher		
Personal-Social	Lower	Female	
Political	Lower		

but not the personal-social dimension are disproportionately likely to be younger men. In Kuwait, neither gender nor age is associated with differing religious attitudes, whereas level of education helps differentiate between those with higher ratings on one attitudinal dimension but not the other.

The data may also be used to examine normative correlates of differing Islamic attachments. Ten items dealing with attitudes toward (1) domestic politics, (2) the United States and the West, and (3) the local application of Western economic and cultural norms were selected for further analysis. The validity and reliability of these items were again established by means of factor analysis, which grouped the items into three unidimensional clusters. For purposes of parsimony, only two items from each cluster are examined here. These are listed below, grouped in the manner established through factor analysis.

1. Domestic Politics

Do you agree or disagree that the government usually ignores the needs of the people? (Agree: Egypt, 68%; Kuwait, 39%)

Do you agree or disagree that public officials usually pursue their own interests first? (Agree: Egypt, 71%; Kuwait, 51%)

2. The United States and the West

Do you agree or disagree that your country should have a strong relationship with the United States? (Agree: Egypt, 57%; Kuwait, 47%)

Do you agree or disagree that Western development is an accomplishment worthy of great admiration? (Agree: Egypt, 59%; Kuwait, 43%)

3. *Local Application of Western Norms*

Do you agree or disagree that Western values have led to moral erosion in your society? (Agree: Egypt, 67%; Kuwait, 68%)

Do you agree or disagree that Western (capitalist) economic forms have been a major cause of inequalities and social problems in your country? (Agree: Egypt, 54%; Kuwait, 71%)

Table 2.6 presents summary information, for both the Egyptian and Kuwaiti samples, showing whether particular responses to any of the six items are overrepresented in any of the four categories based on attitudes toward Islam. Percentages, where shown, indicate the degree to which the proportion of respondents in that category exceeds the proportion of all respondents who answer a question about domestic politics, the West, or the local application of Western norms in the manner indicated. The table thus presents a partial normative profile of individuals who possess a given set of religious attachments. One notable finding, discussed briefly in the text, concerns the differences between more religious and less religious supporters of political Islam. The former but not the latter appear to have negative views about Western values. Another interesting finding is that judgments about Western economic forms do not appear to be influenced by religious attachments.

Table 2.6. Normative Correlates of
Four Categories of Attachment to Islam

		EGYPT	KUWAIT
Personal-Social **Political**	Higher Higher	Government ignores needs, 16%	Not strong relations with U.S., 7%
		Western values erode morals, 19%	Western values erode morals, 20%
Personal-Social **Political**	Higher Lower	Officials self-serving, 10%	Not strong relations with U.S., 8%
		Strong relations with U.S., 8%	Western values erode morals, 11%
		Western development not admirable, 12%	Western economics do not cause problems, 18%
Personal-Social **Political**	Lower Higher	Officials not self-serving, 8%	Western values do not erode morals, 9%
		Western development admirable, 7%	
		Western values do not erode morals, 14%	
Personal-Social **Political**	Lower Lower	Government cares, 11%	Officials self-serving, 9%
		Western values do not erode values, 17%	Strong relations with U.S., 9%
			Western values do not erode morals, 25%

Islam and Democracy in the Middle East: The Impact of Religious Orientations on Attitudes toward Democracy in Four Arab Countries (2002)

Mark Tessler

D iscussions about democracy in the Arab world often include attention to the political orientations of ordinary men and women. In
particular, questions are raised about whether popular attitudes
and beliefs constitute an obstacle to democratization, possibly because the
religious traditions that predominate in most Arab countries inhibit the
emergence of a democratic political culture. But while questions are frequently raised about the views of ordinary citizens, about what is sometimes
described as "the Arab street," answers are most often based on impressionis-
tic and anecdotal information. Indeed, some analyses appear to be influenced
by Western stereotypes about Arabs and Muslims. By contrast, systematic
empirical inquiries into the nature, distribution, and determinants of political attitudes in the Arab world are rare.

This article examines the influence of Islam on attitudes toward democracy using public opinion data collected in Palestine (West Bank and Gaza),
Morocco, Algeria, and Egypt. In surveys conducted by or in collaboration
with Arab scholars, interview schedules containing questions about governance and democracy and also about conceptions and practices relating to
Islam were administered to comparatively large and representative samples
of adults in all four countries, including two samples in Egypt. These data
provide a strong empirical foundation from which to address questions
about the relationship between Islam and democracy at the individual level
of analysis.

Democracy and Political Culture

Despite a few exceptions, the Arab world has made relatively little progress toward political liberalization in recent years. On the contrary, many

of the experiments in democratization that were launched a decade or so ago have been cut back substantially or even abandoned. A prominent American scholar describes the situation as "exceptionally bleak . . . from the spectacular crash and burn of Algeria's liberalization to Tunisia's more subtle but no less profound transformation into a police state, from Egypt's backsliding into electoral manipulation [and repression of Islamic political movements] to the obvious reluctance of Palestinian authorities to embrace human rights."[1]

Yet the importance of political liberalization, and ultimately of democracy, has been emphasized by Arab as well as Western scholars. According to a Lebanese political scientist, unchecked authoritarianism in many Arab countries is "paving the way to a deep crisis in the fabric of society."[2] Similarly, a Jordanian journalist writes that "one of the leading sources of instability and political-economic distortion in the Arab world is the unchecked use of state power, combined with the state's whimsical ability to use the rule of law for its own political ends."[3] An Egyptian sociologist thus argues that "political reform must be initiated, or else there is a real danger of political chaos," while a second Egyptian scholar laments that "although I dreamed of democracy in my youth, I now see that our country is regressing politically."[4]

Studies of democratic transitions and democratic consolidation identify two analytically distinct concerns to which attention must be devoted.[5] One involves political institutions and processes. The other involves citizen attitudes and values, often described as political culture. Institutional and process considerations call attention to the need for mechanisms that make political leaders accountable to those they govern, including free, competitive, and regular elections. Political culture calls attention to the orientations of ordinary men and women and, so far as democracy is concerned, to the need to develop civic and participatory norms at the level of the individual citizen.

The importance of political culture, the focus of this article, has been documented in a growing number of empirical studies carried out in new democracies. This is illustrated, for example, by Mainwaring's conclusions about the reasons democratic consolidation has been more successful in Latin America than many other developing areas. An important factor "that has contributed to the greater survivability of Latin American democracies," he writes, "revolves around changes in political attitudes, toward a greater valorization of democracy."[6] Chu, Diamond, and Shin offer a similar assessment in their study of Korea and Taiwan, stating that the consolidation of democratic transitions requires "sustained, internalized belief in and commitment to the legitimacy of democracy among the citizenry at large."[7] Thus, as summarized by Inglehart, "democracy is not attained simply by making institutional changes or through elite-level maneuvering. Its survival depends also on the values and beliefs of ordinary citizens."[8] The applicability of these conclusions to the Arab world is noted by Harik, who writes that "in the long run, of course, a democratic government needs a democratic political culture, and vice versa."[9]

Research on new democracies also sheds light on the particular attitudes and values that are necessary for successful democratization. Rose, Mishler, and Haerpfer, for example, note that relevant citizen orientations include both support for democratic political institutions and such democratic values as tolerance of diversity and an appreciation of political competition and pluralism.[10] According to Gibson, a democratic citizen is one who "believes in individual liberty and is politically tolerant, has a certain distrust of political authority but at the same time is trusting of fellow citizens, is obedient but nonetheless willing to assert rights against the state, and views the state as constrained by legality."[11]

Despite the importance of such research, there have been few studies of the attitudes and values related to democracy held by ordinary Arab men and women. There has been some relevant research using public opinion data from Palestine,[12] as well as political attitude surveys of more limited scope and relevance in Lebanon,[13] Egypt,[14] and Jordan.[15] Overall, however, the absence of such research has been noted and lamented by students of Middle East politics.[16] With public opinion data from four Arab societies and attitudes toward democracy treated as the dependent variable, the goal of the present study is to help fill this important gap.

Religion and Politics

To what extent do religious orientations account for variance in attitudes related to democracy in the Arab world? Two very different bodies of scholarly research may be consulted for possible insights, and findings from the present chapter may contribute to both of them. The first asks about the relationship between Islam and democracy, focusing for the most part on issues of doctrine and political thought. The second consists of empirical studies that assess the influence of religion and religiosity on various political attitudes in Western countries.

There is much discussion, and considerable disagreement, about the relationship between democracy and Islam. Although stereotypes are sometimes advanced, questions about the influence of Islam are appropriate. There is a strong historic connection between religion and politics in the Muslim world, reflecting Islam's character as a religion of laws pertaining to society's organization as well as individual morality. Thus, as summarized in a recent study, Islam plays a critical role in shaping political culture; no

Middle Eastern Muslim country is "able to escape completely from its over-arching reach." Indeed, this analysis continues, the intersection of culture and politics "may be more pervasive than in other [non-Islamic] contexts."[17]

In addition, Islam has become increasingly influential in Arab cultural and political life during the last quarter century. On the one hand, new Muslim associations, study groups, welfare organizations, and financial institutions have emerged, accompanied by a sharp increase in such expressions of personal piety as mosque attendance and public prayer. On the other, Islam has become an important point of reference in debates about how the Arab world should be governed.[18] Campaigning under the banner "Islam is the Solution," Muslim political organizations have had notable success in attracting new followers, including younger individuals, women as well as men, and many well-educated persons.[19]

So far as democracy is concerned, some observers, particularly some Western observers, assert that democracy and Islam are incompatible. Whereas democracy requires openness, competition, pluralism, and toler-ance of diversity, Islam, they argue, encourages intellectual conformity and an uncritical acceptance of authority. Equally important, Islam is said to be antidemocratic because it vests sovereignty in God, who is the sole source of political authority and from whose divine law must come all regulations governing the community of believers. In the view of some scholars, there-fore, Islam "has to be ultimately embodied in a totalitarian state."[20] The late Elie Kedourie, a prominent student of Arab and Islamic society, gave forceful expression to this thesis in *Democracy and Arab Political Culture.*

> The notion of popular sovereignty as the foundation of govern-mental legitimacy, the idea of representation, or elections, of pop-ular suffrage, of political institutions being regulated by laws laid down by a parliamentary assembly, of these laws being guarded and upheld by an independent judiciary, the ideas of the secularity of the state, of society being composed of a multitude of self-activating groups and associations—all of these are profoundly alien to the Muslim political tradition.[21]

Many others reject the suggestion that Islam is an enemy in the strug-gle for accountable government. They note that Islam has many facets and tendencies, making unidimensional characterizations of the religion highly suspect.[22] They also report that there is considerable variation in the inter-pretations of religious law advanced by Muslim scholars and theologians, and that among these interpretations are expressions of support for democ-racy, including some by leading Islamist theorists.[23] Finally, they insist that openness, tolerance, and progressive innovation are well represented among traditions associated with the religion, and thus entirely compatible with Islam.[24] Such assessments receive institutional expression in the newly established Center for the Study of Islam and Democracy, which in 2000 cosponsored two international conferences at which scholars from five countries sought to demonstrate that the essence of Islam is not antidemocratic. Rather, participants argued, forces of history and economics account for the absence of democratic governance in much of the Arab world.[25]

These various and competing assessments suggest that there are to be found within Islamic doctrine and Muslim tradition both elements that are and elements that are not congenial to democracy. The influence of the religion thus depends to a very considerable extent on how and by whom it is interpreted. There is no single or accepted interpretation on many issues, nor even a consensus on who speaks for Islam. Further, serious doubts have been expressed about the motivation of some religious authorities. As one Arab scholar observes, "there are numerous examples of *ulama* manipulating Islamic teachings. . . . Motivated by political rather than religious considerations, they have offered doctrinal interpretations that are deliberately designed to justify the behavior of political leaders."[26] Systematic empirical research on the connections between religious orientations and political culture in the Arab and Muslim world is therefore needed.

A small but growing number of studies explores these connections with public opinion data from Western countries. Findings from this research are not entirely consistent. Nor are there studies in which attitudes toward democracy is the dependent variable. But these studies offer evidence about whether and how religion and religiosity influence political attitudes.

One of their conclusions is that strong religious attachments usually push toward more conservative political views. Several studies conducted in the U.S. report, for example, that personal religiosity is strongly and positively related to a conservative stance on issues of public policy, especially when these issues involve an ethical or moral dimension.[27] Another study, also using data from the U.S., found that religiosity defined in terms of biblical literalism and a tendency to seek religious guidance are positively correlated with anticommunism and higher levels of support for military and defense-related spending.[28] Research based on survey research in the U.S. has also shown these hawkish foreign policy attitudes to be more pronounced among individuals with strong evangelical beliefs.[29]

In contrast, a study using European data found that greater religiosity was positively correlated with higher levels of internationalism, and specifically with more support for European integration and for aid to developing countries.[30] In this case, religiosity was measured by the degree to which respondents reported that religion was important in shaping their personal outlook. A study based on survey data from twelve European countries found a direct positive correlation between religiosity and support for military security in three countries, a direct but negative correlation between these variables in two countries, and a positive but indirect correlation in seven countries.[31]

A final observation for which there is some evidence is that the explanatory power of religion may vary as a function of demographic characteristics. For example, a study using data from six European countries reported that religion is a more salient independent variable among women than among men, apparently because women are more religious and are thus more likely to be influenced by the teachings of their religion, as they understand them. Although stressing the need for further study, the authors of this study hypothesize that the higher level of religiosity among women helps to account for their greater conservatism relative to men.[32]

Neither of these bodies of scholarly research leads to clear expectations about whether and how attitudes toward democracy will be influenced by the religious orientations of individual Muslim Arabs. Both, however, will benefit from findings based on additional empirical research. Such research has the potential to increase confidence in one position or another in debates about whether Islam is an obstacle to democratization or at least to the emergence of pro-democracy attitudes among ordinary citizens. It will also expand the comparative dimension of social science efforts to determine the nature, extent, and locus of the relationship between religion and political attitudes more generally.

Data and Measures

This study uses survey data from Palestine, Morocco, Algeria, and Egypt to examine the relationship between Islam and democracy at the individual level of analysis. The surveys were conducted between 1988 and 1996 and, some limitations notwithstanding, provide a strong empirical foundation from which to assess whether and how religious orientations influence attitudes toward governance among ordinary citizens in the Arab world.

The Palestinian survey was conducted in August 1995 by the Center for Palestine Research and Studies (CPRS) in Nablus, under the supervision of its director, Dr. Khalil Shikaki, and the head of its polling unit, Dr. Nadir Said. Multistage area probability sampling techniques were employed to select respondents, and the interview schedule was administered to a highly representative sample of 1,184 adults residing in the West Bank and Gaza. Almost all respondents are Sunni Muslim, although a small number of Christians, approximately 4 percent, is included in the sample. CRPS has been conducting opinion polls every six to eight weeks since the Oslo Accords of September 1993 and has developed increasingly rigorous procedures for pretesting survey instruments, selecting respondents, and training interviewers. Additional information about the Palestinian survey has been published elsewhere.[33]

The North African surveys were conducted in Morocco and Algeria in late 1995 and early 1996 under the auspices of the American Institute for Maghrib Studies. The project was directed by an international research team composed of fifteen social scientists from Morocco, Algeria, Tunisia, and the U.S. Each country was represented in approximately equal measure, and all national teams included scholars from at least three different academic disciplines. The group met regularly over a three-year period to develop and then refine both conceptual and methodological aspects of the project.

The surveys were conducted in Rabat, Morocco, and Oran, Algeria. Although limited to a single city in each country, the data are based on carefully drawn random samples of 1,000 households in each city, and they are thus representative of large and very heterogeneous populations. Rabat and Oran are both major urban centers, each with approximately one million inhabitants and populations that are extremely diverse in terms of wealth, lifestyle, culture, and residence patterns. As important centers of administration, finance, and/or commerce, each also contains numerous migrants from rural areas and small towns and villages.

An innovative, multistage procedure was developed to select respondents. One battery of questions was administered to the head of each randomly selected household; another, composed of questions dealing with political, social, and economic attitudes, was given to a second, randomly selected member of each household; and an additional set of questions pertaining to fertility and family planning was asked of all women of childbearing years residing in the household. Extensive care was taken in the training of interviewers, most of whom were university students, and a lengthy "interviewer manual" was prepared for use in each country. Additional information about the study appears in several publications.[34]

There are two Egyptian surveys. The first was carried out in mid-1988 under the direction of Dr. Jamal Al-Suwaidi, who presently directs the Emirates Center for Strategic Studies and Research in Abu Dhabi and who designed the project in collaboration with the present author. Based on stratified samples of 295 adults in Cairo, respondents reflect the extremely heterogeneous nature of the city's population. The sample includes an approximately equal number of men and women, and, despite a slight underrepresentation of poor and less well educated individuals, it is broadly representative with respect to age, education, socioeconomic status, and place of residence. Christians were excluded from the sample for analytical purposes, in order to facilitate comparison of Sunni Muslim populations in other Arab countries. The interviews were conducted by university students and government employees who were given a four-day orientation and then participated in a pretest of the survey instrument. Several publications give additional information about the study.[35]

The second Egyptian survey was carried out in Cairo and Alexandria in late 1992. It was conducted by the Market Research Organization, based in Amman, Jordan, under contract to the United States Information Agency, and the data were later obtained from the archives of the Roper Center. Area probability sampling involving a "random walk" was employed in both cities, with 400 individuals interviewed in Cairo and 100 interviewed in Alexandria. Interviewers, supervised by Market Research Organization personnel, were trained and then given detailed instructions before selecting and interviewing respondents.

The items that may be used to measure attitudes toward democracy vary across the four data sets. The Palestinian survey contained a number of questions about the importance of democratic practices, including government accountability and an elected parliament representing diverse political trends. The Moroccan and Algerian surveys, which used the same interview schedule, asked respondents to rate the importance of openness to diverse political ideas relative to other criteria for political leadership and of developing democratic institutions relative to other priorities for government action. The 1988 Egyptian survey contained a number of questions about the preferred model of government. Respondents were asked, for example, to evaluate parliamentary systems and liberal democracy relative to other political and ideological formulae, including socialism, Arab nationalism, and Islamic government. Finally, the 1992 Egyptian survey asked respondents to rate the importance of having open and competitive elections. These items are listed in the appendix to this chapter.

With the exception of the 1992 Egyptian survey, factor analysis was used to select the items listed in the appendix from a larger battery of questions on each interview schedule that appeared to measure attitudes toward democracy. Factor analysis identifies items that cluster together and hence measure the same underlying concept, thereby increasing confidence in reliability and validity. Confidence is further increased by the fact that the Moroccan and Algerian surveys produced identical results. Only in the case of the 1992 Egyptian survey was it impossible to offer this evidence of reliability and validity. That survey contained only one item pertaining to democracy.

The factor analyses in all instances also included items pertaining to Islam, and it is significant that the same two dimensions emerged in all four cases where the technique was employed. One dimension is based on questions about personal piety, including prayer, other religious observance, and turning to religion when facing important problems or decisions. The other is based on items pertaining to Islam's political role, including questions about Islamist political movements, the political involvement of religious leaders, and Islamic guidance in public affairs. In the 1992 Egyptian survey, there was only one item pertaining to religion. It asked respondents whether or not they agreed that their country should always be guided by Islamic laws and values.

Analysis and Findings

The dependent variable in this analysis is attitude toward democracy. It is measured for Palestine, Morocco, Algeria, and Egypt in 1988 by an additive index constructed from the relevant items shown in the appendix. In each case, responses have been dichotomized and then summed. Based on these measures, Table 3.1 shows for each data set the proportion of respondents attaching various degrees of importance to democracy. Table 3.1 also presents responses to the single item measuring attitudes toward democracy in the 1992 Egyptian survey. Similar procedures have been employed to construct additive indices measuring personal piety and attitudes toward the role of Islam in politics and public affairs.

The differences across data sets shown in Table 3.1 result at least partly from the different survey instruments employed. But Table 3.1 shows that there is also considerable variation within each of the populations surveyed. To determine whether religious orientations are useful in accounting for this variance, regression analysis has been employed to examine the relationship between attitudes toward democracy and each of two Islamic dimensions identified by factor analysis. Age and education are included as control variables, and models are run not only for entire samples but also for subsamples based on sex.

For Palestine, regression analysis shows that personal piety is inversely related to support for democracy, whereas a preference for religious influence in political affairs is not related to the dependent variable to a statistically significant degree. Disaggregation of the data reveals, however, that this pattern characterizes women but not men and, further, that it obtains for women in the West Bank but not for women in the Gaza Strip. These findings are presented in Table 3.2, which gives standardized regression coefficients (betas) since the attitudinal indices are not composed of standard and equivalent units of measurement. The table also reports t-statistics and levels of significance.

In Morocco, there is no statistically significant relationship between attitudes toward democracy and personal piety but support for Islamic guidance

Table 3.1. Importance Attached to Democracy in Morocco, Algeria, Palestine, and Egypt

	PALESTINE 1995	MOROCCO 1995–96	ALGERIA 1995–96	EGYPT 1988	EGYPT 1992
Very important	16.8	18.6	5.5	13.2	38.6
Somewhat important	43.3	26.4	32.8	22.1	39.8
Not important	39.9	55.0	61.7	64.7	21.6
	100%	100%	100%	100%	100%

Table 3.2. Multiple Regression Showing Influence of Islamic Orientations on Attitudes toward Democracy in Palestine in 1995

	FULL SAMPLE	MEN ONLY	WOMEN ONLY	WEST BANK MEN	WEST BANK WOMEN	GAZA MEN	GAZA WOMEN
Personal Piety	−.13 (−3.77)***	−.53 (−1.04)	−.12 (−2.52)***	−.05 (−.70)	−.15 (−2.50)***	−.11 (−1.30)	−.05 (−.67)
Islam and Politics	.26 (−.76)	−.02 (−.46)	.05 (−1.05)	−.08 (−1.18)	−.00 (−.13)	.10 (1.21)	.15 (1.90)
Education	.12 (3.70)***	.09 (1.95)*	.10 (2.15)*	.13 (2.30)**	.11 (1.95)*	−.02 (−.32)	.06 (.76)
Age	−.14 (−4.28)***	.12 (2.81)***	.09 (1.95)*	.09 (1.53)	.10 (1.71)	.22 (3.17)***	.09 (1.04)
Constant	(38.43)***	(26.05)***	(24.48)***	(22.27)***	(20.97)***	(13.37)***	(12.51)***

Note: Table shows standardized coefficients (betas) and gives t statistics in parentheses.

*$p < .05$, **$p < .02$, ***$p < .01$

in public affairs is strongly related to the dependent variable. Specifically, higher levels of support for Islamic guidance are associated with lower levels of importance attached to democratic norms and institutions. These patterns are shown in Table 3.3.

Additional insight is provided by two further analyses. The first replaces the scale measuring attitudes toward Islamic guidance by its two constituent items, one asking about politics and administration and the other asking

Table 3.3. Multiple Regression Showing Influence of
Islamic Orientations on Attitudes toward Democracy
in Morocco in 1995–1996

	FULL SAMPLE	FULL SAMPLE	MEN ONLY	WOMEN ONLY
Personal Piety	−.01 (−.378)	.00 (.08)	.01 (.24)	−.00 (−.09)
Islamic Guidance in Public Affairs	−.09 (−2.50)**			
1. in politics and administration		−.06 (−1.23)	−.11 (−1.67)	-.01 (−.15)
2. in economics and commerce		−.12 (−2.43)**	−.08 (−1.20)	−.15 (−2.17)*
Education	.40 (10.70)***	.38 (9.75)***	.40 (7.54)***	.31 (5.36)***
Age	−.05 (−1.37)	−.06 (−1.48)	−.03 (−.58)	−.11 (−2.00)*
Constant	(19.07)***	(18.24)***	(12.02)***	(13.86)***

Note: Table shows standardized coefficients (betas) and gives t statistics in parentheses.
*$p < .05$, **$p < .02$, ***$p < .01$

about economics and commerce. The regression in this case shows that the item pertaining to guidance in economic and commercial affairs provides the scale's explanatory power; it remains statistically significant in the new regression model, whereas the item pertaining to guidance in political and administrative affairs loses its statistical significance. The second involves separate analyses undertaken for men and women, which reveals that the previously reported pattern holds for the latter but not the former. These findings, too, are shown in Table 3.3.

Findings from Algeria are similar to those from Morocco. Support for Islamic guidance is inversely related to democratic attitudes to a statistically significant degree. Also, as in Morocco, Islamic guidance in economic and

Table 3.4. Multiple Regression Showing Influence of
Islamic Orientations on Attitudes toward Democracy
in Algeria in 1995–1996

	FULL SAMPLE	FULL SAMPLE	MEN ONLY	WOMEN ONLY
Personal Piety	−.06 (−1.55)	−.06 (−1.60)	.03 (.52)	−.15 (−2.82)***
Islamic Guidance in Public Affairs	−.09 (−2.54)***			
1. in politics and administration		.00 (.09)	−.00 (−.13)	.01 (.22)
2. in economics and commerce		−.11 (−2.53)***	−.06 (−.90)	−.15 (−2.56)***
Education	.09 (2.22)**	.10 (2.36)**	.09 (1.41)	.11 (1.93)
Age	.03 (.77)	.04 (.03)	.07 (1.03)	.03 (−.46)
Constant	(4.90)***	(4.37)***	(4.32)***	(1.89)

Note: Table shows standardized coefficients (betas) and gives t statistics in parentheses.
**p < .02, ***p < .01

commercial affairs but not in politics and administration remains significant when the individual items are included in the analysis, and this relationship again holds for women but not men when the data are disaggregated on the basis of sex. In addition, personal piety is inversely related to democratic attitudes, but only for women. These findings are shown in Table 3.4.

The 1988 data from Egypt show that personal piety but not support for a strong connection between religion and politics is inversely related to the degree of importance attached to democracy. Also, as in the other cases, the statistically significant relationship holds for women but not men. The 1992 Egyptian data do not contain any items measuring personal religiosity.

Table 3.5. Multiple Regression Showing Influence of Islamic Orientations on Attitudes toward Democracy in Egypt in 1988

	FULL SAMPLE	MEN ONLY	WOMEN ONLY
Personal Piety	−.20	−.11	−.33
	(−2.81)***	(−1.23)	(−2.87)***
Islam and Politics	−.03	−.00	−.00
	(−.42)	(−.08)	(−.02)
Education	.10	.06	.23
	(1.54)	(.67)	(2.45)**
Age	−.10	.12	.03
	(−1.41)	(1.28)	(.27)
Constant	(15.26)***	(10.33)***	(9.52)***

Note: Table shows standardized coefficients (betas) and gives t statistics in parentheses. **p < .02, ***p < .01

The one item dealing with religion assesses support for political Islam, and, as in the 1988 Egyptian data, this variable is unrelated to attitudes toward democracy, for both men and women and for residents of Alexandria as well as Cairo. Findings from the 1988 Egyptian data are presented in Table 3.5 and those from the 1992 Egyptian data are shown in Table 3.6.

Conclusions

Three sets of conclusions may be tentatively advanced on the basis of these findings. All raise questions that deserve additional research. First, despite a number of statistically significant relationships, Islam appears to have less influence on political attitudes than is frequently suggested by students of Arab and Islamic society. Specifically, among the most complete models presented in Tables 3.2 through 3.6, with male and female respondents treated separately, religious orientations bear a statistically significant relationship to the dependent variable in only five of twenty-two instances. This study is of course limited in both space and time, and it is also restricted to the individual level of analysis. Nevertheless, it strongly suggests that Islam should

Table 3.6. Multiple Regression Showing Influence of Islamic Orientations on Attitudes toward Democracy in Egypt in 1992

	FULL SAMPLE	MEN ONLY	WOMEN ONLY
Islam and Politics	−.07	−.04	−.09
	(−1.28)	(−.56)	(−1.11)
Education	.11	.16	.04
	(2.13)*	(2.21)*	(.50)
Age	.00	.01	−.02
	(.00)	(.20)	(−.26)
Constant	(18.98)***	(14.40)***	(11.57)***

Note: Table shows standardized coefficients (betas) and gives t statistics in parentheses.
*p < .05, ***p < .01

not be reified when attempting to explain Arab political orientations, and, in particular, it offers evidence that support for democracy is not necessarily lower among those individuals with the strongest Islamic attachments. On the contrary, it provides support for those who challenge the thesis that Islam discourages the emergence of political attitudes conducive to democracy.

Second, the locus of those relationships that are and are not statistically significant is noteworthy. Three patterns stand out. One of them concerns sex-linked differences. While there is most often no relationship between Islamic attachments and attitudes toward democracy, all of the exceptions to this pattern occur among women. Personal piety has explanatory power among women in the West Bank, Algeria, and Egypt in 1988, although not among women in Gaza and Morocco. Also, support for Islamic guidance in economic and commercial affairs has explanatory power in Morocco and Algeria, but only among women. Stronger Islamic attachments are inversely related to support for democracy in each of these instances. Although additional research is needed to understand the reasons for this pattern, it appears that Muslim women are at least somewhat more likely than Muslim men to take cues from religion about political affairs. This pattern may be explained by the fact that men tend to be more involved in life outside the home and thus to receive information about political issues from a broader array of sources, whereas women rely on religion to a greater degree.

Another observed pattern is that support for political Islam and religious guidance in public affairs has little explanatory power. Only among Moroccan and Algerian women and only for guidance in economic and commercial affairs, rather than in politics and administration, are relevant measures strongly related to democratic attitudes. This pattern suggests that support for political Islam does not involve a rejection of democracy and that those with a more favorable view of Islamist movements and platforms are no less likely than others to favor political competition and to desire mechanisms to hold leaders accountable. Thus, in the popular mind, at least, there is no necessary incompatibility between democracy and Islamic governance. Rather, deeply discontented with existing political arrangements, many may favor an alternative that incorporates both the democratic principles of choice and accountability and the Islamic principles of justice and protection of the weak.

A final pattern deserving comment is the inverse relationship between a desire for Islamic guidance in economic and commercial affairs and pro-democracy attitudes among women in Morocco and Algeria. Although the other data sets used in this chapter do not contain measures with which to explore this relationship, these identical and unexpected findings from the two North African countries suggest that the pattern may be generalizable. In all probability, women are more discontent with the socioeconomic status quo than are men and thus favor policies guided by the values they associate with Islam, including justice, equality, social welfare, and protection of the weak. If correct, this pattern may reflect women's relatively greater concern with family needs or, possibly, with a social and economic status inferior to that of men. On the strength of the findings from Morocco and Algeria, these propositions would seem to be worthy of further study.

Third, findings presented in this chapter are somewhat but not entirely consistent with those reported in research conducted in the U.S. and Europe. Several areas of similarity may be noted. Religious orientations most often push away from liberal political attitudes; findings vary from one research location to another, suggesting that the nature and extent of religion's impact on political attitudes may be conditioned by system-level attributes; and religion tends to have more explanatory power among women than among men. These similarities suggest that factors which differentiate the Arab world from the U.S. and Europe may be of limited importance with respect to the influence of religion on political attitudes.

At the same time, alternatively, the findings in this chapter also suggest that religious orientations are not as frequently related to political attitudes as appears to be the case in the U.S. and Europe. Despite the variation in findings within each region, a comparison across regions suggests that religion influences political orientations more frequently and consistently in the West than in the Arab world. Levels of personal piety are higher in the Arab world, and there is also a strong and historically legitimated connection between Islam and politics, thereby making religious orientations perhaps less useful in distinguishing between individuals with dissimilar political inclinations. If correct, this analysis leads to the hypothesis that aggregate religiosity at the system level constitutes a conditionality affecting the relationship between religion and politics at the individual level. Specifically, whereas religiosity most often tends to push toward political conservatism in more secular societies, it does so less frequently and less consistently in more religious societies. This proposition, too, deserves further research.

More opinion studies, as well as research at other levels of analysis, are necessary in order to arrive at a fuller understanding of whether and how Islam influences the prospects for democratic transitions in the Arab world. This study aspires to encourage and advance this effort, while at the same time contributing to cross-regional analysis and scientific cumulativeness. In the meantime, the evidence presently available from Palestine, Morocco, Algeria, and Egypt suggests that Islam is not the obstacle to democratization that some Western and other scholars allege it to be. A democratic, civic, and participatory political culture may indeed be necessary for mature democracy, but the findings presented in this chapter suggest that only to a very limited extent is the emergence of such a political culture discouraged by the Islamic attachments of ordinary Arab citizens.

APPENDIX:
Items Used to Measure Attitudes toward Democracy and Islam in Palestine, Morocco, Algeria, and Egypt

PALESTINE, 1995 (WEST BANK AND GAZA)

Attitudes toward Democracy
1. Greater accountability of the government is very important.
2. Freedom of the press without government censorship is very important.
3. Fair and regular elections are very important.
4. The existence of an elected parliament representing all political trends is very important.

Personal Piety

   1. Prays regularly.

   2. Describes self as "religious."

   3. Observes all religious fasting obligations.

Islam and Politics

   1. Men of religion should have a leading role in politics.

   2. Islam is the sole faith by which Palestinians can obtain their rights.

   3. Supports Islamic political parties.

   4. Supports the establishment of an Islamic caliphate state.

MOROCCO AND ALGERIA, 1995–1996

Attitudes toward Democracy

   1. Openness to diverse political ideas is an important criterion for national leadership (ranks first or second on a list that includes experience, a sense of justice, integrity, and human sensitivity).

   2. The development of democratic institutions is a high priority for government (ranks first or second on a list that includes economic well-being, civil peace, and preservation of traditional values).

Personal Piety

   1. Prays regularly.

   2. Consults *imam* or *f'kih* if has a personal problem.

   3. Often reads works on religion (high loading only for Morocco).

Islam and Public Affairs

   1. Believes that religion should guide political and administrative affairs.

   2. Believes that religion should guide economic and commercial affairs.

EGYPT, 1988

Attitudes toward Democracy

   1. Parliamentary government is the preferred political system.

   2. Prefers liberal democracy to Arab nationalism, socialism, and Islamic government.

   3. Prefers a competitive political system along the U.S. or European model.

4. Disagrees that Western values are leading to the moral erosion of our society.

Personal Piety

1. Refers to religious teachings when making important life decisions.

2. Reads the Quran frequently.

3. Prays regularly.

4. Observes all religious fasting obligations.

Islam and Politics

1. Religion and politics should not be separate.

2. Disagrees that religion is a private matter.

3. Is in favor of the religious "awakening" now current in society.

4. Supports present-day organized religious movements.

EGYPT, 1992

Attitudes toward Democracy

Very important to have open parliamentary elections in a country like ours.

Islam and Politics

Our country should always be guided by Islamic law and values.

CHAPTER 4

Political Generations in Developing Countries: Evidence and Insights from Algeria (2004)

Mark Tessler, Carrie Konold, and Megan Reif

Introduction

The replacement of one generation by another with new experiences and attitudes is a common explanation for sociopolitical change. According to this view, historical events define the boundaries of identifiable eras that produce distinct and durable attitudes among individuals who pass through their formative years during this period. These age cohorts constitute political generations and their shared predispositions are described as generation effects or cohort effects. While intuitively appealing, empirical research on political generations has produced mixed findings. Moreover, with few exceptions, this research is based on data from the United States and Europe and focuses on partisanship and other political orientations that are most relevant in democratic polities.

Improving our understanding of generational dynamics is an important task for scholars of developing countries, particularly those who study the Islamic world. There have been dramatic changes in politics and society in many of these countries. Older individuals grew up under colonialism, those who came later passed through their formative years during the period of Third World solidarity and socialism that often followed independence, and those younger still were educated in a climate marked by the political formulae that are today competing for primacy. Moreover, in Muslim-majority countries, Islam has been a prominent part of the political landscape in recent decades and occupies an important place in what are often intense debates about governance, public policy, and cultural norms.

Against this background, the present study inquires into the existence of generation effects in Algeria, a country marked by several distinct historical periods in the last half-century. First, after briefly reviewing the literature on political socialization and historical memory, we summarize recent Algerian history and develop a series of propositions about the predispositions around which cohort effects may have formed. Second, using survey data collected in 1995, we test our expectations about predispositions that may be the focus of cohort effects by comparing the attitudes and values of Algerians who were 18 to 25 years of age during each of five historical periods. We find that cohort effects are not common but do emerge during certain historical periods and with respect to certain types of issues. In concluding, we consider the theoretical implications of our findings and suggest areas for future research on political socialization and political generations in countries like Algeria.

Theoretical Background and Previous Research

Social scientists have sought to test systematically whether certain attitudes, after being formed in late adolescence and early adulthood, persist throughout life, above and beyond whatever political learning continues during later years. Most studies begin with the classic 1928 essay of Karl Mannheim, in which he posits that political socialization during youth is heavily influenced by the prevailing historical circumstances.[1] Shared attitudes should be discernable among men and women who experience the same events during what Mannheim calls their "formative years"—between the ages of 18 and 25—such that a distinguishable political generation emerges and remains identifiable despite the confounding influences of later periods.

According to this "impressionable years" thesis, important political events define what is salient and significant for young people as they first encounter the larger political world. Such events, however, are less important for adults, who tend to assimilate new experiences into an attitudinal framework that is already well developed. This socialization process produces distinct cohorts, or "political generations," which thus respond attitudinally and behaviorally in a similar fashion to new political events. When this occurs, the resulting cohort may be distinguished from earlier or later generations that passed through their formative years under different circumstances. A related area of inquiry has focused on shared memories among cohorts.[2] This literature views generational replacement, whereby one birth cohort is replaced by another with different dispositions, as an engine of gradual social and political evolution.[3]

Although findings from empirical research on political socialization and attitude stability over the life span are inconsistent, there is at least some evidence that late adolescence and early adulthood is a formative period for individual socialization. Tests of the "impressionable years" hypothesis, while mixed, suggest that some attitudes probably do fluctuate most during youth and tend thereafter to be relatively stable,[4] with some possibility of increased fluctuation in old age, described as the "mid-life stability" hypothesis.[5] There is also evidence that attitudes[6] and memories[7] about salient political events acquired during pre- and early adulthood are most likely to be remembered and imbued with importance, thereby contributing to shared characteristics among the members of a birth cohort. Different studies lend support to different hypotheses, indicating that attitudes are in fact influenced by complex combinations of factors.[8]

While intuitively appealing, the existence of cohort effects has thus received only moderate support from empirical research. In addition, several analytical perspectives challenge the proposition that early adult socialization gives rise to political generations. First, some argue that while individuals acquire political attitudes during the impressionable years of youth, exogenous national or international political events may not be the most influential factors. Other considerations, such as family structure, educational attainment, race, class, and economic circumstances, may create a degree of intracohort variability that makes it difficult or even impossible to distinguish intercohort patterns.[9]

Second, the "lifelong openness model" suggests that attitude change occurs continuously throughout adulthood. Some scholars view attitude change primarily as a function of aging, or life-stage. As individuals mature, they encounter new social and personal circumstances, including college, employment, marriage, child rearing, and retirement. Each life-stage brings new roles and responsibilities, altering interests and experiences and modifying attitudes as a result. Moreover, the ages at which such transitions occur may differ across or even within societies because of dissimilar laws and norms.[10] Another challenge posits that major historical events have a similar impact on people of all ages, possibly overwhelming any previously formed cohorts with "period effects."[11]

Finally, a complication arises if the circumstances of a particular period do not have the same impact on all members of a political generation. Events may divide a birth cohort into two or more groups, what Mannheim calls "generation units," making it difficult to identify a given cohort.[12]

These competing perspectives notwithstanding, empirical research provides a measure of support for the existence of cohort effects. This support is limited and inconsistent, however, and several factors can help us understand why political generations are only found in some instances. First, many political events are not highly salient, particularly for young people.[13] Although national politics may play an important role in political socialization, available research suggests that memories and attitudes formed around national events may persist only with respect to high visibility issues that are discussed frequently during an individual's formative years. Such issues attract strong information flows or are subject to continually reproduced interaction and interpretation.[14] For example, Jennings finds that nationally prominent events related to the Vietnam War fostered similar attitudes among a "protest generation" that came of age during the 1960s in the United States.[15] On the other hand, young people are unlikely to form lasting opinions about low-visibility issues, such as government spending priorities or foreign policy decisions, unless they happen to be made unusually salient by a war or some other major event.[16]

A related consideration is that even if political events and issues are highly salient, they may not have a lasting impact on young people if future periods are marked by dramatic change or extended instability. In this instance, continuing upheaval may decrease the salience and influence on attitudes of any event or events that had high visibility during an earlier period and thereby overwhelm cohort effects.[17]

Socialization, then, appears to be episodic. Shaped by the irregular nature and salience of political circumstances, distinguishable cohorts may be formed during certain periods but not during others. To the extent this is the case, political generations may be relatively rare. Further, because major political events occur episodically and discontinuously, one generation may be characterized by similar and stable attitudes pertaining to one set of concerns while a very different set of concerns may characterize another generation. The particular concerns for which the concept of political generation is salient may also vary from one culture to another.[18] It is necessary, therefore, to identify the specific predispositions that may define each individual cohort, recognizing that the same issues and concerns may not be salient across all cohorts. As Schuman and Scott write, "only where events occur in such a manner as to demarcate a cohort in terms of its 'historical-social' consciousness should we speak of a true generation."[19]

These latter observations have implications for cross-national research on political socialization. More specifically, they caution against generalizing results across national boundaries without considering the historical context within which a political generation is formed. Available research supports this caution. For example, the few studies to explore political generation hypotheses outside the United States and Europe suggest that patterns differ from those observed in Western democracies.[20] Similarly, a study comparing seven different birth cohorts in sixty societies using World Values Survey data finds stronger evidence for intergenerational differences in advanced industrial societies than in countries that have experienced collapse and turmoil in their economic, political, and social systems, presumably because period effects supersede cohort effects in such environments.[21]

Despite these theoretical and empirical challenges, we believe that if the concept of political generation has value it should be possible to identify and distinguish birth cohorts in non-Western societies, including those that have experienced regime changes or other important political and social transformations. At the same time, as others have also argued, we believe that hypotheses both about the nature of salient political dispositions and about intergenerational differences in attitudinal expression and predisposition must be based on culture- and context-specific analysis. Accordingly, we expect that cohort effects may be present only for certain attitudes and only under certain circumstances, and, most important, that the issues and concerns around which political attitudes form and persist may not be the same in Algeria as those reported to be important in research carried out in Western democracies.

In developing countries, especially those that have experienced political instability, we believe that the most promising areas for an investigation of socialization and the formation of political generations include views about national leadership and the preferred type of political and economic system. Furthermore, and particularly in societies with Muslim majorities, attitudes about culture, including religion and its political role, the status of women, and the desired level of Western influence, may also be highly salient. Our analysis of the Algerian data is thus guided by assessments that specify both the types of attitudes and the particular historical periods for which we do and do not expect to find generation effects.

The Algerian Case and Empirical Expectations

The Algerian case presents an important opportunity to test hypotheses about socialization and the formation of political generations. Algeria has experienced major political, social, and economic transformations, which provide an opportunity for exploring the extent to which significant political events and the periods they define affect the political and social orientations of most citizens. Yet, only certain periods stand out as most likely to give rise to a recognizable and distinct political generation. These periods are characterized by a broadly consistent political and ideological orientation of substantial duration.

We note five periods in Algeria's history since World War II, each characterized by events of major national importance. These are intense colonial rule prior to 1954 ("Colonialism"), a brutal war for independence between 1954 and 1962 ("Independence War"), followed by three distinct political periods since gaining independence in 1962: the presidency of Houari Boumedienne from 1965 to 1978 ("Boumedienne"); the presidency of Chadli Benjedid from

1979 to 1988 ("Benjedid"); and the most recent period, which began with a short-lived political opening in 1989 and then gave way to intense political violence involving clashes between government security forces, paramilitary forces aligned with the regime, and armed Islamic groups ("Contestation and Violence").

Algeria's colonial experience under the French was longer and more intense than most, lasting over 130 years. Approximately one million French citizens came to live in the territory, expropriating property and suppressing traditional institutions and values. As one scholar notes, "No Islamic society has been so thoroughly pulverized and sociologically deconstructed as Algeria during the nearly century-and-a-half of European occupation, oppression and occultation."[22] Subsequently, from 1954 until 1962, Algerians waged a war of national liberation, ultimately winning independence but at a very high price. Roughly one million Algerians died—one-tenth of the Muslim population—and much of the country's infrastructure—hospitals, schools, factories—was also devastated.[23] The Front de Libération Nationale (FLN) led the revolution and emerged after the war as the dominant political force in the country.[24] Under the FLN, Algeria became a single-party state.

From its independence in 1962 through the 1970s, socialist development policies, including state-driven industrialization, and a relatively egalitarian and effective program of mass education, health care, and social services marked Algeria's political economy. The political system was highly centralized, with a cadre of military and civilian leaders running the country and little grassroots political participation. On the international scene, Algeria identified strongly with the Non-Aligned Movement and became one of its leaders. The first leader of independent Algeria was Ahmed Ben Bella, whose three-year tenure saw the introduction of the country's populist and socialist policies, as well as its single-party political system. Of particular note during this period was a program of self-management through which Algerian workers directed former French farms and factories.

Following a bloodless coup in 1965, Houari Boumedienne took power and held it until his death in 1978. His presidency marked the longest period of political continuity in the history of independent Algeria, and it is also the period with the most consistent set of state policies. The Boumedienne regime relied on the military for support and implemented policies typical of authoritarian and socialist-oriented developing countries at the time, especially those that followed the Soviet "vanguard party" rather than the Chinese and Cuban mass mobilization model. These policies included the nationalization of industry, import-substitution, state funding of the industrial sector at the expense of agriculture, and social welfare policies that provided mass education and health care.[25] Cultural policies emphasized the country's Arab and Islamic identity. Also, as noted, Algeria was an active and militant member of the Non-Aligned Movement.[26]

After Boumedienne's death in 1978, the civilian and military leaders of the FLN selected Colonel Chadli Benjedid, a senior military officer, as his successor. Within a few years and throughout the following decade, spontaneous challenges to the Benjedid regime emerged in many quarters: Berbers, Islamists, workers, students, women's groups, and human rights activists. These communities called for an end to the political silence of the Boumedienne era and, above all, for attention to mounting economic problems, most notably widespread unemployment and a critical shortage of housing. Benjedid responded with modest political liberalization and economic policies that allowed for more autonomy from the state. Discontent continued to mount, however, with a growing gap between rich and poor adding to the complaints of ordinary citizens.[27] In 1988, this discontent exploded in rioting throughout the country, and in response Benjedid initiated a bold experiment in democratization. As reported by one scholar, Algeria's government was "suddenly the most free, most pluralistic, and most enthusiastic defender of democracy in the Arab world."[28]

Algeria's democratic opening was short-lived. The Front Islamique du Salut (FIS) won the 1990 and 1991 elections, whereupon the military voided the results and suppressed the FIS. An increasingly brutal civil war followed, with both Islamists and forces aligned with the regime committing atrocities and contributing to the death of more than one hundred thousand civilians.[29] Order has for the most part been restored at the time of this writing, with power exercised by the military despite the return of some measure of democracy. Thus, a mixture of violence, disorder, authoritarianism, and little progress on pressing economic problems characterized the 1990s.

Given this political history, as well as prior research on political socialization, we may advance the following propositions about the extent and locus of cohort effects in Algeria to guide our analysis of the survey data collected in 1995.

> 1. *Political Efficacy and Trust.* We think it unlikely that historical
>   circumstances have a significant and lasting impact on political
>   efficacy and political trust in Algeria. Nevertheless, given the
>   importance of these dimensions of political culture, as well as
>   the fact that they have received attention in studies of political
>   socialization in the United States, this expectation deserves to
>   be tested. Our expectation is based in part on findings from
>   research in the United States, which suggest that immediate
>   social and economic circumstances have much more influence

on political efficacy than do historical events.[30] Similarly, the
extent to which individuals believe that leaders and institutions
can be trusted to act for the good of the country appears to be
influenced primarily by the response of these leaders and institutions to immediate problems rather than by the performance of
past regimes. The latter pattern is also suggested by studies of
Algeria, which report that the accomplishments of those in
power during one time period have little influence on the evaluation of political leaders during subsequent time periods. In the
1980s and 1990s, for example, several observers reported that
Algerians were no longer impressed by accounts of their leaders'
contribution to the struggle for independence. The younger generation in particular, these observers noted, "feels let down and
marginalized by the post-independence regimes."[31]

2. *Political System Preference.* Questions about how the country
   should be governed are highly salient in developing countries,
   especially in the years following independence and during subsequent periods when many citizens are dissatisfied with prevailing patterns of governance. Accordingly, attitudes about models
   of government, or political system preference, represent the kind
   of political orientation with respect to which cohort effects may
   be found. Democracy more or less along Western lines and
   Islamic governance following the experience of countries like
   Iran and Saudi Arabia are the models of government that have
   received most attention in recent years in Algeria and other Arab
   countries.[32] Each model has its supporters and detractors. In
   addition, some have a positive view of both political formulae,
   perhaps envisioning a political system like that of Iran or even
   Indonesia, rather than that of Saudi Arabia. Finally, some do not
   find either model appealing, presumably believing that the country would be best served by a strong civilian or military leader.
   Should generation-linked attitudes with political content be discernible, they may well involve judgments about one or both of
   these models of government.

3. *Economic Outlook.* Algeria's serious economic problems, which
   have persisted for well over a decade, make it difficult to be opti-
   mistic about the country's economic future. On the other hand,
   the country is rich in land and natural resources, has an overbur-
   dened but still relatively well-developed infrastructure, and has a
   comparatively well-educated population. Thus there is room for
   differing assessments about Algeria's economic prospects. The
   possibility of cohort effects associated with economic outlook in
   such circumstances is suggested by research in post-communist

societies. More specifically, this research finds that present-day economic troubles are more likely to lead to low subjective well-being among individuals who reached adulthood during a period of economic growth.[33] If cohort effects are present, they may thus be found among individuals who have shared memories of times that were either significantly better or significantly worse than the present economic situation.

4. *Cultural Values.* As in other societies experiencing rapid social change, where traditional and nontraditional norms and behavior patterns exist side by side, cultural values have been subjects of debate and disagreement since Algeria became independent. Values and practices pertaining to religion, women, and the appropriate degree of Western influence have been especially salient in this context. Accordingly, these and similar cultural concerns may be the kind of high-visibility issues that attract strong information flows and thus give rise to cohort effects.

While we do not expect to find cohort effects associated with political efficacy or political trust, we suspect that a number of concerns that are central preoccupations in Algeria may give rise to distinctive views among one or more political generations. Among these, in our judgment, are political system preference, specifically relating to democracy and political Islam; economic outlook; and cultural values, such as those pertaining to the status of women.

It is unlikely that every distinguishable period in Algerian history has given rise to cohort effects. Indeed, the existence of cohort effects is probably the exception rather than the rule. In the Algerian case, we believe such effects are most likely to be present among the Boumedienne generation—those who passed through late adolescence and early adulthood during all or most of the years Houari Boumedienne was in power, 1965 to 1978. As noted, this was the period with the greatest degree of ideological salience and coherence, and the highest level of political continuity. Coming shortly after independence, it also occupied a critical temporal position in the history of modern Algeria.

Data

The data for the present study are from a survey of one thousand men and women in Oran, Algeria, conducted in mid-1995 under the auspices of the American Institute for Maghrib Studies. An international research team composed of fifteen social scientists from Algeria, Morocco, Tunisia, and the United States designed and carried out the project in Algeria as well as other countries in North Africa. Each country had approximately equal representation on the overall research team, and all national groups included scholars from at least three different academic disciplines. Professor Abdelbaki Benziane, then vice-rector of the University of Oran, directed the team carrying out fieldwork in Oran.

The timing of the survey should be noted. Since interviews were carried out during a period of turmoil and violence in Algeria, it is almost certain that contemporary events would in some way affect virtually all members of society and thus give rise to period effects. Should generation effects nonetheless be discernable, despite the prospect that they might have been washed away by the dramatic events taking place at the time the survey was conducted, evidence for the existence of political generations will be even stronger than it would have been had the data been collected during a less turbulent period.

Oran had approximately 850,000 inhabitants at the time of the survey, being the second largest city in the country. An important industrial and trading center, the city is the principal focus of urban life in western Algeria. It thus has a significant number of wealthy and middle-class professionals. At the same time, it also has sprawling working-class neighborhoods and *bidonvilles* [shanty towns] inhabited by the urban poor, including at least 100,000 migrants from the surrounding countryside. In this respect, Oran replicates the economic, cultural, and lifestyle diversity that exists in most of the country's large urban centers.

The research team developed a multistage procedure in an effort to construct a representative sample of Oran's population. To begin, it employed area probability sampling involving the successive random selection of districts, neighborhoods, and households. Thereafter, interviewers conducted three separate interviews within each randomly selected household: first, they gave a battery of demographic questions to the household head; second, they administered another interview schedule, composed of questions dealing with political, social, and economic attitudes, to another adult member of each household, selected randomly through the use of a Kish table; and, finally, they presented a third battery of questions, pertaining to fertility and family planning, to all women of child-bearing age residing in the household. The present study employs data from the one thousand randomly selected household members who answered questions about their political, social, and economic attitudes.

The team took extensive care in the training of interviewers, most of whom were university students, and provided a lengthy and detailed "interviewer manual" for use in each country. The language of the interviews was either French or Arabic, depending on the preference of the respondent. In general, better-educated respondents preferred French and less well-educated respondents preferred Arabic. Nonresponse was very low; only about 2 percent of the households or respondents selected did not agree to the interview, and there was about an equal number of households in which respondents could not be contacted.[34] This result is partly due to the careful preparation of interviewers and also, perhaps, because initial interviews with household heads reduced any potential distrust. Additional information about the study appears in several publications.[35] Despite the care taken in drawing the sample, it is not a perfect microcosm of Oran's population. Census data below the provincial (*wilaya*) level are limited, but information about the distribution of age and sex in the *commune* of Oran are available and suggest some discrepancy between the sample and the population on these variables. With respect to the former, population versus sample percentages across the age categories of 18–24, 25–34, 35–49, and over 50 are as follows: 23 versus 18; 29 versus 25; 25 versus 32; and 23 versus 25. This means that individuals under 35 are slightly underrepresented in the sample. There is also a discrepancy with respect to sex. Although 1987 census data report an approximately equal number of men and women in Oran, only 41 percent of the sample is male. In part, this may be attributable to the large number of Algerian men who work abroad and send funds to their families, who remain at home. Nevertheless, it is clear that men are also underrepresented in the sample.

Commune-level information is not available with respect to education, but the sample is very diverse in this respect. The distribution is as follows: no schooling, 19 percent; primary school only, 28 percent; intermediate school, 24 percent; high school, 20 percent; post-secondary schooling, 9 percent. Educational levels are considerably higher among younger Algerians, but this distribution is probably quite representative of Oran's adult population.

Discrepancies between the sample and the population of Oran indicate that findings from the present study should be generalized with caution. This would be the case even were there no discrepancies, however, since Oran is only one city in one developing country. Nevertheless, data about the attitudes and orientations of one thousand individuals who are generally, albeit imperfectly, representative of a large and heterogeneous Third World city provide a solid empirical foundation for an attempt to determine whether cohort effects can be discerned in countries like Algeria and, if so, to contribute to an incremental and cumulative research effort concerned with the formation of political generations.

Methods

Regression analysis has been employed to test for generation effects. The analysis asks whether generation effects are discernible among Algerians who passed through at least six of their eight formative years during any of the five historical periods outlined earlier. Dependent variables are a series of political, economic, and social attitudes relevant to Algeria, some of which resemble those examined in other studies of political socialization. The independent variables, discussed in more detail below, are dummy variables representing each of the five hypothesized political generations, with each respondent assigned to a particular cohort based on his or her age when interviewed in 1995.

Four additional variables have been included in the analysis for purposes of control. These are age, education, gender, and standard of living, the last measured by the number of conveniences and luxury items in a respondent's household. As reported in other research on social and political attitudes, and as the analysis to follow shows for the present study as well, each of these variables is at least sometimes related to one or more of the dependent variables to a statistically significant degree. Some are also related to one or more of the age cohorts. In particular, as expected given the steady expansion of education since Algerian independence, education is disproportionately high among the younger generations and disproportionately low among the older generations.

The political orientations treated as dependent variables include political efficacy, measured by a question asking whether political affairs are too complicated to be understood by ordinary citizens; political trust, measured by a question asking whether national leaders care about the needs of ordinary citizens; and political system preference, based on assessments of democratic and Islamic political systems and with attitudes toward these two political formulae considered both separately and in combination. The first two orientations are similar to dimensions of political culture that have been explored in previous studies of socialization.[36] The third dependent variable—political system preference—represents an evaluation of the most important models of governance competing for support in Algeria and many other Arab and Muslim countries.

Dependent variables concerned with economic and occupational predispositions include an economic outlook index composed of two very strongly correlated items. One asks about the degree to which the national economic situation is improving or deteriorating, and the other asks for a similar assessment of the respondent's personal economic situation.[37] Another dependent variable asks whether hard work at one's job is recognized and rewarded.

The social and cultural orientations examined include personal religiosity, measured by the regularity of prayer; attitudes toward women and gender equality, measured by an item that asks whether it is acceptable for a married woman to work outside the home; and whether the respondent likes Western popular music. Although selected because of their relevance to

Algeria and other post-colonial societies, determinants of attitudes toward the status of women and other cultural norms have also been examined in previous research on intergenerational differences.[38] An appendix gives the exact wording in both French and English of the questions used to measure each of these attitudes, as well as those measuring the political and economic orientations listed above.

Informed by previous studies, we use current age to locate cohorts in relation to historical periods. There is no consensus in the literature on precisely what age span is critical, however, making efforts to operationalize the concept of "formative years" at least somewhat arbitrary.[39] Studies have defined the critical years as the age span between 10 and 30,[40] between 10 and 17,[41] between 18 and 25,[42] and the college years.[43] Moreover, further complicating the situation, some suggest that there are cross-cultural differences in age structuring and, consequently, in the years most relevant for political socialization.[44]

Against this background, we have chosen to define an individual's "formative years" as 18 to 25, not only because this is the age range most frequently used by scholars of socialization but also because, in Algeria as elsewhere, it spans such important life events as the end of secondary schooling, college where relevant, first voting, and first employment. Marriage frequently occurs during this age span as well.[45]

We thus define each cohort as those men and women for whom at least six years of the eight-year span between ages 18 and 25, the "formative years," fall within a given historical period. In the case of the 1965–1978 Boumedienne period, for example, the cohort is composed of men and women between 40 and 50 years of age when the survey was conducted in 1995. At least six of the eight years during which these individuals were between 18 and 25 coincide with the 1965–1978 period. We operationalized membership in each of the four other cohorts in the same way. This method resulted in 72.5 percent of the respondents being assigned to a cohort, with the remainder falling in between two cohorts and not assigned to either. Given the very high birth rate in Algeria, as well as the fact that nearly 10 percent of the Algerian population died in the war for independence, cohorts associated with earlier historical periods are the smallest. The number of respondents assigned to each cohort are as follows: Colonialism, pre-1954, N = 76; Independence War, 1954–1962, N = 67; Boumedienne, 1965–1978, N = 193; Benjedid, 1979 to 1988, N = 184; and Contestation and Violence, 1989–1995, N = 205.

Findings and Implications

Tables 4.1–4.5 present the results of regressions in which political trust, political efficacy, and political system preference are dependent variables.

Table 4.1. Influence of Cohort Membership on Political Trust (Logit)
with Gender, Education, and Living Standard Held Constant

	MODEL 1	MODEL 2	MODEL 3	MODEL 4	MODEL 5
Cohort Membership:					
Colonialism (pre-1954)	.41 (.34)				
Independence War (1954–1962)		−.65** (.27)			
Boumedienne (1965–1978)			.02 (.18)		
Benjedid (1979–1988)				.15 (.18)	
Contestation and Violence (1989–1995)					−.30 (.21)
Age	−.01* (.01)	−.01 (.01)	−.01 (.01)	−.01 (.01)	−.01* (.01)
Higher Educational Level	.01 (.06)	.01 (.06)	.02 (.06)	.02 (.06)	.02 (.06)
Gender (Male = 1)	−.02 (.14)	−.03 (.14)	−.01 (.14)	−.01 (.14)	−.001 (.14)
Higher Standard of Living	.09* (.05)	.10** (.05)	.09* (.05)	.09* (.05)	.09* (.05)
Constant	−.09 (.39)	−.26 (.36)	−.23 (.36)	−.30 (.37)	.02 (.26)
Number of Observations	885	885	885	885	885
Log-likelihood	1200.00	1195.16	1201.37	1200.64	1199.33
χ^2	9.70	14.56	8.35	9.08	10.40

Note: Variables marked (Logit) denote logit coefficients; standard errors are in parentheses.
1 = Respondent agrees that politicians care for citizens.
*Significant at .10 level (two-tailed test).
**Significant at the .05 level.

Table 4.2. Influence of Cohort Membership on Political Efficacy (OLS) with Gender, Education, and Living Standard Held Constant

	MODEL 1	MODEL 2	MODEL 3	MODEL 4	MODEL 5
Cohort Membership:					
Colonialism (pre-1954)	−.14 (.12)				
Independence War (1954–1962)		−.11 (.10)			
Boumedienne (1965–1978)			−.02 (.06)		
Benjedid (1979–1988)				.02 (.06)	
Contestation and Violence (1989–1995)					−.0004 (.07)
Age	.004 (.002)	.003 (.002)	.003 (.002)	.003 (.002)	.002 (.002)
Higher Educational Level	.06** (.02)	.06** (.02)	.06** (.02)	.06** (.02)	.06** (.02)
Gender (Male = 1)	−.05 (.05)	−.05 (.05)	−.05 (.05)	−.05 (.05)	−.05 (.05)
Higher Standard of Living	−.02 (.02)	−.02 (.02)	−.02 (.02)	−.02 (.02)	−.02 (.02)
Constant	1.17*** (.13)	1.22*** (.13)	1.22*** (.13)	1.22*** (.13)	1.22*** (.14)
Number of Observations	893	893	893	893	893
R^2	.01	.01	.01	.01	.01

Note: Variables marked (OLS) denote unstandardized linear regression coefficients; standard errors are in parentheses. 0,3 = Respondent's intensity of agreement that politics is intelligible to ordinary citizens.
**Significant at the .05 level.
***Significant at the .01 level.

Table 4.3. Influence of Cohort Membership on Support
for Democracy (OLS) with Gender, Education,
and Living Standard Held Constant

	MODEL 1	MODEL 2	MODEL 3	MODEL 4	MODEL 5
Cohort Membership:					
Colonialism (pre-1954)	−.06 (.10)				
Independence War (1954–1962)		−.06 (.09)			
Boumedienne (1965–1978)			−.03 (.05)		
Benjedid (1979–1988)				.006 (.05)	
Contestation and Violence (1989–1995)					.02 (.06)
Age	.0009 (.002)	.0006 (.002)	.0005 (.002)	.0004 (.002)	.0007 (.002)
Higher Educational Level	.05** (.02)	.05** (.02)	.04** (.02)	.04** (.02)	.04** (.02)
Gender (Male = 1)	.01 (.04)	.01 (.04)	.01 (.04)	.01 (.04)	.01 (.04)
Higher Standard of Living	−.03 (.02)	−.02 (.02)	−.02 (.02)	−.02 (.02)	−.02 (.02)
Constant	1.28*** (.12)	1.29*** (.11)	1.30*** (.11)	1.30*** (.11)	1.28*** (.12)
Number of observations	839	839	839	839	839
R^2	.01	.01	.01	.01	.01

Notes: Variables marked (OLS) denote unstandardized linear regression coefficients; standard
errors are in parentheses. Index of respondent's support for democratic institutions and diverse
political ideas.
**Significant at the .05 level.
***Significant at the .01 level.

Table 4.4. Influence of Cohort Membership on Support for Islam (OLS) with Gender, Education, and Living Standard Held Constant

	MODEL 1	MODEL 2	MODEL 3	MODEL 4	MODEL 5
Cohort Membership:					
Colonialism (pre-1954)	.11 (.15)				
Independence War (1954–1962)		.10 (.14)			
Boumedienne (1965–1978)			−.05 (.08)		
Benjedid (1979–1988)				−.19** (.08)	
Contestation and Violence (1989–1995)					.18 (.09)
Age	.003 (.003)	.004 (.003)	.004* (.003)	.003 (.003)	.007* (.003)
Higher Educational Level	−.001 (.03)	.0003 (.03)	−.0001 (.03)	.002 (.03)	−.0005 (.03)
Gender (Male = 1)	−.08 (.06)	−.08 (.06)	−.08 (.06)	−.08 (.06)	−.08 (.06)
Higher Standard of Living	−.06** (.02)	−.06** (.02)	−.06** (.02)	−.06** (.02)	−.06** (.02)
Constant	1.95*** (.18)	1.92*** (.17)	1.91*** (.16)	1.98*** (.17)	1.76*** (.18)
Number of Observations	763	763	763	763	763
R^2	.02	.02	.02	.02	.01

Note: Variables marked (OLS) denote unstandardized linear regression coefficients; standard errors are in parentheses. Index of respondent's support for active role of religion in public life.
*Significant at the .10 level (two-tailed test).
**Significant at the .05 level.
***Significant at the .01 level.

Table 4.5. Influence of Cohort Membership on Joint Support
for Democracy and Islam (Logit) with Gender, Education,
and Living Standard Held Constant

	MODEL 1	MODEL 2	MODEL 3	MODEL 4	MODEL 5
Cohort Membership:					
Colonialism (pre-1954)	−.68 (.45)				
Independence War (1954–1962)		−.66 (.44)			
Boumedienne (1965–1978)			.64** (.20)		
Benjedid (1979–1988)				.19 (.20)	
Contestation and Violence (1989–1995)					−.34 (.25)
Age	−.004 (.008)	−.01 (.007)	−.02** (.007)	−.01 (.007)	−.02** (.008)
Higher Educational Level	−.13* (.07)	−.14** (.07)	−.14** (.07)	−.14* (.07)	−.14** (.07)
Gender (Male = 1)	.31* (.17)	.30* (.17)	.31* (17)	.31* (.17)	.31* (.17)
Higher Standard of Living	.09 (.06)	.10 (.06)	.09 (.06)	.10* (.06)	.10 (.06)
Constant	−.90** (.46)	−.66* (.44)	−.65 (.44)	−.74* (.44)	−.38 (.48)
Number of Observations	757	757	757	757	757
Log-likelihood	902.97	905.28	895.82	904.49	903.35
χ^2	9.53	7.22	16.68	8.012	9.15

Note: Variables marked (Logit) denote logit coefficients; standard errors are in parentheses; for
Boumedienne cohort, p = .002. 1 = Respondent supports neither democratic nor Islamic principles
for guidance in public life.
*Significant at .10 level (two-tailed test).
**Significant at the .05 level.
***Significant at the .01 level.

The tables show the relationship between these dependent variables and each one of the five generational cohorts described above. As noted, age, education, sex, and standard of living are included as control variables.

The tables show that cohort membership is very rarely related to a statistically significant degree to any of the dependent variables. Cohort effects are discernible in only three instances: members of the Independence War generation are disproportionately likely to be low in political trust, members of the Benjedid generation are disproportionately likely to have an unfavorable attitude toward political Islam, and members of the Boumdeienne generation are disproportionately likely to have an unfavorable attitude toward *both* democracy and political Islam.[46] By contrast, although not of concern in the present study, each of the dependent variables is related to at least one of the control variables to a statistically significant degree. More specifically, education is positively related to political efficacy and to a favorable attitude toward democracy; standard of living is positively related to political trust and inversely related to support for political Islam; and men are disproportionately likely to have an unfavorable attitude toward both democracy and political Islam.

In addition, our findings provide a basis for informed speculation about connections between the character of political life during a given historical period and any cohort effects exhibited by the generation whose early political learning took place at that time. Three possibilities are deserving of further study, both in Algeria and in other developing nations. First, disproportionately low political trust among members of the Independence War cohort suggests that coming into adulthood during a prolonged and violent decolonization struggle predisposes individuals to be particularly critical of those who lead the independent state, especially during times of political and economic crisis. Second, disproportionately low support for political Islam among members of the Benjedid cohort suggests that passing through pre- and early adulthood during a period of market-oriented economic liberalization fosters among individuals in developing countries such as Algeria a dislike for radical and ideologically oriented political formulae. Last, disproportionately unfavorable attitudes toward both democracy and political Islam among the Boumedienne cohort suggests that if early political socialization occurs during a period of socialist-oriented and state-driven development under a highly centralized and at least somewhat authoritarian government, and especially if this takes place in the early post-colonial period and national leaders enjoy considerable popular approval, cohort effects in developing countries such as Algeria involve lower levels of support for alternative models of government.

With respect to political attitudes, then, our findings indicate that generation effects are uncommon in Algeria, a country that has experienced frequent regime change and significant political instability. These findings also suggest that when cohort effects do form, they are disproportionately likely to involve views about the character of the political system.

Tables 4.6 and 4.7 present the regressions for dependent variables concerned with economic and occupational predispositions. These include views about whether the economic situation is improving or deteriorating and judgments about whether society recognizes and rewards hard work.

The tables show that members of the Boumedienne generation are disproportionately likely to have a negative economic outlook. There are no other statistically significant relationships involving cohort membership and views about economic prospects, and there are none whatsoever involving cohort effects and views about whether hard work is recognized and rewarded. With respect to control variables, both education and standard of living are inversely correlated with negative economic outlook and standard of living is positively correlated with a belief that hard work will bring recognition and reward.

As with political orientations, cohort effects pertaining to economic orientations are rare. An exception, however, is that members of the Boumedienne generation tend to have a gloomy economic outlook. These disproportionately negative economic assessments by the Boumedienne cohort suggest that passing through pre- and early adulthood while a country is emerging from colonialism and newly governed by its own political leaders—and especially if the regime is judged at the time to be honest, hardworking, and making meaningful economic progress—predisposes individuals in developing countries such as Algeria to be particularly disappointed by the disparity between early expectations and the serious economic problems confronting their society at a later time.

Tables 4.8–4.10 display the results of regressions for dependent variables concerned with social and cultural orientations. These include religiosity, appreciation of Western popular music, and attitudes toward women working outside the home.

There are three statistically significant relationships involving cohort membership and social and cultural orientations: members of the Boumedienne cohort are disproportionately unlikely to enjoy Western popular music; members of the Contestation and Violence cohort are disproportionately likely to have a favorable opinion of such music; and members of the Boumedienne cohort are disproportionately likely to favor greater opportunities and equality for women. Although not a focus of the present inquiry, there are also many significant relationships involving control variables. Older individuals and women are disproportionately likely to be religious; a taste for Western popular music is related to a statistically significant degree to younger age, male gender, higher education, and a higher standard of living; and support

Table 4.6. Influence of Cohort Membership on Economic Outlook (Logit) with Gender, Education, and Living Standard Held Constant

	MODEL 1	MODEL 2	MODEL 3	MODEL 4	MODEL 5
Cohort Membership:					
Colonialism (pre-1954)	−.30 (.34)				
Independence War (1954–1962)		.17 (.30)			
Boumedienne (1965–1978)			.68*** (.18)		
Benjedid (1979–1988)				−.14 (.18)	
Contestation and Violence (1989–1995)					.17 (.21)
Age	.002 (.007)	−.002 (.006)	−.004 (.006)	−.001 (.006)	.002 (.007)
Higher Educational Level	−.18** (.06)	−.19** (.06)	−.18** (.06)	−.18** (.06)	−.19*** (.06)
Gender (Male = 1)	.24 (.15)	.23 (.15)	.25* (.15)	.22 (.15)	.22 (.14)
Higher Standard of Living	−.34*** (.05)	−.34*** (.05)	−.35*** (.05)	−.34*** (.05)	−.34*** (.05)
Constant	.92** (.39)	1.06** (.37)	1.02** (.37)	1.09** (.37)	.90** (.40)
Number of Observations	937	937	937	937	937
Log-likelihood	1199.90	1200.33	1187.14	1200.09	1200.05
χ^2	89.14	88.88	102.17	89.22	89.26

Note: Variables marked (Logit) denote logit coefficients; standard errors are in parentheses. 1 = Respondent believes both personal and national economic situations have worsened.
**Significant at the .05 level
***Significant at the .01 level

Table 4.7. Influence of Cohort Membership on Society's Value for Hard Work (OLS) with Gender, Education, and Living Standard Held Constant

	MODEL 1	MODEL 2	MODEL 3	MODEL 4	MODEL 5
Cohort Membership:					
Colonialism (pre-1954)	.18 (.20)				
Independence War (1954–1962)		−.07 (.18)			
Boumedienne (1965–1978)			−.08 (.10)		
Benjedid (1979–1988)				.02 (.11)	
Contestation and Violence (1989–1995)					−.08 (.13)
Age	.005 (.004)	.007** (.003)	.007** (.003)	.007** (.003)	.006 (.004)
Higher Educational Level	.05 (.04)	.05 (.04)	.05 (.04)	.05 (.04)	.05 (.04)
Gender (Male = 1)	.02 (.09)	.02 (.09)	.02 (.09)	.02 (.09)	.02 (.09)
Higher Standard of Living	.07** (.03)	.07** (.03)	.07** (.03)	.07** (.03)	.07** (.03)
Constant	2.20*** (.23)	2.12*** (.22)	2.14*** (.22)	2.13*** (.22)	2.20*** (.24)
Number of Observations	910	910	910	910	910
R^2	.02	.02	.02	.02	.02

Note: Variables marked (OLS) denote unstandardized linear regression coefficients; standard errors are in parentheses. 1,4 = Degree to which respondent believes society rewards hard work.
**Significant at the .05 level.
***Significant at the .01 level.

Table 4.8. Influence of Cohort Membership on Religiosity (Logit) with Gender, Education, and Living Standard Held Constant

	MODEL 1	MODEL 2	MODEL 3	MODEL 4	MODEL 5
Cohort Membership:					
Colonialism (pre-1954)	.92 (.61)				
Independence War (1954–1962)		−.36 (.63)			
Boumedienne (1965–1978)			−.10 (.26)		
Benjedid (1979–1988)				.16 (.19)	
Contestation and Violence (1989–1995)					.19 (.24)
Age	−.08*** (.01)	−.07*** (.01)	−.07*** (.01)	−.07*** (.01)	−.07*** (.01)
Higher Educational Level	−.05 (.07)	−.04 (.07)	−.04 (.07)	−.05 (.07)	−.04 (.07)
Gender (Male = 1)	.53** (.17)	.54** (.17)	.53** (17)	.54** (.17)	.53** (.17)
Higher Standard of Living	−.03 (.06)	−.04 (.06)	−.04 (.06)	−.04 (.06)	−.04 (.06)
Constant	.93* (.49)	.72 (.48)	.74 (.48)	.73 (.48)	.53 (.56)
Number of Observations	979	979	979	979	979
Log-likelihood	904.38	905.99	906.21	905.65	905.74
χ^2	126.35	124.73	124.52	125.08	124.98

Note: Variables marked (Logit) denote logit coefficients; standard errors are in parentheses.
1 = Respondent never prays.
*Significant at the .10 level (two-tailed test).
**Significant at the .05 level.
***Significant at the .01 level.

Table 4.9. Influence of Cohort Membership on Western Influence (OLS) with Gender, Education, and Living Standard Held Constant

	MODEL 1	MODEL 2	MODEL 3	MODEL 4	MODEL 5
Cohort Membership:					
Colonialism (pre-1954)	.17 (.11)				
Independence War (1954–1962)		.03 (.10)			
Boumedienne (1965–1978)			−.14** (.06)		
Benjedid (1979–1988)				−.05 (.06)	
Contestation and Violence (1989–1995)					.17** (.07)
Age	.009*** (.002)	−.007*** (.002)	−.006*** (.002)	−.007*** (.002)	.004** (.002)
Higher Educational Level	.09*** (.02)	.09*** (.02)	.09*** (.02)	.09*** (.02)	.09*** (.02)
Gender (Male = 1)	.15** (.05)	.15* (.05)	.15** (05)	.15*** (.05)	.15** (.05)
Higher Standard of Living	.04** (.02)	.04** (.02)	.04** (.02)	.04** (.02)	.04** (.02)
Constant	−2.96*** (.13)	−3.02*** (.12)	−3.02*** (.12)	−3.01*** (.12)	−3.16*** (.13)
Number of Observations	991	991	991	991	991
R^2	.1	.1	.12	.1	.12

Note: Variables marked (OLS) denote unstandardized linear regression coefficients; standard errors are in parentheses. 1,3 = Degree to which respondent enjoys Western music.
*Significant at the .10 level (two-tailed test).
**Significant at the .05 level.
***Significant at the .01 level.

Table 4.10. Influence of Cohort Membership on Women's Empowerment (Logit) with Gender, Education, and Living Standard Held Constant

	MODEL 1	MODEL 2	MODEL 3	MODEL 4	MODEL 5
Cohort Membership					
Colonialism (pre-1954)	−.44 (.34)				
Independence War (1954–1962)		−.24 (.30)			
Boumedienne (1965–1978)			.34* (.2)		
Benjedid (1979–1988)				.15 (.19)	
Contestation and Violence (1989–1995)					−.10 (.22)
Age	.02*** (.01)	.02*** (.01)	.02** (.01)	.02*** (.01)	.02*** (.01)
Higher Educational Level	.26*** (.06)	.26*** (.06)	.26*** (.06)	.26*** (.06)	.26*** (.06)
Gender (Male = 1)	−.99*** (.15)	−.99*** (.15)	−.99*** (.15)	−.99*** (.15)	−.99*** (.15)
Higher Standard of Living	.11** (.05)	.12** (.05)	.12** (.05)	.12** (.05)	.12* (.05)
Constant	.11 (.40)	.26 (.38)	.27 (.37)	.24 (.38)	.38 (.42)
Number of Observations	989	989	989	989	989
Log-likelihood	1160.37	1161.39	1158.88	1161.42	1161.85
χ^2	69.61	68.60	71.00	68.56	68.14

Note: Variables marked (Logit) denote logit coefficients; standard errors are in parentheses. 1 = Agree that women should work outside the home.

*Significant at .10 level (two-tailed test).

**Significant at the .05 level.

***Significant at the .01 level.

for gender equality is related to a statistically significant degree to older age, female gender, higher education, and a higher standard of living.

Despite controlling for age, it is likely, or at least possible, that the youth of the Contestation and Violence cohort accounts for the fact that its members are disproportionately likely to appreciate Western popular music. The men and women in this cohort were between 18 and 25 when the survey was conducted and are the youngest individuals in the sample. It is also possible that their tastes have been influenced by the turbulent events taking place during their formative years. Perhaps they blame Muslim extremists for Algeria's recent troubles and thus, rejecting militant Islam, embrace a symbol of the West. This is not reflected in their other attitudes, however; and in any event, it is only to the extent that their predispositions and preferences persist and distinguish their generation in the future that it will be possible to speak with confidence about the existence of cohort effects.

By contrast, findings about the Boumedienne generation probably do reflect cohort effects resulting from early socialization. Moreover, they involve both personal orientations, such as musical tastes, and societal norms, such as the role of women outside the home; and they also involve, within the same cohort, a *more* traditional orientation in the sphere of personal affairs and a *less* traditional orientation in the sphere of societal affairs. Linking these patterns to the characteristics of the Boumedienne era suggests that in countries such as Algeria that have had an intense colonial experience, those individuals whose early socialization takes place shortly after independence will be less likely than others to adopt nontraditional habits and cultural preferences in their personal lives. This is particularly likely if the period is also characterized by a national concern with reasserting the country's cultural identity after years of colonial domination. The findings also suggest that in developing countries such as Algeria, those individuals whose early socialization takes place during a period that emphasizes socialist development and mass education, and that possibly also recognizes women's contribution to the achievement of national objectives, will be more likely than others to possess nontraditional values in matters pertaining to societal organization.

Conclusions

Our data present evidence that generation effects are discernible in a country like Algeria, yet these effects are relatively rare. There are cohort effects associated with several historical periods, but in only one case are they discernible for more than a single issue. This is the Boumedienne period. In four different instances, including at least one in each of the substantive areas considered—political, economic, and social—men and women whose early political socialization coincided with the presidency of Houari Boumedienne display attitudinal tendencies that set them apart from other Algerians.

Thus, if we want to identify the attributes of a historical period that would seem to be those most likely to produce cohort effects, we must examine the Boumedienne era. The attributes of this period include substantial duration; centralized political leadership; a coherent socialist orientation; an emphasis on industrial development, mass education, and social welfare; regime legitimacy; and an important temporal position as the period following independence. Yet, it is only possible to speculate about more specific causal linkages and about the relative utility of each of these attributes in accounting for particular cohort effects. For example, were some of the distinctive dispositions of the Boumedienne cohort shaped largely by the ideological orientation that prevailed when its members passed through their formative years, or were they influenced to an equal or even greater degree by the forward-looking and hopeful national mood that prevailed immediately after independence?

The present study also demonstrates that generation effects are limited in substantive scope. They help to account for variance in some normative orientations but are not present in many other instances. It is possible that disaggregation might have yielded additional significant relationships, revealing cohort effects for some time periods or orientations among only one sex, only one educational level, and so forth. Nevertheless, while this is another subject for future research, it seems clear that in countries like Algeria, as in the West, the concept of political generation has only limited explanatory and predictive power.

Our findings demonstrate the importance of contextual knowledge in formulating and testing hypotheses about political generations. With respect to both historical periods and the content of period effects, familiarity with the Algerian case has informed what was expected and, equally important, has been essential to understanding what was actually observed. The present study has also been informed, and to an extent inspired, by research on political socialization and political generations carried out in the United States. Nevertheless, the concerns of this research could not have been meaningfully pursued in Algeria without knowledge of the country's history and the issues confronting its citizens.

Additional research is needed not only to reduce uncertainly and shed light on causal pathways; it is also needed to assess the generalizability of insights derived from our study of Oran. To what extent is our sample representative of Algeria's urban population? Would data from Algerians living in small towns and villages lead to different conclusions? And how representative is the overall Algerian experience? We believe that in the areas of politics, economics, and culture, Algeria resembles many of the Third World countries that became independent in the 1950s and 1960s. Other scholars agree. Quandt, for example, argues that Algeria is similar to many postcolonial countries and should be examined in comparative perspective.[47] We also believe that the demographic and economic heterogeneity of Oran makes it at least reasonably representative of the country as a whole. Nevertheless, propositions derived from the study of one Algerian city cannot be assessed without research in other locations. Furthermore, having emphasized the importance of contextual knowledge, we would add that an understanding of the history, politics, and culture of any society in which scholars investigate generation effects must inform such research.

Finally, as illustrated by relationships involving the control variables of age, education, gender, and standard of living, it should be emphasized that generation effects are only one determinant of variance in political, economic, and social attitudes. Moreover, the amount of variance for which they account is relatively modest. A different kind of study would be needed if accounting for attitudinal variance were the primary objective. The focus of the present investigation, by contrast, is an inquiry into the existence and character of generation effects. And although many questions remain unanswered, the Algerian case offers evidence that political generations do emerge in response to certain conditions, that their characteristics are discernible, and that the content of cohort effects can be plausibly linked to the characteristics of the time period during which members of the generation passed through their formative years.

Appendix

We have provided below the exact question wording and response choices in the French language version of the Oran survey, followed by an English-language translation.

POLITICAL ORIENTATIONS

Political System Preferences
Support for democracy

(1) Classez dans l'ordre de leur importance (de 1 à 4), *selon votre opinion,* les besoins des citoyens qu'un gouvernement doit chercher à satisfaire:

   1. Conditions matérielles (travail, logement)

   2. Paix civile

   3. Sauvegarde des traditions et valeurs culturelles

4. Développement des institutions démocratiques

5. Pas d'opinion

Place in the order of their importance (from 1 to 4), *in your opinion*, the needs of citizens that the government should satisfy [coded 1 according to whether respondent selected #4, 0 otherwise]:

1. Material conditions (work, lodging)

2. Civil peace

3. Protecting cultural traditions and values

4. Developing democratic institutions

9. No response

(2) Classez dans l'ordre de leur importance (de 1 à 5), *selon votre opinion*, les qualités que doit posséder un homme politique:

1. Expérience (compétence)

2. Intégrité morale

3. Sens de la justice

4. Sensibilité humaine

5. Esprit ouvert aux idées politiques diverses

9. Pas d'opinion

Place in the order of their importance (from 1 to 5), *in your opinion*, the qualities a politician should possess [coded 1 according to whether respondent selected #5, 0 otherwise]:

1. Experience (competence)

2. Moral integrity

3. A sense of justice

4. A humane sensibility

5. Openness to diverse political ideas

9. No response

Support for political Islam

(3) Selon vous, la religion doit-elle guider les décisions dans la vie administrative et politique?

1. Beaucoup

2. Un peu

3. Non

4. Ne sait pas

9. Pas d'opinion

In your opinion, should religion guide political and administrative decisions?

1. A lot

2. Some

3. None

4. Don't know

9. No response

(4) Selon vous, la religion doit-elle guider les décisions dans la vie économique et commerciale?

1. Beaucoup

2. Un peu

3. Non

4. Ne sait pas

5. Pas d'opinion

In your opinion, should religion guide economic and commercial decisions?

1. A lot

2. Some

3. None

4. Don't know

9. No response

Political Efficacy

(5) Selon vous, la vie politique est-elle trop compliquée pour être comprise par les citoyens ordinaries?

1. Oui, trop compliquée

2. Un peu compliquée

3. Non, pas trop compliquée

4. Ne sait pas

9. Pas d'opinion

In your opinion, is politics too complicated for ordinary citizens to understand?

    1. Yes, too complicated

    2. Somewhat complicated

    3. No, not too complicated

    4. Don't know

    9. No response

Political Trust

(6) A votre avis, les décideurs du pays se soucient-ils des besoins des citoyens?

    1. Souvent

    2. Parfois

    3. Rarement

    4. Jamais

    9. Pas d'opinion

In your view, do politicians care about the needs of citizens?

    1. Often

    2. Sometimes

    3. Rarely

    4. Never

    9. No response

ECONOMIC ORIENTATIONS

National Economic Assessment

(7) Par rapport aux 5 dernières années, la situation économique du pays:

    1. S'est amélioré beaucoup

    2. S'est amélioré un peu

    3. N'a pas beaucoup changé

    4. S'est dégradé un peu

    5. S'est dégradé beaucoup

    8. Ne sait pas

    9. Pas d'opinion

In the last 5 years, the economic situation of the country has:

1. Improved a lot

2. Improved a little

3. Hasn't changed

4. Deteriorated a little

5. Deteriorated a lot

8. Don't know

9. No response

Personal Economic Assessment

(8) Par rapport aux 5 dernières années, votre niveau de vie personnel:

1. S'est amélioré beaucoup

2. S'est amélioré un peu

3. N'a pas beaucoup changé

4. S'est dégradé un peu

5. S'est dégradé beaucoup

8. Ne sait pas

9. Pas d'opinion

In the last 5 years, your standard of living has:

1. Improved a lot

2. Improved a little

3. Hasn't really changed

4. Deteriorated a little

5. Deteriorated a lot

9. No response

The Reward of Hard Work

Selon vous, l'effort dans le travail paie-t-il (sur le plan moral et matériel)?

1. Souvent

2. Parfois

3. Rarement

4. Jamais

8. Ne sait pas

In your opinion, hard work is rewarded (morally and materially):

    1. Often

    2. Sometimes

    3. Rarely

    4. Never

    8. Don't know

SOCIAL AND CULTURAL ORIENTATIONS

Women and Gender Equality

(10) Etes-vous pour le travail de la femme (hors domicile)?

    1. Oui, en général

    2. Oui, avant le mariage

    3. Oui, avant la naissance des enfants

    4. Absolument contre

Do you favor women working (outside the home)?

    1. Yes, in general

    2. Yes, before marriage

    3. Yes, before having children

    4. Absolutely against

Personal Religiosity

(11) Ou faites-vous d'habitude vos prières?

    1. A la mosquée

    2. A la maison

    3. Au travail

    4. Ne fait pas la prière

    9. Pas d'opinion

In general, where do you pray?

    1. At the mosque

    2. At home

    3. At work

    4. Do not pray

    9. No response

Preference for Western Music

(12) Quel genre de musique aimez-vous?

    a. Arabe classique

        1. Beaucoup

        2. Un peu

        3. N'aime pas

    b. Variété du pays

        1. Beaucoup

        2. Un peu

        3. N'aime pas

    c. Occidentale classique

        1. Beaucoup

        2. Un peu

        3. N'aime pas

    d. Occidentale populaire

        1. Beaucoup

        2. Un peu

        3. N'aime pas

What kind of music do you like?

    a. Classical Arabic

        1. A lot

        2. A little

        3. Don't like

    b. Algerian music

        1. A lot

        2. A little

        3. Don't like

    c. Western classical

        1. A lot

        2. A little

        3. Don't like

    d. Western popular

        1. A lot

        2. A little

        3. Don't like

CHAPTER 5

The Democracy Barometers:
Attitudes in the Arab World (2008)

Amaney Jamal and Mark Tessler

Over the course of the last quarter-century, democratic currents have swept across much of the developing and post-communist worlds. The Arab world, however, has remained largely untouched by this global democratic trend. The first *Arab Human Development Report,* published by the United Nations Development Programme in 2002, lamented that political systems "have not been opened up to all citizens" and that "political participation is less advanced in the Arab world than in other developing regions."[1] The 2003 report reiterated this assessment, stating that the Arab world's freedom deficit "remains critically pertinent and may have become even graver" since the 2002 report was issued.[2] A series of articles in the January 2004 issue of *Comparative Politics* described the "resilient and enduring authoritarianism" in the Arab world, and later that same year Thomas Carothers and Marina Ottaway concluded that in most Arab countries "real progress toward democracy is minimal."[3] Nor has the situation changed very much in the last few years, as the 2005 Arab Human Development Report confirms.

Despite—or perhaps because of—the persistence of authoritarianism across the Arab world, popular support for democracy there is widespread. The evidence for this may be gleaned from twenty different surveys carried out in nine Arab countries between 2000 and 2006.[4] Indeed, cross-regional data from the World Values Survey indicate that support for democracy in the Arab world is as high as or higher than in any other world region.[5] While this might appear anomalous in a region where ordinary citizens have had little experience with democracy, the absence of democracy may be the very factor that leads so many citizens to desire a democratic alternative to the political systems by which they are currently governed.

The most recent of these surveys were carried out in 2006 as part of the Arab Barometer survey project.[6] Data were collected through face-to-face interviews with representative national samples in Morocco, Algeria,

Palestine, Jordan, and Kuwait. The Arab Barometer survey instrument was jointly developed by the present authors and team leaders from the five countries in which the surveys have thus far been carried out.[7] The interview schedule also included items used in the regional Barometers in Africa, Asia, and Latin America, with which the Arab Barometer is cooperating as part of the Global Barometer project.

As suggested above, data from the Arab Barometer, as yet unreported elsewhere, once again reveal high levels of support for democracy. More specifically, 86 percent of those interviewed believe democracy is the best form of government, and 90 percent agree that democracy would be a good or very good system of governance for the country in which they live. These findings are shown in Table 5.1, which also provides percentages for the individual participating countries. It shows that, despite some cross-national variation, there is overwhelming support for democracy in every country.

The Arab Barometer also provides data that shed light on political participation and can help us to probe how respondents understand democracy and think about democratization. Many but not all citizens are politically engaged. For example, 52 percent of the Arab citizens surveyed report that they have voted in elections, and 56 percent report that they regularly follow the news. Notably, despite their preference for democratic governance, 83 percent believe that political reforms should be implemented gradually. Some also state that democracy has a number of important drawbacks, even if they nonetheless consider it to be the best political system. For example, 31 percent state that democracy is bad for the economy and 33 percent state that it is bad at maintaining order. These findings are shown in Table 5.2, which also presents percentages for the individual countries.

There is considerable variation in the way that citizens in the Arab world think about democracy. On the one hand, a solid majority expresses support not only for democracy as an abstract concept but also for many of the institutions and processes associated with democratic governance. For example, 62 percent of those interviewed believe that competition and disagreement among political groups is good for their country, and 64 percent believe the government should make laws according to the wishes of the people. On the other hand, when asked to identify the most important factors that define a democracy, about half the respondents emphasized economic considerations rather than political rights and freedoms.

In Algeria, Jordan, and Palestine (the question was not asked in Kuwait and Morocco) only about half the respondents stated that the most important aspect of democracy is the opportunity "to change the government through elections" or the "freedom to criticize the government." The other half attached greatest importance to democracy's (presumed) ability to

Table 5.1. Support for Democracy

	ALL COUNTRIES	JORDAN	PALESTINE	ALGERIA	MOROCCO	KUWAIT
Despite drawbacks, democracy is the best system of government	86% N = 5,740	86% N = 1,143	83% N = 1,270	83% N = 1,300	92% N = 1,277	88% N = 750
Having a democratic system of government in our country would be good	90% N = 5,740	93% N = 1,143	88% N = 1,270	81% N = 1,300	96% N = 1,277	93% N = 750

Note: See question wording at http://www.arabbarometer.org (accessed September 21, 2010).

"provide basic necessities like food, clothing, and shelter for everyone" or "decrease the income gap between rich and poor."[8]

Such findings suggest that economic issues are central to the way that many Arab citizens think about governance and, accordingly, that many men and women probably have an instrumental conception of democracy. When asked to identify the most important problem facing their country, fully 51 percent of the entire five-country sample described that problem in economic terms, citing such considerations as poverty, unemployment, and inflation. Only 5 percent stated that authoritarianism is the most important problem. Slightly higher percentages mentioned the U.S. occupation of Iraq (8 percent) and the Arab-Israeli conflict (7 percent) as the most important problem.

Coupled with the finding that most Arabs want political reform to be implemented gradually, this suggests that majorities in the Arab world attach higher priority to solving economic problems than to securing the political rights and freedoms associated with democracy. One way to read this is that Arab-world majorities support democracy, at least in part, because it promises to make governments more accountable and more attentive to the concerns of ordinary citizens, particularly their economic concerns. In other words, for at least some respondents, it is not so much that democracy is the "right" political system in a conceptual sense but rather that democracy is a "useful" form of government that has the potential to address many of a country's most pressing needs.

Table 5.2. Political Engagement and Evaluations of Democracy

	ALL COUNTRIES (%)	JORDAN (%)	PALESTINE (%)	ALGERIA (%)	MOROCCO (%)	KUWAIT (%)
Voted in the last election	52	59	71	45	50	23
Follows news about politics often or very often	56	49	78	45	49	23
Political reform should be introduced gradually	83	77	91	79	81	88
In a democracy, the economy runs badly	31	38	41	38	10	28
Democracies are bad at maintaining order	33	36	42	43	12	33
Competition and disagreement are not a bad thing for our country	62	60	50	61	67	79
The government should make laws according to the wishes of the people	61	58	59	59	81	62
Percentage of people giving a political feature of democracy as most important*	48	39	58	50	—	—

*Percentage of people choosing "opportunity to change government" or "freedom to criticize government" rather than "reduce income gap between rich and poor" or "provide basic necessities like food."

This conclusion is reinforced by other findings from the Arab Barometer surveys. Respondents were much more likely to be critical of their government for poor economic performance than for a lack of freedom. Indeed, slender majorities view their governments favorably on political grounds. For example, 54 percent believe that they have the power to influence government decisions; 50 percent believe that the courts are fair; 53 percent believe that they can criticize the government without fear; and 57 percent believe that they can join organizations without fear. By contrast, only 33 and 31 percent, respectively, believe that their government is doing a good job of fighting unemployment and narrowing the gap between rich and poor.

Democracy and Islam

Across all sectors of the Arab world, as in other Muslim-majority countries, there is a vibrant and nuanced discourse on the compatibility of Islam and democracy. Although some Muslim clerics and religious thinkers contend that democracy is not possible in a political system guided by Islam, others disagree. Equally important, it appears that neither Arab intellectuals nor ordinary citizens accept the view that Islam and democracy are incompatible. Rather, from mosque sermons to newspaper columns, from campus debates to coffee-shop discussions, large numbers of Arabs and other Muslims contend that the tenets of Islam are inherently democratic.[9]

In Western discourses, by contrast, it has often been asserted that Islam is opposed to democratic rule, and assertions along these lines are frequently advanced to explain the persistence of authoritarianism in the Arab world. The argument that Islam stifles democracy includes several interrelated assertions. First, some contend, as does Samuel P. Huntington in *The Clash of Civilizations,* that Islam and democracy are inherently incompatible because Islam recognizes no division between "church" and "state" and emphasizes the community over the individual.[10] Individualism, Huntington maintains, is a necessary component of a liberal-democratic order. Second, some scholars assert that Islamic law and doctrine are fundamentally illiberal and hence create an environment within which democracy cannot flourish. Francis Fukuyama, among others, makes this argument.[11] Finally, some claim that Islam fosters antidemocratic attitudes and values among its adherents. On the one hand, according to this argument, the religion does not advocate a commitment to political freedom. On the other, Islam is said to promote fatalism, the unquestioning acceptance of "Allah's way," and thus to nurture acceptance of the status quo rather than the contestation needed for a vibrant democracy.[12] As a result, according to this collection of arguments, the religious orientations and attachments of Muslim citizens create a normative climate that is hostile to democracy.

Arab Barometer data permit an examination, admittedly limited to the individual level of analysis, of these competing views of the relationship between democracy and Islam. To the extent that religious orientations and attachments do discourage democracy, support for democracy should be lower among more religious men and women. This is not the case, however. In fact, more religious Muslims are as likely as less religious Muslims to believe that democracy, despite its drawbacks, is the best political system. The Barometer has identified the frequency of Koran reading as a valid and reliable measure of religiosity. Respondents are categorized according to whether they read the Koran every day, several times a week, sometimes, or rarely or never. Strikingly, at least 85 percent of the respondents in each category state that democracy is the best political system. Thus, since public support for democracy is necessary for a successful and consolidated democratic transition, and since available evidence indicates that religiosity does not diminish this support for democracy among Muslim publics, it seems clear that the persistence of authoritarianism in the Arab world cannot be explained by the religious orientations and attachments of ordinary men and women.

A different question bearing on the relationship between democracy and Islam concerns the role of Islam in political affairs. Many Arab citizens express support for the influence of Islam in government and politics. This is not the view of all citizens, however. In contrast to support for democracy, which is expressed by the overwhelming majority of the respondents in the Arab Barometer and other recent surveys, men and women in every country where surveys have been conducted are divided on the question of whether Islam should play an important political role. For example, whereas 56 percent of the respondents in the Arab Barometer surveys agree with the statement that men of religion should have influence over government decisions,[13] 44 percent disagree, indicating that they believe Islam should *not* play an important political role.

Further, the division of opinion observed among all respondents is present to the same degree among those who express support for democracy. Among respondents who believe democracy to be the best political system, despite any possible drawbacks, 54 percent believe that men of religion should have influence over government decisions while 46 percent disagree. This is shown in Table 5.3, which juxtaposes these items measuring support for democracy and support for a political role for Islam. Although there is modest variation from country to country, Table 5.3 shows that respondents who support democracy are divided more or less equally between those who favor secular democracy and those who favor a political system that is both democratic and gives an important role to Islam. Consistent with findings reported earlier, the table also shows that among the relatively few

Table 5.3. Variations in the Support for Democracy
by Attitudes toward a Political Role for Islam

	PERCENTAGE SAYING THAT, DESPITE DRAWBACKS, DEMOCRACY IS THE BEST SYSTEM OF GOVERNMENT	
	STRONGLY AGREE/AGREE THAT MEN OF RELIGION SHOULD INFLUENCE GOVERNMENT DECISIONS	STRONGLY DISAGREE/ DISAGREE THAT MEN OF RELIGION SHOULD INFLUENCE GOVERNMENT DECISIONS
All Countries	54	46
Jordan	52	48
Palestine	55	45
Algeria	58	42
Morocco	63	37
Kuwait	39	61

respondents who do not support democracy there is also a division of opinion regarding a political role for Islam.

How do Muslim Arabs who express support for democracy but also want their religion to have a meaningful role in political life understand what might be called "Islamic democracy"? Aspects of this question pertaining to Islam itself—to views about the particular ways that democratic political life might incorporate an Islamic dimension—are beyond the scope of this essay.

More pertinent to the present study is the question of whether those who support Islamic democracy possess democratic values, both in absolute terms and relative to those who support secular democracy. Table 5.4 presents data with which to address this question. The table compares respondents who favor secular democracy to those who favor Islamic democracy with respect to three normative orientations that relevant scholarship has identified as necessary (along with support for democracy) to the long-term success of a democratic transition. These values are (1) respect for political diversity and dissent, measured by the importance that respondents attribute to the presence of political leaders who are open to different political opinions; (2) social tolerance, measured by respondents stating that they would harbor no objection to having neighbors of a different race; and (3) gender equality, measured by a question asking whether men and women should have equal job opportunities and wages. Although these are only some of the values that are important for democracy, responses to questions about them will offer insights about the presence or absence of democratic values among Muslim Arab men and women in general and, in particular, about similarities or differences in the values of citizens with dissimilar preferences regarding the place of Islam in democratic political life.

Several conclusions may be drawn from Table 5.4. First, most men and women in every country express democratic values. Almost all respondents consider it important that political leaders be open to diverse ideas. Social tolerance, as reflected in openness to having neighbors of a different race, is also very high. Indeed, overall, there is only one instance in which less than two-thirds of those surveyed answered in a manner inconsistent with democracy. This instance occurs among those Algerian respondents who say that they favor Islamic democracy. Of these, only 57 percent say that they favor equal job opportunities and wages for men and women (compared to 71 percent among secular democrats).

Second, there are very few significant differences between respondents who favor secular democracy and those who favor Islamic democracy. The former are more likely to endorse a norm that is consistent with democracy in most instances, but differences are almost always very small. In only two of the fourteen country-specific comparisons shown in Table 5.4 is the difference between those who favor secular democracy and those who favor Islamic democracy greater than 10 percent (12 percent in one instance and 14 percent in the other). In almost all the remaining comparisons, the difference is actually 5 percent or less. Thus, the overall conclusion suggested by Table 5.4 is that democratic values are present to a significant degree among Muslim Arab citizens, most of whom support democracy, and that this is the case whether or not an individual believes that his or her country should be governed by a political system that is Islamic as well as democratic. These observations reinforce previous assessments related to Arab Muslims' views regarding the compatibility of democracy and Islam.

A final question pertaining to the relationship between democracy and Islam concerns the reasons why some respondents favor secular democracy while others prefer a political system that is democratic and also incorporates an Islamic dimension. Of particular concern is whether a preference for democracy that has an Islamic dimension reflects the influence of religious orientations, political judgments and evaluations, both, or neither. One hypothesis is that piety and religious attachments may lead Muslim Arabs to favor Islamic democracy. Another is that discontent with governments and regimes that are essentially secular may predispose citizens to favor a system that incorporates an Islamic dimension. It is also possible that a preference

Table 5.4. Democratic Values and Support of a Political Role for Islam among Respondents Who Support Democracy

THOSE WHO SUPPORT DEMOCRACY		PERCENTAGE AGREEING WITH STATEMENT ABOUT DEMOCRATIC VALUES		
		IT IS IMPORTANT TO HAVE POLITICAL LEADERS WHO ARE OPEN TO DIFFERENT POLITICAL OPINIONS	DO NOT MIND HAVING NEIGHBORS OF A DIFFERENT RACE	MEN AND WOMEN SHOULD HAVE EQUAL JOB OPPORTUNITIES AND WAGES
All Countries	Secular Democracy	95	86	76
	Islamic Democracy	95	82	70
Jordan	Secular Democracy	94	79	66
	Islamic Democracy	92	67	66
Palestine	Secular Democracy	96	NA	79
	Islamic Democracy	97	NA	72
Algeria	Secular Democracy	95	83	71
	Islamic Democracy	96	80	57
Morocco	Secular Democracy	93	94	78
	Islamic Democracy	95	89	77
Kuwait	Secular Democracy	96	88	85
	Islamic Democracy	98	92	84

for Islamic democracy reflects concern with preserving a measure of continuity—that is, with keeping a measure of tradition in place even as a shift to something new (democracy) is taking place.

We tested these propositions via a regression analysis that assesses the impact on political-system preference of personal religiosity and political evaluations. Frequency of Koran reading is again used as a measure of personal religiosity. Political evaluations include an item that asks about trust in the head of the government, another that asks whether ordinary citizens have the ability to influence the policies and activities of the government, and a third that asks whether democracies are not good at maintaining order. Binary logistic regression is used since only those who favor democracy (whether with or without an Islamic dimension) are included in the analysis.[14] Age, educational level, and economic well-being served as control variables.

The regression analysis shows that personal religiosity is not significantly related to political-system preference in any of the five countries in which Arab Barometer surveys were conducted. This is consistent with earlier findings; not only does religiosity not lead men and women to be less supportive of democracy, it does not lead them to be more supportive of a political system that incorporates an Islamic dimension.

Political evaluations, by contrast, are significantly related to political-system preference in every country. There is some cross-national variation in the particular evaluations that are most salient, and the direction of the relationship is not the same in every instance. A preference for a democratic system that incorporates an Islamic dimension is disproportionately likely among (1) Jordanian respondents who have little trust in the head of government, believe that ordinary citizens have the ability to influence the activities and policies of the government, and believe that democracies are not good at maintaining order; (2) Palestinians who have these same sentiments; (3) Algerians who believe that democracies are not good at maintaining order; (4) Moroccans who believe that democracies *are* good at maintaining order; and (5) Kuwaitis who have little trust in the head of government, believe that ordinary citizens have little ability to influence the activities and policies of the government, and believe that democracies are not good at maintaining order.

These differences invite inquiry into the ways that particular national circumstances determine how political judgments shape citizens' attitudes about the desired connection between democracy and Islam. Even in the absence of such inquiry, however, findings from the Arab Barometer make clear that explanatory power is to be found in political judgments rather than religious orientations.

The Desire for a Strong Leader

Despite the support for democracy that overwhelming majorities of respondents express in the Arab Barometer surveys, some respondents state that it would be good or very good for their country to have a strong non-democratic leader who does not bother with parliament and elections. This opinion is expressed by 17 percent of the respondents in the five surveys taken together, although it is somewhat higher in some countries and somewhat lower in others, ranging from 26 percent in Jordan to 10 percent in Algeria. Further, this undemocratic attitude is expressed only slightly less frequently among individuals who express support for democracy, being about 15 percent overall and ranging from 25 percent in Jordan to 8 percent in Algeria and Kuwait. These findings are shown in Table 5.5.

Since these percentages are fairly low, they are consistent with the finding that most ordinary citizens in the Arab world believe that democracy, whatever its drawbacks, is the best political system—and the one by which they believe their own country should be governed. On the other hand, the inverse correlation between support for democracy and approval of a strong leader who does not have to bother with parliament and elections is not as strong as might be expected. In other words, as noted above, some men and women support democracy and also state that an undemocratic leader would be good for their country.

How should this apparent contradiction be understood? Although at least some of these individuals may simply not understand what democracy involves, in many cases the juxtaposition of these contradictory attitudes probably reflects concern that a democratic transition could be destabilizing or disproportionately harmful to some citizens even if it helps the country overall, and that it should therefore be implemented in a "guided" fashion by a strong leader who is able to ensure that political change will be carried out in an orderly fashion. This is consistent with the finding, reported earlier, that almost all respondents want political reforms to be implemented gradually. It may also be significant that support for an undemocratic leader is expressed most frequently, both among all respondents and among those who support democracy, in Jordan and Morocco, two poor countries in which a monarch who is not responsible to the electorate is the guarantor of political order and political continuity.

We have also carried out a regression analysis (similar to that presented with respect to the connection between attitudes toward democracy and political Islam) to shed light on the connection between support for a democratic political system and support for an undemocratic leader. Again, binary

Table 5.5. Support for Democracy and Attitudes about Strong
Leaders Who Do Not Have to Bother with Parliament and Elections

THOSE WHO SAY THAT HAVING A STRONG LEADER WHO DOES NOT HAVE TO BOTHER WITH PARLIAMENT AND ELECTIONS IN OUR COUNTRY WOULD BE GOOD	DESPITE DRAWBACKS, DEMOCRACY IS THE BEST SYSTEM OF GOVERNMENT	
	STRONGLY AGREE/ AGREE (%)	STRONGLY DISAGREE/ DISAGREE (%)
All Countries	15	25
Jordan	25	37
Palestine	14	14
Algeria	8	18
Morocco	16	37
Kuwait	8	30

logistic regression has been used, since the analysis includes only those who support democracy and do not approve of undemocratic leadership and those who support democracy and do approve of undemocratic leadership. Also, once again, the same measures of personal religiosity and political evaluations are employed, as are the control variables of age, educational level, and economic well-being.

The results are consistent both with the conclusions about religiosity reported above and with the hypothesis offered to explain why some individuals who favor democracy might also express approval of an undemocratic leader. On the one hand, in *none* of the five countries for which data are available is this combination of supposedly contradictory attitudes more common among individuals who are more religious.

On the other hand, political assessments have explanatory power in four of the five countries, Kuwait being the exception. In Algeria, Jordan, and Palestine, individuals who believe that democracies are not good at maintaining order are more likely than others to couple support for democracy with support for strong leadership. In Morocco, those who believe that democracies are not good at maintaining order are less likely than others to combine a preference for strong leadership with support for democracy. In Jordan and Morocco (both of which are monarchies), individuals who believe that citizens have the ability to influence government activities and policies are disproportionately likely to favor democracy but also to express support for a strong leader who does not have to bother with parliament and elections. Thus, as the Arab Barometer data have shown with respect to all the questions investigated, the political-system preferences and views about governance held by ordinary men and women are not shaped to a significant degree by religious orientations or attachments. By contrast, these preferences and views do appear to be influenced in important ways by people's judgments and perceptions relating to political considerations.

Support for Democracy, But of What Kind?

Data from the Arab Barometer surveys make clear that there is broad support for democracy in the Arab world. In a way that is perhaps fed by the very persistence of authoritarianism in Arab polities, the vast majority of Arab men and women believe that democracy is the best political system and that it would be a good way for their country to be governed. This is not the whole story, however. People understand democracy in different ways. Often, they value it mainly as an instrument. They want to see it implemented gradually, and they disagree among themselves about whether it should include an important role for Islam. Thus, an understanding of political-system preferences and popular views about governance requires attention to multiple dimensions of support for democracy.

The Arab Barometer data also illuminate debates about the compatibility of Islam and democracy. More specifically, findings from these surveys suggest that Islam does not foster antidemocratic attitudes. On the one hand, personal religiosity does not diminish support for democracy. Nor even does it foster a preference for a political system that is Islamic as well as democratic. On the other hand, those who do favor Islamic democracy are not significantly less likely than those who favor secularism to embrace democratic norms and values. But while Islamic orientations appear to play no significant role in shaping citizens' attitudes toward democracy, the Arab Barometer data offer strong evidence that judgments pertaining to political circumstances and performance do make a difference.

It is unclear whether popular support for democracy can and will actually become transformed into pressure for political reform and democratic openings in the Arab world. Earlier surveys also found a widespread preference for democratic governance, which is a sign that undemocratic regimes and popular desires for democracy can coexist for considerable periods of time. Findings from the Arab Barometer suggest the possibility that this may be partly the result of a desire for stability that parallels the desire for democratic governance. This is reflected in the widespread emphasis on gradualism, as well as the support of some Arabs for a strong leader who does not have to bother with parliament and elections—a support fostered, in part, by a belief that democracies are poor at maintaining order. Concerns about stability almost certainly reflect the geostrategic situation in the region, particularly the destabilizing developments that have shaped politics in Iraq, Palestine, Lebanon, and Algeria in recent years. In some countries, concerns about stability may also be encouraged by political leaders who justify their opposition to reform by insisting that democratization will bring divisiveness and disorder. All of this may reduce the pressure from below for a democratic transition and serve the interests of regimes committed to preserving the status quo.

But while findings from the Arab Barometer say little about whether there are likely to be transitions to democracy in the Arab world in the years ahead, they do offer evidence that citizens' attitudes and values, including those relating to Islam, are not the reason that authoritarianism has persisted. Indeed, the Arab Barometer indicates that if and when progress toward democracy does occur, most Arab-world citizens will welcome it even as they debate the precise character and content of the democratic political systems that they believe should be established. As a result, those who wish to advance the cause of democracy in the Arab world should focus their investigations not on the alleged antidemocratic impulses of ordinary women and men but rather on the structures and manipulations, and perhaps also the supporting external alliances, of a political leadership class that is dedicated to preserving its power and privilege.

PART 2

Political
Culture
and Islam

CHAPTER 6

Political Culture in Turkey: Connections between Attitudes toward Democracy, the Military, and Islam (2004)

Mark Tessler and Ebru Altinoglu

The importance of a democratic political culture has been noted by many scholars and documented in a growing number of empirical studies. For example, research in Latin America shows that an important factor contributing to democratic survivability "revolves around changes in political attitudes, toward a greater valorization of democracy."[1] Similarly, a recent analysis of survey data from Taiwan and Korea concludes that a "crucial dimension [in the consolidation of democracy] involves sustained, internalized belief in and commitment to the legitimacy of democracy among the citizenry at large."[2] Linz and Stepan thus contend that "a democratic regime is consolidated when a strong majority of public opinion, even in the midst of major economic problems and deep dissatisfaction with incumbents, holds the belief that democratic procedures and institutions are the most appropriate way to govern collective life."[3] And again, according to Przeworski, "democracy becomes the only game in town when no one can imagine acting outside the democratic institutions, when all losers want to do this again with the same institutions under which they have just lost."[4]

The importance of political culture has similarly been emphasized by Turkish scholars, including Esmer, who coordinated the 1997 World Values Survey in Turkey. Like others, Esmer calls attention to the need to examine the normative orientations of ordinary citizens in order to understand fully the nature and functioning of a political system. He also contends that definitions of political culture should not be limited to beliefs and values. He asserts, convincingly, that political attitudes are an equally important component of political culture.[5]

Turkey's Experience with Democracy

Turkey has regularly held free and competitive elections since 1946. During this period, the number and influence of political parties has changed frequently. The country has had a two-party political system at some times and a multiparty system at others. Electoral politics has at times been dominated by highly ideological rival parties. Following the most recent election, parties range across the ideological spectrum from center-left to extreme-right. Party competition and electoral politics are only part of the story, however. Turkish politics has also been marked by a number of military interventions.

In the elections of 1950, the center-right Democratic Party (DP) defeated the Republican People's Party (RPP), which had been established by Kemal Atatürk and thus represented the Turkish revolution. Partisan competition was interrupted by a military coup in 1960, however. A new constitution was promulgated the following year, and one of its most important provisions was the establishment of a National Security Council (NSC). Composed of senior military leaders, as well as top government officials, the NSC is an extra-political institution. It is not accountable to elected policy makers; even though some of its members have been elected to their positions in the government, the NSC is essentially an instrument through which the military can exert political influence or even intervene in the political process when it judges government actions to be injurious to the national interest.[6]

With the resumption of electoral politics, competition between the DP and the RPP gave way to a multiparty system in the 1960s. Then, in the 1970s, following a military ultimatum in 1971, the political landscape began to change with the emergence of two new parties: the pro-Islamic National Order Party (NOP) and the ultra-nationalist National Action Party (NAP). In 1980 the military again intervened, claiming that coalition instability and political unrest required it to act in order to safeguard democracy. The military ruled until 1983, at which time it permitted new legislative elections. It also modified the electoral code, requiring that a party receive at least 10 percent of the national vote to be represented in parliament, thereby diminishing the prospects for small extremist movements.

The Motherland Party (MP) of Turgut Özal captured an absolute majority of the seats in parliament in the 1983 elections, but fragmentation and polarized multipartyism reemerged in the elections of 1987. In the elections of 1991 and 1995, support for centrist parties diminished as voters increasingly displayed a preference for either the pro-Islamic Welfare Party (WP), a descendant of the NOP and later reformed as the Virtue Party, or the highly nationalistic NAP. Indeed, the WP became the dominant party after the 1995 elections and established a coalition with the True Path Party (TPP) of Tansu Çiller. Some scholars consider these developments a turning point in Turkish politics.[7]

Once again, however, the military concluded that there was a threat to democracy, this time in the form of the WP's pro-Islamic policies. In February 1997, demands by the NSC forced the resignation of WP leader and then prime minister Necmettin Erbakan, after which a new coalition government was formed under NSC supervision. In 1998, in response to an ultimatum from military leaders, the cabinet adopted measures designed to limit the influence of Islamic parties and movements.

As a result of these measures, a new political configuration emerged following the election of 1999. As Çarkoğlu notes, the election was marked by the "poor showing of the center-right Motherland Party and True Path Party."[8] Similarly, the Virtue Party lost influence, coming in third behind the left-of-center Democratic Left Party and the National Action Party of the extreme right.[9] The latter two parties thus became the dominant members of the government coalition, which also included the Motherland Party. Accordingly, as summarized by Çarkoğlu, at the end of the 1990s much of the electorate remained at or around centrist positions on a left-right continuum, a majority was nonetheless situated at least somewhat to the right of center, and at least 15 percent of the electorate placed itself at the extreme right of the ideological spectrum.[10]

Early elections in November 2002 brought important changes, however. All three parties in the governing coalition, as well as the center-right TPP, then in opposition, failed to meet the 10 percent threshold for representation in parliament. These parties were punished by voters for failing to make progress in the fight against poverty and corruption, and in response some of their leaders resigned and then retired from political life. Only two parties surpassed the 10 percent threshold: the Justice and Development Party (JDP) led by R. Tayyip Erdogan, which obtained 34 percent of the vote and won the right to form a government; and the RPP led by Deniz Baykal, which received 19 percent of the vote and became the opposition. The origins of the JDP are in the Virtue Party; and while the party describes itself as a "conservative democratic" movement and rejects the label "Islamist," its impressive electoral victory led some to wonder whether the emerging political configuration would assign a more central role to Islam.

Despite its history of competitive elections, Turkey does not appear to be a consolidated democracy.[11] It should probably be placed in the category of countries that possess some but not all of the characteristics of democratic political systems. Such countries have been variously described as "unconsolidated," "incomplete," or "electoral" democracies.[12] A Turkish political scientist recently described his country's political system as a "delegative democracy."[13] These and other assessments point to a number of factors that compromise Turkish democracy, including human rights violations, political corruption, and the prohibition of some political parties.

At the same time, this does not mean that democracy in Turkey is destined to remain unconsolidated. Heper and Güney write, for example, that neither political Islam nor military rule is likely to predominate in the long run. Rather, they predict that sooner or later, and possibly sooner, the military's "occasional indirect presence will be replaced by consolidated democracy."[14] The accuracy of this prediction will be known in the years ahead. For the present, it is only possible to identify and assess the factors on which the future of Turkey's democratic transition will depend. Three such considerations, and the interrelationships between them, are of particular concern to the present inquiry.

Research Concerns

The question of most immediate relevance to the present study concerns the degree to which Turkey possesses a democratic political culture. As noted above, many scholars consider the existence of pro-democracy attitudes among a majority of the population to be a necessary condition for democratic consolidation. Inglehart writes, for example, that "democracy is not attained simply by making institutional changes through elite-level maneuvering. Its survival depends also on the values and beliefs of ordinary citizens."[15] As summarized by Rose, Mishler, and Haerpfer, "a new democratic regime can become established only as and when there is a popular consensus favoring a democratic culture."[16] Therefore, unless and until it can be established that a significant proportion of Turkey's citizens possess attitudes and values supportive of democracy, the country's democratic transition should be considered incomplete. Indeed, even the continuation of this transition remains uncertain.

A second important consideration is the military's involvement in political life. More specifically, are the prospects for democratic consolidation either advanced or retarded by the military's recurring intervention? Most students of democratization consider political involvement by the military to be an obstacle, calling attention to the problem of "privileged enclaves" and "extra-political authority." For example, Linz and Stepan observe that

> in many cases . . . in which free and contested elections have been
> held, the government resulting from elections . . . lacks the de jure
> as well as de facto power to determine policy in many significant
> areas because the executive, legislative, and judicial powers are still
> decisively constrained by an interlocking set of reserve domains,
> military prerogatives, or authoritarian enclaves.[17]

Observers of present-day Turkey give particular attention in this connection to the issue of "military prerogatives." On the one hand, they note that there have indeed been frequent military interventions, thwarting the will of the electorate, restricting political freedoms and, on occasion, resulting in human rights abuses. According to a recent analysis, the Turkish military enjoys superior political status: "it has placed itself above the restrictions, scrutiny, and public criticism that apply to all other sectors of society, placing it virtually above the state."[18] On the other hand, the military's involvement in political affairs is sanctioned by the constitution and in this sense is not extra-legal. Further, the contribution of the military to safeguarding secular democracy has been emphasized by both Turkish and American scholars.[19] Equally important, there appears to be broad popular approval of the military. Public opinion polls consistently report that ordinary citizens have more confidence in the military than in any other political institution, suggesting that it may not be perceived as contravening the will of the people and protecting its own interests rather than those of the nation.[20]

Third, questions have been raised about the compatibility of Islam and democracy. Some allege that Islamic political parties are inherently anti-democratic and suggest that popular support for these parties reflects an anti-democratic impulse. Others argue more generally that the religion tends to produce a mind-set hostile to democracy among ordinary Muslims. Whereas democracy requires openness, competition, pluralism, and tolerance of diversity, Islam, they argue, encourages intellectual conformity and an uncritical acceptance of authority. Equally important, Islam is said to be anti-democratic because it vests sovereignty in God, who is the sole source of political authority and from whose divine law must come all regulations governing the community of believers. As expressed by Kedourie, "the notion of popular sovereignty as the foundation of governmental legitimacy, the idea of representation, or elections, of popular suffrage, of political institutions being regulated by laws laid down by a parliamentary assembly, of these laws being guarded and upheld by an independent judiciary, the ideas of the secularity of the state, of society being composed of a multitude of self-activating groups and associations—all of these are profoundly alien to the Muslim political tradition."[21]

At the same time, many others reject the suggestion that Islam is an enemy in the struggle for democracy. They note that Islam has many facets and tendencies, making unidimensional characterizations of the religion highly suspect.[22] They also point out that openness, tolerance, and progressive innovation are well represented among the religion's traditions.[23] Indeed, there are even expressions of support for democracy by some Islamist theorists.[24]

Similarly divergent analyses are offered by students of Islam and politics in Turkey. While many regard the Welfare Party and its successors as a threat to the country's secular democracy, others note that behind its radical rhetoric the party has shown the same kind of flexibility and pragmatism displayed by other political parties.[25] Further, while research suggests that religiosity is a very strong predictor of party preference among Turkish voters,[26] there is also evidence that Welfare Party voters include many citizens who, though religious, have no desire to see an Islamic state established in their country.[27] Thus, the impact of Islamic attachments on the attitudes toward governance held by ordinary Turkish Muslims remains an open question.

These concerns inform the present study, which, as noted, seeks to shed light on the nature and determinants of the attitudes relating to democracy held by ordinary Turkish citizens. The analysis to follow gives special attention to the influence on these attitudes of views about the military and personal religious attachments.

Data, Variables, and Measures

The analysis to follow uses data from the World Values Survey conducted in Turkey in 1997. The Turkish survey, which is based on a national random sample of 1,907 respondents, was carried out by a team of scholars at Bogaçizi University in Istanbul.

Dependent Variables

Dimensions of political culture relating to democracy are the dependent variables in this study, with conceptual and operational definitions informed by prior research on democratization. According to one study, relevant orientations include both generalized support for democratic political forms and the embrace of specific democratic values, such as respect for political competition and tolerance of diverse political ideas.[28] Thus, as summarized in another empirical investigation, a democratic citizen is one who "believes in individual liberty and is politically tolerant, has a certain distrust of political authority but at the same time is trusting of fellow citizens, is obedient but nonetheless willing to assert rights against the state, and views the state as constrained by legality."[29]

Esmer offers a similar assessment, writing that a person who has democratic values is an individual who trusts others and participates, who is liberal and tolerant, who compromises, who is moderate and non-extremist, and who criticizes legal authority but does not totally reject it.[30] In addition, however, Esmer observes that it is important to examine the relationships between these attitudes and values, which will shed light not only on levels of support but also on the meaning citizens attach to democracy. More specifically, he suggests that many people may express a preference for democratic political forms at the same time that they hold attitudes and values that are inconsistent with a democratic political culture.[31] This point has also been made in studies of the new democracies in Eastern Europe and elsewhere.[32] Thus, it is important to identify and examine the relationship between empirically distinct clusters of pro-democracy attitudes.

Factor analysis has been employed to select items measuring the dependent variables and other variables. For the dependent variables, those items in the interview schedule that appear to be tapping attitudes and values pertaining to democracy are included in the analysis and, following rotation, the items with the highest factor loadings are selected and then combined to form additive indices.

Used in this way, factor analysis has a number of important advantages.[33] First, it provides an objective basis for selecting the items used to measure the dependent variable. While selection is, of course, limited by the composition of the interview schedule, factor analysis identifies those items that are most closely associated with whatever conceptual property or properties characterize the collection of items that ask about democratic institutions and values. Second, factor analysis constitutes a scaling technique and offers evidence of reliability and validity. High loadings on a common factor indicate reproducibility, and hence reliability. They also indicate unidimensionality, meaning that the items measure a common conceptual property, which is a basis for inferring validity. Third, factor analysis identifies empirically distinct clusters of items, which not only addresses concerns of measurement but also helps to clarify the conceptual locus of various normative orientations. In this case, factor analysis will demonstrate whether items pertaining to democracy are or are not indicators of a single conceptual dimension, and, if the latter, it will shed light on the character of each distinct dimension.

Two independent clusters of items emerge from the analysis, and in both cases two different items have particularly high loadings on one and only one factor. This is shown in Table 6.1, which also presents the bivariate correlations among these items. As with the factor loadings, the coefficients show that the two items in each cluster are strongly intercorrelated but that neither is strongly correlated with either item in the other cluster. The four items selected in this manner are shown below.

V157. I'm going to describe various types of political systems and ask what you think about each as a way of governing this country. For each one, would you say it is a very good, fairly good, fairly bad, or very bad way of governing this country? Coded according to the evaluation of a democratic political system.

V163. Democracy may have problems but it's better than any other form of government. Do you: Agree Strongly, Agree, Disagree, Disagree Strongly?

V106. If you had to choose, which one of the things on this card would you say is most important: Maintaining order in the nation, Giving people more say in important government decisions, Fighting rising prices, Protecting freedom of speech? Coded according to whether or not respondent chose "Giving people more say in important government decisions" or "Protecting freedom of speech."

V159. If you had to choose, which would you say is the most important responsibility of government: To maintain order in society, To respect freedom of the individual? Coded according to whether or not respondent chose "To respect freedom of the individual."

As shown in Table 6.1, the first two of these items, V157 and V163, are strongly intercorrelated and have high loadings on a common factor. Similarly, the next two, V106 and V159, are also strongly intercorrelated and have high loadings on a common factor. V157 and V163 measure level of support for democracy, and, as noted, they have been combined to form an additive index. V106 and V159 measure importance attached to political liberty, and they, too, have been combined to form an additive index. The two indices, support for democracy and importance attached to political freedom, are treated as dependent variables in the analysis to follow. It is noteworthy, as discussed above, that past research on cultural aspects of democratization calls attention to both of the conceptual dimensions that these indices appear to measure. Their importance has been demonstrated in studies carried out in the new democracies of Eastern Europe,[34] and their statistical independence has also been shown in a cross-national analysis of World Values Survey data from seventeen countries.[35] A similar pattern, based on survey data from several Arab countries, has also been reported by one of the authors of the present study.[36]

Table 6.2 presents percentage distributions for each index, showing that there is considerable variance on both variables. At the same time, the two distributions are skewed in different directions. While there is fairly widespread popular support for democracy, at least in the abstract, a much smaller proportion of individuals attaches importance to political freedom and, to that extent, possesses a normative orientation conducive to democracy.

In addition to treating each index as a separate dependent variable, the two measures have been combined to form a two-dimensional typology. This will be treated as a third dependent variable. Table 6.3 presents this typology by cross-tabulating dichotomized measures of support for democracy and the importance of political freedom. The table indicates, as expected given the patterns shown in Tables 6.1 and 6.2, that respondents are no more likely to be either high or low on both indices than to be high on one and low on

Table 6.1. Factor Analysis and Correlations between
Attitudes and Values Relating to Democracy

	V157 DEMO–CRATIC SYSTEM	V163 DEMO–CRACY: BETTER	V159 GOVERNMENT: SOCIETY VS. INDIVIDUAL	V106 GOVERNMENT: ORDER VS. FREEDOM
Correlations				
Democratic System				
Pearson Correlation	1.000	0.424	−0.075	−0.077
Sig. (2-tailed)	—	0.000	0.002	0.001
N	1,775	1,684	1,747	1,752
Democracy: Better				
Pearson Correlation	0.424	1.000	−0.045	−0.020
Sig. (2-tailed)	0.000	—	0.061	0.418
N	1,684	1,720	1,692	1,701
Government: Society vs. Individual				
Pearson Correlation	−0.075	−0.045	1.000	0.226
Sig. (2-tailed)	0.002	0.061	—	0.000
N	1,747	1,692	1,844	1,806
Government: Order vs. Freedom				
Pearson Correlation	−0.077	−0.020	0.226	1.000
Sig. (2-tailed)	0.001	0.418	0.000	—
N	1,752	1,701	1,806	1,851
Factor Analysis				
Rotated Component Matrix				
Component 1	0.85	0.84	−0.02	−0.04
Component 2	0.02	−0.08	0.78	0.78

the other. Rather, with each index dichotomized so as to give categories of relatively equal size, the proportion of respondents in each of the typology's four categories is also approximately equal.

Independent Variables

Three conceptually distinct categories of independent variables are examined in an effort to account for variance in attitudes and values relating

Table 6.2. Levels of Support for Democracy and
Importance Attached to Political Freedom

	SUPPORT FOR DEMOCRACY (%)	IMPORTANCE OF POLITICAL FREEDOM (%)
High	53.4	16.6
Somewhat High	33.1	35.9
Low	13.5	47.5

to democracy. The selection of independent variables has been guided both by considerations of availability, meaning the items included on the World Values Survey interview schedule, and by prior research on democratization. Although findings from prior research are neither comprehensive nor entirely consistent, these studies offer insights not only about which factors are likely to have explanatory power but also about the direction of significant variable relationships.[37] In cases where a variable refers to a normative or behavioral orientation that is measured by a multi-item index, items have been selected using the same factor analytic procedures discussed in connection with the dependent variables.

The first category of independent variables deals with personal status. It includes education, age, sex, and a measure of personal well-being. The later is an additive index composed of intercorrelated items that ask about financial satisfaction, general life satisfaction, and income. Based on past research, it is expected, other things being equal, that support for democracy and attachment to democratic values will be higher and more widespread among individuals who are better educated, younger, male, and characterized by higher levels of personal well-being and life satisfaction.

A second category deals with cultural and normative orientations. It includes a measure of religiosity in the form of an additive index based on six highly intercorrelated items from the interview schedule: self-assessed religiosity, belief in God, importance of God, belief in life after death, belief in the soul, and taking comfort in religion. This measure is of particular interest given questions that have been raised about the influence of Islamic attachments on attitudes toward governance and democracy. Other independent variables in this category include individualism, measured by two intercorrelated items that ask about the importance of emphasizing independence and imagination in child rearing; a five-item measure of traditionalism, which includes questions about the importance of traditional values pertaining to family life and a preference for continuity over change in other areas; and

Table 6.3. Percent in Each Category of Typology Based on Support for Democracy and Importance Attached to Political Freedom

	IMPORTANCE OF POLITICAL FREEDOM	
Support for Democracy	Lesser	Greater
Lesser	25.4	21.2
Greater	22.2	31.2

social tolerance, which is measured, following Esmer,[38] by a willingness to have people of a different race or religion as neighbors. The items used to measure all of these variables are given in the appendix to this chapter.

It is expected, other things being equal, that support for democracy and attachment to democratic values will be higher and more widespread among individuals who are higher on the measures of individualism and social tolerance and lower on the measure of traditionalism. Expectations regarding religiosity are less clear; while some scholars posit an inverse relationship between strong Islamic attachments and pro-democracy attitudes, this has not been documented by empirical research among ordinary citizens in Muslim societies.[39]

The final category of independent variables deals with political experiences and assessments. Of particular note is an index measuring confidence in the military and other institutions of order. Once again guided by Esmer's analysis of the World Values Survey data, this index is composed of three highly intercorrelated items: one asks about confidence in the military, another about confidence in the police, and a third about confidence in the legal system. Other independent variables in this category are trust in ordinary citizens, rather than a preference for either a strong political leader or technocratic leadership; an evaluation of government performance at the time of the survey; confidence in the institutional structure of the political system at the time of the survey; and a three-item measure of political attentiveness based on expressed political interest, frequency of discussing politics, and the importance attached to political affairs. Again, the questions used to create multi-item indices are presented in the appendix to this chapter.

Based on past research, it is expected, other things being equal, that support for democracy and attachment to democratic values will be higher and more widespread among individuals who have higher levels of trust in ordinary citizens, more positive assessments of the government, more confidence in the institutional structure of the political system, and higher levels of political attentiveness. Expectations are less clear with respect to confidence in the military and other institutions of order. While the non-democratic character of these institutions suggests an inverse relationship, this may not be the case since the military presents itself as the guardian of democracy.

In addition to identifying the relative importance of specific independent variables in accounting for variance on the dependent variables, the analysis to follow will also shed light on the relative explanatory power of *categories* of independent variables. More specifically, it will help to determine the degree to which attitudes and values related to democracy are influenced by demographic characteristics, normative orientations, and/or political experiences and assessments. This, in turn, will contribute to a fuller understanding of the way that particular political attitudes are acquired and of the factors likely to promote or retard the emergence of a democratic political culture.

As noted, factor analysis has been used to select and validate the items used to construct indices measuring these independent variables. In cases where appropriate, a response of "don't know" has been coded as the midpoint along an agree-disagree or important-unimportant continuum. This has been done to maximize the number of useable responses. Factor analyses have been run both with and without this recoding, and no item used to construct an index was recoded in this way if to do so significantly altered the pattern of factor loadings. In fact, however, this very rarely occurred.

Analysis and Findings

Regression analysis has been used to assess the relationship between these independent variables and the two one-dimensional dependent variables described above. Ordinal logistic regression has been employed for this purpose since there is no standard unit of measurement and, accordingly, the categories of each dependent variable are ordinal rather than interval. Table 6.4 presents the results of an analysis in which the support for democracy index is the dependent variable, and Table 6.5 presents the results of an analysis in which the importance attached to the political liberty index is the dependent variable. In addition, logistic regression has been used to examine the relationship between the independent variables and the third dependent variable, the two-dimensional typology based on support for democracy and importance attached to political liberty taken together. Separate logistic regressions are run for each of the four categories of this typology, which were shown in Table 6.3. The results are presented in Tables 6.6–6.9.

In one important case, that of religiosity, approximately 20 percent of the respondents did not answer at least one question in the six-item index. Mean substitution was employed in this instance, and two assessments were performed to make sure this did not introduce distortions. First, regressions were run both with and without the cases for which mean substitution was employed. The results were identical. Second, when the cases for which mean substitution was employed were included in the regressions, a with/without mean substitution dummy variable was added as an additional control.

Support for Democracy

Table 6.4 presents the results of an analysis in which the support for democracy index is the dependent variable. Four models, each involving a different set or combination of independent variables, are examined in an effort to account for variance on the dependent variable. The first model includes only independent variables pertaining to personal status. As expected, support for democracy is higher among individuals who are better educated and male. Contrary to expectations, however, older individuals are more likely than younger individuals to support democracy. Further, although a positive relationship between personal well-being and support for democracy had been expected, regression results indicate that this variable has no effect on the dependent variable.

The second model deals with cultural and normative orientations. While at least some scholars argue that support for democracy will be higher and more widespread among individuals who are less religious, Table 6.4 indicates that religiosity has no effect on support for democracy. The table also shows, contrary to expectations, that individualism is unrelated to support for democracy. On the other hand, consistent with expectations, both lower levels of traditionalism and higher levels of social tolerance are related to support democracy to a statistically significant degree.

The third model examines the impact of political experiences and assessments. As expected, support for democracy is higher among individuals who have higher levels of trust in ordinary citizens, as opposed to a strong leader or government technocrats, and also among individuals who are more politically attentive. Alternatively, contrary to expectations, support for democracy is higher among individuals who have an unfavorable view of government performance. Finally, confidence in the institutional structure of the political system has no effect on support for democracy, whereas confidence in the institutions of order, which includes the military, the police, and the legal system, is positively related to support for democracy.

Model 4 includes all the categories of independent variables. It shows only one change in the relationships that are statistically significant; evaluation of government performance loses the significant relationship to the dependent variable observed in Model 2. Given that all other significant relationships remain unchanged, it is possible to conclude both that hardly any of the relationships observed in Models 1–3 is spurious and that all three categories of independent variables are important in accounting for variance on the dependent variable. Specifically, then, support for democracy is higher among individuals who are male, older, and better educated; who are higher in social tolerance and lower in traditionalism; and who are higher in political attentiveness, higher in trust in ordinary citizens, and higher in confidence in the country's institutions of order.

Two points deserve additional comment in view of the character of the Turkish case. First, the fact that religiosity is not significantly related to support for democracy lends support to those who take the view that democracy and Islam are not incompatible. This is notable given debates about the influence of Islam on political culture. In addition, however, several cautions are in order. On the one hand, with its long tradition of secularism, findings from Turkey may not be indicative of trends in other Muslim countries. On the other, the pro-Islamic Welfare Party was in power at the time the survey was conducted, being the senior partner in a coalition with the center-right True Path Party, and this raises the possibility of a temporal conditionality that also limits the generalizability of findings from the present study.

Second, although it may appear anomalous that support for democracy is associated with confidence in such institutions of order as the military and the police, which themselves are not democratic, this, too, reflects a particularity of the Turkish case. The military played a critical role in establishing the Turkish Republic, and since that time it has considered itself the guardian of democratic governance. As discussed earlier, the military has frequently intervened in political life, asserting that it was doing so to ensure the survival of Turkish democracy. The military's role and intention in this connection are also noted by several scholars. Özbudun writes, for example, that "the soldiers' intention on each [military intervention] was a 'moderating coup' rather than the creation of a lasting bureaucratic-authoritarian regime."[40] Some believe the military acts on behalf of a certain political class, however, and that its involvement in political life, whatever the intention, is an obstacle to democratic consolidation. The present study suggests that this view may not be widespread among ordinary citizens, however, since greater support for democracy is associated with greater confidence in the military and other institutions of order.

Importance of Political Liberty

Table 6.5 presents the regressions in which importance attached to political liberty is the dependent variable. Model 1, with demographic characteristics as independent variables, shows a pattern similar in most respects to the one observed in Table 6.4. Consistent with expectations, importance attached to political liberty is higher among male and better-educated individuals. Also as in Table 6.4, but in contrast to expectations, personal well-being has

Table 6.4. Support for Democracy

	MODEL 1	MODEL 2	MODEL 3	MODEL 4
Personal Status				
Education	.2040 (.021)***			.1225 (.024)***
Personal Well-being		.0125 (.009)	.0136 (.009)	
Sex (Men)		.1898 (.087)*		.2502 (.095)**
Age	.0189 (.003)***			.0148 (.003)***
Cultural and Normative Orientations				
Religiosity		.0014 (.021)		.0245 (.024)
Individualism		.1195 (.064)		.0636 (.070)
Traditionalism		−.0638 (.023)**		−.0723 (.026)**
Social Tolerance		.3781 (.055)***		.2699 (.062)***
Political Experiences and Assessments				
Confidence in Institutional Structure of Political System			−.0196 (.012)	−.0114 (.013)
Confidence in Institutions of Order			.0494 (.018)**	.1023 (.020)***
Trust in Ordinary Citizens			.1962 (.021)***	.1763 (.023)***
Political Attentiveness			.1985 (.030)***	.1226 (.035)***
Government Performance			−.0577 (.023)*	−.0247 (.026)
Number of Observations	1,783	1,733	1,827	1,627

Note: Robust standard errors in parentheses.

*p < 0.05, **p < 0.01, ***p < 0.001

no effect on the importance attached to political liberty. The relationship between age and the dependent variable is different, however. Younger age is related to a statistically significant degree to attaching greater importance to liberty, whereas Table 6.4 showed that older age was associated with support for democracy.

In Model 2, all the cultural and normative orientations treated as independent variables are statistically significant at the 0.001 level of confidence. In accordance with expectations, the importance attached to liberty is higher and more widespread among citizens who have higher ratings on the measures of individualism and social tolerance and lower ratings on the measure of traditionalism. Religiosity is also inversely related to the dependent variable. The finding with respect to religiosity deserves special note because it differs from that reported in Table 6.4 and supports a different position in debates about the compatibility of democracy and Islam. While the overall conclusion about the influence of Islamic attachments on pro-democracy attitudes thus remains ambiguous, one implication of the present analysis is that the impact of religiosity may vary from one dimension of political culture to another.

Political experiences and assessments are the independent variables in Model 3. This model shows that individuals who are less content with the present government, who are more attentive to politics, or who have lower levels of confidence in institutions of order are more likely to attach importance to political liberty. Relationships involving trust in ordinary citizens and confidence in the institutional structure of the political system are not statistically significant. It is notable that the relationship between confidence in institutions of order and importance attached to political liberty is inverse, in contrast to the finding when support for democracy was the dependent variable. This suggests that although the military may be regarded by much of the public as the guardian of a political system that is democratic at least to some degree, citizens among whom democratic values are most pronounced actually have a less favorable opinion of the military.

When all variables are included, in Model 4, education and individualism cease to be related to the dependent variable to a statistically significant degree. All other relationships remain significant, although the level of confidence associated with social tolerance declines. Thus, with spurious relationships eliminated, the data show that attachment to political liberty is higher among individuals who are male, younger, less religious, less traditional, more attentive to politics, higher in social tolerance, have an unfavorable assessment of the government, and have less confidence in institutions of order.

Given the nature of the Turkish case, it is noteworthy that both religiosity and confidence in institutions of order are related to the dependent variable with a high level of statistical confidence. Religiosity was not related to support for democracy, as shown in Table 6.4. Since it is inversely related to attachment to liberty, however, it may be that religiosity among Muslims, at least in Turkey, does discourage the emergence of at least some values associated with democracy. Taking findings from Tables 6.4 and 6.5 together, as a proposition for future research, it may be that Islamic attachments have an impact on some dimensions of political culture but not others so far as democracy is concerned.

The inverse relationship between confidence in institutions of order and attachment to political liberty is instructive in view of the anomaly noted in the discussion of Table 6.4: that support for democracy is associated with confidence in political institutions that themselves are not democratic. But while confidence in institutions of order tends to increase support for a pattern of governance on whose behalf the military has frequently intervened, Table 6.5 suggests that it tends to *decrease* support for the more fundamental norms of political culture that are necessary for democracy to mature. Democratic consolidation, in other words, depends in the final analysis on a supportive political culture, not on military intervention, and those who possess political values conducive to democracy are more likely than others to see a contradiction in relying on anti-democratic institutions to ensure democracy's survival.

Democracy and Political Liberty

A single model including all independent variables has been run for each of the four categories associated with the third dependent variable, which is a two-dimensional typology based on support for democracy and importance attached to political liberty taken together. These are shown in Tables 6.6–6.9. Table 6.6 presents the results of an analysis in which the category of lesser support for democracy and lesser importance attached to political liberty is the dependent variable. Respondents in this category may be labeled "non-democrats." As shown in Table 6.3, with the cutting points employed they constitute 25.4 percent of the sample. Table 6.6 shows that individuals in this category are more likely than individuals who are not in this category, to a statistically significant degree, to be less educated, female, lower in personal well-being, higher in religiosity, higher in traditionalism, lower in political attentiveness, and more trusting of strong leaders and government technocrats than are ordinary citizens.

This profile suggests that non-democrats are apolitical, with little interest in public affairs and a restricted political horizon. Less educated and higher in both religiosity and traditionalism, they very probably have a limited social horizon as well. They are also disproportionately likely to be

Table 6.5. Importance Attached to Political Liberty

	MODEL 1	MODEL 2	MODEL 3	MODEL 4
Personal Status				
Education	.1822 (.022)***			.0259 (.026)
Personal Well-being	−.0037 (.009)			.0073 (.010)
Sex (Men)	.2376 (.092)**			.2831 (.102)**
Age	−.0208 (.003)***			−.0232 (.004)***
Cultural and Normative Orientations				
Religiosity		−.1697 (.025)***		−.1155 (.027)***
Individualism		.2941 (.078)***		.1210 (.082)
Traditionalism		−.1745 (.027)***		−.1258 (.029)***
Social Tolerance		.2937 (.060)***		.1459 (.069)*
Political Experiences and Assessments				
Confidence in Institutional Structure of Political System			−.0202 (.013)	.0007 (.015)
Confidence in Institutions of Order			−.1653 (.020)**	−.0948 (.022)***
Trust in Ordinary Citizens			.0446 (.023)	.0373 (.025)
Political Attentiveness			.1561 (.030)***	.1214 (.034)***
Government Performance			−.1362 (.026)***	−.1187 (.030)***
Number of Observations	1,764	1,714	1,801	1,607

Note: Robust standard errors in parentheses.

*$p < 0.05$, **$p < 0.01$, ***$p < 0.001$

economically disadvantaged, as suggested by their lower levels of personal well-being. Apparently, then, as expected, non-democrats tend to be found outside the more modern, dynamic, affluent, and outward-looking sectors of Turkish society. Individuals in this category possess few of the attitudes and values conducive to democracy, nor even confidence in the political capability of ordinary citizens like themselves. They are apparently content to stand apart from the political process and leave the direction of their society to a strong leader or government technocrats.

Table 6.7 presents the results of an analysis in which the category of greater support for democracy and lesser importance attached to political liberty is the dependent variable. Respondents in this category appear to support the prevailing political order and may be described as politically satisfied. As shown in Table 6.3, they constitute 22.2 percent of the sample. Table 6.7 shows that individuals in this category are more likely, to a statistically significant degree, to be better educated, older, and religious and also to have confidence in institutions of order, more trust in ordinary citizens than in strong political leaders or government technocrats, and a positive assessment of government performance.

Older and better educated, these individuals are probably the most established and secure of the population categories examined. Accordingly, as their satisfaction with the status quo also suggests, they appear to be among those who benefit most from prevailing political and social arrangements. This is reflected in their confidence in institutions of order and their positive assessment of government performance. Against this background, it is possible that they identify good government, and hence democracy, with the present regime, regardless of the degree to which it has undemocratic as well as democratic characteristics. They are not hostile to democracy, as indicated by their greater trust in ordinary citizens than in strong political leaders or government technocrats. They are not true democrats, however, but rather appear to be establishment-oriented political conservatives. They may be social conservatives as well, a possibility suggested by their higher levels of religiosity.

Table 6.8 presents the results of an analysis in which the category of lesser support for democracy and greater importance attached to political liberty is the dependent variable. These men and women, who constitute 21.2 percent of the sample, appear to represent a segment of the country's youth that is alienated from the political system. Individuals in this category are more likely to a statistically significant degree to be younger, less religious, and have lower levels of confidence both in institutions of order and in ordinary citizens. Their profile may be characterized as "anti-establishment."

Table 6.6. Logit Results for the Category of Lesser Support for Democracy and Lesser Importance Attached to Political Liberty

Personal Status		
Education	−.1053	(.034)**
Personal Well-being	−.0246	(.012)*
Sex (Men)	−.5735	(.127)***
Age	.0059	(.004)
Cultural and Normative Orientations		
Religiosity	.1358	(.053)*
Individualism	−.0549	(.107)
Traditionalism	.0752	(.039)*
Social Tolerance	−.1410	(.084)
Political Experiences and Assessments		
Confidence in Institutional Structure of Political System	.0120	(.018)
Confidence in Institutional Structure of Political System	.0206	(.027)
Trust in Ordinary Citizens	−.1649	(.030)***
Political Attentiveness	−.1474	(.043)***
Government Performance	.0589	(.035)
Constant	−1.8134	(1.15)
Number of Observations	1,595	

Note: Robust standard errors in parentheses.
*$p < 0.05$, **$p < 0.01$, ***$p < 0.001$

Although these young men and women attach importance to political liberty, this may be more of a protest against those in power than a genuine expression of democratic values. This interpretation is suggested by their low confidence in institutions of order, which claim to be, and are, guardians of the status quo. It is also suggested by their low trust in political bodies elected by ordinary citizens. Indeed, their greater trust in a strong leader or government technocrats suggests potential receptivity to anti-establishment, and

Table 6.7. Logit Results for the Category of Greater Support for Democracy and Lesser Importance Attached to Political Liberty

Personal Status		
Education	.0777	(.034)*
Personal Well-being	.0141	(.013)
Sex (Men)	.2048	(.130)
Age	.0213	(.004)***
Cultural and Normative Orientations		
Religiosity	.0799	(.038)*
Individualism	−.0597	(.112)
Traditionalism	.0733	(.039)
Social Tolerance	−.0648	(.083)
Political Experiences and Assessments		
Confidence in Institutional Structure of Political System	−.0219	(.017)
Confidence in Institutions of Order	.0979	(.028)***
Trust in Ordinary Citizens	.1107	(.032)***
Political Attentiveness	.0107	(.043)
Government Performance	.1005	(.035)**
Constant	−6.9483	(1.04)***
Number of Observations	1,595	

Note: Robust standard errors in parentheses.
*$p < 0.05$, **$p < 0.01$, ***$p < 0.001$

very possibly anti-democratic, movements that promise radical change. That these individuals tend to be less religious suggests an alienation that may be social as well as political. They apparently lack the strong religious attachments that might compensate for their estrangement from the prevailing political order.

Table 6.9 treats the category of greater support for democracy and greater importance attached to political liberty as the dependent variable. Respondents in this category, who constitute 31.2 percent of the sample, may

Table 6.8. Logit Results for the Category of Lesser Support for
Democracy and Greater Importance Attached to Political Liberty

Personal Status	
Education	−.0612 (.034)
Personal Well-being	−.0037 (.013)
Sex (Men)	.1458 (.129)
Age	−.0250 (.005)***
Cultural and Normative Orientations	
Religiosity	−.0703 (.031)*
Individualism	−.0046 (.102)
Traditionalism	.0313 (.038)
Social Tolerance	−.0975 (.088)
Political Experiences and Assessments	
Confidence in Institutional Structure of Political System	.0133 (.018)
Confidence in Institutions of Order	−.1250 (.026)***
Trust in Ordinary Citizens	−.0941 (.029)**
Political Attentiveness	−.0016 (.043)
Government Performance	.0070 (.037)
Constant	2.4007 (.891)**
Number of Observations	1,595

Note: Robust standard errors in parentheses.
*$p < 0.05$, **$p < 0.01$, ***$p < 0.001$

be described as "true democrats." They favor democracy and also posses at least some of the political values necessary for successful democratization. Table 6.9 shows that these individuals are more likely to be male, politically attentive, lower on the measure of traditionalism, higher on the measures of social tolerance and trust in ordinary citizens, and have an unfavorable assessment of government performance.

True democrats appear to be progressive, open-minded, forward-looking, and politically conscious individuals. Tolerant of diversity and lower in traditionalism, they look to the future rather than the past. They are also politically engaged, being attentive to politics, impatient with the present regime, and desirous of a political system that is genuinely accountable to ordinary citizens. Their attitudes and values are consistent with expectations based on prior research on democratization. They conform to the model of a "democratic citizen," whose presence in substantial numbers is probably necessary for the maintenance and eventual consolidation of democratic transitions.

Conclusion

Against the background of Turkey's continuing but unconsolidated democratic transition, the present study examines the nature and determinants of attitudes toward democracy held by ordinary Turkish citizens. Four interrelated questions have been of particular concern:

- To what extent does the Turkish population hold attitudes supportive of democracy?
- What are the most important determinants of popular support for democracy; what factors account for any observed variance in relevant political attitudes?
- What is the relationship between attitudes toward the military and attitudes toward democracy and governance?
- What is the relationship between personal religious attachments and attitudes toward democracy and governance?

Two attitudinal dimensions relating to democracy have been identified and each has been measured with a two-item additive index. On one of these, support for democracy as a political system, pro-democracy attitudes are held by a substantial proportion of ordinary men and women. Specifically, 53.4 percent of those interviewed have a high rating on this index. The distribution of ratings on the second index is quite different, however. This index measures importance attached to political liberty, and in this case only 16.6 percent of the respondents express strongly pro-democracy attitudes. The two dimensions have also been considered in combination, and 31.2 percent of those interviewed have high or at least fairly high ratings on both measures and are classified as "true democrats." This latter figure, however, is not an absolute measure; rather, it is somewhat inflated since it is based on a typology formed by combining two dichotomized indices.

These findings suggest that attitudes conducive to democracy and democratization are held by a relatively limited number of Turkish men and women, and that, accordingly, an appropriate political culture probably does not yet exist to the extent necessary for democratic consolidation. A majority

Table 6.9. Logit Results for the Category of Greater Support for Democracy and Greater Importance Attached to Political Liberty

Personal Status	
Education	.0536 (.030)
Personal Well-being	.0116 (.012)
Sex (Men)	.2404 (.120)*
Age	−.0083 (.004)
Cultural and Normative Orientations	
Religiosity	−.0183 (.030)
Individualism	.0469 (.093)
Traditionalism	−.1257 (.033)***
Social Tolerance	.3700 (.084)***
Political Experiences and Assessments	
Confidence in Institutional Structure of Political System	−.0094 (.017)
Confidence in Institutions of Order	.0318 (.025)
Trust in Ordinary Citizens	.1197 (.030)***
Political Attentiveness	.1166 (.041)**
Government Performance	−.1573 (.037)***
Constant	−1.2797 (.829)
Number of Observations	1,595

Note: Robust standard errors in parentheses.
*p < 0.05, **p < 0.01, ***p < 0.001

of Turkish citizens do express support for democracy as a political system, but, as discussed, at least some of these individuals are probably expressing satisfaction with the status quo rather than a genuine commitment to democracy. Even more important, both the limited importance attached to political liberty and the fact that importance attached to political liberty is not related to support for democracy suggests that Turkey does not at present possess a democratic political culture.

Findings about the determinants of pro-democracy attitudes not only help to account for variance; they also shed light on prospects for the emergence and expansion of a democratic political culture in the future. Significantly, and consistent with the preceding assessment, there are important differences, as well as some similarities, between the determinants of support for democracy and the determinants of importance attached to political liberty. The similarities include male gender, higher social tolerance, lower traditionalism, and greater attentiveness to politics. This suggests that experiences which promote a favorable predisposition toward social change and diversity tend to encourage pro-democracy attitudes, and that such attitudes are thus likely to become more widespread with the acceleration of modernization and social change.

Differences in the two sets of determinants are equally instructive. Variance in support for democracy is associated with older age, a higher educational level, and greater confidence in the country's institutions of order, whereas variance in importance attached to political liberty is associated with younger age, less religiosity, an unfavorable assessment of government performance, and less confidence in institutions of order. Both profiles suggest that social circumstances are of critical importance. Individuals who are more established and in a relatively favorable position, who benefit from the status quo, in other words, are more likely to express support for democracy. Alternatively, those who are more likely to attach importance to political liberty are young people with unfavorable views of both the modern and traditional sociopolitical system. They are youthful protesters who do not have confidence in institutions of order and judge government performance harshly. At the same time, they are not strongly connected to either religion or traditional society.

These interpretations, if correct, suggest that political attitudes are strongly influenced by social status and perceived self-interest, and that to some extent attitudes toward democracy and liberty are thus a proxy for support or opposition to the existing political system. Accordingly, there are limits to the inferences about political culture that can be drawn when attitudes toward democracy and political liberty are considered separately. These two political orientations have also been examined in combination, however, making it possible to identify determinants of support for democracy *and* importance attached to political liberty, to investigate factors that separate "true democrats" from other citizens.

The profile of true democrats is consistent with expectations. These individuals possess the kinds of values associated with a democratic political culture, being politically attentive and higher on the measures of social tolerance and trust in ordinary citizens. They are also critical of the present quasi-democratic regime, having an unfavorable assessment of government performance. Finally, and significantly, they are lower in traditionalism, suggesting that the expansion of modernization and development may increase their numbers in the future.

The data also shed light on the two remaining issues that are of interest in the Turkish case: the significance for democracy of attitudes toward the military and of religious attachments. Confidence in the military, associated with confidence in institutions of order more generally, tends to encourage support for democracy and discourage attaching importance to political liberty. These findings may say as much about attitudes toward the prevailing political system as they do about democracy, however, since views about the military do not have an impact on the political orientations of true democrats but rather on the orientations of those who possess some pro-democracy attitudes but not others. The military is committed to the present political order, regardless of the degree to which that order is or is not democratic, and it apparently inspires confidence among those who benefit from the status quo and is judged critically by those who are less established and less secure.

This suggests that the anomaly of an anti-democratic institution presenting itself as the guardian of democracy may neither trouble most Turkish citizens nor be taken especially seriously. True democrats have neither a more favorable view of the military because of its espoused commitment to democracy nor a less favorable view because of its anti-democratic character. Rather, whether justified or not, the common view seems to be that the military acts to preserve a quasi-democratic status quo, and it is by this standard, rather than by the implications for democratic consolidation, that the military and other institutions of order tend to be judged.

With respect to religion, it does not appear that strong Islamic attachments discourage the emergence of pro-democracy attitudes. With other factors held constant, religiosity is inversely related to importance attached to political liberty. As noted, however, this may be more a reflection of youthful alienation than an indication that religiosity fosters anti-democratic attitudes. Religiosity is not associated with support for democracy, and, most important, religious individuals are no less likely than others to be true democrats.

These findings tend to support those who challenge the proposition that Islam is hostile to democracy. Admittedly, the present study's location in space and time raises questions about the generalizability of its conclusions. On the one hand, a strong tradition of secularism suggests that findings based on the Turkish cases may not shed light on other Muslim societies. On the other, the survey was conducted at a time when the pro-Islamic Welfare Party led the governing coalition, raising the possibility that the relationship between religiosity and democratic attitudes may depend on the nature of the regime in power. Nevertheless, religiosity among Turkish Muslims is not strongly and consistently associated with anti-democratic attitudes, and similar results reported in other recent investigations lend confidence to the conclusion that Islam and democracy are not incompatible.[41]

In sum, findings from the present investigation indicate that Turkey does not at present possess a broadly based democratic culture and leave unanswered questions about the prospects for its emergence in the future. The low traditionalism of true democrats suggests that an intensification of social change and development might help to promote democratic values. The extent and rapidity of this intensification is unknown, however, and it is also significant that pro-democracy attitudes are no more prominent among younger and better-educated individuals than among others. Thus, neither the expansion of education nor generational change is likely, by itself, to increase the proportion of ordinary citizens who hold the political orientations necessary for democratic consolidation. Against this background, with no serious obstacles provided by Islam but with the military's interventions on behalf of democracy having little impact on the political attitudes of ordinary men and women, the best guess is that Turkey's democratic transition will continue at an uneven pace and remain unconsolidated for the foreseeable future.

Appendix: Indices Measuring Independent Variables

PERSONAL STATUS

Education

V217. What is the highest educational level that you have attained? Code based on a 1–10 scale from low to high.

Personal Well-being

V64. How satisfied are you with the financial situation of your household? If 1 means you are completely dissatisfied on this scale, and 10 means you are completely satisfied, where would you put your satisfaction with your household's financial situation?

V65. All things considered, how satisfied are you with your life as a whole these days? Please use this card to help with your answer. Code based on a 1–10 scale, with 1 being completely dissatisfied.

V227. Here is a scale of incomes. We would like to know in what group your household belongs, counting all wages, salaries, pensions, and other incomes that come in. Just give the letter of the group your household falls into, before taxes and other deductions. Code based on a 1–10 scale, with 1 being the lowest.

CULTURAL AND NORMATIVE ORIENTATIONS

Religiosity

V182. Independent of whether you go to church (mosque) or not, would you say you are a religious person, not a religious person, or a convinced atheist?

Which, if any, of the following do you believe in? Code based on a 1–3 scale, with 1 being "Yes," 3 being "No," and "Don't Know" coded as 2.

V183. Do you believe in God?

V184. Do you believe in life after death?

V185. Do you believe people have a soul?

V190. How important is God in your life? Code based on a 1–3 scale, with 1 being least important (original 1–10 scale: 1–3 = 1, 4–7 = 2, 8–9 = 3).

V191. Do you find that you get comfort and strength from religion? Code based on a 1–3 scale, with 1 being "Yes," 3 being "No," and "Don't Know" coded as 2.

Individualism

Here is a list of qualities that children can be encouraged to learn at home. Which, if any, do you consider to be especially important? Coded according to whether respondent did or did not mention a particular quality.

V 15. Independence

V 18. Imagination

Traditionalism

V12. With which of these two statements do you tend to agree?
A. Regardless of the qualities and faults of one's parents, one must always love and respect them.

B. One does not have the duty to respect and love parents who have not earned it by their behavior and attitudes.

Here is a list of qualities that children can be encouraged to learn at home. Which, if any, do you consider to be especially important? Coded according to whether respondent did or did not mention a particular quality. (Only the one item from the list used in the present analysis is given here.)

V14. Good manners

For each of the following pairs of statements, please tell me which one comes closest to your own views:

V47. (1) We should emphasize tradition more than high technology.

(2) We should emphasize high technology more than tradition.

I'm going to read a list of various changes in our way of life that might take place in the near future. Please tell me for each one, if it were to happen, whether you think it would be a good thing, a bad thing, or you don't mind?

V114. Greater respect for authority

V115. More emphasis on family life

Social Tolerance

On this list are various groups of people, Could you please sort out any that you would not like to have as neighbors? Code based on whether or not respondent mentioned the following groups.

V52. People of a different race

V56. Christians

POLITICAL EXPERIENCES AND ASSESSMENTS

Confidence in the Political System

I am going to name a number of organizations. For each one, could you please tell me how much confidence you have in it: a great deal, quite a lot, not very much, or none at all.

V142. The government in Ankara

V143. Political parties

V144. Parliament

V145. The Civil Service

Confidence in Institutions of Order

I am going to name a number of organizations. For each one, could you please tell me how much confidence you have in it: a great deal, quite a lot, not very much, or none at all.

V136. The armed forces

V137. The legal system

V141. The police

Trust in Ordinary Citizens

I am going to describe various types of political systems and ask what you think about each as a way of governing this country. For each one, would you say it is a very good, fairly good, fairly bad, or very bad way of governing this country?

V154. Having a strong leader who does not have to bother with parliament and elections

V155. Having experts, not the government, make decisions according to what they think is best for the country

Political Attentiveness

Please say, for each of the following, how important it is in your life. Would you say it is very important, rather important, not very important, or not at all important? (Only the one item from the list used in the present analysis is given here.)

V7. Politics

V37. When you get together with your friends, would you say you discuss political matters frequently, occasionally, or never?

V117. How interested would you say you are in politics? Are you very interested, somewhat interested, not very interested, or not at all interested?

Government Performance

V152. People have different views about the system governing this country. Here is a scale for rating how well things are going: 1 means very bad and 5 means very good. Where on this scale would you put the political system as it is today?

V165. How satisfied are you with the way the people now in national office are handling the country's affairs? Would you say you are very satisfied, fairly satisfied, no opinion, fairly dissatisfied, or very dissatisfied?

CHAPTER 7

Assessing the Influence of Religious Predispositions on Citizen Orientations Related to Governance and Democracy: Findings from Survey Research in Three Dissimilar Arab Societies (2006)

Mark Tessler

Studies of democracy and democratic transitions place emphasis on the attitudes, values, and behavioral patterns of ordinary citizens. More specifically, this research argues that successful democratization requires the existence of a "democratic" political orientation among a significant proportion of a country's population. Some analysts suggest that this is a precondition for a democratic transition.[1] More common is the view that democratic norms and behavior need not precede, but rather can follow, an elite-led transition involving the reform of political institutions and procedures.[2] Indeed, according to this argument, citizen orientations conducive to democracy may emerge in response to the experience of a democratic transition.

Debates about timing and sequence notwithstanding, there is general agreement that sustainable democracy depends not only on the commitments and actions of political elites but also on the political orientations of ordinary men and women. This thesis was advanced more than four decades ago by Almond and Verba in their seminal work, *The Civic Culture*. They observed in 1963 that, "if the democratic model . . . is to develop in new nations, it will require more than the formal institutions of democracy—universal suffrage, the political party, the elective legislature. . . . A democratic form of participatory political system requires as well a political culture consistent with it . . . [of which] the norms and attitudes of ordinary citizens are subtler cultural components."[3] Inglehart is among the many scholars of democratization who have made the same point more recently. He wrote in 2000 that "democracy is not attained simply by making institutional changes or through elite level maneuvering. Its survival depends also on the values and beliefs of ordinary citizens."[4]

Against this background, it is important to investigate the factors that either encourage or discourage the emergence of democratic attitudes and values, and, in Arab and other Muslim societies, the influence of Islam is of particular interest. Although some scholars suggest that Islam is hostile to democratic values,[5] empirical research at the individual level of analysis finds no evidence that religiosity and Islamic involvement diminish support for democracy.[6] The relationship between religious predispositions and a normative political orientation supportive of democracy has not been investigated, however, and the present study seeks to fill this gap by examining the relationship between religious predispositions and political orientations related to governance and democracy among Muslims in Jordan, Palestine (West Bank and Gaza), and Algeria.

Data and Method

Data from national surveys carried out in Jordan, Palestine (West Bank and Gaza), and Algeria in 2003–2004 are used to examine the political orientations of ordinary citizens in these three Arab countries. Surveys were conducted in Jordan and Palestine in December 2003 and in Algeria in the summer of 2004. These three countries were chosen for both practical and analytical reasons. Practical reasons include the availability of local scholars and institutions with substantial experience in the conduct of rigorous survey research and, as reflected in Freedom House ratings of "Partly Free," a political climate that permits the conduct of public opinion research. Jordan, Palestine, and Algeria are among the relatively few Arab countries where political attitude research is possible at the present time.

Analytical considerations include system-level differences that make cross-national comparison instructive. Within the context of the Arab world, the three countries constitute something of a "most different systems" research design. Although none of them resembles the small, oil-rich countries of the Arab Gulf, they are otherwise at least somewhat representative of the region's republics, monarchies, and strong presidential systems. Any patterns observed in all three countries may thus be generalizable to other parts of the Arab world. It is also possible that patterns common to Jordan, Palestine, and Algeria will be applicable to nondemocracies in other world regions, since they will have been found to obtain under widely differing conditions. Alternatively, the unique attributes and circumstances of each country will help to define in conceptual terms the locus of applicability of patterns found only in that country.

Algeria, a republic, is one of the largest states in the Arab world, has considerable wealth from oil and natural gas, and possesses a tradition of state socialism and centralized planning. For much of the time since it gained independence in 1962, Algeria has been governed by a cohort of military and civilian leaders, with military officers having preponderant influence. Jordan, a monarchy, tends to be socially conservative, is organized to a considerable extent along tribal lines, and is among the less populous and also the poorer countries of the Arab world. Jordanian society is also marked by an important cleavage between Jordanians of Palestinian origin and other Jordanians, the so-called East Bankers. Palestine, which is struggling for statehood, has a tradition of secular nationalism and strong relations with its diaspora. Until very recently, the Palestine national movement had been symbolized and led for nearly four decades by a single individual. The three political communities also differ with regard to their history of foreign relations. Algeria has a legacy of intense French colonialism and continues to have very important ties to France; the British were the dominant imperial power prior to Jordanian independence, and Jordan is today one of the most important American allies in the Arab world; and the Palestinian political experience is shaped by its historical and continuing relationship with Zionism and Israel.

The surveys in Jordan and Palestine were funded by a grant from the National Science Foundation, and the survey in Algeria was funded by the American Institute for Maghrib Studies. All are based on representative national samples. The survey in Jordan was conducted by the Center for Strategic Studies at the University of Jordan, the survey in Palestine was conducted by the Palestinian Center for Policy and Survey Research in Ramallah, and the survey in Algeria was conducted by a team at the University of Algiers. All three surveys involved three-stage cluster sampling based on the most recent national census, 1994 in Jordan, 1997 in the West Bank and Gaza, and 1998 in Algeria. The same interview schedule was administered in Jordan and Palestine. It was used in Algeria as well, although supplemented by a number of items dealing with domestic policy issues in that country.

Political orientation is the dependent variable in the analysis to follow, and respondents were rated according to whether or not they possess an orientation composed of attitudes, values, and behavior patterns supportive of democracy—whether, in other words, they possess a "democratic" political orientation. For purposes of the present analysis, ratings are based on items from the survey instrument that measure the following six normative and behavioral dimensions: (1) political tolerance, (2) support for gender equality, (3) political interest, (4) political knowledge, (5) civic participation, and (6) interpersonal trust. To measure each dimension, two or more highly correlated items were combined to form an additive index; the six resulting indices were then factor analyzed, which generated a two-factor solution; and, finally, respondents above the midpoint on both sets of factor scores produced by this analysis have been classified as having a democratic political orientation. The specific items used to measure each of the six dimensions are listed in the appendix to the chapter.

The independent variables in the analysis are two different kinds of Islamic predispositions. The first is the degree to which an individual seeks personal guidance and support from religion, measured by the degree to which respondents report finding comfort in religion and by the likelihood they consult religious officials when seeking guidance in personal affairs. The second, which has not been examined in previous research concerning political attitude but is no less important, is liberalism-conservatism in the interpretation of religious codes. As in other instances where a body of law must be interpreted and applied to present-day and changing real-life circumstances, there is disagreement and debate among Muslims, including devout Muslims, about whether to be guided by a strict, literal, and historically dominant construction of Islamic law or by a construction that emphasizes adaptability and looks for the underlying spirit and intent of the law. Islamic interpretation is measured by an item that reminds respondents that "Muslim scholars and jurists sometimes disagree about the proper interpretation of Islam in response to present-day issues," and then asks them to evaluate three issues on which there is disagreement about what Islam requires and prohibits: coeducation at universities, charging interest on bank loans, and citizenship in the Muslim *umma*.

The same two items measuring importance of religious guidance in personal affairs and the same three items measuring liberalism-conservatism in religious interpretation, all of which are listed in the appendix, in each case have high loadings on a single factor in the three countries for which data are available. All but four of the fifteen loadings exceed .700, and the lowest of the remaining four loadings is .624. The analysis also includes several other non-dependent variables. These may be considered control variables since the primary purpose of this essay is to assess the influence of religious predispositions on political orientations. They may also be regarded as independent variables, since their own explanatory power may be of interest as well. One of these variables is judgment about the regime in power, measured by correlated items that ask respondents to evaluate how good a job the government is doing in running the country and to indicate how much confidence they have in the government. Factor scores based on these items have been generated and are employed in the analysis. The other variables are sex, education, and age.

Findings

Table 7.1 shows the proportion of Jordanians, Palestinians, and Algerians who possess a democratic political orientation. The proportions are similar in the Jordanian and Palestinian cases; in both countries only 11–12 percent of the respondents have such an orientation. By contrast, the Algerian case stands out from Jordan and Palestine; 37 percent have a democratic political orientation. Some minor question wording and coding differences were introduced by the Algerian research team on one item, but it is unlikely that this contributed more than marginally to the difference between Algeria and the other two countries. Accordingly, it seems reasonable to conclude that some of the history and political experience that set Algeria apart from Jordan and Palestine have contributed to the greater emergence, in relative terms, of a democratic political culture. Among these aspects may be the mobilization and modernization resulting from Algeria's extended experience with centralized planning and socialist development after independence or, closer to the present, its deeper experience with partisan diversity and competitive elections.

Table 7.2 presents the results of binary regression analyses for Jordan, Palestine, and Algeria in which the presence or absence of a democratic political orientation is the dependent variable. The primary independent variables, again, are the importance of religion in personal affairs and liberalism-conservatism in Islamic interpretation. Other variables include assessment of the governing regime, sex, age, and educational level.

Table 7.2 shows both differences and similarities across the three countries. In Jordan, liberalism in Islamic interpretation and higher educational level are related to the presence of a democratic political orientation to a statistically significant degree, with $p = .002$ or less in both instances. In Palestine, liberalism in Islamic interpretation and higher educational level are again related to the dependent variable to a statistically significant degree, with $p = .005$ or less. In addition, lesser importance of religious guidance in personal affairs, male sex, and older age are also related to a statistically significant degree to the presence of a democratic political orientation. The three p values are between .006 and .039. Finally, in Algeria, the independent variables in statistically significant relationships are importance of religion in personal affairs, sex, age, and educational level. Specifically, greater importance of religion in personal affairs, male sex, older age, and higher educational level are all associated with the presence of a democratic political orientation. Probability values are .016 or lower.

It is notable that neither of the two identical variable relationships found in all three countries concerns Islam. One of these involves education. Better-educated individuals are disproportionately likely to possess a democratic political orientation. Given the important differences between Jordan, Palestine, and Algeria, it would appear that this relationship is not condition-specific. Rather, following the logic of a most different systems

Table 7.1. Proportion of Jordanian, Palestinian, and Algerian
Respondents with a Democratic Political Orientation

		JORDAN	PALESTINE	ALGERIA
Political Orientation	Democratic	11.2%	11.9%	37.0%
	Nondemocratic	88.8%	88.1%	63.0%
	All	100%	100%	100%

Table 7.2. Logistic Regression Showing Influence on
Political Orientations Related to Governance and Democracy
of the Importance of Religion in Personal Affairs, Liberalism-
Conservatism in Islamic Interpretation, Assessment of the
Governing Regime, and Sex, Age, and Educational Level

	JORDAN	PALESTINE	ALGERIA
Religion more important in personal affairs	.070 .128	−.233 .095**	.243 .092**
Greater liberalism in Islamic interpretation	.372 .120**	.275 .097**	.087 .087
More negative assessment of governing regime	.159 .121	−.153 .105	−.148 .089
Female sex	−.288 .267	−.568 .208**	−.420 .175**
Older age	.010 .010	.017 .006*	.152 .042***
Higher educational level	.391 .099***	.546 .074***	.454 .083***

Note: Dependent variable is coded 0 = not a democratic political orientation, 1 = a democratic political orientation. Table presents logit coefficients (B) with standard errors in parentheses.

*p < .05, **p < .02, ***p > .01

research design, it is probably reasonably generalizable. The other identical finding is the absence of any significant relationship involving assessment of the governing regime. In no instance is either a positive or a negative evaluation of the government strongly related to the presence of a political orientation supportive of democracy. This finding, for the same reason, would also appear to be somewhat generalizable, refuting the plausible hypothesis that antipathy to the government in a nondemocratic political setting tends to give rise to democratic values and behavioral norms.

With respect to norms pertaining to Islam, the primary concern of the present inquiry, both of the relevant independent variables are related to political orientations to a statistically significant degree in two of the three countries. But it is not the same two countries in each instance, and, in one case, the direction of the relationship differs. In Palestine, men and women for whom religious guidance is less important are disproportionately likely to possess a democratic political orientation, whereas, in Algeria, those for whom religious guidance is more important are disproportionately likely to possess such an orientation. Coupled with the finding that the importance of religious guidance has no explanatory power in Jordan, this suggests that the influence of personal religious involvement is not consistent but rather highly conditional in Arab societies, and most likely in other Muslim and perhaps even non-Muslim societies as well.

There is too much overdetermination to do more than offer informed speculation about some of the conditionalities associated with each observed relationship. Attributes and experiences shared by Palestine and Algeria but not Jordan are a strong tradition of secular nationalism; a political system that is republican rather than monarchical; and particularly intense involvement with a Western democracy, Israel in the Palestinian case and France for Algerians. The two countries, in contrast to Jordan, have also been marked in recent years by extensive turmoil and violence. Some of these considerations, singly or in combination, may define the conditions under which personal religious involvement has explanatory power. Palestine and Algeria also differ from one another in important respects. Palestine is more traditional, being marked to a much greater degree by the prominence of extended notable families, by the influence of Islamic trusts and other religious institutions, and by the importance of patron-client relationships. Algeria, by contrast, is more mobilized and proletarian as a result of its intense colonial experience and, after independence, by the government's emphasis on centralized planning and socialist development.

Taken together, these characteristics suggest several hypotheses deserving further study: personal religious involvement is more likely to influence political orientations related to governance and democracy in Arab and Muslim societies with a tradition of secular nationalism and intense interaction with Western democracies; personal religious involvement discourages the emergence of a democratic political orientation when a society with these characteristics is more traditional; and personal religious involvement contributes to the emergence of a democratic political orientation when a society with these characteristics is more mobilized and developed.

Liberalism-conservatism in the interpretation and application of Islamic strictures, an important religion-related variable that has not been studied previously at the individual level of analysis, also has significant explanatory power in two of the three countries for which data are available. In Jordan and Palestine, but not in Algeria, men and women with a more liberal perspective are disproportionately likely to possess a democratic political orientation. Again, it is only possible to speculate about the attributes shared by the two countries but not by Algeria that might constitute conditions under which this relationship obtains. Jordanian society, like that of Palestine, is much more traditional than that of Algeria. Although by no means absent in Algeria, religious institutions, notable families, and clan-based social structures are much less influential than in Jordan and Palestine, having declined in importance first under the French and then under the centralized planning and state socialism that followed the achievement of independence. This suggests, plausibly enough, that differing tendencies in the interpretation and application of religious prescriptions to everyday life have a much greater impact on political norms and values in societies that are more traditional than in societies that are less traditional.

Finally, male sex and older age are associated with the presence of a democratic political orientation in Palestine and Algeria but not in Jordan. Attributes that distinguish Palestine and Algeria from Jordan, as noted, include a tradition of secular nationalism, a republican political system, intense involvement with a Western democracy, and turmoil and violence in recent years. A tradition of secular nationalism and greater exposure to Western democracy would seem to be the most important of these characteristics so far as conditions that specify when male gender and older age are associated with a political orientation supportive of democracy. Another possibility, suggested by an earlier study in Algeria,[7] is that older men constitute a political generation and that their disproportionate likelihood to possess a democratic political orientation reflects values shaped not only by secular nationalism and exposure to Western democracy but also by the fact that the society characterized by these attributes was relatively peaceful when they were in their late teens and early twenties.

Conclusion

Research on democratic transitions and consolidation indicates that successful democratization requires the existence of a democratic political orientation among a significant proportion of a country's citizens. Accordingly, there have been many data-based studies of political attitudes, values, and behavior patterns in countries where a democratic transition is taking place. By contrast, there has been little empirical research on the political orientations of ordinary men and women in nondemocracies, particularly in the Arab world. The present study contributes to filling this gap by presenting findings about the determinants of orientations related to governance and democracy among ordinary citizens in Jordan, Palestine, and Algeria. It investigates, in particular, the degree to which, and the conditions under which, norms and predispositions associated with Islam either promote or discourage the emergence of a democratic political orientation.

Whereas several previous investigations suggest that personal religious involvement has relatively little influence on political attitudes in Arab countries, survey data from Jordan, Palestine, and Algeria in 2003–2004 indicate that this frequently is not the case with respect to values and behavioral patterns associated with democracy. Rather, these data suggest that more than one kind of religious predisposition is relevant; that greater reliance on religion in personal affairs sometimes pushes toward, sometimes pushes away from, and sometimes is unrelated to the possession of a democratic political orientation; that liberalism in the interpretation of Islamic legal codes and prescriptions, a heretofore neglected dimension of views pertaining to Islam, often pushes toward and never pushes away from a democratic political orientation; and that the importance of each of these predispositions in accounting for variance in political orientations related to governance and democracy is conditional upon country-level attributes and experiences. Sorting out which religious predispositions shape political orientations in which ways and under which conditions, and whether the same relationships obtain when the religion is not Islam, is a promising avenue for future research.

Appendix: Items Used to Measure Dependent and Independent Variables

Political Tolerance

People sometimes talk about the factors that make a person qualified for national leadership. On this card are listed six of the qualifications to which different people would give priority. Would you please say which one of these you consider the most important? Which would be the next most important? And which would be third? Coded according to whether "Openness to Diverse Political Ideas" ranks first or second.

Jordan and Palestine only: Do you disagree or agree with this statement: Christian citizens of our country should have the same rights as Muslim citizens to hold any political office, including the president of the state.

Algeria only: People sometimes talk about what the aims of this country should be for the next ten years. On this card are listed four of the goals to which different people would give priority. Would you please say which one of these you consider the most important? Which is the second-most important, and which is the third-most important? Coded according to whether "Assuring equal rights for all citizens, regardless of religion or gender" ranks first or second.

Support for Gender Equality

Do you disagree or agree with this statement? "On the whole men make better political leaders than women do."

Do you disagree or agree with this statement? "A university education is more important for a boy than a girl."

Do you disagree or agree with this statement? "A woman may work outside the home if she wishes."

Political Interest

How important is politics in your life?

When you get together with your friends, would you say that you discuss political matters frequently, occasionally, or never?

Political Knowledge

Can you name the Foreign Minister?

Can you name the Minister of Finance?

Can you name the Speaker of Parliament?

How often do you read the newspaper?

Civic Participation

How often do you interact with people in social, cultural, or youth groups?

How often do you interact with people at your mosque or church or in religious associations?

How often do you interact with people in political groups, clubs, or discussion groups?

How often do you interact with people in your professional associations?

How often do you interact with people in sports or recreation groups?

Political Trust

Generally speaking, would you say that most people can be trusted or that most people cannot be trusted?

I will read some statements about social and political issues. Please indicate your agreement or disagreement with each. (Only the one statement from the list used in the present analysis is given here.)

You can trust no one these days.

Importance of Religion in Personal Affairs

Do you find that you get comfort and strength from religion? Very much, Some, A little, Very little, or None.

When you need advice about a personal problem, how often do you consult each of the following? An *imam* or *f'kih*.

Liberalism-Conservatism in Islamic Interpretation

Today, as in the past, Muslim scholars and jurists sometimes disagree about the proper interpretation of Islam in response to present-day issues. For each of the statements listed below, please indicate whether you agree strongly, agree, disagree, or disagree strongly with the interpretation of Islam that is presented.

It is a violation of Islam for male and female university students to attend classes together.

Banks in Muslim countries must be forbidden from charging even modest interest on loans because this is forbidden by Islam.

Nationalism (like Arabic, Turkish, or Kurdish) is incompatible with Islam because Islam requires that Muslims be united in a single political community (the *ummah*) rather than be citizens of different states and loyal to different governments.

Evaluation of Governing Regime

People have different views about the system for governing the country. In your opinion, how good a job is the government doing?

I am going to name a number of public and civic institutions. For each one, could you tell me how much confidence you have in it: a great deal of confidence, quite a lot of confidence, a little, very little, or none at all. (Only the one institution from the list used in the present analysis is given here.)

The government.

CHAPTER 8

Democracy and the Political Culture Orientations of Ordinary Citizens: A Typology for the Arab World and Perhaps Beyond (2009)

Mark Tessler and Eleanor Gao

Political Culture Orientation and Its Relevance for Democracy

Studies of democracy and democratic transitions place emphasis on the attitudes, values, and behavior patterns of ordinary citizens. This research argues that successful democratization requires not only support for democracy among a significant proportion of a country's population but also that its citizens possess norms and behavior patterns that are conducive to democracy—in other words, that they possess a democratic political culture orientation. Some analysts suggest that this is a precondition for a democratic transition.[1] More common is the view that democratic norms and behavior need not precede, but rather can follow, an elite-led transition involving the reform of political institutions and procedures.[2] Indeed, according to this argument, citizen orientations conducive to democracy may emerge in response to the experience of a democratic transition. Debates about timing and sequence notwithstanding, there is general agreement that sustainable democracy ultimately depends not only on the commitments and actions of political elites but also on the normative and behavioral predispositions of ordinary citizens.

These insights are derived primarily from the study of new democracies. Less commonly examined are the politically relevant attitudes, values, and behavior patterns of citizens in non-democracies, especially those in the Arab world. Against this background, the present analysis uses recent survey data from Jordan, the Palestinian Territories (West Bank and Gaza), and Algeria, three very different Arab polities, to investigate the nature and structure of citizen orientations related to democracy and governance. It also considers the degree to which patterns and relationships observed in these three political communities may be generalizable to other Arab countries and perhaps beyond.

Almond and Verba's work, *The Civic Culture*, was the first major attempt at understanding the relationship between citizen orientations and democracy.[3] Among the particular orientations they explore are obligation to participate, sense of efficacy, and level of interpersonal trust. Although Almond and Verba's study was later criticized for a number of limitations, such as a failure to examine subcultures, it was the first large-scale comparative survey of its kind and established the importance of studying the attitudes, values, and behavior patterns of ordinary men and women. Since that time, especially during the last decade and a half, there have been many empirical investigations of citizen orientations and their relationship to democratization. The general conclusion, as summarized by Inglehart, is that "culture plays a crucial role in democracy . . . its survival depends on the values and beliefs of ordinary citizens."[4]

These studies have examined a broad array of attitudes, values, and behavior patterns. Almond and Verba focused on political cognition, feelings toward government and politics, levels of partisanship, sense of civic obligation, and political efficacy. Using World Values Survey data from 1990 and 1995, Inglehart investigated the relationship between democratic achievement and adherence to self-expression values, including trust, tolerance, and political activism. In another empirical study based on data from Eastern Europe, the authors examined support for freedom of expression, political tolerance, respect for competing ideas and preferences, political interest, and a willingness to participate in the political process.[5] Dimensions of political culture that have received attention in other studies include political interest, political tolerance, valuation of liberty, rights consciousness, support for civil disobedience, support for media independence, and political participation.[6]

Although many analyses have focused on the extent and distribution of these and other democratic norms throughout a population, it is possible that these dimensions of political culture do not form a coherent syndrome. In other words, there may be no one-dimensional democratic political culture orientation, meaning that a citizen who possesses one kind of democratic norm is not necessarily likely to possess others. This seems particularly probable in countries, such as those in the Arab world, where ordinary men and women have had relatively little experience with democratic governance. On the other hand, there is no reason to assume that there are no interconnections at all among relevant attitudes, values, and behavior patterns. In light of these possibilities, a goal of the present investigation is to understand the degree to which normative and behavioral predispositions relevant for democracy are associated with one another and, more specifically, to offer insights about conceptual meaning of the patterns that are observed.

Elements of Democratic Political Culture Orientation

As noted, different authors have emphasized different attitudes, values, and behavior patterns when discussing the elements of a democratic political culture orientation. Among these are six that may be examined with the data available for the present study: support for gender equality, tolerance, interpersonal trust, civic participation, political interest, and political knowledge. The importance and relevance of each of these is briefly discussed.

The most recent Arab Human Development Report published by the United Nations Development Programme discusses the importance of gender equality and women's empowerment both in general and with respect to the Arab world in particular.[7] Democracy is meaningless if half the citizens of a country do not have equal rights and equal access to political influence and power. But granting these rights is not sufficient to promote the involvement and inclusion of women in public life: rights can be granted without removing the social barriers that prevent women from becoming full citizens. For a polity to be truly democratic there also needs to be broad public support for the principle and practice of gender equality: ordinary citizens need to appreciate that gender equality is desirable for ethical reasons and is in the public interest. It is in this connection that a recent study by Inglehart and Norris documents the difference between Western and Muslim societies in public attitudes toward women's rights and opportunities and suggests that a lower level of support for gender equality is among the reasons that democracy lags in Muslim countries.[8] Similar findings are presented by Fish.[9]

Not only should all citizens be accorded equal rights; their diverse ideas and preferences should be respected as well. Tolerance and respect for diversity are necessary in order for democracy to function effectively. At the most basic level, a tolerant citizenry can prevent civil strife, since the abridgement of minority rights by a dominant majority can lead to violence and conflict.[10] Beyond this, however, tolerance is an indispensable feature of democracy for two interrelated reasons. On the one hand, democracy requires the equality of all citizens before the state and under the law, and, for this to be accepted as legitimate, the right to hold and express views with which one disagrees must be accepted as well. On the other hand, tolerance for diverse and opposing viewpoints is necessary for the political contestation and open exchange of ideas that are essential for democracy.[11] Without respect for the right to advocate, argue, dissent, and debate, citizens would be unable to hold their leaders accountable and government by the consent of the governed would not be possible.

Along with tolerance, citizens must trust one another in a functioning democracy; they must believe that most men and women are fair-minded and reasonable and, accordingly, that citizens like themselves are the best judges of how a country should be governed. Otherwise, they are unlikely to distinguish respect for the rule of law from uncritical deference to those in authority.[12] In addition, interpersonal trust is necessary for citizens to coalesce and engage in collective political action, which is also essential for democracy to function effectively. Putnam is among those who make this point, arguing that trust is a requirement for strong civic organizations, which in turn improve the quality of governance in two important ways.[13] On the demand side, citizens in communities with high levels of trust can insist upon better government. They can engage in collective action if the government is unresponsive to their needs. On the supply side, representative government benefits from a reserve of citizens as potential lawmakers. Trustful citizens understand the necessity of cooperation and compromise in a democratic regime.

Civic participation is another important component of a democratic political culture orientation. First, a vibrant civil society is an important check on the power of the government. Interest groups and other civic associations allow citizens to monitor government actions, articulate and aggregate interests, and exert political influence. This is important in new democracies, as norms of governance have not been well established and power can be easily abused.[14]

Second, civic participation fosters the development of some of the skills that are useful for democratic citizens. Those who have learned how to organize activities, direct meetings, and prioritize goals are more likely to be effective in organizing a demonstration, circulating a petition, or preparing a ballot initiative. Civic engagement can also increase feelings of efficacy, which, in turn, promotes political involvement.[15]

On a cognitive level, political interest and political knowledge are also very important for effective democracy. Individuals who are interested in politics are more likely to follow political affairs and to participate in civic activities.[16] Engaged citizens are also likely to be effective monitors of public policy and government action. Political knowledge, which is associated with political interest, is important for the same reasons. Citizens are more likely to learn about politics and make informed assessments when an issue is important to them and if they possess relevant political knowledge.[17] Political interest and political knowledge can thus improve the quality as well as the quantity of participation by allowing citizens to make enlightened choices and helping them to resist elite manipulation.[18]

Cases and Data

Data from representative national surveys carried out in Jordan, the Palestinian Territories (West Bank and Gaza), and Algeria in 2003–2004 are used to examine the political orientations of ordinary citizens in these three Arab non-democracies. Surveys were conducted in Jordan and the Palestinian Territories in December 2003 and in Algeria in the summer of 2004. These three countries were chosen for both practical and analytical reasons. The practical reasons include the availability of local scholars and institutions with substantial experience in the conduct of rigorous survey research and, as reflected in Freedom House ratings as partly free, a political climate that permits the conduct of public opinion research.

The analytical considerations include system-level differences that make cross-national comparison instructive. Algeria, a republic, is one of the largest states in the Arab world, with considerable wealth from oil and natural gas and possessing a tradition of state socialism and centralized planning. For much of the time since its independence in 1962 Algeria has been governed by a cohort of military and civilian leaders, with military officers having preponderant influence. Jordan, a monarchy, tends to be socially conservative, is organized to a considerable extent along tribal lines, and is among the less populous and also the poorer countries of the Arab world. Jordanian society is also marked by an important cleavage between the Jordanians of Palestinian origin and other Jordanians. The Palestinian Territories, which is struggling for statehood, have a tradition of secular nationalism and strong relations with the Palestinian diaspora. Until very recently the Palestinian national movement had been symbolized and led for nearly four decades by a single individual.

The three political communities also differ with regard to their history of foreign relations. Algeria has a legacy of intense French colonialism and continues to have very important ties to France. The British were the dominant imperial power prior to Jordanian independence, and Jordan is today one of the most important American allies in the Arab world. The Palestinian political experience is shaped by its historic and continuing relationship with Zionism and Israel.

In the context of the Arab world, these three countries constitute something of a "most different systems" research design. Although none resembles the small, oil-rich countries of the Arab Gulf, they are otherwise at least somewhat representative of the region's republics, monarchies, and strong presidential systems. Any pattern observed in all three countries may thus be at least somewhat generalizable to other parts of the Arab world, since it will have been found to obtain under widely differing conditions. For the same reason, patterns common to Jordan, the Palestinian Territories, and Algeria may also be applicable to non-democracies in other world regions. Alternatively, the unique attributes and circumstances of each country will help to define in conceptual terms the locus of applicability of patterns found only in that country. With only three cases, it is not possible to eliminate multi-colinearity and differences between the countries will thus remain overdetermined. But Jordan, the Palestinian Territories, and Algeria are nonetheless sufficiently different to be able to offer plausible propositions about the country-level attributes associated with particular within-system patterns and relationships.

The surveys in Jordan and the Palestinian Territories were funded by a grant from the National Science Foundation, and the survey in Algeria was funded by the American Institute for Maghrib Studies. All are based on representative national samples. The three surveys were conducted, respectively, by the Center for Strategic Studies at the University of Jordan, the Palestinian Center for Policy and Survey Research in Ramallah, and a team at the University of Algiers. All three surveys involved three-stage cluster sampling based on the most recent national census; 1994 in Jordan, 1997 in the West Bank and Gaza, and 1998 in Algeria. In Jordan and the Palestinian Territories, districts or clusters were first randomly selected from the list of all clusters in the national census, followed by a random selection of households within each of the selected clusters, and a Kish table was finally used to choose the person in each household to be interviewed. In Algeria, governorates and then communes were selected randomly, and quota sampling based on age, sex, and education was employed at the commune level. Census data were used to establish the quotas.

The same interview schedule was administered in Jordan, the Palestinian Territories, and Algeria, although in Algeria it was supplemented by a number of items dealing with domestic policy issues in that country.

The survey instrument contained items measuring the six normative and behavioral orientations discussed above, including support for gender equality, tolerance, interpersonal trust, civic participation, political interest, and political knowledge. Each of these orientations is measured by an additive index constructed by combining two or more highly inter-correlated items from the interview schedule. Further, in all three countries, each index is constructed using the same items, all of which are given in the appendix to this article. All the items possess face validity.

In addition, evidence of reliability, further confidence in validity, and an indication of cross-national conceptual and measurement equivalence are provided by the consistently significant inter-correlations among the items; the same items are related to one another to a statistically significant degree for each one of the six indices in each one of the three countries.

Analysis and Findings

Dimensions and Types of Political Culture Orientation

Factor analysis was used to explore interrelationships among the six indices of normative and behavioral orientations discussed above. As stated, each index is composed of the same significantly inter-correlated items in Jordan, the Palestinian Territories, and Algeria, thus maximizing conceptual and measurement equivalence across the three countries. Strikingly, the results of the factor analyses, shown in Table 8.1, are the same for the three countries. In each case, a two-factor solution emerges. Both prior to and after rotation, political tolerance and support for gender equality load highly on one factor; political interest, political knowledge, civic participation, and interpersonal trust load highly on a second factor. All factor loadings are robust, with the partial exception of interpersonal trust, which loads most strongly on the same factor but at a somewhat lower level in all three cases.

Table 8.1 shows that the elements of political culture explored in this investigation neither form a one-dimensional political culture orientation nor are completely unrelated to one another. Rather, they consistently subdivide into two identifiable clusters. One, composed of political tolerance and support for gender equality, might be characterized as a pluralism or diversity dimension. The other, composed of political interest, political knowledge, civic participation, and interpersonal trust, might be characterized as an involvement dimension. The data not only permit the delineation of these conceptually distinct dimensions; they also demonstrate their empirical independence. Whereas some citizens possess the orientations associated with both dimensions or neither dimension to a significant degree, the political culture orientation of other citizens is characterized by the norms of one dimension but not the other.

Table 8.2 shows the four possible ways in which these two normative and behavioral dimensions might intersect: (a) a strong pluralism orientation and a strong involvement orientation; (b) a strong pluralism orientation and a weak involvement orientation; (c) a weak pluralism orientation and a strong involvement orientation; and (d) a weak pluralism orientation and a weak involvement orientation. For convenience, and also as a step toward conceptual clarification, these combinations may be described, respectively, as (a) democratic, (b) indifferent, (c) activist, and (d) parochial.

Although they are to an extent ideal types, each represents a particular political culture orientation that characterizes a subset of ordinary citizens in

Table 8.1. Factor Loadings of Indices Measuring Political Tolerance, Support for Gender Equality, Political Interest, Political Knowledge, Civic Participation, and Interpersonal Trust in Jordan, the Palestinian Territories, and Algeria

	UNROTATED SOLUTION		ROTATED SOLUTION	
	FIRST	SECOND	FIRST	SECOND
Political Tolerance				
Jordan	.132	**.728**	.149	**.725**
Palestinian Territories	.173	**.657**	.076	**.675**
Algeria	−.176	**.578**	.093	**.597**
Support for Gender Equality				
Jordan	−.131	**.757**	−.113	**.760**
Palestinian Territories	.050	**.730**	−.057	**.729**
Algeria	−.323	**.677**	.003	**.750**
Political Interest				
Jordan	**.674**	.025	**.675**	.009
Palestinian Territories	**.698**	−.145	**.712**	−.042
Algeria	**.676**	.379	**.773**	.047
Political Knowledge				
Jordan	**.752**	.148	**.755**	.130
Palestinian Territories	**.738**	.192	**.703**	.298
Algeria	**.666**	.394	**.771**	.066
Civic Participation				
Jordan	**.722**	−.216	**.717**	−.233
Palestinian Territories	**.674**	−.094	**.680**	.005
Algeria	**.697**	−.150	**.562**	−.438
Interpersonal Trust				
Jordan	**.217**	.144	**.220**	.139
Palestinian Territories	**.383**	−.334	**.427**	−.274
Algeria	**.434**	−.216	**.297**	.383

Note: Figures are in bold for items that have a high factor loading and consequently help to show what the factor measures.

Jordan, the Palestinian Territories, and Algeria, and, quite possibly, in other non-democratic societies in the Arab world and elsewhere.

An individual whose political cultural orientation may be described as democratic is tolerant of diverse political views, supports gender equality, is interested in politics, is knowledgeable about politics, participates in civic and associational life, and is trusting of fellow citizens.

Table 8.2. Political Culture Orientation Based on Pluralism and
Involvement Dimensions Taken Together

| | | PLURALISM DIMENSION | |
		STRONG	WEAK
Involvement Dimension	**Strong**	***Democratic:*** A democratic citizen is tolerant of diverse political views, supports gender equality, is interested in politics, is knowledgeable about politics, participates in civic and associational life, and is trusting of fellow citizens.	***Activist:*** An activist citizen is not tolerant of diverse political views and does not support gender equality but is interested in politics, is knowledgeable about politics, participates in civic and associational life, and is trusting of fellow citizens.
	Weak	***Indifferent:*** An indifferent citizen is tolerant of diverse political views and supports gender equality but is not interested in politics, is not knowledgeable about politics, does not participate in civic and associational life, and is not trusting of fellow citizens.	***Parochial:*** A parochial citizen is not tolerant of diverse political views, does not support gender equality, is not interested in politics, is not knowledgeable about politics, does not participate in civic and associational life, and is not trusting of fellow citizens.

One whose orientation may be described as activist is not tolerant of diverse political views and does not support gender equality but is interested in politics, is knowledgeable about politics, is active in civic and associational life, and is trusting of fellow citizens. Perhaps reflecting a more ideological perspective, this person engages with political and public life but does not accord legitimacy to alternative views, preferences, and lifestyles.

An individual whose political cultural orientation may be described as indifferent is tolerant of diverse political views and supports gender equality but is not interested in politics, is not knowledgeable about politics, does not participate in civic and associational life, and is not trusting of fellow citizens. This person is both disengaged and nonjudgmental, unconcerned with either political affairs or the behavior of others.

Finally, an individual whose political cultural orientation may be described as parochial is not tolerant of diverse political views, does not support gender equality, is not interested in politics, is not knowledgeable about politics, does not participate in civic and associational life, and is not trusting of fellow citizens.

Three possibilities were explored to combine, respectively, the two inter-correlated indices associated with a pluralism dimension and the four inter-correlated indices associated with an involvement dimension: first, factor scores were generated; then a scale was constructed by adding indices, each of which was first adjusted to a range between 1 and 10 to provide measurement equivalence; and, finally, an additive scale was constructed in the same way with adjusted indices weighted in proportion to their factor loadings. These three possibilities yielded virtually identical results. In no case was the correlation coefficient between any two of the three possible involvement dimension measures or any two of the three possible pluralism dimension measures lower than 0.950.

In the additive measures as well as the factor scores, and regardless of which measures are used, the two political culture dimensions are independent of each other. In no case was the correlation coefficient between any measure of the pluralism dimension and any measure of the involvement dimension greater than 0.050. It is thus the case that there are a significant number of respondents in all four of the categories described in Table 8.2. Although some respondents are either high or low on both the pluralism and involvement dimensions, many others have dissimilar tendencies on the two dimensions.

Cross-National Variation in Political Culture Orientation

It is necessary to specify cutting points that distinguish between strength and weakness on the pluralism and the involvement dimensions in order to juxtapose the two dichotomized measures and classify individuals with respect to the four types of political culture orientation described above. For purposes of the present analysis, the cutting point selected is the midpoint between the highest and lowest score of the unrotated factor scores for each dimension.

Table 8.3 shows the proportion of Jordanian, Palestinian, and Algerian respondents with strong and weak ratings on the pluralism and the involvement dimensions based on these cutting points. Table 8.4 shows the distribution of political culture orientations among Jordanians, Palestinians, and Algerians that results from a juxtaposition of these dichotomized measures of the pluralism and involvement dimensions.

Table 8.4 shows both similarities and differences in the distribution of political culture orientations across the three countries. The distributions are

Table 8.3. Pluralism and Involvement Dimensions of Political Culture of Jordanian, Palestinian, and Algerian Respondents

		JORDAN (%)	PALESTINIAN TERRITORIES (%)	ALGERIA (%)
Pluralism	Strong	26.4	31.5	70.1
Dimension	Weak	73.6	68.5	29.9
Involvement	Strong	36.9	33.2	53.5
Dimension	Weak	63.1	66.8	46.5

Table 8.4. Types of Political Culture Orientation of Jordanian, Palestinian, and Algerian Respondents

		JORDAN (%)	PALESTINIAN TERRITORIES (%)	ALGERIA (%)
Political	Democratic	11.2	11.9	37.0
Culture Orientation	Activist	15.2	21.3	16.5
	Indifferent	25.7	19.6	33.1
	Parochial	47.9	47.2	13.3
	All	100	100	100

fairly similar in the Jordanian and Palestinian cases. In both countries only 11–12 percent of the respondents have a democratic orientation, whereas 47–48 percent have a parochial orientation. Among those who have neither orientation, an activist pattern is somewhat more common among Palestinians and an indifferent pattern is somewhat more common among Jordanians. This former finding may be the result of the particular Palestinian situation, with a heightened degree of political consciousness and ideological militancy developing in response to the Israeli occupation.

More generally, however, the findings suggest that comparatively few individuals in either country possess a political culture orientation that is democratic with respect to both the dimensions examined, and that nearly half the ordinary men and women in each country do not have a democratic orientation with respect to either dimension.

The Algerian case stands out from Jordan and the Palestinian Territories in that a strong rating is more common than a weak rating with respect to both the pluralism and the involvement dimensions, and so there is also a higher proportion of citizens with a democratic political culture orientation. Specifically 37 percent of the Algerian respondents possess a democratic orientation. This may be partly explained for the pluralism dimension by some wording differences introduced on one question by the Algerian research team.[19] But the difference between Algeria and the other two cases is similar for the involvement dimension, for which question wording and coding were identical in all three countries. Thus, even allowing for some minor measurement-related variation, it seems reasonable to conclude that some of the history and political experience that set Algeria apart from Jordan and the Palestinian Territories have contributed to the greater emergence, in relative terms, of a democratic political culture.

Among the factors that may help to explain the difference between Algeria and the other two countries are Algeria's prolonged and intense colonial experience, which introduced severe social dislocation and undermined traditional institutions and relationships, the mobilization and modernization resulting from Algeria's extended experience with centralized planning and socialist development after independence, and, closer to the present, the country's relatively deeper experience with partisan diversity and competitive elections.

The latter observation, if correct, suggests that experience with partisan competition helps to foster a democratic political culture orientation, which would be an important finding given debates in the literature about whether such an orientation is a precondition for democratic transitions or rather can follow elite-led transitions involving the reform of political institutions and procedures.

Conclusion

The preceding comments are not intended to be an adequate explanation of the observed cross-national variation in political culture orientation patterns. Such a discussion is beyond the scope of the present inquiry. Nor should it be assumed that the distributions reported in Table 8.4 are unchanging, since global, regional, or country-specific events might alter the relative importance of some political culture orientation categories in one or more countries. But while these are subjects for future investigation, with both longitudinal data and data from more countries, the present analysis provides evidence for several significant conclusions.

First, although the literature identifies a number of attitudes, values, and behavior patterns associated with a democratic political culture, in none of the three countries considered in this study do these norms constitute a one-dimensional orientation. Rather, the six normative and behavioral measures that have been examined consistently subdivide into two distinct and independent dimensional clusters, and these clusters are the same in Jordan, the Palestinian Territories, and Algeria.

One dimension, which we have termed pluralism, is composed of political tolerance and support for gender equality. The other, which we have termed "involvement," is composed of political knowledge, political interest, civic participation, and interpersonal trust. That identical patterns should be found in these three countries with very different political, economic, and social attributes suggests that this dimensional structure may be present in a broader array of non-democracies, including, perhaps, some outside the Arab world.

Second, the analysis also suggests the utility of juxtaposing the dimensions of pluralism and involvement in order to form a two-dimensional typology of political culture orientations associated with democracy. Individuals with strong ratings on measures of both pluralism and involvement resemble the ideal democratic citizen described in the literature. Their political culture orientation may be termed "democratic." Other individuals, however, have strong ratings on the measure of only one dimension, or on measures of neither pluralism nor involvement. Their political culture orientations may be termed, respectively, "activist," "indifferent," and "parochial." Although the proportion of citizens who posses each political culture orientation depends, to a degree, on the way the two dimensions are dichotomized and juxtaposed, it is significant that there are substantial cross-national differences in these proportions when the same classification procedures are employed. This suggests that although the typology may be useful for mapping political culture orientations, future research should undertake to identify the country-level attributes and experiences that account for variance in the distribution of these orientations. Future research may also refine this typology by incorporating dimensions that go beyond pluralism and involvement.

Finally, the analysis shows that there is significant cross-national variation in the within-country distributions across the four political culture orientation categories. This, in turn, raises important questions for future research, both about the causes and about the consequences of variation across and within countries. On the one hand, it will be instructive to investigate why a particular kind of political culture orientation is more common in some countries and less common in others. It will be similarly instructive to ask why some citizens in a country exhibit one kind of political culture orientation while others in the same country exhibit a different orientation—and in particular, in this connection, to investigate the factors that either promote or discourage a democratic political culture orientation. On the other hand, the consequences of particular distributions deserve attention as well. For example, are some distributions of political culture orientation more conducive to democracy than others, or to particular kinds of ideological tendencies or policy preferences? These questions offer a rich agenda for future research.

Appendix: Items Used to Measure Dependent and Independent Variables

Political Tolerance

People sometimes talk about the factors that make a person qualified for national leadership. On this card are listed six of the qualifications to which different people would give priority. Please say which one of these you consider the most important? Which would be the next most important? And which would be third? Coded according to whether "Openness to Diverse Political Ideas" ranks in first or second place.

Jordan and the Palestinian Territories only: Do you disagree or agree with this statement: Christian citizens of our country should have the same rights as Muslim citizens to hold any political office, including head of the government.

Algeria only: People sometimes talk about what the aims of this country should be for the next ten years. On this card are listed four of the goals to which different people would give priority. Would you please say which of these you consider the most important? Which is the second in importance, and which the third? Coded according to whether "Assuring equal rights for all citizens, regardless of religion or gender" ranks first or second.

Support for Gender Equality

Do you disagree or agree with this statement? "On the whole men make better political leaders than women do."

Do you disagree or agree with this statement? "A university education is more important for a boy than a girl."

Do you disagree or agree with this statement? "A woman may work outside the home if she wishes."

Political Interest

How important is politics in your life?

When you get together with your friends, do you discuss political matters frequently, occasionally, or never?

Political Knowledge

> Can you name the Foreign Minister?
> Can you name the Minister of Finance?
> Can you name the Speaker of Parliament?
> How often do you read the newspaper?

Civic Participation

How often do you interact with people at social, cultural, or youth groups?

How often do you interact with people at your mosque or church or at religious associations?

How often do you interact with people at political groups, clubs, or discussion groups?

How often do you interact with people at your professional associations?

How often do you interact with people at sports or recreation groups?

Political Trust

Generally speaking, would you say that most people can be trusted or that most people cannot be trusted?

I will read some statements about social and political issues. Please indicate your agreement or disagreement with each. (Only the one statement from the list used in the present analysis is given here.)

> You can trust no one these days.

PART 3

Interna–
tional
Conflict

Gender, Feminism, and Attitudes toward International Conflict: Exploring Relationships with Survey Data from the Middle East (1997)

Mark Tessler and Ina Warriner

Gender studies, which separate the socially constructed roles and orientations of women and men from biological definitions of sex, are increasingly being combined with international studies at the theoretical level.[1] Scholars working in this area seek to determine whether and how the dynamics of international politics are influenced by gender-specific agendas, and also whether there are gender-specific consequences associated with particular patterns of international political behavior. The field is at present marked by considerable diversity, with clear and in some instances sharp disagreements among analysts who are identified with differing approaches to inquiry, including liberal, standpoint, and postmodernist feminism.

In an effort to contribute to the dialogue between gender studies and international studies, this report presents findings from an investigation based on the integrated secondary analysis of survey data collected in Israel, Egypt, Palestine,[2] and Kuwait. In broad terms, the goal of this research is a contribution to rigor and cumulativeness. It seeks to provide systematic empirical evidence in order to evaluate hypotheses that are most commonly supported with deductive reasoning or interpretative historical analysis, and it also seeks to bring a comparative perspective that incorporates data and insights from non-Western as well as Western societies. More specifically, the analysis assesses the utility of both gender and attitudes pertaining to the circumstances of women in accounting for variance in views about war and peace, and thereafter examines the degree to which political system attributes constitute conditionalities associated with important individual-level variable relationships.

Based on data from the Arab world and Israel, with attitudes about a peaceful resolution of the Arab-Israeli conflict treated as the dependent

variable, this research also aspires to shed light on more practical considerations pertaining to the international relations of the Middle East. Although
the major preoccupations of the analysis remain theoretical, with a specific
concern for generalizable variable relationships, the report additionally seeks
to present findings that have implications for the Arab-Israeli conflict.

Theoretical Context

Two interrelated bodies of theoretical literature shape much of the current interest in gender and international studies. The first, which includes
attempts to link feminism and globalism, hypothesizes that women are more
pacifistic than men in their approach to international relations, that they are
more accepting of compromise to resolve interstate disputes and less likely
than men to believe that war is necessary or appropriate in particular conflict
situations. Competition, violence, intransigence, and territoriality are thus
associated with a "male" approach to human relations, including relations
between sovereign states, whereas moderation, compromise, tolerance, and
pacifism are seen as a "female" perspective on world affairs.

Public opinion research provides some evidence in support of these
propositions. Evidence from such research is limited to the United States,
however, and even here findings are not entirely consistent. For example, while
several systematic studies have found American men to be more supportive
of militarism and war involvement than American women by an average of
seven to nine percentage points,[3] a recent data-based analysis by Conover and
Shapiro reports no sex-linked differences in general militarism.[4]

The Conover and Shapiro investigation, which analyzed data from the
1991 American National Election Study Pilot Study, did note that women
were less supportive than men of U.S. involvement in the 1990–91 Gulf War,
and it speculated accordingly that sex-linked differences may exist in relation to concrete but not hypothetical war situations. But even in the former
instance, the authors added, differences are "by no means large enough to
divide men and women into different camps, and they are certainly not large
enough to warrant making the kinds of statements differentiating women
and men that have long been part of [the popular] stereotype." Overall, the
authors thus conclude, "Stereotypes [about male-female differences] turn
out to be only partial truths, and the hypotheses [about the explanatory
power of gender are] only partially confirmed."[5]

Findings from research on the differences between men and women in
several related fields are also sometimes offered in support of efforts to establish a connection between gender and international studies. For example,
Gilligan reported a distinctly feminine sensibility based on studies undertaken with small children, college students, and adults.[6] In these studies,

women repeatedly demonstrated a predilection to care for others and to prefer harmonious human relations to individual achievement and conquest. Men, by contrast, were more likely to value and pursue behavior involving rivalry and competition, even when this resulted in interpersonal conflict.

Also sometimes cited in support of hypotheses about differences between women and men are findings from earlier anthropological studies of tribal societies. McGuigan has shown, for example, that communal violence and aggressive behavior vary in proportion to male control of the public sphere, and also as a function of the degree to which paramount gods are male.[7] To the extent that these attributes are present, aggression and violence predominate in the resolution of conflicts. Alternatively, the level of violence is significantly lower in tribal societies that draw less of a distinction between the roles of men and women and worship female gods.

More common than studies presenting empirical evidence in support of "feminist-pacifist" propositions are analyses based on deductive reasoning, most of which emphasize the uniquely female experience of motherhood.[8] Two overlapping visions of the motherhood experience and its salience are found in those feminist and other discourses that seek to establish a link between gender and international affairs. The first celebrates a cultural feminism, or feminism of identity, in which the "female" values of caring and nurturance are given prominence. The second introduces the concept of "moral motherhood," which is said to incline women toward "preservative love" and the elimination of violence in human relations.

The caregiver approach to international relations stresses empathy and compromise, observing that these values are associated with social roles that in most societies are played primarily by women. Women are the principal caregivers in most cultures, attending to the needs of children, ailing friends, elderly parents, and others. Cultural feminism argues that this has relevance for the international arena. Emphasizing the universal applicability of a predisposition toward nurturance, it links women's roles as domestic caregivers to a more tolerant approach to relations between communities and states. Men, by contrast, being less involved in caregiving, are said to be less moderate and pacifistic and more likely to be concerned with hierarchy, hegemony, and justice in intercommunal and international relations.

Although these hypotheses associated with caregiving are advanced by some feminist scholars, others express reservations, not only challenging the evidence on which they are based but also dissenting from their philosophical and political assumptions. In particular, critics charge that attributions of empathy, nurturance, and caring reinforce traditional stereotypes about women and retard the feminist goal of emancipation. On the one hand, some postmodern feminist theorists insist that there are no "essential components" which characterize all women.[9] On the other, some assert that the emphasis on caring is itself misplaced, either seeing this as patronizing or disputing the hypothesized link to public and international affairs.[10]

A second and closely related feminist discourse emphasizes the concept of "moral motherhood," which asserts that women as mothers have a responsibility to eliminate violence in the resolution of conflicts. Advancing the concepts of "maternal thinking" and "preservative love," which are said to be consequences of the social practice of mothering, this discourse distinguishes between "bureaucratic-administrative abstractionism" and an empathetic and loving approach to human relations.[11] Maternal thinking about world affairs thus rejects a distinction between individual and collective forms of violent conflict, viewing both as equally abhorrent. Elshtain describes the political implications of maternal thinking as "social feminism." An approach to international relations shaped by maternal thinking, she argues, is significantly more pacifistic and tolerant than one founded on abstract and hierarchical conceptions of justice.[12]

This discourse, too, has critics among some feminist and other scholars. Some argue that men as well as women are capable of maternal thinking, even though the male voice is largely absent in discussions of this concept. Some also raise questions about women who do not have children, noting that they are not considered in the conversation about maternal thinking. Still another reservation, echoing a complaint about the caregiver paradigm, is that an emphasis on motherhood and material thinking reduces women to unidimensional actors and obscures the diversity of the factors that influence their attitudes and behavior.

Whether there is indeed a distinctly female approach to international relations, and, if so, whether it is characterized by an inclination toward compromise, tolerance, and pacifism, thus remain open questions. Hypotheses to this effect are advanced by some scholars but challenged by others, with debates for the most part uninformed by the results of systematic empirical research. Moreover, consistent and unambiguous conclusions do not emerge from the empirical research that has been conducted, and, in addition, this research has been limited almost entirely to the United States. Finally, even should it eventually become clear that significant sex-linked differences do exist, these might be the result of factors other than caregiving and maternal thinking. For example, as one analyst points out, women might be more predisposed than men toward the peaceful resolution of international conflicts because they are the principal users of social programs that compete with the military for governmental funds.[13]

A second body of theoretical literature has also contributed to current interest in the connections between gender and international studies. The focus in this instance is on the relationship between nationalism and feminism, particularly, although not exclusively, in the dependency situations of external or internal colonialism and in circumstances of ethnic or cultural conflict.

A major concern of scholars interested in the relationship between nationalism and feminism is whether support for gender equality enhances or diminishes the struggle of a political community for its collective or national rights, and whether that struggle in turn advances or retards the achievement of feminist goals. Some scholars argue in this connection that culture and politics reinforce each other; these analysts hypothesize that political struggles aimed at either altering or maintaining existing political relationships will bring a similar attitude toward issues of gender, particularly when male dominance and patriarchy are part of the status quo. Others, by contrast, suggest that individuals tend to compartmentalize and set priorities among political and cultural concerns, with most men, and many women, attaching greater importance to political objectives and avoiding gender-related issues so as not to undermine national or communal solidarity.[14]

The relationship between feminist and nationalist agendas is highly contextual. Since the ideologies and strategies of women's organizations are usually fashioned within the framework of wider social or political movements, this relationship is dependent upon cultural, political, and era-specific conditions. In some circumstances, a push for gender equality complements the political goals of communal emancipation or development. In many newly independent countries, for example, where women's unions were frequently linked to nationalist movements, the leftist ideologies that predominated in the 1950s and 1960s incorporated feminist concerns and advanced the idea, accepted by many men as well as by women, that modernization and progress require a national commitment to improving the circumstances of women.[15] In this context, feminist and nationalist goals were linked within a broader framework of political mobilization and reform, and hence were mutually reinforcing.

Under other conditions, feminist aims may have no link to nationalist agendas or may even be explicitly denounced as contrary to the collective good. For example, efforts to forge a coherent communal identity may involve an emphasis on conservative traditional values. In this situation, nationalism is not associated with reform but rather may seek the reaffirmation of a patriarchal status quo.[16] Indeed, nationalism's antipathy toward feminist goals may be particularly intense; since women are often considered to be the guardians of culture and tradition—wardens of the community's sacred heritage and authenticity, as it were—reforms relating to women may be judged injurious to nationalist efforts to protect or unify the community.[17]

This is also the case in countries where nationalism and national identity are strongly influenced by religious fundamentalism. In addition, as in a number of former communist states, women may sometimes even be called upon to serve the nation by bearing offspring in order to reverse a declining birth rate.[18] In this instance, as in some others, nationalist rhetoric urges women to make their "special and unique contribution" but then restricts this contribution to the domestic sphere.

Other considerations may also produce tension between feminist and nationalist goals, such as calls for gender solidarity in order to forge a unified nationalist movement. In this case, many men, and perhaps also many women, will favor the subordination or at least the deferment of attention to the needs of women. Believing that to do otherwise would divide the community at a time when unity is necessary if the struggle for national rights is to succeed, this reasoning is particularly likely to be advanced by political leaders, most of whom are men. Among Palestinians, for example, rhetoric about the revolutionary character of the resistance movement notwithstanding, feminists frequently complain that men engaged in the national struggle rarely show any interest in the concerns of women; when pressed, these men reply that attention to these concerns is divisive and will thus have to wait until political and national goals have been achieved.[19] Nor is this situation unique to the Third World. Pointing to efforts to create a supranational European Community, feminist scholars assert that women's issues have been similarly marginalized, ghettoized, or dismissed as extraneous by a male-dominated leadership.[20]

Also worth noting are the implications of women's participation in the military dimension of a nationalist struggle, as in the war for Algerian independence or some aspects of the Palestinian resistance movement during the 1970s or even later. Sometimes called "integrationist feminism," or "feminism of reality," this holds out the prospect of greater equality between women and men, but it also reinforces the military as an institution and warfare as a strategy of progress, thereby encouraging the view that women are of value and merit consideration to the extent that they behave like men.[21] Accordingly, whatever the potential for a partnership between women and men in the pursuit of national objectives, there is not a fusing of feminism and nationalism in this situation but rather, again, the subordination of the former to the latter.

Research Design and Cases

The preceding discussion suggests the absence of a clear consensus about the utility of either gender or attitudes pertaining to the circumstances of women in accounting for variance in views about war and peace. Logical arguments have been advanced for opposing hypotheses: that conceptions of international relations are heavily influenced by considerations of gender and feminism, and also that both differences between men and women and considerations of feminism are largely irrelevant in this domain.

Support for these various arguments is usually the product of either deductive reasoning or inferences from aggregate case-study material; typically, it is not based on rigorous and systematic empirical research in which the individual is the unit of analysis. The present investigation, by contrast, uses survey data from four Middle Eastern societies to explore the connections between gender, feminism, and attitudes toward war and peace. And although there is no a priori reason to assume that findings from the Middle East may be generalizable to other regions, neither is there reason to assume that findings are not applicable more broadly. Rather, until hypothesized variable relationships have been tested rigorously and widely, the primary purpose of individual studies, whatever their database, should be an incremental contribution to discovering the nature and determinants of particular attitudes and behavior patterns. The present study seeks to make such a contribution. Variable relationships of potentially general applicability will be examined with data from the Middle East so that evidence from this region becomes part of the empirical foundation being constructed to discern the nature, determinants, and locus of relevant social processes.

In addition, the data in the present study, based on surveys in Israel, Egypt, Palestine, and Kuwait, permit a comparative analysis in which both the degree of generalizability across political systems may be assessed and system-level conditionalities may be identified. To the extent that there are important similarities in the findings from several or all of the four populations surveyed, there will be evidence that these findings are not idiosyncratic. Indeed, it will be plausible in this instance to suggest that conclusions based on the study of the Middle East are likely to be applicable more broadly. Given the very significant differences between the four societies from which data have been gathered, a comparison of these societies possesses elements of a "most different systems" research design, which increases confidence in generalizability when similar findings are reported. Taken together, Israel, Egypt, Palestine, and Kuwait encompass almost all the political, economic and cultural diversity of the Middle East.

Several different interpretations will be possible should some or all of the cases produce dissimilar findings. It may be that some or all of the cases are unique, raising the possibility that there are no patterns of general applicability. A finding of differences is by no means an analytical dead end, however. On the contrary, although much additional research will be needed before firm conclusions can be drawn, there will meanwhile be an important opportunity to contribute to theoretical elaboration. More specifically, characteristics that differentiate between the cases may be incorporated into the analysis as system-level variables, thereby producing testable hypotheses about the conditionalities associated with particular normative or behavioral patterns.

Further, each of the societies included in the present study differs from the others in several critical ways, narrowing the range of relevant system-level variables that might explain why it is not characterized by the same patterns as the others, should this in fact occur. In other words, despite the diversity of the four cases taken together, giving the analysis, as noted, elements of a most-different systems research design, a comparison between any single society and the others also involves elements of a most-similar systems research design. This is an important advantage in seeking to specify conditionalities in terms of system-level variables.[22]

Israel, for example, is the only democratic and developed county in the present study and the only one that is not exclusively or predominantly Arab and Muslim. Egypt is the only "typical" Third World country, characterized by overpopulation, mass poverty, and an inefficient, corrupt, and at least somewhat authoritarian government. It is also the only Arab country in the present study with a sophisticated, centuries-old, and cosmopolitan urban culture. Palestinians provide the only instance of statelessness, where the society being studied remains under occupation and where a nationalist movement is still actively engaged in the struggle for self-determination and independence. Finally, Kuwait is the only monarchy and the only rentier state, characterized by the juxtaposition of a small population, the majority of whom are not even Kuwaiti citizens, and massive wealth from the export of natural resources.

There are also important and noteworthy differences between the four societies with respect to issues and institutions associated with women, both in general and as they relate to questions of war and peace. These differences may be briefly summarized, not only to call attention to additional system-level properties that may help to account for country-specific findings, should there be any, but also to provide an introduction to issues of gender and peace in the particular societies from which data for the present analysis have been drawn.

Israel

In Israel, feminism has only recently emerged as an important and activist social movement. Women have long been visible in many professions and in political institutions. Women have also for many years served in the Israeli military. But while these experiences have given legitimacy to female participation in public life since the pre-state period, women in Israel have not historically organized in pursuit of objectives in either the arena of legislation or the domain of public opinion.[23]

The Israeli women's movement has made important gains during the last decade and a half, however, becoming more successful in fostering social activism and, in particular, articulating a connection between feminism and a peaceful resolution of the Arab-Israeli conflict. Israeli feminists explicitly argue that those who support the struggle for equality and self-fulfillment within the Jewish state should be equally sensitive to these struggles in the Palestinian context.[24] An organizational as well as ideological connection between feminism and peace has also developed. Since the 1982 Israeli invasion of Lebanon, and particularly since the outbreak of the Palestinian intifada, which began in December 1987, feminists have become noticeably active in the Israeli peace movement. Indeed, several all-women peace groups have recently come into existence.[25]

These developments have placed feminism in opposition to nationalism in Israel, or at least that is the perception of many Israelis. In particular, some Israelis, including most nationalists, assert that any linkage between feminism and international peace poses a threat to national security. One argument is that such a linkage fosters sympathy for the country's enemies, who, according to nationalist analyses, cannot be trusted and in all probability remain committed to the destruction of the Jewish state. Another is that it could, if pursued to its logical conclusion, result in a feminist-inspired pacifism that would reduce support for the military, at least among women and possibly among many men as well. And still a third assertion, common to other countries faced with a foreign enemy, is that feminism may accentuate societal divisions and undermine national solidarity. For all these reasons, recent gains notwithstanding, the analyses of Israeli feminists have frequently been brushed aside in the name of national security.[26]

Egypt

In Egypt, calls for expanded opportunities for women were heard at the end of the nineteenth century, and women organized within the nationalist movement shortly after World War I.[27] Moreover, although dominated by upper-class women, this long-standing and well-established tradition of feminism, or protofeminism, included many Egyptian women who were not of bourgeois origin.[28] But although women worked alongside men in the struggle for independence, organizing strikes and protest demonstrations, for example, feminist goals were of limited importance to the nationalist movement and later to the state. Even Gamal Abdel Nasser's program of Arab socialism, although it extended women's rights, prohibited women from organizing politically. In the ensuing decades, women made gains in education and professional life but registered far less progress in the political arena, the only notable exception being the partial reform of personal status laws carried out by Anwar Sadat, Nasser's successor, at the urging of his wife. The women's movement in postcolonial Egypt has thus been characterized by sustained independence from the state, there being no progressive alliance with a political leadership committed to eradicating practices that subordinate or demean women.

Even as they complain about indifference or lethargy on the part of political leaders, many Egyptian feminists are at pains to point out that their movement is indigenous, that their core values are to be found in Islam, and that normative influences from the West, including Western feminism, are only one of the sources from which they draw inspiration, and by no means the most important.[29] Egyptian feminists frequently argue in this connection that the patriarchal structure of society, rather than Islam, bears primary responsibility for the oppression of women. In view of these considerations, as well as the historic association of the women's movement with Egyptian nationalism, it is not surprising that many Egyptian women are attracted to Islamist organizations. Muslim political organizations not only receive rank-and-file support from women as frequently as men;[30] in recent years they have encouraged the growth of voluntary groups that compete with secular feminist associations for recruits among politically conscious women.[31]

As the preceding summary suggests, issues of war and peace have been noticeably absent from the agenda and discourse of Egyptian feminism. In contrast to the situation in Israel, where there are both ideological and organizational links between feminism and peace, the women's movement in Egypt has been concerned almost exclusively with domestic considerations, including increased opportunities for women in public life and a reduction in those aspects of poverty that fall heaviest on women. Further, feminist efforts in these domains are for the most part non-ideological, marked by practical and low-key outreach activities that are either unaccompanied by any philosophical grounding or explained and justified with reference to Islam.[32]

Palestine

Two discourses have traditionally characterized Palestinian women, and each continues to be important. The first, which is widely embraced, affirms the primacy of the Palestinian struggle for self-determination and independence. The view that nothing is more important than this existential struggle, and that, in any event, women cannot be liberated unless all Palestinians are liberated, is almost universally held by both women and men. For some, this view also brings a rejection of Western notions of women's emancipation, including an assertion that in the Third World, or at least in Palestine, women's liberation *is* national liberation.[33] This analysis has been particularly common among women's organizations affiliated with the Palestine Liberation Organization (PLO).[34] In recent years some women, although a minority, have also chosen to work for their simultaneous liberation as Palestinians and women within the framework of Islamic political organizations. For example, women are as likely as men to support Hamas and Islamic Jihad, the two most important Islamist movements in Palestine.[35]

In addition, however, there is a small but growing core of politically conscious women who see the nationalist struggle through a more explicitly feminist lens. Although they accept the primacy of this struggle, they also argue that those aspects of Palestinian society that oppress women should be attacked during, as well as after, the battle for national liberation.[36] Further, they frequently complain that this is not occurring largely because of the social conservatism that characterizes the nationalist movement and many of the men who lead it. They often charge that these men possess a "revolutionary political consciousness" coupled with a "reactionary social-gender consciousness."[37] Such complaints, which have been articulated for nearly two decades, assert that women (and men) are oppressed not only by the Israeli occupation but also by a conservative class structure and patriarchal social institutions that national liberation alone will not modify. Moreover, although criticism has been directed primarily at men, those who articulate this view have sometimes charged that the female leaders of traditional charitable societies and established women's organizations also tend to be social conservatives who favor the existing class structure.[38] More recently, there have also been complaints about the glorification of women's homebound roles as the mothers or wives of resistance fighters and martyrs.[39]

Although neither of these discourses has traditionally articulated a link between issues of gender and issues of peace, both an ideological and an organizational connection has recently begun to emerge among women unwilling to subordinate the interests of their gender to those of national emancipation. On the one hand, while no less committed than other Palestinians to the goal of self-determination, these women have concluded that the nationalist struggle has not brought progress on women's issues and may indeed have retarded the struggle for women's rights, and that the achievement of peace is therefore essential for the fulfillment of their aspirations as women as well as Palestinians. On the other hand, particularly since the outbreak of the intifada and in response to parallel developments within the Israeli women's movement, an incipient but nonetheless important cooperation between Palestinian feminists and the peace movement in Israel has begun to take shape, overcoming at least some of the historic divide between oppressor and oppressed. There are a number of women's peace groups in which Palestinians and Israelis cooperate, for instance, as well as activities in which both Palestinian women and men join their Israeli counterparts in the pursuit of a just and peaceful resolution of the Arab-Israeli conflict.[40]

Kuwait

Kuwait is a deeply conservative society. Unlike Egypt and many other Arab and Muslim countries, Kuwait has no tradition of women organizing in an effort either to improve their own circumstances or to advance a nationalist struggle. Among the reasons for this is Kuwait's historic isolation from the currents of modernization and development experienced elsewhere in the Middle East, an isolation that ended only when oil exports assumed significant proportions in the 1950s and 1960s. An important related consideration is the absence of progressive political leadership; the country has been ruled by a conservative monarchy since its independence in 1961. As a result, not only is there no tradition of an organized struggle for women's rights, but participation in public life even by individual women has long been limited.[41] According to a 1984 UNESCO study, for example, work outside the home is neither sought nor valued by native Kuwaiti women.[42] Women are also legally prohibited from joining the armed forces, voting, or becoming members of the National Assembly.[43]

This conservative legacy notwithstanding, the last decade or so has witnessed the beginning of a change in the circumstances of women, including the formation of an embryonic women's movement. On the one hand, women's participation in the labor force has slowly begun to rise, and this has in fact increased somewhat more sharply since the Gulf crisis of 1990–91. On the other hand, several nongovernmental women's organizations were formed in the 1980s and have been lobbying, although without success thus far, for various legal reforms, including voting rights for women.[44] Women have also strengthened their position and increased their political consciousness through participation in the resistance against Iraq's occupation during the Gulf crisis. While there is no discernible concern for issues of war and peace associated with these developments, beyond that involving condemnation of the Iraqi invasion, there is an emerging feminist sensibility. For example, publications of the new organizations break with the older view that confined women to activities within the family; rather, they cover political events of relevance to women and examine the ways that "life in patriarchal societies distorts a woman's definition of herself and her relationship to society."[45]

Data and Measurement

Against this background, and with the previously discussed possibilities for comparative analysis in mind, data from survey research carried out in Israel, Egypt, Palestine, and Kuwait have been collected for the present study. The data from each country are from a heterogeneous and generally representative sample of the active, urban, adult population. The data set from each country also includes items dealing with both the Middle East conflict and the circumstances of women.

Israel

The Israeli data to be analyzed in this study were collected in 1989 and are from a national sample of persons over the age of eighteen residing in four hundred randomly selected urban Jewish households. Polling was done by the Dahaf Agency, which conducted the survey as part of a broad program of research on women and war designed by Professors Galia Golan and Naomi Chazan of the Hebrew University of Jerusalem. Arab citizens of Israel were not included in the sample. Nor were Israeli Jews living in kibbutzim or other agricultural communities. The sample yielded usable responses from 985 individuals, including 534 women and 451 men.

The interview schedule administered in Israel included a large number of questions about the Arab-Israeli conflict, among them items designed to assess attitudes toward the Palestinians and toward the possibility of territorial compromise in the West Bank and Gaza. It also included many items dealing with gender equality and other issues relating to the circumstances of women. Factor analysis was employed to select from among these larger batteries of questions two subsets of items to be utilized in the present study. More specifically, five items dealing with the conflict between Israel and the Palestinians loaded highly on a common factor and were accordingly combined to form a single attitudinal scale; and four additional items pertaining to the role and status of women loaded highly on another common factor and were thus combined to form a second attitudinal scale.

In fact, factor analysis has been useful on two counts: it provides a mechanism for item selection, and it contributes to measurement reliability and validity. Reliability is assured since only reliable items will load highly on a common factor; further, because this will occur only if all items pertain to the same underlying normative or behavioral dimension, it is also highly likely that the items are valid. The two sets of items identified through factor analysis and combined to form scales measuring attitudes toward the Arab-Israeli conflict and attitudes toward gender equality are shown in Table 9.1, along with their respective factor loadings following rotation. Most questions require that an answer be selected from a list of four or five possible responses, and the wording of several questions has accordingly been modified slightly in order to incorporate information about the available responses.

Egypt

The Egyptian data to be analyzed in this study were collected in 1988 and are from a stratified and broadly representative sample of Muslim adults residing in Cairo. The survey was carried out under the supervision of Professor Jamal Sanad Al-Suwaidi of the Center for Strategic Studies and Research in Abu Dhabi, who designed the project in collaboration with Mark Tessler,[46] and it is part of a larger, continuing study of Arab attitudes toward domestic and foreign policy issues. The actual interviews were conducted by a team of research assistants, or intermediaries, who were selected on the basis of previous experience in survey research administration. Some were university students and others were government employees. Intermediaries were also given a four-day orientation, after which they participated in the pretest of the survey instrument.

The sample constructed in Cairo contains 292 respondents, including an almost equal number of men and women. All respondents are over the age of eighteen. More generally, the sample was stratified and designed to be representative with respect to gender, age, education, socioeconomic status, and neighborhood, although individuals who are poorly educated and unemployed or economically disadvantaged are slightly underrepresented. Non-Muslim Egyptians were not surveyed, which makes the sample somewhat less representative of the total population but appropriate in view of the study's strong interest in Islamic issues and in comparisons with Muslim Arabs in other countries. Overall, although not a strict random sample, the Egyptian data are generally representative of the country's adult, urban, and Muslim population.

The survey instrument administered in Egypt includes many items dealing with the status and circumstances of women, as well as other social issues, particularly those bearing on the practice and interpretation of Islam. The survey also dealt with issues of domestic politics and foreign policy, and among the latter are several questions about the Arab-Israeli conflict. For the present investigation, the factor-analytic procedures described with respect to the Israeli data were also employed in the Egyptian case, where they again permitted the formation of scales measuring attitudes toward the Arab-Israeli conflict and toward gender equality. The factor analysis also permitted the formation of a four-item scale measuring the strength of Islamic attachments, including personal piety and attitudes toward the social salience of

Table 9.1. Factor Analysis of Items from the Israeli Survey

	FACTOR LOADINGS*	
	ATTITUDES TOWARD THE ARAB-ISRAELI CONFLICT	ATTITUDES TOWARD GENDER EQUALITY
ITEM		
Would you be willing to return either all or some of the occupied territories in return for a peace agreement with the Arabs?	**.74931**	.05366
Do you prefer to address the problem of the West Bank and Gaza by exchanging them for peace, by giving the Palestinians partial autonomy, or by removing the Arab population from these territories?	**.73406**	.02799
Do you agree or disagree that Israel should consider permitting the establishment of a Palestinian state?	**.66018**	.12193
Do you think the real aim of the Palestinians is to establish a state alongside Israel or to destroy the Jewish state and drive out its population?	**.64889**	.00002
Do you define the Palestinians as a nation?	**.59568**	.07926
Do you agree or disagree that a woman should be laid off of a job before a man?	−.08094	**.70713**
Do you believe that men and women should receive equal pay for equal work or that men should have higher salaries because they are the major breadwinners?	.01352	**.69310**
Do you support or oppose a woman's right to choose to have an abortion?	.18322	**.62655**
Do you agree or disagree that men and women should share everything in an ideal marriage?	.10166	**.54804**

Directional differences in items and/or response codes have been removed through recoding, so that positive values for factor loadings always indicate more positive attitudes toward Arab-Israeli peace and more positive attitudes toward gender equality. The figures in boldface type in each column identify those items with high factor loadings. These items, which define the factor's conceptual content, have been combined to form a unidimensional attitudinal scale.

Table 9.2. Factor Analysis of Items from the Egyptian Survey

Item	FACTOR LOADINGS[*]		
	ATTITUDES TOWARD THE ARAB-ISRAELI CONFLICT	ATTITUDES TOWARD GENDER EQUALITY	STRENGTH OF ISLAMIC ATTACH-MENTS
Do you agree or disagree that peace with Israel is both desirable and possible?	**.86411**	−.08016	−.11416
Do you believe that the Arab-Israeli conflict can be resolved by diplomacy, or is a military solution required?	**.84614**	.09527	−.03108
Do you agree or disagree that full-time housework is the best area of work for a woman?	−.08830	**.75641**	.16867
Should women be required to cease work after marriage in order to devote full time to their homes and families?	.19187	**.73300**	−.00053
Do you think it is more important for a boy to go to school than a girl?	.21893	**.69596**	.15314
Do you agree or disagree that there should be equality between men and women in jobs, wages, and promotion?	.15092	**.69064**	−.16196
Do you support the application of Islamic law in social life?	−.11644	.24017	**.81899**
Do you support the application of Islamic law to deal with civil and criminal matters?	.03852	.12045	**.80240**
How often do you refer to religious teachings when making important decisions about your life?	−.15011	−.06406	**.71752**

Table 9.2. Factor Analysis of Items from the Egyptian Survey (continued)

	FACTOR LOADINGS[*]		
	---	---	---
	ATTITUDES TOWARD THE ARAB-ISRAELI CONFLICT	ATTITUDES TOWARD GENDER EQUALITY	STRENGTH OF ISLAMIC ATTACH-MENTS
Item			
Would you support anyone in your family who wants to study in a religious institution?	.13882	.25564	**.66492**

[*]*Directional differences in items and/or response codes have been removed through recoding, so that positive values for factor loadings always indicate more positive attitudes toward Arab-Israeli peace, more positive attitudes toward gender equality, and stronger Islamic attachments. The figures in boldface type in each column identify those items with high factor loadings. These items, which define the factor's conceptual content, have been combined to form a unidimensional attitudinal scale.*

Islam. The three sets of items and their respective factor loadings are shown in Table 9.2.

It will be noted that the first Egyptian scale focuses on the Arab-Israeli conflict in general rather than the Palestinian question in particular. This is also part of a more inclusive scale measuring foreign policy orientation that was generated by a factor analysis of the Egyptian data. Even though items used in the Egyptian and Israeli surveys are not identical, the similarity and conceptual equivalence of the scales developed in the two countries are readily apparent. Both measure respondent views about the most salient dimensions of the conflict and, specifically, about a peaceful resolution of the Middle East dispute through diplomacy, compromise, and mutual recognition. Additional information pertaining to sampling, survey administration, and measurement has been reported in greater detail in previous publications.[47]

Kuwait

The Kuwaiti data used in the present study were collected as part of the comparative research project that also produced the Egyptian data described above. The same procedures related to sampling and survey administration were employed, and again the result was a heterogeneous and broadly representative sample of the country's active, adult, and urban population of Kuwaiti citizens. For reasons related to the analytical goals of the research, only Sunni Muslims were sampled, which again reduces representativeness

Table 9.3. Factor Analysis of Items from the Kuwaiti Survey

	FACTOR LOADINGS*		
	ATTITUDES TOWARD THE ARAB-ISRAELI CONFLICT	ATTITUDES TOWARD GENDER EQUALITY	STRENGTH OF ISLAMIC ATTACH- MENTS
ITEM			
Do you agree or disagree that peace with Israel is both desirable and possible?	**.76336**	.25572	.10206
Do you believe that the Arab-Israeli conflict can be resolved by diplomacy, or is a military solu- tion required?	**.83185**	−.08331	−.09435
Do you agree or disagree that full-time housework is the best area of work for a woman?	.22365	**.80811**	.06399
Should women be required to cease work after marriage in order to devote full time to their homes and families?	.00843	**.80533**	.00802
Do you think it is more impor- tant for a boy to go to school than a girl?	−.07892	**.67290**	.02340
Do you agree or disagree that there should be equality between men and women in jobs, wages, and promotion?	−.10435	**.67833**	.19076
Do you support the application of Islamic law in social life?	.10306	.04578	**.82762**
Do you support the application of Islamic law to deal with civil and criminal matters?	−.09989	.12534	**.71202**
How often do you refer to reli- gious teachings when making important decisions about your life?	.19142	−.02954	**.60269**

Table 9.3. Factor Analysis of Items from the Kuwaiti Survey (continued)

	FACTOR LOADINGS[*]		
	ATTITUDES TOWARD THE ARAB-ISRAELI CONFLICT	ATTITUDES TOWARD GENDER EQUALITY	STRENGTH OF ISLAMIC ATTACH- MENTS
Item			
Would you support anyone in your family who wants to study in a religious institution?	−.00070	.12675	**.72326**

[*]*Directional differences in items and/or response codes have been removed through recoding, so that positive values for factor loadings always indicate more positive attitudes toward Arab-Israeli peace, more positive attitudes toward gender equality, and stronger Islamic attachments. The figures in boldface type in each column identify those items with high factor loadings. These items, which define the factor's conceptual content, have been combined to form a unidimensional attitudinal scale.*

but provides comparability with the other Arab populations included in the study. The total number of Kuwaiti respondents is three hundred, and, as in the Egyptian case, this includes an approximately equal number of women and men.

The Kuwaiti survey employed the same interview schedule that was administered in Egypt, the only difference being in the response codes of a small number of items. Moreover, the factor analytic procedures employed to select and validate items in the cases of Egypt and Israel were employed in Kuwait as well, with nearly identical results. As shown in Table 9.3, the items again yielded three distinct factors with consistently high loadings, making it possible to construct multi-item scales measuring attitudes toward the Arab-Israeli conflict, attitudes toward gender equality, and strength of Islamic attachments.

Palestine

The Palestinian data used in the present study were collected early in the fall of 1994 by the Center for Palestine Research and Studies (CPRS) in Nablus. Under the supervision of its director, Khalil Shikaki, and the head of its polling unit, Nader Said, trained field-workers administered an interview schedule to an area probability sample of 1,251 West Bank and Gaza residents. CPRS has conducted polls every month or two since the signing of the September 1993 agreement between the PLO and Israel. Limited in substantive scope but increasingly accurate with respect to sampling and measurement procedures, CPRS polls have a slight urban bias but are otherwise very highly representative. Christians as well as Muslims are included among respondents, but the former constitute less than 4 percent of the sample. Moreover, subsequent analysis confirmed that findings pertinent to the present study are the same even when Christian respondents are removed from the database. Data from the CPRS poll of fall 1994, the eleventh it had conducted, have been selected for the present investigation because this poll includes an item pertaining to the use of armed operations against Israel.[48]

The survey instrument employed in Palestine has a more restricted scope than the instruments used to collect data in Israel, Egypt, and Kuwait. Accordingly, there are not enough items dealing with either the Israeli-Palestinian conflict or attitudes toward the circumstances of women to use factor analysis. Respondent views about the conflict have thus been measured with an index composed of two highly intercorrelated items. One asks about partisan preferences, with respondents divided into those who do and those who do not favor factions that support territorial compromise and mutual recognition. The other asks about support or opposition with respect to the conduct of armed operations against Israeli targets in Gaza and Jericho. Attitudes toward women's circumstances have been measured using an item that asks about the participation of women in Palestinian elections, including voting, running for office, and having seats on the Palestinian Council reserved for women. This is the only item on the survey instrument that asks specifically about women. The Palestinian interview schedule does not contain any items measuring the strength of religious attachments, and this variable accordingly is not included in analyses of the data from Palestine.

The data from these four samples provide a strong foundation for examining the relationships between gender, feminism, and attitudes toward war and peace in the Middle East. As noted, all four samples are highly representative, at least of the urban populations from which they are drawn, and all accordingly possess male and female respondents in almost equal proportions. Thus, even though only one of the four data sets is based on a strict random sample, they nevertheless constitute an unusually solid empirical foundation, indeed one that is extremely rare in the study of the Middle East or other developing areas at the individual level of analysis.

A second very important strength, discussed earlier, is the cross-national character of the data, and, in particular, the advantages for comparative analysis derived from the dissimilar nature of the four societies from which data have been drawn. To the extent that observed variable relationships are similar in all four societies, confidence in the generalizability of these findings will increase significantly since they will have been produced with data from widely differing environments. Alternatively, should there be important differences in the variable relationships observed in some or all of the societies under study, knowledge will be gained about the system-level attributes upon which particular findings are conditional.

Finally, the limitations as well as the strengths of the available data should be noted. For one thing, there are not enough questions in several of the data sets, particularly those from Egypt and Kuwait, to provide a complete picture of respondent attitudes toward issues of war and peace. Although it is possible to situate respondents along a militarism-pacifism continuum, and hence test hypotheses, a fuller attitudinal profile is beyond the capabilities of the Egyptian and Kuwaiti data. For another, it is important to emphasize that the data provide attitudinal but not behavioral measures, and to point out in this connection that there are constraints on the ability of respondents to act in accordance with their views, particularly in the relatively undemocratic political systems of Egypt and Kuwait.

Analysis and Findings

In analyzing the data from Israel, Egypt, Palestine, and Kuwait, the first relationship to be examined is that between gender and attitudes toward the Arab-Israeli conflict. Specifically, do men and women have similar or different views about whether the long-standing dispute can and should be resolved peacefully, that is, through diplomacy and compromise leading to mutual recognition between Israelis and Arabs, including, of course, the Palestinians? The scales measuring these attitudes in each of the four societies have been trichotomized, with respondents accordingly divided into those who are more supportive of compromise and reconciliation, those who are somewhat supportive or unsure, and those who are less supportive of a peaceful resolution of the conflict.

Findings are presented in Table 9.4, which compares the attitudes of men and women in each of the four societies. In reading the table, it should be recalled that the relationship between gender and attitudes is being assessed within each country and that comparisons across the four societies involve only this relationship, not the attitudes being measured by the dependent variable. Because the specific items used to measure the dependent variable vary from country to country, respondent categories should be considered relative, rather than absolute, and distributions across these categories are thus not comparable from one sample to another. The only exception involves Egypt and Kuwait, where the same survey instrument was employed.

Table 9.4 shows that women and men do not have differing views about the Arab-Israeli conflict in any of the four societies examined. On the contrary, not only are gender-linked differences statistically insignificant, there

Table 9.4. Relationship between Gender
and Attitudes toward the Arab-Israeli Conflict

		SUPPORTS NONVIOLENT MEANS OF RESOLVING ARAB-ISRAELI CONFLICT	FEMALE	MALE	TOTAL
Israel	$X^2 = .44$, $df = 2, p > .05$	Highly Supportive	35%	33%	34%
		Somewhat Supportive	31%	33%	32%
		Not Supportive	34%	34%	34%
		TOTAL	475	382	857
Egypt	$X^2 = 3.86$, $df = 2, p > .05$	Highly Supportive	64%	74%	70%
		Somewhat Supportive	19%	16%	17%
		Not Supportive	17%	10%	13%
		TOTAL	135	148	283
Palestine	$X^2 = 1.14$, $df = 2, p > .05$	Highly Supportive	51%	53%	52%
		Somewhat Supportive	35%	35%	35%
		Not Supportive	14%	12%	13%
		TOTAL	619	609	1228
Kuwait	$X^2 = .69$, $df = 2, p > .05$	Highly Supportive	24%	25%	25%
		Somewhat Supportive	33%	29%	31%
		Not Supportive	43%	46%	44%
		TOTAL	148	136	284

is for the most part a remarkable similarity in the attitudinal distributions
of the two sexes. The only exception is the case of Egypt, where men are
actually more pacifistic than women, although the difference is not statistically significant at the generally accepted .05 level. Thus, notwithstanding the
contrary hypotheses advanced by some scholars, there is no evidence that
women are less militaristic than men or more oriented toward diplomacy

and compromise in their judgments about the most important international conflict in the region in which they reside.

Furthermore, as noted in the discussion of research design, these parallel observations from Israel, Egypt, Palestine, and Kuwait increase confidence in the generalizability of the finding that gender is not related to attitudes about international conflict, perhaps in general and at least about the disputes affecting one's own country and region. This proposition naturally needs to be tested further, with survey data drawn from other societies and pertaining to other international conflicts. Nevertheless, with comparable findings from surveys carried out in countries that differ significantly in their political, economic, and cultural attributes, as well as their histories, the present study provides strong evidence that men and women have similar attitudes toward issues of war and peace regardless of the political and social environment within which they reside.

A second relationship to be explored concerns a possible association between attitudes toward the status of women and attitudes toward issues of war and peace. Such a relationship is suggested by pertinent social science literature; and it is indeed possible that attitudes toward gender equality, if not gender itself, will be useful in accounting for variance in attitudes toward the Middle East conflict. Table 9.5 presents relevant findings from Israel, Egypt, Palestine, and Kuwait. The measures of attitudes toward gender equality are dichotomized: respondents who are more supportive of equality between women and men are compared to those who are less supportive.

Table 9.5 reveals the existence of a strong and positive relationship between attitudes toward gender equality and attitudes toward the Arab-Israeli conflict in all four of the societies for which data are available. Specifically, Israelis, Egyptians, Palestinians, and Kuwaitis who are more supportive of equality between women and men are also more favorably disposed toward diplomacy and compromise in the Arab-Israeli dispute, whereas those who are less supportive of gender equality are in each case less likely to favor resolving the conflict on this basis. The relationship is highly statistically significant in all four instances, indicating that, in this sense at least, there is a clear connection between feminism and issues of gender, on the one hand, and concerns related to international conflict, on the other. Moreover, again, the dissimilar characteristics of the four societies in which the same relationship has been observed strongly suggests that this relationship is of broad applicability.

Some respondents in each of the four countries examined are highly supportive both of resolving the Middle East conflict through compromise and diplomacy and of striving for greater equality between women and men, and the final set of relationships to be investigated concerns the degree to

Table 9.5. Relationship between Attitudes toward Gender Equality and Attitudes toward the Arab-Israeli Conflict

		SUPPORTS NON-VIOLENT MEANS OF RESOLVING ARAB-ISRAELI CONFLICT	MORE SUPPORTIVE OF GENDER EQUALITY	LESS SUPPORTIVE OF GENDER EQUALITY	TOTAL
Israel	$X^2 = 20.02$, $df = 2, p < .001$	Highly Supportive	44%	29%	34%
		Somewhat Supportive	29%	34%	32%
		Not Supportive	27%	37%	34%
		TOTAL	290	567	857
Egypt	$X^2 = 14.53$, $df = 2, p < .001$	Highly Supportive	78%	58%	70%
		Somewhat Supportive	14%	21%	17%
		Not Supportive	8%	21%	13%
		TOTAL	170	113	283
Palestine	$X^2 = 25.19$, $df = 2, p < .001$	Highly Supportive	57%	41%	52%
		Somewhat Supportive	32%	42%	35%
		Not Supportive	11%	17%	13%
		TOTAL	880	341	1,221
Kuwait	$X^2 = 11.26$, $df = 2, p < .01$	Highly Supportive	29%	20%	25%
		Somewhat Supportive	36%	25%	30%
		Not Supportive	35%	55%	45%
		TOTAL	141	141	282

which this normative orientation is associated with various personal status attributes. The proportion of respondents in this category is not of particular interest in the present study, since the scales derived through factor analysis provide relative rather than absolute ratings and since the cutting points selected are inevitably somewhat arbitrary. Of interest, rather, are the reasons why some individuals but not others embrace this combination of attitudes. Specifically, to what degree is the possession of this orientation a function of particular respondent characteristics?

There would appear to be a common theme underlying support for a peaceful resolution of the Arab-Israeli dispute and support for gender equality. Individuals who embrace this combination of attitudes would seem to have a generalized predisposition in favor of reconciliation, extending their concern for justice and equality to individuals and political communities alike. They also appear willing to challenge traditional and established ideas about right and wrong, or, perhaps more accurately, about the "natural" order of human interaction, and thus to reject the notion that existing conflicts and differences are inescapable. This orientation is sometimes characterized as "feminist-pacifist." As discussed earlier, it is an important focus of the theoretical literature seeking to link gender, feminism, and international studies. Some scholars also describe this perspective as one of "global feminism," arguing, as one analyst does, that there is a connection between feminism and international relations because "a world committed to domination at its intimate core in the home more readily accepts ever-escalating levels of domination and imperialism between peoples."[49]

The personal attribute variables, whose relationship to this normative orientation will be assessed, are gender, age, education, religiosity, and interest in current affairs, the latter based on the frequency of newspaper readership. Religiosity has been measured in the Israeli survey by items indicating whether a respondent is ultraorthodox (Haredi), orthodox, traditional, or nonreligious. Religiosity has been measured in the Egyptian and Kuwaiti surveys by a scale composed of five items dealing with Islamic attachments. These items, which are shown in Tables 9.2 and 9.3, were selected using the factor-analytic procedures discussed earlier. There is no measure of religiosity in the Palestinian case, since no salient items were included on the interview schedule.

Logistic regression, which assesses the explanatory power of each independent variable while all others are held constant, has been used to determine whether these personal attributes help to explain why some respondents possess a feminist-pacifist orientation and others do not. Accordingly, the dependent variable is a dichotomous "dummy" variable based on whether or not a respondent is high in support both for peace through compromise and for gender equality. Among the independent variables, age, education, and newspaper readership involve ordinal categories, as religiosity does in the Israeli case. The direction of each independent variable is indicated in parentheses, with the sign of the coefficients showing whether associations with that value are positive or negative.

Tables 9.6, 9.7, 9.8, and 9.9 present the logistical regressions for Israel, Egypt, Palestine, and Kuwait, respectively. As seen in Table 9.6, Israelis who favor both peace through compromise and gender equality are more likely than other Israelis to be older, better educated, less religious, and more interested in current affairs. All these relationships are statistically significant. Among Egyptians, as shown in Table 9.7, a feminist-pacifist orientation is more common among those who are female, better educated, and less religious. Table 9.8 shows that in the Palestinian case there is a statistically significant relationship between this orientation and older age and interest in current affairs, with an association with female gender falling just short of statistical significance. Finally, as shown in Table 9.9, Kuwaitis who favor both peace through compromise and gender equality are more likely than other Kuwaitis to be female and less religious.

The logistical regressions reveal both similarities and differences between the cases examined, with the former suggesting conclusions that are, at least to some extent, generalizable. Indeed, as noted with respect to findings about gender, the observation of comparable relationships in countries that differ significantly in their political, economic, cultural, and historical circumstances strongly suggests that these relationships are unaffected by, and thus apply regardless of, the system-level attributes that characterize a country's political and social environment.

In the present analysis, the most important instance of similar findings concerns the inverse relationship between religiosity and a feminist-pacifist normative orientation. The relationship is the same whether the pertinent religion is Judaism or Islam, and in the latter case whether it is the Islam of Cairo, a large, ancient, and cosmopolitan city with the world's most important Islamic university, or the Islam of a conservative sheikhdom with an essentially tribal tradition. The importance of low religiosity is also independent of conflict involvement, being the same for the heavily engaged Israelis as for the more distant Kuwaitis and the Egyptians, whose country had already been at peace with Israel for a decade when data for the present study were collected. In view of these findings, future research should seek to explicate the pathways that link low religiosity to a feminist-pacifist orientation, undertaking to identify, for example, the substantive content of those dimensions of religiosity that are most important in accounting for variance.

Table 9.6. Logistical Regression for Israeli Data Showing the Relationship between Selected Personal Attributes and Support for Both Peace through Compromise and Gender Equality

VARIABLE	B	S.E.	WALD	SIG	R
Gender (Female)	−.4285	.2586	2.7463	.0975	−.0363
Age (Older)	.2075	.0840	6.1003	.0135	.0850
Education (Higher)	.7219	.1505	22.9977	.0000	.1923
Religiosity (Lower)	1.7423	.2970	34.4069	.0000	.2389
Reads Newspapers (More)	.3218	.1591	4.0926	.0431	.0607

Table 9.7. Logistical Regression for Egyptian Data Showing the Relationship between Selected Personal Attributes and Support for Both Peace through Compromise and Gender Equality

VARIABLE	B	S.E.	WALD	SIG	R
Gender (Female)	.8551	.2564	11.1250	.0009	.1524
Age (Older)	.0788	.0903	.7611	.3830	.0000
Education (Higher)	.3164	.1464	4.6702	.0307	.0824
Religiosity (Lower)	.8145	.0632	8.5145	.0035	.1288
Reads Newspapers (More)	−.0991	.1129	.7704	.3801	.0000

Table 9.8. Logistical Regression for Palestinian Data Showing the Relationship between Selected Personal Attributes and Support for Both Peace through Compromise and Gender Equality

VARIABLE	B	S.E.	WALD	SIG	R
Gender (Female)	.2311	.1221	3.5837	.0584	−.0312
Age (Older)	.0978	.0290	11.1003	.0008	−.0758
Education (Higher)	.0150	.0626	.0574	.8107	.0000
Reads Newspapers (More)	−.1463	.0657	4.9659	.0259	.0427

Table 9.9. Logistical Regression for Kuwaiti Data Showing the Relationship between Selected Personal Attributes and Support for Both Peace through Compromise and Gender Equality

VARIABLE	B	S.E.	WALD	SIG	R
Gender (Female)	1.0708	.4071	6.9181	.0085	.1465
Age (Older)	−.1293	.1708	.5737	.4488	.0000
Education (Higher)	.3008	.3056	.9689	.3249	.0000
Religiosity (Lower)	.2047	.0741	7.6427	.0057	.1570
Reads Newspapers (More)	−.1270	.2289	.3078	.5971	.0000

Also suggestive are findings pertaining to gender, which involve both similarities and differences among the four cases. Female gender is related to a feminist-pacifist orientation among Egyptians and Kuwaitis, and the relationship falls just short of statistical significance in the case of the Palestinians. This suggests that the relationship may be broadly applicable to Arab and Muslim societies, and perhaps to other non-European societies. Another possibility is that the relationship is dependent upon the degree of gender equality that characterizes a society. This is suggested by comparisons with Israel, where a significant relationship involving gender was not observed. On the one hand, despite their continuing problems and the limits of feminism in the Jewish state, Israeli women are not disadvantaged relative to men to the same extent as their Egyptian, Palestinian, and Kuwaiti counterparts. On the other hand, more specifically, differences between the Israeli and Arab cases may be explained by the fact that only in the former do women serve in the military.

Finally, findings pertaining to education, which again involve both similarities and differences, offer possibilities for theoretical elaboration. Education is positively related to a feminist-pacifist orientation in Israel and Egypt, which are the two most cosmopolitan, politically developed, and culturally heterogeneous of the four societies examined. Although other explanations are possible and additional study is needed, this suggests that the socialization experiences associated with education tend to produce a feminist-pacifist perspective only among the citizens of those countries marked by a meaningful measure of social diversity and political development.

Conclusion

The comparative analysis of data from four highly dissimilar Middle Eastern societies suggests interesting conclusions about the connections between gender, feminism, and international relations. Evidence from four societies suggests that women are not more pacifistic than men in their attitudes toward international conflict. And while this finding contradicts the argument advanced in some feminist literature, the likelihood of its validity is strengthened by the fact that a connection between gender and attitudes toward war and peace was found to be absent in diverse political, economic, and social environments.

On the other hand, findings from the present study do suggest a connection between *attitudes* related to gender and attitudes about war and peace, between feminism and pacifism, as it were. Specifically, regardless of the sex of the individual, persons who express greater concern for the status and role of women, and particularly for equality between women and men, are more likely than other individuals to believe that the international disputes in which their country is involved should be resolved through diplomacy and compromise. This pattern, too, was observed in all four of the societies examined, suggesting that it may also be broadly applicable.

In addition, the data shed light on the personal circumstances that lead individuals to support both peace through compromise and equality between women and men, an orientation that some scholars describe as "pacifist-feminist," and the data also make it possible to offer testable propositions about the locus of applicability of significant variable relationships. Specifically, this orientation appears to be a function of low religiosity under highly diverse conditions, of gender in societies with higher levels of inequality between women and men, and of education in countries that are relatively politically developed and cosmopolitan.

All these relationships must, of course, be additionally tested and refined through research in other countries. In the meantime, however, findings reported in the present study offer an unusually strong empirical foundation for insights about the interconnections between gender, feminism, and international conflict. Whereas scholarly inquiries seeking to connect gender studies and international studies rely most frequently on deductive reasoning and historical interpretation, and focus only on Western societies when they do involve more rigorous analyses, the present study offers evidence based on the comparative analysis of cross-national survey data in support of its conclusions about the nature, generalizability and locus of important variable relationships.

Finally, it may be worthwhile in concluding to comment briefly on the practical as well as the theoretical implications of the findings reported above. The latter remain the primary concern of this report, but findings about attitudes toward the Arab-Israeli conflict will be of interest to students of the Middle East as well as to students of gender and international relations.

Three summary observations may be offered in this connection, put forward without elaboration as a stimulus to reflection and further research. First, the absence of sex-linked differences in attitudes toward the Arab-Israeli conflict suggests that neither advocates nor opponents of territorial compromise are likely to find one sex more receptive to their message than the other. Particularly in Israel and Palestine, where this issue is of central concern, the partisan and ideological struggles surrounding questions of war and peace are thus unlikely to find women more frequently than men in any particular political camp.[50] Second, the strong association between attitudes toward war and peace and attitudes toward gender equality suggests that the former are part of a more comprehensive worldview. If this is correct, the promotion of progressive values in other areas is likely to increase support in the Middle East for peace through diplomacy and compromise. Third, the emergence of a progressive and globalist worldview is tied to secularism or, more accurately, to the privatization of religion, and also to education under conditions of greater political development and social diversity. This in turn suggests that gains in the Middle East with respect to development, political tolerance, and citizen equality, to the extent they are realized, will also increase support for Arab-Israeli peace.

Some of these propositions may be disputed, and none is accompanied by a fully developed rationale. But although their further consideration is beyond the scope of the present inquiry, they are offered in conclusion in order to invite and inform speculation not only about theoretical considerations but also about the practical implications of findings pertaining to gender and international conflict. They are also offered as a stimulus to further research at the individual level of analysis, in the hope that more and better-quality survey research will be undertaken in the Middle East, and particularly in the Arab world, in order to understand better the nature, determinants, and consequences of citizen attitudes about issues of war and peace.

CHAPTER 10

Islam and Attitudes toward International Conflict: Evidence from Survey Research in the Arab World (1998)

Mark Tessler and Jodi Nachtwey

D efying all expectations of modernization theory, the 1970s and 1980s witnessed a reawakening of religious ideas and social movements. This has been particularly true in the Middle East, which provided the setting for important early research on modernization but has demonstrated more recently that economic development and social change are not necessarily associated with an increase in secularism. In the Islamic countries of the Middle East, and in Israel as well, it is today more important than ever to devote attention to religion and religious movements when examining social and political phenomena.

Despite religion's increasing salience, both within the Middle East and more generally, a systematic and coherent understanding of the connections between religion and politics remains elusive. First, studies are often highly descriptive, confined to particular cultural or sociopolitical settings and concerned with explicating the causes and consequences of specific events rather than contributing generalizable theoretical insights. Second, only rarely are studies cross-national and genuinely comparative, with a concern for discovering systemic variables that condition social and political relationships. Third, and perhaps most important, there has been little research in which the individual is the unit of analysis, and accordingly very few systematic, data-based investigations that focus on the link between the religious and political orientations of ordinary citizens.

To these deficiencies may be added the paucity of information about the relationship between religion and international conflict, which is the focus of the present report. A small body of research in the United States is beginning to examine this relationship, and some hypotheses have been examined in European countries as well. This research is in an early stage, however, and is even more underdeveloped in the Islamic countries of the Middle East. Accordingly, to contribute to an understanding of whether and how religion influences the way that ordinary men and women think about international events, and at the same time to shed light on politics and international relations in the Middle East, this study uses original public opinion data from several Arab and Islamic countries to examine the degree to which, and the conditions under which, personal religiosity and support for political Islam account for variance in attitudes toward the Arab-Israeli conflict.

Theoretical Considerations and Previous Research

The theoretical linkage between religion and international politics is based on the assumption that religion plays a critical role in shaping both the normative orientations of individuals and their understanding of the surrounding world. Religious beliefs provide answers in unpredictable surroundings and guide behavior through compelling ethical or moral prescriptions.[1] This is especially true among adherents and believers because, as Leege notes, religion "characterizes its answers as sacred, eternal, [and] implicated with the ultimate meaning of life."[2]

With respect to political processes more particularly, at least three different roles have been suggested for religion: a priestly role, a prophetic role, and a mediating societal function.[3] In its priestly role, religion is a force that legitimates government action by justifying policies on the basis of a superior, transcendent, morality.[4] If a religious belief system is widely shared, these common norms may be emphasized in order to build support for the government and its policies.[5] In a prophetic role, by contrast, religious ideals provide criteria by which to judge governmental authority and, in many instances, to criticize decisions or policies deemed inconsistent with divine purposes. In this way, religion provides support for advocates of political change. Finally, as a mediating institution, religion offers protection from excessive government control and authoritarian tendencies. By providing a focus of identity that rivals state loyalties, and also through the provision of services that reduce dependence on the state, religious institutions contribute to the vitality of civil society and allow individuals to maintain an independent or even critical stance toward the government and its actions.[6]

On the other hand, it can also be argued that religion has little or no influence on political orientations. This thesis, at least as applied to Western societies, rests in part on the assumption that religion has been privatized, that religion increasingly has meaning only in the private sphere of the individual. It also rests on the assumption that most individuals have embraced secularism as a model for state-society relations. As expressed in one recent study, if institutional modernization has routinized and specialized social relations and removed from the state any legitimate concern with maintaining a religious worldview, then the search for religious fulfillment becomes a personal quest for spiritual meaning and is quite detached from the daily functioning of political affairs.[7] Thus, to the extent these assumptions about privatized religion and secularism are correct, religious norms may be influential only in matters of personal ethics and morality.

These competing perspectives suggest that the utility of religious variables in explaining political attitudes and behavior may depend on the kinds of religious orientations that individuals hold and the broader societal and cultural context within which they reside. Findings from a number of empirical studies, although not entirely consistent, also suggest a more nuanced and conditional relationship between religion and politics, one in which religious orientations are neither consistently useful nor consistently irrelevant in accounting for variance in political attitudes and behavior. Several opinion surveys report, for example, that personal religiosity is strongly and positively related to the degree of importance that individuals attach to issues of public policy pertaining to personal conduct, especially when, as in the case of abortion, homosexuality, and gender roles, this conduct is deemed to involve an ethical or moral dimension.[8] Some of these studies are based on data from Europe as well as the United States.

In another study, using data from the United States, researchers Benson and Williams constructed attitudinal scales measuring four different normative dimensions associated with religion and then examined the correlation between each and a series of political attitudes.[9] Two scales exhibited particularly strong correlations. One assessed whether respondents viewed the "human problem" primarily as a personal struggle or a societal challenge. The other measured the degree to which respondents' religious behavior focused primarily on their private relationship with God or, alternatively, on their relationships with other people. In each case, the more individualistic orientations were correlated with greater conservatism, as normally defined in Western countries, both in general and with respect to various public policy concerns. Similar findings were also reported in another, more recent study, which found individualism to be related to conservatism in ideology, partisanship, and policy preferences.[10] These studies are of particular interest because their conceptualization of religiosity is based on normative interpretation rather than church affiliation or other institutional considerations; thus, this conceptualization is readily applicable to the world of Islam.

A few opinion studies in the Middle East have also examined the relationship between religiosity and attitudes toward politics and public policy, and they, too, report that some religious orientations have more explanatory power than others. For example, a recent analysis of public opinion data from Egypt observed a negative correlation between religious activism, as measured by support for religious dress, censorship, religious instruction in schools, and

Islamic revival, and support for economic liberalism in such areas as price controls and subsidies. On the other hand, religiosity defined in terms of piety and measured on the basis of prayer and ritual performance bears no relationship to attitudes toward these issues of political and economic policy.[11]

Other studies have explored the relationship between religious piety and partisan preferences using survey data from Egypt, Palestine, and Lebanon, and in each case there was at best a weak relationship not only between religiosity and political preferences in general but between religiosity and support for Islamic political movements in particular. In Egypt, more than one-third of those classified as more pious did not support Islamic parties, whereas approximately half of those who did support these parties were not personally observant and devout.[12] In Lebanon, the relationship between religiosity and support for the Islamic political party, Hezbollah, was only moderately strong.[13]

Although only a few studies have sought to link religion to international concerns at the individual level of analysis, available research once again suggests that relationships are complex and conditional. Guth and Green, using data from the United States, looked at religiosity defined in terms of a tendency to seek religious guidance and biblical literalism and found a positive correlation with anti-communism and higher levels of support for military and defense-related spending.[14] But, although this finding suggests that religiosity pushes toward conservative and nationalistic political views, a study using European data found that greater religiosity was positively correlated with higher levels of internationalism and specifically with more support for European integration and for aid to developing countries.[15] In this case, religiosity was measured by the degree to which respondents reported that religion was important in shaping their political outlook.

The findings of yet another scholar are similarly diverse. In studies based on data from the United States, Jelen found that respondents with Evangelical beliefs associated with Protestantism were more likely to display hawkish foreign policy attitudes related to defense spending, the use of military power to achieve foreign policy goals, and the bombing of civilian targets in wartime situations.[16] Roman Catholics, by contrast, took more dovish positions on a number of foreign policy questions. A less consistent pattern emerged from his analysis of European data, however. With an index of attitudes toward NATO and the U.S. military presence in Europe treated as the dependent variable, and using church attendance, which was the only available indicator, to measure religiosity, Jelen found (1) a direct positive correlation between religiosity and support for military security in three countries, (2) a direct but negative correlation between religiosity and support for military security in two countries, and (3) a positive but indirect correlation between religiosity and support for military security in seven countries.[17]

The findings by Benson and Williams illuminate further the complex role of religiosity as an independent variable.[18] Of the two normative dimensions noted previously, the religious orientations associated with political conservatism were also correlated with conservatism in foreign policy attitudes. Specifically, support for defense spending and a reduction in foreign aid were associated with more individualistic orientations on both religious dimensions. In this instance, it is not the degree of religiosity but rather the type of religious orientation that accounts for variance in individual political attitudes, thus suggesting that it is not possible to draw simple and straightforward conclusions about an association between levels of personal religiosity and particular political attitudes.

The findings from these various studies suggest that religious orientations do play an important role in shaping political attitudes, including attitudes toward foreign policy and world affairs. Furthermore, more often than not, they suggest that religiosity pushes toward a more conservative and nationalistic view of politics and international relations. In addition, however, this body of research also shows that religiosity can sometimes lead to a more liberal and internationalist political perspective, that the salience and direction of relationships vary as a function both of the particular dimension of religiosity treated as an independent variable and of the particular political attitude treated as a dependent variable, and, finally, that all this variation is itself influenced by the spatial and temporal setting. More research is needed to resolve inconsistencies about relationships and conditionalities and to increase theoretical coherence in this area of scholarship. It is against this background that the present study aspires to make a contribution.

Religion and Politics in the Middle East

Beyond a contribution to the general empirical foundation required for theoretical development, research about religion and politics in the Arab and Islamic countries of the Middle East is important in at least two additional, interrelated respects. First, it expands the range of conditions under which salient variable relationships may be explored. Second, and equally important, it permits consideration of the possibility that the diversity and inconsistency noted in studies conducted in Western societies are at least partly a consequence of the ambiguous political role that religion plays in largely secular societies. This would be indicated should a different pattern, and especially a more coherent one, be observed in societies where there has long been a much stronger connection between religion and political life.

Only a brief summary of the aggregate and historical connections between religion and politics in the Arab-Islamic world is required in the present context. These connections are for the most part familiar, and the concern of the present report is in any event limited to an examination of variable relationships at the individual level of analysis. But because this also includes consideration of the differences and similarities between patterns observed in Arab and Islamic countries and those reported in studies conducted in more secular societies, it may be useful to offer a short and very general account of Islam's political significance in the Arab Middle East.

The association between religion and politics can be seen at several levels in the Arab world. On the one hand, constitutions declare Islam to be the official state religion in almost all Arab countries and, accordingly, religious holidays are national holidays, religion is part of the curriculum in state-run schools, the government has responsibility for mosques and other Islamic institutions, and, most important perhaps, substantial segments of national legal codes are based on the Quran. As summarized recently by an Arab scholar, "Secularism and the privatization of religion are alien to the Muslim conception. Muslims have continued to assume that only a 'religious leader' can provide good government for the Muslim community and that the main function of an Islamic government is to ensure obedience to God's law as explained in the Quran and the Sunnah."[19] This strong and historically validated connection between religion and politics contrasts dramatically with the established patterns of secularism that, however imperfect, characterize most Western societies.

On the other hand, Islam contributes significantly to both the ideological and the institutional axes according to which government and opposition play themselves out in most Arab countries. Although there is some variation across political systems and also over time, it is common for governments to employ Islamic symbols in an attempt to shore up their legitimacy and to use government-appointed religious officials to justify the regime and its policies. In the latter connection, there are numerous examples of Islamic jurists and scholars issuing pronouncements that are deliberately designed to serve the interests of political leaders,[20] such as the statement that Anwar Sadat obtained in 1979 from Islamic scholars at Cairo's Al-Azhar Mosque University to the effect that peace with Israel is compatible with Islam.[21] This illustrates the "priestly" role of religion, noted earlier, wherein religion is used to give legitimacy to actions of the government.

Similarly, Islam provides a frame of reference and an institutional structure for political movements opposed to established regimes, in this case playing a "prophetic" role. This has been particularly apparent in recent decades, although it is not a new phenomenon. Indeed, nationalist movements often carried out resistance to colonialism during the pre-independence period under the ideological banner of Islam, and they often used mosques and brotherhood lodges for organizational purposes. More recently, Islamic groups have been in the forefront of challenging the governments of many Arab countries, sometimes using extralegal or even violent means in pursuit of their objectives but more often working within the political system.[22] These groups use mosques and other Muslim institutions to recruit followers and disseminate their message, the content of which is usually that the government is not only repressive and corrupt but has also deviated from Islamic principles and is therefore illegitimate.[23]

Islamic opposition movements have assumed increased importance in recent decades for a number of reasons.[24] Some have to do with deteriorating economic and political conditions, which lead ordinary citizens to support those political movements they believe are best able to put pressure on the government. In this instance, especially in view of the political vacuum that exists in countries ruled by authoritarian governments, the organizational and mobilizational advantages of Islamic movements are particularly important. So, too, is the fact that many of these movements carry out an extensive array of welfare and development activities at the grassroots level, especially in poorer neighborhoods. As one Arab scholar reports in this connection, groups associated with political Islam use socioeconomic institutions and programs, particularly those that target the poor, to gain "greater access to the masses and through them access to power."[25] On the other hand, factors having to do with Islam itself are also important. These include the religion's strong emphasis on justice, equality, and assistance to those in need, as well as the fact that Islamic law is regarded by Muslims as a guide and blueprint for societal organization in all spheres of human activity, including the political sphere.

The obvious point is that Islam and politics are intimately connected in the Arab world, making it reasonable to expect that the influence of religion on foreign policy attitudes will be stronger and more consistent than the ambiguous pattern of relationships observed by studies carried out in the United States and other Western societies. If this is indeed the case, the hypothesis that follows is that the utility of religious orientations in accounting for variance in political attitudes is itself dependent on contextual considerations, such as the degree to which a society is more or less secular.

Methodology

The objective of the present analysis is to examine the influence of Islamic orientations on attitudes toward international conflict using survey data from Arab societies, and then to compare findings from this research with those based on studies conducted in Western societies. The primary data are from public opinion surveys carried out in Egypt, Kuwait, and Palestine. Survey data from Jordan and Lebanon are available for a more limited analysis.

Data Sources

The Egyptian and Kuwaiti surveys were carried out in mid-1988 under the direction of Jamal Al-Suwaidi, who presently directs the Emirates Center for Strategic Studies and Research in Abu Dhabi. Based on stratified samples of 295 adults in Cairo and 300 adults in Kuwait City, respondents reflect the heterogeneous nature of the general population. Each sample includes an approximately equal number of men and women and, despite a slight under-representation of poor and less well-educated individuals, each is broadly representative with respect to age, education, socioeconomic status, and place of residence. Egyptian Christians and Kuwaiti Shi'ites were excluded from the samples for analytical purposes to facilitate comparison of Sunni Muslim populations in other Arab countries. The same survey instrument was employed in each country.

The Palestinian survey was conducted in August 1995 by the Center for Palestine Research and Studies in Nablus, under the supervision of its director, Khalil Shikaki, and the head of its polling unit, Nadir Said. Multistage area probability sampling techniques were employed to select respondents, and the interview schedule was administered to 1,184 adults residing in the West Bank and Gaza. Almost all respondents are Sunni Muslim, although a small number of Christians, approximately 4 percent, are included in the sample.

The Jordanian and Lebanese surveys were carried out in 1994 by the Market Research Organization of Amman, Jordan, under the supervision of its director, Tony Sabbagh. They are based on random samples in major cities—Amman, Zarqa, and Irbid in Jordan, and Beirut, Tripoli, and Sidon in Lebanon. All respondents, 251 in Jordan and 252 in Lebanon, are over the age of eighteen. The same survey instrument was employed in the two countries, but this instrument contains items dealing with only some of the religious orientations of interest to the present study.

Despite some limitations, including the relatively small size of four of the samples, these data constitute an empirical foundation possessing considerable strength. First, the availability of opinion data dealing with religion and politics from five different Arab societies is itself a very notable strength, not only because of the potential for cross-national comparisons but also because surveys dealing with political attitudes are extremely rare in the Arab world. Second, the data have all been collected by indigenous scholars and institutions, indicating a knowledge of local conditions that inspires confidence in the application of survey methods. Third, there has been attention to rigor as well as respect for local conditions. In all cases, representative samples were constructed, survey instruments were pretested and refined, and interviewers were carefully trained and monitored.

Furthermore, the diversity of the samples with respect to place and time is also an important strength. Among the five societies from which data are available are both rich and poor countries, both monarchies and republics, more competitive and less competitive political systems, and states with and without a long history of cosmopolitanism and contact with the West. There is also diversity with respect to temporal considerations, with some surveys conducted before and others after the Gulf crisis of 1990–91 and the Israel-PLO accord of 1993. As a result of this diversity, it is possible to examine variable relationships under widely differing conditions. This will increase confidence in the generalizability of observed relationships should there be similar findings in all the cases. Alternatively, it will facilitate the identification of spatial or temporal system-level conditionalities should these relationships differ in some or all of the countries. Additional information about these and other aspects of data collection is given elsewhere.[26]

The Dependent Variable

The dependent variable in this analysis is attitudes toward the resolution of international conflict and specifically toward a peaceful resolution of the Arab-Israeli dispute. For each country, these attitudes are measured by a scale composed of two intercorrelated items from the survey instrument. Table 10.1 lists the items used to construct these measures, all of which deal with the desirability or possibility of achieving Arab-Israeli peace through diplomacy and compromise. Table 10.2 presents the response distribution on these measures of the dependent variable for each of the five countries.

Evidence in support of the validity and reliability of these measures comes from several sources. Face validity is high in all cases, and strong intercorrelations inspire confidence in reliability. This logic is further supported by the use of factor analysis; in each case, these items load highly on a separate factor when varimax rotation is used to extract factors from a large matrix of items.

In addition, there appears to be a high level of conceptual equivalence across the samples, meaning that the same concept has been validly and reliably measured in each instance. This is indicated by the content of the survey items, which inquire about processes and relationships whose salience is not limited to a particular country or a particular stage of the Arab-Israeli conflict. Equally significant is the dimensional structure of the three pairs of intercorrelated items; in each case one item asks about a resolution of the conflict through diplomacy and negotiation, whereas the other assesses

Table 10.1. Survey Items Used to Measure the Dependent Variable

Egyptian and Kuwaiti Surveys

Which is the best solution to the Arab-Israeli conflict: military or diplomatic?

Which of the following best describes your attitudes toward relations with Israel? Egypt: Peace treaty should be canceled, or Peace treaty should continue; Kuwait: Peace is impossible, or Peace efforts are desirable.

Palestinian Survey

Do you support the continuation of current peace negotiations between the PLO and Israel?

I expect the achievement of a lasting peace between Palestinians and Israelis. Do you agree or disagree with this statement?

Jordanian and Lebanese Surveys

The PLO and Israel have recently signed an agreement on mutual recognition and on a transitional period of autonomy for Palestinians in the Occupied Territories, starting with Gaza and Jericho. Do you approve or disapprove of this agreement?

If there is an overall Arab-Israeli settlement, would you favor or oppose our country having normal diplomatic and other relations with Israel?

Table 10.2. Attitudes toward Peace with Israel

	FAVORS PEACE (%)	SOMEWHAT FOR PEACE (%)	OPPOSES PEACE (%)
Egypt	70	16	14
Kuwait	25	30	45
Palestine	33	48	19
Jordan	35	21	44
Lebanon	46	16	39

Note: The items listed in Table 10.1 have been combined to form an index for each sample. Favors peace indicates a positive response on both items; opposes peace indicates a negative response on both items.

general receptivity to peaceful coexistence between Arabs and Israelis. It is true that the items do not establish *measurement* equivalence, which would permit the direct comparison of responses from one sample to the next. This would be possible only if the three survey instruments included identical items. This is not the object of the present analysis, however. Rather, it is to compare findings, and for this it is sufficient to know that the dependent variables measured in all cases are *conceptually* equivalent.

Primary Analysis

As discussed, the present analysis seeks to determine the utility of religious orientations in accounting for variance in attitudes toward the Arab-Israeli conflict. The Egyptian, Kuwaiti, and Palestinian surveys contain a large number of items dealing with Islam and Islamic attachments, which permits a more refined and multidimensional assessment of religious influences and which accordingly makes these cases the primary focus of this study's empirical contribution. In these three cases, factor analysis has been employed to identify different kinds of religious orientations. Factor analysis provides conceptual guidance and also has statistical and methodological advantages. On the one hand, it contributes to parsimony and increases the ability of a regression equation to stand up to cross validation.[27] On the other, as noted, it increases confidence in the reliability and validity of the items selected to measure particular orientations.

Two theoretically distinct and empirically independent dimensions of religious attitudes emerge from the factor analysis of Egyptian, Kuwaiti, and Palestinian data. Furthermore, these dimensions are conceptually equivalent in all three cases. The first factor revolves around aspects of personal piety (i.e., frequency of prayer), whereas the second concerns the relationship between religion and sociopolitical life and includes support for Islamist political movements. The survey items that cluster together to measure each dimension are shown in Tables 10.3 and 10.4. It is noteworthy that a similar pattern was found in another study, which increases confidence in the results of the factor analysis in the present instance. Using survey data from Egypt, Palmer, El Safty, and Sullivan found that religiosity may relate to private or largely "passive" ritual experiences, or it may tap into a concern for how religious principles are actively followed in society.[28] It is also notable that some work in the United States has found a similar differentiation between religious attitudes. In particular, Benson and Williams report a distinction between attitudes concerned with an individual's personal relationship with God and views emphasizing the role of religion in creating societal harmony.[29] This suggests that there may be important similarities in the dimensional structure, if not necessarily the associated political attitudes, of religious orientations in the Muslim Middle East and the more secular West.

Table 10.3. Survey Items Used to Measure Religious Orientations in Egypt and Kuwait and Factor Analysis Using Varimax Rotation of Survey Items Regarding Religious Attitudes

Personal Aspects of Islam

1. Would you support anyone in your family who wants to study in a religious institution?

2. How often do you refer to religious teachings when making important decisions about your life?

3. How often do you read the Koran?

4. Do you observe your five daily prayers?

Political Aspects of Islam

1. Do you agree or disagree that religion and politics should be separate?

2. What do you think of the following statement: religious practice must be kept private and separated from sociopolitical life?

3. Do you support current organized Islamic movements?

4. What do you think of the religious awakening now taking place in society?

ITEM NUMBER	EGYPT		KUWAIT	
	FACTOR 1: PERSONAL ASPECTS OF ISLAM	FACTOR 2: POLITICAL ASPECTS OF ISLAM	FACTOR 1: PERSONAL ASPECTS OF ISLAM	FACTOR 2: POLITICAL ASPECTS OF ISLAM
1	**.65**	.13	**.59**	.14
2	**.77**	.02	**.67**	.24
3	**.76**	.17	**.73**	.04
4	**.67**	.26	**.76**	.19
5	−.02	**.75**	.08	**.83**
6	.25	**.61**	.08	**.84**
7	.09	**.71**	.27	**.57**
8	.29	**.55**	.41	**.49**

Note: The first and second factors explained 35 percent and 16 percent of the variance, respectively, in Egypt. The first and second factors explained 38 percent and 15 percent of the variance, respectively, in Kuwait. Because of missing data, Question 8 was not included in the piety and political Islam factors used in the Kuwaiti model in the analysis to follow.

Table 10.4. Survey Items Used to Measure Religious
Orientations in Palestine and Factor Analysis Using
Varimax Rotation of Survey Items

Personal Aspects of Islam

1. A Muslim is considered a Muslim even if he does not pray the five times.

2. Do you describe yourself as religious?

3. To what extent does the phrase, "I Pray" apply to you?

Political Aspects of Islam

4. How important is it for men of religion to have a leading role in the government?

5. Islam is the sole faith by which Palestinians can obtain their rights.

6. I support Islamic political parties.

7. I support the establishment of an Islamic Caliph state.

ITEM NUMBER	FACTOR 1: POLITICAL ASPECTS OF ISLAM	FACTOR 2: PERSONAL ASPECTS OF ISLAM
1	.05	**.50**
2	.18	**.79**
3	.20	**.82**
4	**.65**	.11
5	**.65**	.21
6	**.61**	.11
7	**.74**	.09

Note: The first and second factors explain 34 percent and 15 percent of the variance, respectively.

These two religious orientations, personal piety and views about political Islam, are the primary independent variables in this analysis. Whether either one or both is related to attitudes toward the Arab-Israeli conflict remains to be determined, however. Although it might be assumed that Islamic attachments imply a rejection of peace with Israel, creating a situation of endogeneity involving independent and dependent variables in the present study, the actual situation is much more complex. Muslim officials have issued contradictory statements about whether Islam permits accommodation with the Jewish state,[30] and even theoreticians and politicians affiliated with militant Islamic movements advance different views about whether peace is permissible in the context of a freely negotiated settlement between Israelis and Palestinians.[31]

Other independent variables are also included in the analysis, both to address the problem of spuriousness in causal inference through statistical controls and to assess the explanatory power of Islamic attachments relative to that of other factors. Linear regression is used to examine these relationships, with the following additional independent variables included in the models for each country: gender, age, education, income, and perceived economic security, the latter measured through items asking about the economic circumstances of respondents and their country.

Secondary Analysis

The survey instrument administered in Jordan and Lebanon is more limited, permitting the examination of some but not all of the independent variables of interest in the present study. More specifically, there is a good measure of attitudes toward the relationship between Islam and politics but not of piety and religious observance. Thus, the explanatory power of personal religiosity cannot be assessed, nor can this variable be held constant when seeking to determine whether attitude toward political Islam accounts for variance on the dependent variable. Also, the Jordanian and Lebanese data contain information about perceived economic security but not about respondent income. Nevertheless, despite these limitations and the caution they necessitate, the data from Jordan and Lebanon do provide an additional opportunity to examine some important variable relationships. The item used to measure attitudes toward political Islam in Jordan and Lebanon asks about the degree of importance attached to the proposition that "our country should always be guided by religious values and Islamic law."

Analysis and Findings

The results of the analyses for Egypt, Kuwait, and Palestine are presented in Table 10.5. With respect to the influence of religious orientations, findings are the same in all three countries. First, support for political Islam consistently exhibits a very strong negative relationship with support for Arab-Israeli peace. In other words, respondents are much less likely to support peace and/or the normalization of relations with Israel if they favor a prominent role for religion in political and public affairs, if they support religious political movements, or if they are less critical of Islamic militants. Indeed, these relationships are almost always stronger than those involving any other independent variable. Second, in no case does personal Islamic piety bear a significant relationship to the dependent variable. Individuals who report high levels of religious devotion in their personal lives do not

Table 10.5. Multiple Regression of Factors Influencing
Attitudes toward Peace in Egypt and Kuwait

	EGYPT	KUWAIT	PALESTINE
Piety (Factor 1)	−.08	−.04	.01
	(−1.60)	(−.70)	(.84)
Political Islam (Factor 2)	−.18	−.14	−.60
	(−3.72)**	(−2.87)**	(−7.80)**
Sex	.13	−.10	−.06
	(1.36)	(−.92)	(−1.22)
Education	−.01	.08	.06
	(−.30)	(1.72)	(3.00)**
Age	−.20	−.07	−.00
	(−3.49)**	(−.74)	(−.26)
Income	.02	−.01	.05
	(1.14)	(−.55)	(1.62)
Economic Security	.13	.04	−.21
	(2.60)*	(−.51)	(7.10)**
Constant	2.42	3.11	2.82
	(8.49)	(8.03)	(17.22)
R^2	0.17	0.06	.16
N	225	254	823

Note: Numbers in parentheses are t statistics.
*$p < .05$, **$p < .01$.

possess attitudes toward the Arab-Israeli conflict that differ from those held by persons with lower levels of religious devotion.

Although the first of these findings is perhaps to be expected, the latter is more surprising and noteworthy. It is also at variance with the arguments advanced by some scholars, to the effect that Islam breeds militant attitudes and antipathy toward the West and accordingly pushes toward international conflict. This argument is present in the "clash of civilizations" thesis, for example, which contends that Islam is a force for strife among peoples and states.[32] A similar argument is present in debates about the universal applicability of the hypothesis that democracies do not fight one another. In this connection, some have asserted that democratization would make Arab and Islamic countries more rather than less prone to go to war, at least against non-Islamic democracies, since their governments would be more responsive to the allegedly militant and belligerent Muslim masses.[33]

Findings from the present study do not lend support to these arguments. Attachment to Islam, defined in terms of piety, observance, and an inclination to seek guidance from religious sources, bears no relationship to attitudes about the most important interstate conflict in the Middle East. It is true that support for Islamist movements and political formulae is associated with opposition to peace, but the basis of such support is to a considerable extent political, as much or often more than it is religious or ideological. Indeed, as noted earlier, the bivariate correlation between support for political Islam and personal religiosity is usually weak and in some cases does not attain even minimal statistical significance.

As discussed earlier, this finding derives additional significance from the national and temporal differences encompassed by the data. Although additional tests would of course be desirable, confidence in both the accuracy and generalizability of the relationships reported above is enhanced significantly by the fact that they were observed in three very different political and social settings and also both before and after such watershed events in recent Middle Eastern history as the crisis in the Gulf and the Oslo Accord.

The data from Jordan and Lebanon permit further examination of the relationship between attitudes toward political Islam and those pertaining to the Arab-Israeli conflict. They also extend the database for some observations about the explanatory utility of other independent variables, those not involving religious orientations. The regression analyses for these two countries are presented in Table 10.6.

In both the Jordanian and Lebanese cases, support for political Islam bears the same highly significant and inverse relationship to support for Arab-Israeli peace that was observed in the Egyptian, Kuwaiti, and Palestinian cases. Confidence in the accuracy and generalizability of this finding is thus further enhanced. Moreover, the constancy of this pattern across five different societies and two different time periods hints at another, broader conclusion about the relationship between religion and attitudes toward international conflict. Whereas research on the connection between religious and political attitudes has not produced consistent findings in more secular Western societies, the pattern observed in the Arab countries of the Middle East is notable for its uniformity across space and time. The consistent finding of no relationship between personal piety and attitudes toward international conflict in the Arab world, in those instances where data are available, offers additional

Table 10.6. Multiple Regression of Factors Influencing
Attitudes toward Peace in Jordan and Lebanon

	JORDAN	LEBANON
Political Islam	−1.02	−2.18
	(−3.31)**	(−4.15)**
Sex	−.18	−.38
	(−.594)	(−1.14)
Education	−.12	−.06
	(−1.065)	(−.45)
Age	−.11	−.00
	(−.902)	(−.00)
Economic Security	.88	.28
	(2.434)*	(1.38)
Constant	3.80	4.88
	(3.493)	(5.23)
R^2	0.13	0.29
N	135	160

Note: Numbers in parentheses are t scores.
*$p < .05$, **$p < .01$

evidence that the impact of religious orientations tends to be more uniform and constant than in countries that are less secular.

Although more research in both the Middle East and the West is obviously required, it is reasonable to suggest, on the basis of available evidence, that the nature and salience of religion's explanatory power may not be the same in the Muslim Middle East and the more secular West. Accordingly, in the language of comparative analysis, this means that attributes that differentiate these world regions must be incorporated as systemic variables into attempts to derive generalizable insights. One hypothesis suggested by the present study is that relationships between particular religious orientations and attitudes toward international conflict are more consistent over space and time in regions where secularism is less pronounced.

To conclude, some brief observations pertaining to other independent variables may be offered. Findings about these variables are not always consistent and, in any event, are of only secondary interest to the present study.

Nevertheless, there are several interesting relationships, some of which identify promising areas for future research. To begin, the absence of any significant relationship involving sex deserves mention. Although some scholars hypothesize that women are more pacifistic than men,[34] it appears that this is not the case in the Middle East. This point has been elaborated elsewhere and demonstrated with survey data from Israel as well as the Arab world.[35]

The explanatory power of perceived economic security is also significant. In Egypt, Palestine, and Jordan, but not in Kuwait or Lebanon, respondents having more economic worries express less support for Arab-Israeli peace. This demonstrates both that economic considerations help to shape attitudes toward international conflict and that this may be the case only under certain conditions. Furthermore, because Kuwait and Lebanon are the more prosperous of the counties considered in this study, it may be hypothesized that perceived economic insecurity pushes toward opposition to peace in countries that are less prosperous but not in countries that are more prosperous.

A related consideration is that income, unlike perceived economic security, is not related to attitudes about the conflict in any of the cases for which data are available. This suggests that national as opposed to personal economic issues may be important in shaping attitudes toward international affairs. This proposition, which deserves further study, is consistent with findings about the determinants of political attitudes in Western countries.[36] It also receives support from a recent investigation that found similar results using survey data from Israel.[37] Coupled with the present study's finding that support for political Islam but not personal religiosity accounts for variance in attitudes toward the Arab-Israeli conflict, this suggests that assessments pertaining to society as a whole have a much greater impact on attitudes toward international conflict than do the attributes and circumstances of respondents themselves.

Conclusion

The principal goal of this study has been to assess the impact of religious orientations on attitudes toward international conflict using survey data from Arab countries. The results are clear and consistent. An empirical distinction between personal and political dimensions of religion emerges in all cases where the data permit relevant analysis, and the relationship between each dimension and attitudes toward the Arab-Israeli conflict is the same in all the Arab countries examined. Specifically, support for political Islam is consistently associated with unfavorable attitudes toward a peaceful resolution of the conflict, and personal piety is consistently unrelated to attitudes toward the conflict.

These findings indicate that while religion influences political attitudes in the Arab world, a conclusion that is hardly surprising to those familiar with Muslim societies, not all dimensions of religion are equally important. They also suggest a more focused conclusion about the kinds of religious orientations most likely to have explanatory power. Judgments and prescriptions pertaining to societal affairs in general and to considerations of political economy in particular appear to be more important than those concerned with personal normative codes in shaping attitudes toward international conflict. This proposition, which receives support from findings about the importance of perceptions relating to national but not personal economic security, offers a promising area for future research.

Beyond this, the present study has asked whether and with what theoretical implications the nature and salience of religious influences appear to be different in the Arab Middle East and the more secular West. Given that empirical research is at an early stage both in the Arab world and the West, any serious response to this question is premature. At the same time, it is notable that the ambiguous and inconclusive character of the findings from research in the United States and Europe has not been replicated by the present study. This suggests, as another general proposition worthy of future research, that the role played by religion in shaping attitudes toward international and foreign policy concerns may be more uniform and consistent in societies without a strong tradition of secularism and less uniform and consistent in societies where religion is more fully privatized and separated from political life.

CHAPTER 11

Further Tests of the Women and Peace Hypothesis: Evidence from Cross-National Survey Research in the Middle East (1999)

Mark Tessler, Jodi Nachtwey, and Audra Grant

This research report replicates, extends, and adds a longitudinal dimension to a recently published analysis focusing on the relationship between sex and attitudes toward international conflict, and specifically on the hypothesis which asserts that women are more peace-oriented than men.[1] The study being replicated utilized public opinion data from Israel, Egypt, Palestine, and Kuwait. The present report extends the analysis, employing one additional data set from Israel, two additional data sets from Palestine, and new data sets from Jordan and Lebanon. The interrelated goals of the analysis are (1) to test further a social science hypothesis that purports to have explanatory power in diverse social and cultural contexts; (2) to compare findings from different Middle Eastern societies and different points in time in order to determine whether aggregate societal circumstances affect the applicability of this hypothesis; and (3) to compare findings from the Middle East to published findings based on research in the U.S. and Europe in order to investigate further the conditionalities associated with the women and peace hypothesis.

The Women and Peace Hypothesis

The women and peace hypothesis need only be considered briefly. It is discussed in a growing body of social science literature, much of which is reviewed in the research report referenced above. The hypothesis posits a distinction between the orientations of men and women regarding issues of war and peace. More specifically, it asserts that women are more pacifistic than men in their approach to international relations, being more accepting of compromise to resolve interstate disputes and less likely than men to believe that war is necessary or appropriate in particular conflict situations.

Competition, forcefulness, dominance, violence, intransigence, and territoriality are thus associated with a "male" approach to human relations, including relations between sovereign states, whereas moderation, accommodation, compromise, tolerance, and pacifism are seen as a "female" perspective on world affairs. The gendered division of power and violence to which this hypothesis calls attention is summarized in the following terms in a recent volume titled *Global Gender Issues:*

> Throughout history there have been numerous examples of women warriors, and women fighters exist today. In spite of this, there is a pervasive gender dichotomy that divides women and men into "life-givers" and "life-takers." . . . As life givers, women are not only prevented from engaging in combat, but are also expected to restore "life" after a death dealing war is over. Women are expected to mourn dutifully the loved ones who fell in war and then to produce new lives for the nation to replace its lost members. [Thus] in spite of their participation, women remain associated with war's opposite—peace.[2]

Feminist theorists offer a number of theoretical arguments in support of the women and peace hypothesis. Some emphasize the uniquely female experience of motherhood, seeking to establish a link between women and peace by celebrating the traditionally "female" attributes of caring and nurturance. Extended to the sphere of international relations, this "caregiving" perspective emphasizes the universal applicability of a predisposition toward nurturance and links women's roles as domestic caregivers to a more tolerant attitude toward the resolution of international conflicts.[3] Also advanced in this connection is the concept of "moral motherhood," which asserts that women as mothers have a responsibility to eliminate violence as a means for the resolution of conflict and to put in its place an orientation toward "maternal thinking" and "preservative love." This assertion, based on the proposition that maternal thinking derives from the social practice of mothering, reflects an effort to supplement or counterbalance theories of international relations that give priority to such "male" concepts as power, hegemony, and hierarchy.[4] While these theorists recognize that men are also capable of "maternal thinking," they point out that women usually have primary responsibility for child rearing and, accordingly, are more likely than men to develop the nurturing values hypothesized to be associated with nonviolent approaches to conflict resolution.

An alternative perspective argues that the orientations of women toward international relations are rooted less in maternal and other "female" experiences and more in women's marginality with respect to both the definition and exercise of political power. As one scholar notes, "since women have had less access to the instruments of coercion, they have been more apt to rely on power as persuasion."[5] As explained more fully in another analysis, "most male-dominated societies have constructed elaborate sanctions and even taboos against women fighting and dying in war. As a result, men have gained almost exclusive control over the means of destruction worldwide, often in the name of protecting women and children, who are either discouraged from or not allowed to take up arms to protect themselves."[6]

Still other theorists emphasize exposure to feminist politics as the basis for more peace-oriented attitudes among women.[7] Committed to values of freedom and equality, feminism seeks to expose and undermine social and political structures based on hierarchy, domination, and exploitation. The military is judged from this feminist perspective to embody these characteristics and is thus rejected as a legitimate instrument of foreign policy. This, in turn, encourages anti-militarism among individuals with feminist commitments, and for this reason women are more likely than men to have dovish views about issues of war and peace.

Finally, some theorists hypothesize that women's pacifistic tendencies are the result of economic marginality.[8] Because women make up a disproportionate share of the economically disadvantaged, they may be more sensitive to the cost of a militaristic foreign policy. In other words, high military expenditures may be viewed as a drain on the resources available for domestic social programs that are particularly important for women.

While the women and peace hypothesis has had a significant impact on contemporary thinking about the relationship between sex and international relations, it has also met with considerable criticism, including some by feminist scholars. For one thing, critics charge that an emphasis on the central experience of motherhood in the formation of normative predispositions and conceptions of citizenship fails to differentiate between women who do and do not have children. A related criticism is that approaches that emphasize caregiving and moral motherhood are unduly mechanistic, attributing cause and effect but failing to develop a coherent model of the pathway linking caregiving and maternal thinking to tolerance, compromise, and other peace-oriented political norms.[9]

A different kind of criticism is the contention that discourses that reify motherhood and family membership tend to reduce women to unidimensional actors and obscure the complex origins of their political orientations, including whatever tendency toward pacifism they may possess. In particular, critics charge that attributions of empathy, nurturance, and caring reinforce traditional stereotypes about women and retard the goal of emancipation. On the one hand, some postmodern feminist theorists insist that there are no "essential components" that characterize all women.[10] On the other, some assert that the emphasis on caring is itself misplaced, either seeing this as patronizing or disputing the hypothesized link to public and international affairs.[11]

It is also sometimes asserted in this connection that tolerance, empathy, and pacifism are not "female" norms, even socially constructed ones, but rather the norms of any population category that has traditionally had little opportunity to exercise power. According to this view, which is articulated by some feminist scholars as well as others, there is an association but not a causal connection between gender and peace. As expressed by one analyst, to the extent that women are more predisposed toward peace than men, it is at least partly because "the exercise of power has generally been a masculine activity: women have rarely exercised legitimate power in the public domain."[12]

Prior Research in the U.S. and Elsewhere

Beyond the question of *why* women and men have different attitudes toward issues of war and peace, an entirely different concern is *whether* the hypothesized sex-linked difference actually exists. The basis of this concern is neither epistemological nor philosophical but rather empirical. Until fairly recently, few studies provided rigorous and systematic tests of the women and peace hypothesis. Further, those available provided inconsistent findings and were largely limited to the United States.

More recent scholarship has expanded the empirical foundation for assessing the hypothesized relationship, although the findings from this research do not lead to unambiguous conclusions. On the one hand, polls conducted in the 1980s found significant differences between American men and women with respect to military aid, the use of U.S. troops, and the containment of communism.[13] Other studies have found that American men are more supportive of militarism and war involvement than American women by an average of seven to nine percentage points.[14]

Alternatively, other data-based investigations report no sex-linked differences in general militarism. Among these is a study based on data from the 1991 American National Election Study Pilot Study.[15] Conover and Sapiro report in this study that women were less supportive than men of U.S. involvement in the 1990–91 Gulf War but not of militarism in general, and they accordingly speculate that sex-linked differences may exist in relation to concrete but not hypothetical war situations. But even in the former instance, the authors add, differences are "by no means large enough to divide men and women into different camps, and they are certainly not large enough to warrant making the kinds of sweeping statements differentiating women and men that have long been part of [the popular] stereotype."[16]

Other analyses of attitudes toward the Gulf War are consistent with the Conover and Sapiro findings. For example, Bendyna et al. report gender gaps in responses to almost fifty questions about the war's initiation and conduct.[17] These items measure support for the war, support for military force, evaluations of the war's impact, optimism about war costs, concern about casualties, emotional reactions, and attentiveness to Gulf War news. Earlier research on the Gulf War has also reported statistically significant gender differences regarding the use of military force.[18] In both studies, however, the authors point out that sex-linked differences are not large and that men and women are much more likely to agree than disagree on matters of military action.

Evidence from other countries also sheds light on the women and peace hypothesis. In Denmark, for example, polls conducted in the 1980s revealed women to be more supportive of defense budget cuts and the peace movement, as well as aid to developing countries.[19] Another study reported a tendency for women to be more "dovish" on issues of war and peace in four of the six European countries examined.[20] Patterns in the latter study were not consistent, however, varying not only across countries but also according to such issues as support for peace movements, military spending, and expectations about future war and increasing violence.

Cross-national research is needed not only to test the generalizability of conclusions drawn from studies conducted in the United States; it can also help to uncover the conditions under which gender differences do and do not exist. This is illustrated by a comparative study of cities in eleven different countries, in which Wilcox, Hewitt, and Allsop found that women were significantly less likely than men to support military action in nine of the eleven countries, even after controlling for demographic characteristics and political views.[21] The exceptions to this pattern were Turkey and Nigeria, two of the three developing countries in the study. The third developing country was Mexico.

The comparative dimension of the Wilcox, Hewitt, and Allsop study indicated that the existence of a gender gap in attitudes toward war and peace was not consistently related either to the presence of a strong feminist movement or to the local salience of the Gulf War. Alternatively, since sex-linked differences were not observed in the two predominantly Muslim countries, Turkey and Nigeria, the authors speculated that either cultural factors associated with Islam or the existence of strong anti-imperialist sentiments may constitute conditions under which the women and peace hypothesis does not apply.

Comparison and Replication

Expanding research beyond the U.S. and Europe is necessary both to assess the generalizability of gender differences observed in Western countries and to identify the conditions under which these differences do and do not exist. It is within this comparative framework that the present study, as well as the research here being replicated and extended, seeks to make a contribution.

Using nine public opinion data sets collected through surveys in six Middle Eastern societies, the present study involves something of a "most different systems" research design.[22] Included in the study are monarchies, autocracies, democracies, and one stateless society. The countries also differ significantly with respect to size, level of economic development, religion, religious and ethnic heterogeneity, and strength of the domestic women's movements. Thus, if the same pattern is found in all the countries examined, this pattern will have been demonstrated to obtain under widely varying conditions and confidence in its generalizability will be high. Depending on the specific nature of the findings, similar patterns observed in each country will significantly increase confidence either that the women and peace hypothesis is correct or that it is incorrect and has no explanatory power.

Different findings in the cases will lead to different conclusions. Should the hypothesized attitudinal differences between men and women be found in some countries but not others, the distribution of these dissimilar findings can be linked to aggregate political and social system attributes in order to identify conditionalities associated with the hypothesis. For example, if findings about the relationship between sex and attitudes toward international conflict are not the same in countries that are more developed and less developed, more democratic and less democratic, or more secular and less secular, the characteristics of those national systems where a positive association has been observed constitute conditions under which sex is of value in accounting for attitudinal variation.

Further, the identification of conditionalities can help to determine not only *when* but also *why* there are or are not significant differences between the attitudes of women and men toward issues of war and peace. For example, as noted above, the Wilcox, Hewitt, and Allsop study suggested that cultural factors associated with Islam and/or the existence of anti-imperialist sentiments may explain the absence of gender differences in attitudes toward the Gulf War. These and other possibilities can also be tested with the present study's data from the Middle East. These data are drawn from both Muslim and non-Muslim Middle Eastern populations, and from countries in which anti-imperialist sentiments are present to varying degrees.[23]

Longitudinal comparison provides an additional opportunity to identify systemic factors associated with the women and peace hypothesis. This includes a comparison of findings based on data from Israel collected at two different points in time, one during the *intifada* and before the Gulf War and the other after the Gulf War and at a time when the Palestinian uprising had lost much of its momentum. A temporal dimension is also present in the Arab data sets, two of which are from the earlier period and five of which are not only from the latter period but from the period following the 1993 Israel-PLO agreement as well. Despite a measure of overdetermination, this makes it possible to address the question of generalization not only across space but also across time and, in particular, to determine whether important conflict-related events, such as the *intifada,* the Gulf War, and the Oslo Accord between the PLO and Israel, affect the relationship between sex and attitudes toward war and peace. If this is found to be the case, these events, like the national characteristics investigated in cross-sectional comparisons, will shed light on conditionalities defining the locus of the relationship between gender and attitudes toward international conflict.

Finally, the importance of replication and cumulativeness may be briefly noted in this context. Extending and replicating earlier analyses provides a basis for assessing the confidence that published findings deserve. Moreover, replications serve this purpose not only when they challenge existing findings but also when they validate earlier research.[24] In addition, replication permits expanding the range of points in space and time from which observations are drawn, which is essential for generalization and also, when appropriate, for identifying conditionalities that define the locus of variable relationships.[25] Replication is thus an indispensable component of the scientific method and an absolute requirement for the cumulative production of knowledge.

Data and Findings

Detailed information about data sources, research design, and methodology is presented in the publication referenced earlier, as well as in several other papers based on some of the available data sets.[26] Accordingly, only a summary account of these considerations is presented here.

One of the two Israeli data sets was collected in 1989 and is from a national sample of persons over the age of eighteen residing in four hundred randomly selected urban Jewish households. Polling was done by the Dahaf Agency, which conducted the survey as part of a broad program of research on women and war designed by Professors Galia Golan and Naomi Chazan of the Hebrew University of Jerusalem. The sample yielded usable responses from 985 individuals, including 534 women and 451 men. The second Israeli data set was collected in 1991 and is from a national random sample commissioned by the German magazine *Der Spiegel.* A total of 993 Jewish Israelis were interviewed.

The Egyptian and Kuwaiti data were collected in 1988 and are from stratified and broadly representative samples of Muslim adults residing in

Cairo and Kuwait City. The surveys were conducted under the supervision of Professor Jamal Sanad Al-Suwaidi of the Emirates Center for Strategic Studies and Research, who designed the project in collaboration with one of the authors of the present study. The actual interviews, based on a stratified quota sample of 295 Egyptians and 300 Kuwaitis, were conducted by research assistants selected on the basis of previous experience in survey research administration.

The Jordanian and Lebanese data were collected in 1994 and are based on random samples in major cities—Amman, Irbid, and Zarqa in Jordan and Beirut, Sidon, and Tripoli in Lebanon. The surveys, which include interviews with 251 Jordanians and 252 Lebanese over the age of eighteen, were carried out by the Market Research Organization of Amman, Jordan. The data were subsequently purchased off-the-shelf by the Office of Research of the United States Information Service and made available to the authors of the present study.

The Palestinian data were collected by the Palestine Center for Research and Studies (CPRS), which has been using area probability sampling to conduct regular polls of West Bank and Gaza residents since September 1993. The Palestinian data employed in the previously published study were collected in 1994 and are from a sample of 1,228 adults, including 754 residents of the West Bank and 474 residents of Gaza. The present report also uses two subsequent CPRS surveys, one conducted in 1995 and the other in 1996. The 1995 survey instrument was administered to a representative sample of 1,184 respondents, including 740 residents of the West Bank and 444 residents of Gaza. The 1996 survey instrument was administered to a representative sample of 980 respondents, including 607 residents of the West Bank and 373 residents of Gaza.

The dependent variable in the present analysis is attitude toward the conflict between Israel and the Palestinians and other Arabs, with respondents rated according to the degree of their support for, or opposition to, a peaceful resolution of the conflict based on territorial compromise and mutual recognition between Israelis and Palestinians. As in the earlier study, factor analysis has been employed to identify items from the survey instruments that provide a reliable measure of attitudes toward the conflict, and the items that ask about the conflict and have high loadings on a common factor have in each case been combined to form an attitudinal scale. Table 11.1 lists the items that have been used to construct this scale for each of the data sets used in the present study. The factor loadings of these items are given as well.

Table 11.2 shows the relationship between gender and attitudes toward the Arab-Israeli conflict for all nine of the data sets. Ratings on the scale

Table 11.1. Item Loadings on Factor Measuring Attitudes
toward the Israeli-Palestinian Conflict

Israel 1989

Would you be willing to return either all or some of the occupied
territories in return for a peace agreement with the Arabs?   .69419

Do you prefer to address the problem of the West Bank and Gaza
by exchanging them for peace, by giving the Palestinians partial
autonomy, or by removing the Arab population from these territories? .64914

Do you agree or disagree that Israel should consider permitting the
establishment of a Palestinian state?   .54507

Do you think the real aim of the Palestinians is to establish a state
alongside Israel or to destroy the Jewish state and drive out its
population?   .52313

Israel 1991

Use the following 11-point scale, ranging from 5 (highly sympathetic)
to −5 (highly unsympathetic) to express the degree of your support
for the Palestinian cause.   .76550

In your opinion, which of the following solutions, ranging from
Palestinian statehood to complete Israeli annexation, is the best way
to resolve the status of the West Bank (Judea and Samaria) and Gaza? .74283

Egypt 1988

Do you believe that the Arab-Israeli conflict can be solved by
diplomacy or is a military solution required?   .86036

Do you agree or disagree that peace with Israel is both desirable
and possible?   .62474

Kuwait 1988

Do you believe that the Arab-Israeli conflict can be solved by
diplomacy or is a military solution required?   .79864

Do you agree or disagree that peace with Israel is both desirable
and possible?   .78454

Table 11.1. Item Loadings on Factor Measuring Attitudes toward the Israeli-Palestinian Conflict (continued)

Palestine 1994

Which political faction do you prefer, one that does or one that does
not favor territorial compromise to resolve the conflict with Israel?   .77115

Do you support or oppose the conduct of armed operations against
Israeli targets in Gaza and Jericho?   .76479

Palestine 1995

Do you agree or disagree that peace negotiations with Israel
should continue?   .72057

Do you or do you not expect the achievement of a lasting peace
with Israel?   .60347

Palestine 1996

Do you agree or disagree that peace negotiations with Israel
should continue?   .76717

Do you support or oppose the current peace process?   .78939

Do you believe that final status negotiations can produce an
acceptable solution to the conflict with Israel?   .59224

Jordan 1994

To what extent do you favor diplomatic relations with Israel?   .91676

To what extent do you approve of the PLO-Israel agreement?   .87477

To what extent are you satisfied with the policies being pursued
by Yasir Arafat?   .85009

Lebanon 1994

To what extent do you favor diplomatic relations with Israel?   .92109

To what extent do you approve of the PLO-Israel agreement?   .93366

To what extent are you satisfied with the policies being pursued
by Yasir Arafat?   .45131

measuring the dependent variable have been trichotomized, as in the earlier analysis, and chi square has been computed in each instance to determine whether there is a statistically significant difference between the attitudes of men and women. The earlier study found that neither in the 1989 Israeli sample nor in the Egyptian, Kuwaiti, and 1994 Palestinian samples was there a significant difference in the attitudes expressed by men and women toward issues of war and peace. As shown in Table 11.2, this same pattern, that of no significant relationship, characterizes all the additional data sets included in the present investigation. In the absence of any significant bivariate relationships, it has not been necessary to address the issue of spuriousness in causal inference through the use of multivariate statistical techniques. In fact, however, sex has been included in regression models using many of the same data sets to examine other determinants of attitudes toward the Arab-Israeli conflict, and in no case has it been related to the dependent variable to a statistically significant degree.[27]

Table 11.3 adds to the analysis a within-system dimension that was not present in the earlier inquiry. Specifically, it disaggregates each sample on the basis of religiosity and then examines the relationship between gender and attitudes toward the conflict separately for more and less religious respondents. Religiosity is measured in both Israeli samples through a self-identification question. There is no item dealing with religiosity in the 1994 and 1996 Palestinian samples, which accordingly are not included in Table 11.3. The other Arab samples, including the 1995 Palestinian survey, contained a number of items dealing with religiosity and religious attachments, and in each case factor analysis was employed and the item loading highest on a religiosity factor was then dichotomized to form the categories used in Table 11.3.

The rationale for this disaggregation is the possibility that religiosity influences attitudes toward war and peace to such an extent that other independent variables, such as sex, will have explanatory power only among less religious individuals. This possibility seems particularly likely given the strong association between religion and politics in both Israel and the Arab world. In fact, however, as Table 11.3 demonstrates, in no instance, neither among less religious respondents nor among more religious respondents in any of the samples, is there a statistically significant relationship between sex and attitudes toward the Arab-Israeli conflict.

Conclusion

The consistent finding of no relationship provides compelling evidence that the women and peace hypothesis does not apply in the Middle East, or at least not in the case of the Arab-Israeli conflict. This conclusion is reinforced

Table 11.2. Relationship between Gender and Attitudes toward the Arab-Israeli Conflict among Israeli, Egyptian, Kuwaiti, Palestinian, Jordanian, and Lebanese Respondents

	SUPPORTS COMPROMISE, DIPLOMACY, AND/OR NONVIOLENT MEANS OF RESOLVING ARAB-ISRAELI CONFLICT	FEMALE	MALE	TOTAL
Israel 1989	Highly Supportive	35%	33%	34%
$X^2 = .44$	Somewhat Supportive	31%	34%	32%
$df = 2$				
$p > .05$	Not Supportive	34%	33%	34%
	TOTAL	475	382	857
Israel 1991	Highly Supportive	35%	32%	34%
$X^2 = 1.74$	Somewhat Supportive	37%	35%	36%
$df = 2$				
$p > .05$	Not Supportive	28%	33%	30%
	TOTAL	498	495	993
Egypt 1988	Highly Supportive	83%	90%	87%
$X^2 = 3.13$	Somewhat or not	17%	10%	13%
$df = 1$	Supportive			
$p > .05$				
	TOTAL	133	141	274
Kuwait 1988	Highly Supportive	24%	25%	25%
$X^2 = .69$	Somewhat Supportive	33%	29%	31%
$df = 2$				
$p > .05$	Not Supportive	43%	46%	44%
	TOTAL	148	136	284
Palestine 1994	Highly Supportive	51%	53%	52%
$X^2 = 1.14$	Somewhat Supportive	35%	35%	35%
$df = 2$				
$p > .05$	Not Supportive	14%	12%	13%
	TOTAL	619	609	1228

Table 11.2. (continued)

	SUPPORTS COMPROMISE, DIPLOMACY, AND/OR NONVIOLENT MEANS OF RESOLVING ARAB-ISRAELI CONFLICT	FEMALE	MALE	TOTAL
Palestine 1995	Highly Supportive	24%	26%	25%
$X^2 = .77$	Somewhat Supportive	57%	54%	55%
$df = 2$				
$p > .05$	Not Supportive	19%	20%	20%
	TOTAL	504	522	1026
Palestine 1996	Highly Supportive	35%	34%	35%
$X^2 = .98$	Somewhat Supportive	36%	37%	36%
$df = 2$				
$p > .05$	Not Supportive	29%	29%	29%
	TOTAL	476	491	967
Jordan 1994	Highly Supportive	33%	34%	33%
$X^2 = 3.78$	Somewhat Supportive	15%	26%	21%
$df = 2$				
$p > .05$	Not Supportive	52%	40%	46%
	TOTAL	79	83	162
Lebanon 1994	Highly Supportive	36%	36%	36%
$X^2 = 3.26$	Somewhat Supportive	19%	28%	23%
$df = 2$				
$p > .05$	Not Supportive	45%	36%	41%
	TOTAL	107	103	210

by the comparative dimension of the present study. As noted, the cases, taken together, constitute something of a most different systems research design. The countries from which data have been drawn differ significantly with respect to political, economic, and cultural characteristics. Further, there is temporal as well as cross-national diversity, with some data sets collected before and other data sets collected after several watershed events in recent

Table 11.3. Relationship between Gender and Attitudes toward the Arab-Israeli Conflict among More Religious Respondents and Less Religious Respondents from Israel, Egypt, Kuwait, Jordan, and Lebanon

Israel 1989	More religious	$X^2 = 0.63, df = 2, p > .05$
	Less religious	$X^2 = 0.35, df = 2, p > .05$
Israel 1991	More religious	$X^2 = 2.05, df = 2, p > .05$
	Less religious	$X^2 = 1.52, df = 2, p > .05$
Egypt 1988	More religious	$X^2 = 3.14, df = 2, p > .05$
	Less religious	$X^2 = 0.62, df = 2, p > .05$
Kuwait 1988	More religious	$X^2 = 3.04, df = 2, p > .05$
	Less religious	$X^2 = 0.64, df = 2, p > .05$
Palestine 1995	More religious	$X^2 = 0.92, df = 2, p > .05$
	Less religious	$X^2 = 0.36, df = 2, p > .05$
Jordan 1994	More religious	$X^2 = 1.53, df = 2, p > .05$
	Less religious	$X^2 = 2.34, df = 2, p > .05$
Lebanon 1994	More religious	$X^2 = 1.15, df = 2, p > .05$
	Less religious	$X^2 = 4.28, df = 2, p > .05$

Middle Eastern history. Finally, level of personal religiosity has been introduced as a within-system "specification" variable, with the hypothesized relationship examined among both more religious and less religious respondents. All these characteristics define conditions under which, at least in a Middle Eastern context and at least with respect to one specific and highly salient international conflict, the women and peace hypothesis does not apply.

This conclusion is at variance with findings from research in the United States and other Western countries, which has begun to provide evidence that men and women may indeed have different attitudes toward international conflict. These findings are not entirely consistent, and more research in the West, as well as elsewhere, is needed to determine the extent and locus of attitudinal differences between women and men. Nevertheless, recent research in the U.S. and Europe tends to point to a different conclusion than does the present study based on data from the Middle East about sex-linked differences in attitudes toward issues of war and peace.

There are two possible ways to account for this disparity of findings, and each can only be pursued through additional comparative research. The first is that one set of conclusions is inaccurate, presumably because the data are unrepresentative or because results are biased by other limitations. In the case of Western surveys, for example, the observed gender differences have tended to be small and are based to a significant degree on attitudes toward a particular international conflict, the Gulf War. Seen from this perspective, the present study's findings from the Middle East raise serious questions about the accuracy of the women and peace hypothesis. They reinforce the assessment of Conover and Sapiro, noted earlier, that available evidence does not "warrant making the kinds of sweeping statements differentiating women and men that have long been part of [the popular] stereotype."[28]

The second possibility, which seems equally likely if not more so and which also is potentially more instructive, is that both sets of findings are accurate and that theory construction can be advanced by seeking to identify conditions under which the attitudes of men and women do and do not differ. Religion represents one potentially important conditionality, since there are clear religious differences between the Middle East and the West. Moreover, this is consistent with the speculation advanced by Wilcox, Hewitt, and Allsop to explain the cross-national differences found in their eleven-country study. This explanation is not fully convincing, however. Sex-linked differences failed to emerge in non-Muslim Israel as well as in Arab and Islamic countries. They also failed to emerge when the attitudes of less religious and more religious individuals were examined separately. If religion did constitute an important conditionality, attitudinal differences between women and men would presumably have been more pronounced among less religious respondents.

The anti-imperialism thesis proposed by Wilcox and his coauthors might seem to offer a more persuasive interpretation. A fear that peace will increase the dominance of imperialist powers, which is how the United States and Israel are seen by many Arabs and Muslims, might constitute a conditionality that accounts for differences between the Middle East and the West. According to this thesis, anti-imperialism overrides gender and thus eliminates sex-linked differences in regions that perceive themselves to be victims of Western imperialism. Again, however, the present study does not support this interpretation. Not only were gender differences absent in Israel, which does not share the anti-imperialist impulses of the Arab world, they were also absent in Kuwait, a wealthy Arab state whose citizens for the most part support the status quo and benefit from the projection of U.S. power into the Middle East.

Another possibility is that variation in the relative strength of feminist movements explains why attitudinal differences between men and women are greater in the West than in the Middle East. This, too, is not entirely convincing. There is much variation among the Middle Eastern countries included in the present study with respect to the strength and influence of feminism, and gender differences in attitudes toward international conflict are absent in those with stronger as well as those with weaker feminist movements. Nor did the Wilcox et al. study find cross-national variation in the strength of feminist movements to be correlated with different findings about the women and peace hypothesis. On the other hand, despite considerable variation among Western countries and among Middle East countries, it is at least possible that between-region variance substantially exceeds within-region variance, and that this difference does help to explain why competing conclusions are reached by studies in these different parts of the world. Lending credibility to this suggestion is the fact that even in Israel, which is among the Middle Eastern countries where opportunities for women are greatest, the feminist movement is not particularly well developed.[29]

A final possibility concerns salience, which has been discussed elsewhere as having the potential either to increase or to diminish sex-linked differences in attitudes toward international conflict.[30] In the present study, it may be the high salience of the Arab-Israeli conflict, compared to the lesser salience of the conflicts considered in research in the West, that explains why men and women do not have differing attitudes in Middle Eastern countries but do in some Western settings.

The Arab-Israeli conflict is a central preoccupation in the Middle East to a degree that far exceeds that of the Gulf War or issues of military spending in the U.S. and Europe. Most Arabs and Israelis have grown up with this conflict, which is a, and in most cases the, primary foreign policy issue for both individuals and states. In this context, it is possible that the immediacy and intensity of concerns about national security, collective identity, and resource allocation override the influence of gender and explain why, for this particular conflict, the sex-linked differences found in the West have not been observed in the Middle East.

This explanation is not without problems. If salience is an important factor, it might be expected that gender differences would be absent in Israel and Palestine but existent in some countries, such as Kuwait. As emphasized above, however, concern about the conflict is intense throughout the Arab world. Further, in the case of Kuwait, data were collected at the height of the Palestinian *intifada,* giving the conflict a particularly high level of visibility. Finally, a recent study in Northern Ireland also found no gender differences in attitudes toward the intense and highly salient conflict in that country. According to the author, "it is not possible to draw a simple distinction between women and men in terms of their attitudes toward the violent conflict [in the country]. In terms of attitudes toward violence, [other factors are] more important than gender in shaping individual responses."[31]

The notion of salience suggests that the characteristics of the conflict about which attitudes are held may be more important than country or regional attributes in accounting for differences in findings about the women and peace hypothesis. More research is needed, of course, to assess this and the other explanations that have been considered. Further, it is at least possible that such research may eventually demonstrate that there are no significant differences between patterns in the West and patterns in the Middle East, the appearance of difference having been the result of data limitations. Assuming this is not the case, however, the conclusion to which the present study points is that men and women will not hold different attitudes toward international conflict when this concerns a conflict that is concrete, intense, long-standing, familiar, and perhaps to some extent existential, and for these reasons highly salient.

CHAPTER 12

The Political Economy of Attitudes toward Peace among Palestinians and Israelis (2002)

Jodi Nachtwey and Mark Tessler

The Arab-Israeli dispute has played a critical role in shaping the political landscape of the Middle East and has been the focus of considerable social science research. Only a small portion of this research has explored the determinants of popular attitudes toward the conflict, however, and the factors that shape Palestinian public opinion have been particularly neglected. The present study responds to this gap by investigating factors that influence how ordinary Palestinian and Israeli citizens think about the conflict.

Understanding popular attitudes toward issues of war and peace may be approached from different theoretical perspectives. The political culture approach, for instance, is prevalent among scholars who argue that shared norms and values are the basis of political attitudes. In the context of the Middle East, this approach often regards religion and religiosity as critical influences on views about conflict, and it often links strong religious attachments to aggressiveness, militancy, and opposition to compromise. We have pursued this approach elsewhere in some detail, focusing on the influence of Islamic orientations and finding that religious piety has little explanatory power among Muslims in Palestine and four other Arab countries.[1]

By contrast, support for political Islam does have an impact on attitudes toward the conflict, but this nonetheless leaves most of the variance unexplained. Finally, we have also tested the hypothesis that women are more predisposed toward peace than men are. We analyzed nine data sets from Israel and five Arab countries, including Palestine, and found no evidence of a significant sex-linked difference in any of the analyses.[2]

Against this background, with considerable variance remaining unexplained, we use the present analysis to explore economic, rather than cultural or demographic, influences. This approach, often described as a political economy perspective, is based on the belief that political attitudes are shaped at least partly by economic conditions and by judgments about the ability of political leaders to promote economic well-being. This belief is supported by research in the United States and other Western democracies, which has been useful in delineating the conceptual and empirical linkages between economic variables and various political attitudes and behavior patterns. Economic influences are likely to be important in other settings, too, including not only democratic Israel but also the non- or quasi-democratic Palestinian case. On the one hand, economic problems have contributed to increasing public dissatisfaction with government leaders and policies, especially among Palestinians. On the other hand, financial considerations have become an increasingly important aspect of Palestinian-Israeli relations.

In applying this political economy perspective, the present analysis assesses the degree to which economic evaluations help to explain attitudes toward the Palestinian-Israeli conflict in the years following the 1993 Oslo Accords. It first applies insights from political science and economics to the Israeli-Palestinian context, deriving testable hypotheses that are applicable both to the conflict and to social science inquiry more broadly. The proposed relationships are then tested using recent survey data from Israel and Palestine. Findings show that economic evaluations are indeed important to understanding views about the conflict and its resolution.

The Economics of Political Behavior

Strategic Calculations

A rational choice perspective offers the most direct way to conceptualize the relationship between economic considerations and opinions about international conflict. This approach is grounded in the assumption that political judgments result from individual cost-benefit calculations. Citizens consider how policy outcomes will affect their well-being and then give or withhold their support based on these expectations. Research in the United States, for example, demonstrates that Americans often perceive trade-offs between foreign policy and domestic objectives. One study shows that decreased support for defense spending coincides with increases in the national deficit, indicating that economic constraints influence views about foreign affairs.[3] Other research reports that Americans are less likely to support an interventionist foreign policy if they believe that domestic issues, especially economic ones, are the nation's priorities.[4]

The nature of the relationship between economic perceptions and attitudes toward international conflict may depend on the particular way that individuals link domestic conditions to foreign policy goals. Those who blame economic problems at least partly on an international dispute may be more likely to support efforts to reach a timely and peaceful resolution of that dispute. In this case, prolonged conflict is viewed as a drain on resources, a constraint on the free flow of trade and capital, or some other impediment to economic improvement. Alternatively, citizens may view an international conflict as a means to improve the economic situation, possibly through the acquisition of resources or by challenging the existing domestic or international economic power structure.

Such calculations become more complicated when evaluated in relative rather than absolute terms. Scholars of international political economy often contrast liberal and realist ideological perspectives in this regard.[5] To liberals, international economics and politics run largely independent courses. The nature of the market, if left unencumbered by political obstacles, will foster productive economic relationships as states seek to enhance their comparative advantage. The result is increased wealth and economic growth for all actors. The political consequences are advantageous as well. To sustain a mutually advantageous economic situation, states have a great incentive to cooperate and peacefully resolve any conflicts that arise.

For realists, political and economic objectives are interwoven, with political power, rather than wealth, the most important national objective. Although economic relations may enhance political and military power, they may also reduce state power. For example, powerful states may benefit disproportionately from economic arrangements, thereby perpetuating existing inequalities and making other states more vulnerable. For this reason, realists are less concerned with the absolute benefits that economic cooperation may bring than with the distribution of such benefits and its effect on the overall balance of power. Accordingly, they are more likely than liberals to anticipate the possible negative consequences of economic interaction.

Thus, in addition to considering the potential for economic advantage, citizen attitudes toward international conflict may reflect strategic calculations about the consequences of a particular foreign policy. Citizens with a realist outlook would tend to evaluate foreign policy less on the basis of absolute socioeconomic benefits and more in terms of relative gain or loss in the political as well as the economic arena. Potential economic gain in this case would not be sufficient to produce support for either pursuing or seeking to resolve an international conflict if to do so would increase the relative political power of an adversary.

The Importance of Confidence

A less direct but no less useful way to theorize about the relationship between economic perceptions and international conflict is through the linkages examined by scholars of political behavior. Their research has demonstrated that economic conditions and perceptions of these conditions have considerable influence on voting behavior, incumbent satisfaction, and policy support.[6] In general, these studies demonstrate that economic problems and citizen dissatisfaction with economic performance reduce support for the political status quo.

Economic performance influences more than judgments about government officials and policies, however. A number of scholars contend that economic concerns, including perceptions of poor economic performance, are associated not only with lower levels of incumbent support but also with diminished trust in public institutions and reduced satisfaction with democracy.[7] Similarly, a cross-national study of European countries reports that inflation and unemployment have a direct influence on support for political reform, as well as an indirect impact through such variables as life satisfaction and satisfaction with democracy.[8] Confidence in the political order is thus grounded in the government's ability to meet public needs by ensuring a stable and healthy economy. Persistent failure to do so, by contrast, may undermine government legitimacy and erode confidence in the regime itself.

Constraints on public policy, including foreign policy, may be an additional consequence of distrust and dissatisfaction. If citizens distrust the motives of their leaders and doubt their ability or desire to defend the public good, they are less likely to give these leaders discretion in policy making, thereby limiting their room for maneuver and innovation.[9] Put differently, a government's inability to solve economic problems may foster doubt about its policies more broadly. Many of its policies may be discredited in the eyes of those who believe it is misguided, corrupt, or both.

In sum, the theoretical linkage between economic considerations and attitudes toward foreign policy may be direct or indirect. In the former case, citizens judge foreign policy alternatives by weighing costs and benefits and then give or withhold support according to the socioeconomic consequences they expect to result from a particular policy. Moreover, this calculation may be made with strategic considerations in mind, so that costs and benefits are also considered in relation to the implications for other actors, particularly adversaries. In the latter case, support or opposition to a particular foreign policy may be determined to a greater degree by confidence in the government. The substantive qualities of an individual policy mean little if the government is viewed as being too inept or dishonest to implement it effectively and with the public interest at heart. Policy alternatives thus may not be evaluated independently, with respect to their merits, but rather in terms of confidence in the policy's architects. Although distinct, these theoretical approaches are not mutually exclusive. Citizens may use or combine both types of reasoning when formulating opinions about foreign policy, including issues of war and peace.

Although grounded primarily in research conducted in Western societies, these theoretical perspectives have implications for analyzing political attitudes in the Middle East. The following section thus considers how concerns of economic well-being, political vulnerability, and government legitimacy may influence attitudes toward compromise and reconciliation among Israelis and Palestinians.

The Economics of Attitudes toward the Israeli-Palestinian Conflict

Recent experience indicates that economic circumstances and perceptions may have significant political implications in the Middle East. Two arguments are presented below to link the economic concerns of ordinary citizens to their attitudes about the Israeli-Palestinian conflict. The first focuses on views about the economic dimension of Arab-Israeli relations. Fundamental to this approach is an understanding of the ways that citizens assess the economic costs and benefits of peace based on territorial compromise and mutual recognition. The second argument emphasizes perceptions of government legitimacy, considering whether and how judgments about government performance influence views about public policy, including foreign policy.

The Economics of Peace

Although attitudes toward the Palestinian-Israeli dispute are sometimes understood in moral, religious, or even existential terms, everyday socioeconomic concerns are also likely to influence the way that ordinary citizens view the conflict. The conflict is a daily reality, and attempts to resolve it have concrete implications. Thus, not surprisingly, previous research suggests that cost-benefit considerations are very useful in understanding Arab and Israeli attitudes. For example, a survey in Israel found that individuals are more likely to support the establishment of a Palestinian state if they expect this to increase their personal safety or improve their economic and social circumstances.[10]

THE PALESTINIAN CASE

The economic conditions of most Palestinians are dire. In 1998, 20 percent of Palestinian households earned incomes below the poverty line, and 21 percent of Palestine's citizens were either unemployed or underemployed.[11] Palestinians most likely have different views about the best strategy to improve their economic situation. For some, Israel is a potential source of income and economic development. By encouraging joint ventures and free trade with Israel, as well as labor mobility, the Palestinian economy can obtain desperately needed capital, technology, and employment opportunities.[12] Movement toward peace and normalized political relations are necessary to secure these economic benefits, however. Accordingly, Palestinians who emphasize these economic concerns should be more likely to support efforts at compromise and reconciliation in the expectation that this will improve Palestine's economic situation.

Reinforcing this perspective may be the perception of economic benefits associated with the Oslo peace process. Although employment and income levels declined immediately following the 1993 Oslo Accords, they subsequently increased.[13] These improvements are often linked to the peace process, which reduced closures and other security measures that restrict the movement of Palestinian goods and labor.[14] Many individuals may thus link continuing improvement in the economic arena to further progress in the political realm. A survey conducted in July 2000 shows that a large majority of Palestinians in the West Bank and Gaza favor an open economic relationship with Israel, presumably in the hope that the Palestinian economy will benefit.[15]

An alternative viewpoint considers the peace process a danger to Palestine's economic well-being. As reported in a survey conducted in 1999, it appears that many Palestinians, as well as Syrians, Jordanians, and Lebanese, believe that one of Israel's objectives in pursuing peace is to enhance its economic dominance.[16] According to another study, many Arabs fear that open economic relations with Israel would reinforce existing inequalities and exacerbate regional disparities in economic power.[17] Strong economic ties would also render Palestinian businesses dependent on Israel's economic cycles and political calculations, a relationship that is not reciprocal. It is probable that the reluctance of some Palestinians to endorse a negotiated settlement with Israel stems from concern about these disadvantageous economic consequences.

Existing economic patterns undoubtedly reinforce these Palestinian fears. A recent United Nations (UN) report expressed concern about the increased concentration of Palestinian trade with Israel. Although Palestinian exports were already heavily targeted toward Israel in 1990, representing 85 percent of all exports, 95 percent of all Palestinian products were intended for the Israeli market by 1998.[18] This situation almost certainly leads at least some Palestinians to conclude that normalized relations with Israel would be a threat to their own economic and political independence.

THE ISRAELI CASE

Israel is a prosperous country. Most citizens enjoy an adequate standard of living and economic conditions have been improving steadily in recent years. Furthermore, the country is democratic, so ordinary citizens have ample opportunity to express their views and organize in an effort to influence public policy and the selection of national leaders. Nevertheless, as in the Palestinian case, economic concerns may be important in shaping attitudes toward conflict resolution and peace.

On the one hand, territorial compromise and mutual recognition may have greater appeal among Israelis who believe their country will benefit economically from peace. First, peace holds out the prospect of Israel's integration into the Middle East, thereby offering larger markets, cheaper labor sources, and increased trade.[19] In addition, the cost of occupying the West Bank and Gaza has taken a toll on the Israeli economy. The military budget has generated a balance-of-payments deficit and contributed to a rise in external debt.[20] Military spending also diverts funds from important social programs. These anticipated economic benefits led many Israelis to discuss the possibility of a "peace dividend" following the 1993 Oslo Agreement, and support for peace may thus be disproportionately strong among those who believe that an end to the Israeli-Palestinian conflict will bring economic gains to the Jewish state.

On the other hand, there is a view that Israel has little to gain from expanding economic ties with its Palestinian neighbors. This view points out that the market potential of the Palestinian economy is limited, foreign labor within Israel is actually less expensive than Palestinian labor, and open economic ties may undercut labor-intensive industries within Israel.[21] Moreover, even if Israelis do believe that normalized relations with a Palestinian state would be economically advantageous, they may also believe that these economic benefits are outweighed by security costs associated with a strong connection between the Israeli and Palestinian economies. Thus, in both absolute and relative terms, Israelis may conclude that the potential economic gains of peace are insignificant, in which case economic concerns will have little or no effect on attitudes toward the conflict.

The Political Status Quo

The linkage between economic perceptions and attitudes toward the Israeli-Palestinian conflict can also be indirect, contingent upon the level of confidence in political leaders. If citizens do not trust their leaders' intentions or capacity to implement effective economic or social policies, they may distrust their foreign policy initiatives as well. This trust depends, in part, on whether citizens believe that the government can effectively handle the economic and social concerns that are central to their lives. For much of the Palestinian population and for at least some Israelis as well, socioeconomic problems may have had a damaging impact on the legitimacy of government leaders.

THE PALESTINIAN CASE

There is a great deal of evidence about citizen discontent with the economic status quo in the Arab world. In Palestine, as in many other Arab societies, a familiar litany of grievances begins with the fact that many people live in impoverished conditions. Furthermore, for many individuals, especially the young, prospects for social mobility and a higher standard of living are declining rather than improving. Unemployment is the most important part of this picture. Although employment levels in the West Bank and Gaza have risen in recent years, overall unemployment and underemployment rates remain high. Since 1995, unemployment has ranged between 12 percent and 28 percent, and even many with work do not earn enough to lift their families out of poverty.[22] From 1992 to 1996, real per capita income rates declined by 36 percent, and although real income levels began to rise in 1998, the gross domestic product (GDP) per capita purchasing power parity was only $1,060 in 1999.[23]

At the same time, there is a large and growing gap between rich and poor, meaning that the burdens of underdevelopment are not shared equitably. Equally important is the widespread belief that elite membership is determined in most instances not by ability, dedication, or service to society but by personal and political connections. The result is a system where patronage and clientelism predominate in decisions about public policy and resource allocation. Recent polls report that a majority of Palestinians in the West Bank and Gaza believe that corruption exists in the institutions of the Palestinian Authority, that such corruption will increase in the future, and that jobs are obtained largely through personal connections and nepotism.[24]

Frustration is further intensified by the political context, which provides few mechanisms by which the populace can express discontent in a way that will have a meaningful impact. Freedom House considers the areas administered by both Israel and the Palestinian Authority (PA) to be lacking most basic political rights and civil liberties.[25] Other international agencies have also documented human rights abuses, suppression of political dissent, and extra-legal behavior by both Palestinian and Israeli officials.[26] Thus, one of the surveys cited above found that 65 percent of those interviewed do not believe people can criticize the PA without fear.[27] Taken together, these circumstances erode the legitimacy of Palestinian leadership in the eyes of many ordinary citizens.

These questions about legitimacy may have an impact on attitudes toward negotiations and peace with Israel. To the extent that Palestinians believe that peace is championed by leaders in whom they have confidence, as part of a sincere effort to bring changes that will benefit ordinary citizens as well as elites, it may be hypothesized that support for compromise and accommodation will be high. Alternatively, to the extent that peace initiatives are viewed as part of a policy designed by self-interested political leaders and intended to perpetuate a status quo that is disadvantageous for most ordinary citizens, such initiatives are unlikely to find support at the grassroots level.

THE ISRAELI CASE

Concerns of government legitimacy are much less intense in Israel. The country has long been an established democracy, with political leaders regularly voted out of office when their performance or policies lose popular support. But trust in government and regime support may nonetheless vary as a function of real or perceived economic conditions. This has been demonstrated by research carried in affluent Western democracies, and it has been documented in Israel as well. Israeli and other analysts describe periods of uncertainty during which economic concerns contributed to shifts in public opinion and voting patterns.[28]

For Palestinians, it has been hypothesized that citizens who are discontent with their economic situation will have less confidence in their political leaders and, as a result, be less likely to support the peace negotiations in which their leaders are engaged. A somewhat similar analysis has been advanced to explain support for a hard-line foreign policy among segments of Israel's Jewish population, particularly those Jews who emigrated from other Middle Eastern countries during the 1950s and 1960s. These "Afro-Asian" Jews tended to be discontent with their economic and social position, and they tended to blame the leftist and centrist political parties in power during this period for not doing enough to meet the needs of new immigrants. Moreover, they were particularly outraged when some political leaders responded that the problems of Afro-Asian Jews were largely the result of their own backwardness.[29] As David Gurion, Israel's first prime minister, once remarked about Jews of Moroccan origin, "The culture of Morocco I would not like to have here . . . Maybe in the third generation something will appear from the Oriental Jew that is different. But I don't see it yet."[30]

Israeli Jews of Afro-Asian origin have tended to support right-wing political parties and a hard-line foreign policy. Various explanations have been advanced to explain these attitudes, and among these are analyses that emphasize the juxtaposition of economic grievances and distrust of political leaders. As expressed in one recent study:

> The appeal of the right to Middle Eastern Jewish voters was not ideological or intellectual primarily, but more attitudinal and emotional. Support for the [right-wing] Likud was a way of breaking

the hegemony of the Western-oriented elite . . . of even turning the
tables on those who had been disdainful of them.[31]

It follows from this assessment that Israeli Jews of Afro-Asian origin may
reject a compromise-oriented foreign policy, at least in part, because it is
advocated by political leaders whom, for reasons having to do with their own
situation, they dislike and distrust.[32]

   This analysis may or may not apply in the post-Oslo period. There have
been important changes in Israel with respect to politics, economics, and
demography, to say nothing of the evolution of the Israeli-Palestinian conflict itself. Nevertheless, there continue to be Israelis with important economic concerns. Between 1995 and 1999, for example, the country's growth
rate declined from roughly 7 percent to 2 percent, and unemployment rose to
almost 9 percent.[33] To the extent that economic discontent leads to political
distrust, this juxtaposition may foster an attitude toward Israeli-Palestinian
peace that is at variance with that of the government. And in the context
of negotiations associated with the Oslo agreement, especially during the
period from 1993 to 1996 when Labor was in power, this may mean that
those who are unhappy with the economic situation will be more likely than
other Israelis to oppose making concessions in order to achieve peace. A
recent analysis along these lines suggests that it may indeed apply in the
post-Oslo period. Moreover, this possibility is discussed with respect to Afro-
Asian Jews in particular:

> The transition to a peace economy and economic growth will bene-
> fit in particular the elite and the upper middle class of professionals,
> managers, business leaders, and industrialists who are well equipped
> to seize the new opportunities . . . On the other hand, these eco-
> nomic transformations will inflict a serious blow on the working
> class and the poor . . . [and this] will most likely hit Mizrahim [Jews
> of Middle Eastern origin] particularly hard [since they are] mem-
> bers of the lower strata.[34]

Hypotheses

   The two approaches discussed above help to explain possible linkages
between economic variables and the way citizens view conflict resolution in
the Palestinian-Israeli context. The first perspective presents a cost-benefit
rationale, linking attitudes toward the conflict to economic consequences
anticipated from its resolution. As discussed, men and women may anticipate
that an end to the Israeli-Palestinian conflict will lead to economic circumstances that are more favorable, less favorable, or no different than the pres-

ent situation. Thus, following the logic of this cost-benefit assessment, the following hypothesis may be offered for testing with Palestinian and Israeli public opinion data.

> *Hypothesis 1:* Citizens who believe that a resolution of the Israeli-Palestinian conflict will improve national or personal economic well-being are more likely than others to support negotiations and peace based on territorial compromise and mutual recognition.

Or, conversely, citizens who believe that a resolution to the conflict will have unfavorable national or personal economic consequences are less likely to support negotiations and peace based on territorial compromise and mutual recognition.

Perceptions of present-day national and personal economic circumstances may also influence attitudes about resolution of the conflict. One possibility is that support for compromise and peace will be more common among those who are satisfied with present-day economic conditions. The reason for this, presumably, is that these citizens are more likely to believe that their satisfactory situation will enable them to benefit from any economic opportunities that peace provides and be shielded from any associated costs. Alternatively, it is also possible that support for an accommodation will be more common among those who are dissatisfied with the current economic situation. In this case, presumably, perceived economic need leads individuals to support peace in the hope that their situation will improve, and perhaps also to believe that they would have little to lose even if peace does not bring economic benefits. Because these possibilities include both a positive and an inverse relationship between economic satisfaction and support for Israeli-Palestinian peace, they may be expressed in the following alternative propositions.

> *Hypothesis 2a:* Citizens who are more *satisfied* with national or personal economic circumstances are more likely than others to support negotiations and peace based on territorial compromise and mutual recognition.

> *Hypothesis 2b:* Citizens who are more *dissatisfied* with national or personal economic circumstances are more likely than others to support negotiations and peace based on territorial compromise and mutual recognition.

The second approach argues that attitudes toward conflict resolution are heavily influenced by confidence in political leaders. Such confidence extends to the government's role in conducting foreign policy and peace negotiations. It is grounded, however, in judgments about the effectiveness and motivation of political leaders more generally, including their ability and willingness to address socioeconomic needs. Accordingly, citizens will probably believe that the potential economic benefits of peace are more likely to be realized and used productively or that the potential costs of peace are more likely to be minimized and shared equitably, if they have confidence in their leaders. Without such confidence, citizens are less likely to support negotiations and peace because, in their judgment, this will not significantly improve and may even worsen economic conditions.

At the time when some of the data used in the present study were collected, Israel and the Palestinians were conducting peace talks within the framework of the 1993 Oslo Agreement, or Declaration of Principles. Moreover, both Palestinian and Israeli leaders were at the time committed to the Oslo principles of territorial compromise and mutual recognition. Thus, confidence in political leaders at the time these surveys were conducted most likely involves support for negotiations and peace. This is expressed in the following hypothesis:

> *Hypothesis 3:* Citizens who have higher levels of confidence in their political leaders are more likely than others to support negotiations and peace based on territorial compromise and mutual recognition.

It follows from Hypothesis 3 that confidence is important as an intervening as well as an independent variable. If citizens do not trust their leaders' intentions or capacity to implement effective economic and social policy, they probably distrust the foreign policy initiatives of these leaders as well. Moreover, as demonstrated by past research, this trust depends at least partly on whether citizens believe the government can effectively handle the economic and social concerns that are central to their own lives. This means that the degree to which economic evaluations account for variance in attitudes toward negotiations and peace may in part be dependent on confidence in political leaders. Put differently, in the context of the present study, the relationships proposed in hypotheses 1, 2a, and 2b may be weaker when a measure of confidence in political leaders is included in the analysis. This may be stated in the form of the following hypothesis:

> *Hypothesis 4:* Economic judgments influence citizen attitudes toward negotiations and peace indirectly by contributing to the level of confidence citizens have in government leaders.

An emphasis on economic factors, and on considerations of political economy more broadly, is not intended to suggest that issues of religion and culture are unrelated to attitudes toward the Israeli-Palestinian conflict. On the contrary, religion is an important part of the political discourse in both the Arab world and Israel. As noted, our prior research has examined whether and how religious orientations influence attitudes toward conflict.[35] Moreover, these analyses distinguish between religious piety and observance, on the one hand, and support for political movements with a religious orientation, on the other. Given their importance, these two sets of religious orientations are included in the present study as control variables to determine whether economic factors account for attitudinal variance independent of religious influences.

Data and Measurement

These hypotheses have been tested using public opinion data collected in Palestine and Israel in 1996, 1999, and 2001. The earliest survey was directed by scholars at Haifa University and Tel Aviv University in Israel and carried out in May 1996, just prior to that year's elections. The randomly selected sample includes 1,168 Israeli adults. The second survey was carried out in the West Bank and Gaza Strip in May 1999 by the Jerusalem Media and Communications Centre (JMCC) and is based on a random sample of 1,200 Palestinian adults. The most recent survey is a cross-national project conducted in both Israel and the Palestinian territories during July 2001. The survey was jointly designed and implemented by Khalil Shikaki of the Center for Policy and Survey Research in Ramallah and by Jacob Shamir of Hebrew University in Jerusalem. The samples include 1,318 Palestinian and 519 Jewish Israeli adults.

Because the data sets were collected by different institutions for different purposes, the measures used to operationalize the dependent and independent variables are not identical and thus not always as equivalent as desired. Nevertheless, despite this limitation, it is possible to examine the explanatory power of economic orientations while controlling for religious and demographic variables, thus testing the hypotheses presented above.

The dependent variable in the present analysis is attitudes toward resolving the Palestinian-Israeli conflict. Respondents are rated according to the degree of their support for, or opposition to, a peaceful resolution based on territorial compromise and mutual recognition. The dependent variable in all cases is an additive index composed of three or more questions relating to support for peace negotiations and desire for peaceful coexistence. The exact questions are listed in Table 12.1 with reliability coefficients for each scale.

Economic orientations are the principle independent variables of the present analysis. Table 12.2 lists the survey items used to measure different dimensions of economic behavior, the corresponding hypotheses they test, and the data sets for which they are available. Data limitations do not permit simultaneous testing of all the hypotheses involving economic variables in either the Palestinian or Israeli case. Taken together, however, the models and data presented below permit a broad examination of several important connections between economic assessments and foreign policy attitudes.

To test Hypothesis 1, it is necessary to ascertain views about the economic consequences of peace. Two measures are available in the 2001 Palestinian and Israeli surveys that examine both national and personal economic expectations. The first ascertains whether respondents expect the national economy to improve or worsen in the event of a peace settlement. The second asks whether respondents expect that their personal financial situation will improve or worsen if the conflict is peacefully resolved. Both questions probe respondent views about the potential economic costs and benefits of a peace agreement.

Perceptions of present-day economic circumstances may also influence attitudes about resolution of the conflict (hypotheses 2a and 2b). Items with which to measure respondent evaluations of national and personal economic circumstances are available for the 1996 Israeli and 1999 Palestinian data sets. The Palestinian items ask respondents to rate the economic situation in the West Bank and Gaza Strip and also to rate their own standard of living. Two comparable proxies are used in the Israeli case. The first asks respondents whether they believe that economic issues are the most critical problems facing their country. Respondents who consider the country's primary concern to be socioeconomic problems (such as the economy, unemployment, poverty, housing, etc.) are more likely than others to be less satisfied with the national economic situation. The second item asks respondents to rate their personal situation. Although the latter item captures more than economic satisfaction, financial status is most likely a central element in this evaluation.

Other important independent variables include confidence in government, religious attitudes and behavior, demographic attributes, and, in the Israeli case, feelings of personal security. Government confidence is measured by items that ask respondents to rate government performance. In the 2001 Palestinian survey, an index is created by combining respondent evaluations of Yasir Arafat, corruption in the Palestinian Authority, and the degree to which the PA is democratic. In the 1999 Palestinian data set, this is operationalized by two items that ask about the government's overall performance and the extent of government corruption. Although no measure is available for the 2001 Israeli survey, government confidence is measured in the 1996

Table 12.1. Survey Items Utilized to Measure
Attitudes toward Peace

Palestinian and Israeli Surveys, 2001

1. Now that both the Israeli and Palestinian sides have accepted the Mitchell report and the cease-fire, do you support or oppose the immediate return to Palestinian-Israeli negotiations?
   (1 = *strongly oppose* to 4 = *strongly support*)

2. After reaching a peace agreement between the Palestinian people and Israel and the establishment of a Palestinian state that is recognized by Israel, do you support or oppose the process of reconciliation between the state of Palestine and the state of Israel?
   (1 = *strongly oppose* to 4 = *strongly support*)

3. After reaching a peace agreement between the Palestinian people and Israel, do you support or oppose opening borders to the free movement of people and goods?
   (1 = *strongly oppose* to 4 = *strongly support*)

Reliability Coefficient: alpha = .58 (Palestinian survey)
Reliability Coefficient: alpha = .67 (Israeli survey)

Palestinian Survey, 1999

1. Do you support or oppose the current peace process?
   (1 = *strongly oppose* to 4 = *strongly support*)

2. Is it necessary to support the peaceful coexistence of Palestinians and Israelis?
   (1 = *strongly oppose* to 4 = *strongly support*)

3. Is it necessary for Palestinians and Israelis to know each other better?
   (1 = *strongly oppose* to 4 = *strongly support*)

Reliability Coefficient: alpha = .66

Israeli Survey, 1996

1. Should Israel return territories for peace?
   (1 = *approve*, 0 = *disapprove*)

2. What is your attitude toward the Oslo Agreement?
   (1 = *support*, 0 = *oppose*)

3. Should negotiations with the PLO be stopped?
   (1 = *no, only successful negotiations will end terrorism*; 0 = *yes, as long as terrorism continues*)

Table 12.1. Survey Items Utilized to Measure
Attitudes toward Peace (continued)

---

4. Opinion of evacuation of Jewish settlements in territories:
   (1 = *willing to evacuate all territories/willing to evacuate if they raise security problems*, 0 = *not willing to evacuate under any conditions*)

5. Is it true that "most Palestinians really want peace"?
   (1 = *true*, 0 = *false*)

6. Will a peace contract end the conflict?
   (1 = *yes*, 0 = *no*)

7. Do you think Israel should agree to the establishment of a Palestinian state?
   (1 = *yes*, 0 = *no*)

Reliability Coefficient: alpha = .84

Israeli survey by an item that asks respondents to rate the government's ability to handle national problems. To the extent possible, the analyses also include two measures pertaining to religious attachments, one reflecting personal piety and another assessing support for religious political movements or for increased religious influence in political affairs. Demographic variables include sex, age, income, and education. The complete survey items used to operationalize the demographic as well as political and religious variables are listed in Table 12.2.

In the Israeli analyses, an additional variable is included in order to control for the influence of security concerns. Because security has been a central issue in Israeli thinking about the conflict, the 1996 analysis includes a measure of the degree to which respondents believe that their personal security has either improved or worsened as a result of the peace process. The 2001 analysis also includes a measure to control for respondent concerns about security. Based on a survey item that asks respondents to rank five issues according to their national importance, the measure dichotomizes responses according to whether they identify security as the most critical issue facing Israel today. Inclusion of these measures is necessary to provide a reliable test of the impact of economic evaluations on Israeli attitudes toward peace and reconciliation.

Findings

The first hypothesis tests whether attitudes toward peace and reconciliation are influenced by cost-benefit considerations. In other words, do citi-

Table 12.2. Survey Items Utilized to Measure Economic
Orientations and Other Independent Variables

Economic Variables

Palestinian Survey, 2001

Hypothesis 1	If a peace agreement is reached, what will its economic impact be for the Palestinian people in general? (1 = *very harmful* to 5 = *very beneficial*)
	If a peace agreement is reached, what will its economic impact be for you and your family? (1 = *very harmful* to 5 = *very beneficial*)

Israeli Survey, 2001

Hypothesis 1	If a peace agreement is reached, what will its impact be for Israel's economic situation? (1 = *very harmful* to 5 = *very beneficial*)
	If a peace agreement is reached, what will its impact be for your personal economic situation? (1 = *very harmful* to 5 = *very beneficial*)

Palestinian Survey, 1999

Hypotheses 2a, 2b, 4	Rate the economic situation in the West Bank and Gaza. (1 = *very bad*, 2 = *somewhat bad*, 3 = *somewhat good*, 4 = *very good*)
	Rate your own family's standard of living. (1 = *very bad*, 2 = *somewhat bad*, 3 = *somewhat good*, 4 = *very good*)

Israeli Survey, 1996

Hypotheses 2a, 2b, 4	Rate your current personal situation. (1 = *worst* to 9 = *best*)
	What is the main problem that the government has to handle? (1 = *economy or socioeconomic issue* [e.g., housing, unemployment, poverty, education], 0 = *all other issues* [e.g., peace, security, terrorism])

Government Confidence

Palestinian Survey, 2001

Hypotheses 3, 4	Additive Index (0 low to 3 high): What is your evaluation of the status of

Table 12.2. (continued)

	democracy and human rights under the PA? (1 = *good/fair*, 0 = *bad*)
	Do you think there is corruption in the PA? (1 = *no*, 0 = *yes*)
	If separate elections for the president were held today, for whom would you vote? (1 = *Arafat*, 0 = *other*)
Israeli Survey, 2001	N/A
Palestinian Survey, 1999	
Hypotheses 3, 4	Additive Index (2 low to 8 high):
	Rate the overall performance of the PA. (1 = *very bad*, 2 = *bad*, 3 = *good*, 4 = *very good*)
	Rate the level of corruption within PA institutions. (1 = *much corruption* to 4 = *no corruption*)
Israeli Survey, 1996	
Hypotheses 3, 4	Rate the way the government handles national problems. (1 = *very badly*, 2 = *badly*, 3 = *good*, 4 = *very good*)
Religious Orientations	
Palestinian Survey, 2001	
Political Islam	Additive Index (0 low to 2 high):
	Which form of government would you want for an established Palestinian state? (1 = *Islamic*, 0 = *nationalist, democratic, or other*)
	Do you support Islamic political parties? (1 = *yes*, 0 = *no*)
Personal piety	Additive Index (3 low to 12 high):
	How important is religion in your life? (1 = *very unimportant* to 4 = *very important*)
	How often do you read the Quran? (1 = *never* to 4 = *every day*)
	Generally to what extent do you observe religious rules and traditions? (1= *none* to 4 = *all the time*)

Table 12.2. (continued)

Israeli Survey, 2001

Political religious affiliation	Which party would you vote for if the election were held today? (1= *religious party* [Shas, Mafdal, Yhadut Hathora, or Hayhud Haleumi], 0 = *nonreligious party*)
Personal piety	Additive Index (2 low to 8 high):
	How religious would you describe yourself? (1 = *not religious* to 4 = *very religious*)
	What is your religious identity? (1 = *secular*, 2 = *traditional*, 3 = *orthodox*, 4 = *ultra-orthodox*)

Palestinian Survey, 1999

Political Islam	Additive Index (4 low to 16 high):
	Religion should be separate from government policy. (1 = *strongly oppose* to 4 = *strongly support*)
	A Shari'a-based Islamic state is best form of government. (1 = *strongly oppose* to 4 = *strongly support*)
	Religious leaders should play a larger role in politics. (1 = *strongly oppose* to 4 = *strongly support*)
	Islamic values should play a larger role in government policy. (1 = *strongly oppose* to 4 = *strongly support*)
Personal piety	Additive Index (3 low to 12 high):
	How important is religion in your life? (1 = *very important* to 4 = *not very important*)
	How often do you pray? (1 = *never* to 4 = *five times daily*)
	How often do you read the Quran? (1 = *never* to 4 = *every day*)

Israeli Survey, 1996

Political religious affiliation	Which party would you vote for if the election were held today? (1 = *religious party* [Mafdal, Agudat Israel and Degel HaTora, or Shas], 0 = *nonreligious party*)
Personal piety	How obedient are you to the Jewish religious traditions? 1 = *not at all*, 2 = *a little*, 3 = *a lot*, 4 = *thoroughly*

Table 12.2. (continued)

Other Controls

Palestinian Survey, 2001

Sex	What is your gender? (1 = *male*, 2 = *female*)
Age	What is your exact age?
Income	Rate your level of income. (1 = *low* to 4 = *high*)
Education	What is your educational level? (1 = *illiterate* to 7 = *MA and above*)

Israeli Survey, 2001

Sex	What is your gender? (1 = *male*, 2 = *female*)
Age	What is your exact age?
Income proxy	What are your average monthly expenditures? (1 = *much below average* to 5 = *much above average*)
Education	How many years did you attend school?
Security	What is the most important issue facing Israel today? (1 = *security*, 0 = *other issues* [e.g., economic prosperity, democracy, peace, Jewish state])

Palestinian Survey, 1999

Sex	What is your gender? (1 = *male*, 2 = *female*)
Age	What is your exact age?
Income	Rate your income level. (1 = *a lot less than average* to 5 = *a lot more than average*)
Education	What is your educational level? (1 = *primary* to 5 = *college and above*)

Israeli Survey, 1996

Sex	What is your gender? (1 = *male*, 2 = *female*)
Age	What is your exact age?
Family expenditures	Rate your family expenditures. (1 = *much below average* to 5 = *much above average*)
Education	How many years did you attend school?
Personal security	What effect has the peace process had on your personal security? (1 = *now it is much better*, 2 = *now it is better*, 3 = *now it is worse*, 4 = *now it is much worse*)

zens form their opinions toward peace, in part, by considering the economic consequences of reconciliation? The findings indicate that they do. Model 1 in Table 12.3 and the model shown in Table 12.4 present the results of the regression analyses completed for the 2001 Palestinian and Israeli surveys. Palestinians and Israelis who believe that the peace process will be beneficial to the national economy are more likely than others to support negotiations and peace based on territorial compromise and mutual recognition. Conversely, respondents who expect national economic conditions to deteriorate with the conclusion of an agreement are less likely to support negotiations and peace. Moreover, in the Palestinian case, respondents who expect their own standard of living to improve from peace are more likely to support a peaceful resolution to the conflict. Personal financial considerations are not, however, significant in the Israeli case.

The second hypothesis considers the influence of perceptions of present-day national and personal economic circumstances. In contrast to Hypothesis 1, the relationship between these economic evaluations and attitudes toward a compromise-oriented peace settlement can be anticipated in different directions (hypotheses 2a and 2b). The findings, presented in Tables 12.5 and 12.6 under Model 1, show that among both Palestinians and Israelis, individuals with a positive evaluation of the economy or of their personal situation are more likely to support compromise and reconciliation than are individuals with a negative evaluation. Put differently, citizens who are dissatisfied with economic circumstances are less likely than others to support negotiation and compromise. It is possible to surmise from these findings that many respondents believe that peace will perpetuate existing economic conditions, either by improving a generally satisfactory economic situation or by worsening an already unsatisfactory economic situation.

Some variation in the explanatory power of national and personal economic assessments should also be noted. National economic orientations are significantly related to attitudes toward peace in all but the 1996 Israeli analysis shown in Table 12.6, whereas relationships involving personal economic orientations are significant in only half the models—those based on the 2001 Palestinian and 1996 Israeli surveys. Although further research is necessary, it is possible to suggest some reasons for these findings. In the1996 Israeli case, it is possible that a better measure of satisfaction with the national economic situation would produce different results. The finding that personal economic assessments are more important than national economic assessments is at variance with studies in Western countries, which report that national economic orientations have greater explanatory power. This is often described as a "sociotropic" pattern. The reason for this, presumably, is that national economic health is more likely than personal economic

Table 12.3. Regression Analyses of the Influence of
Economic Orientations on Attitudes toward Peace
in the West Bank and Gaza Strip, July 2001

	MODEL 1	MODEL 2	MODEL 3
Economic Orientations			
Evaluation of national economic situation after peace	.20*** (2.58)		.18** (2.28)
Evaluation of personal standard of living after peace	.33*** (4.20)		.32*** (3.88)
Government confidence		.37*** (6.09)	.33*** (5.61)
Control Variables			
Political Islam	−.48*** (−7.38)	−.44*** (−6.13)	−.41*** (−5.84)
Personal religiosity	.05* (1.65)	.04 (1.04)	.04 (1.12)
Education	−.18*** (−5.16)	−.15*** (−3.85)	−.16*** (−4.01)
Income	−.02 (−.34)	.01 (.19)	.02 (.29)
Sex	.21** (2.28)	.23** (2.17)	.20** (1.99)
Age	.00 (1.01)	.01* (1.85)	.01 (1.31)
R^2	.15	.10	.18
N	1,196	1,076	1,059

Note: t scores are in parentheses.

*p < 0.10, **p < 0.05, ***p < 0.01

Table 12.4. Regression Analysis of the Influence of Economic Orientations on Attitudes toward Peace in Israel, July 2001

Economic Orientations		
Evaluation of national economic situation after peace	.70***	(6.20)
Evaluation of personal standard of living after peace	.18	(1.58)
Control Variables		
Personal security	−.37**	(−2.01)
Political religious affiliation	−.82***	(−2.67)
Personal religiosity	−.28***	(−3.85)
Education	.05*	(1.68)
Income	−.00	(−.02)
Sex	.01	(.04)
Age	.02***	(2.85)
R^a	.31	
N	411	

Note: t scores are in parentheses.

*p < 0.10, **p < 0.05, ***p < 0.01

well-being to be considered a responsibility of the government. Thus, had the 1996 Israeli survey contained a more direct measure of satisfaction with the national economy, a different pattern might have emerged.

The Palestinian case, by contrast, suggests that a more thorough look at the relationship between personal and national economic orientations may be warranted in future research. The 2001 Palestinian analysis shows that both personal and national economic considerations are positively related to attitudes toward peace. The reason may be that widespread poverty and severe and worsening economic problems affecting the entire country foster an overlap between personal and national economic assessments to a degree that does not exist in Israel or developed Western countries. In such a situation, which prevailed in the Palestinian territories in 2001, both national and personal economic considerations may influence the way that individuals evaluate the potential outcomes of government policy. The possibility that

Table 12.5. Regression Analyses of the Influence of
Economic Orientations on Attitudes toward Peace
in the West Bank and Gaza Strip, May 1999

	MODEL 1	MODEL 2	MODEL 3
Economic Orientations			
Evaluation of national economic situation	.64*** (6.39)		.20* (1.92)
Evaluation of personal standard of living	.02 (.23)		−.05 (−.51)
Government confidence		.68*** (13.27)	.64*** (11.61)
Control Variables			
Political Islam	−.17*** (−5.42)	−.11*** (−3.57)	−.11*** (−3.59)
Personal religiosity	−.04 (−.91)	−.07* (−1.71)	−.07* (−1.85)
Education	−.24*** (−3.30)	−.10 (−1.46)	−.10 (−1.38)
Income	−.02 (−.30)	−.13** (−1.95)	−.12* (−1.67)
Sex	−.14 (−.90)	.07 (.49)	.05 (.36)
Age	.01 (1.16)	.01 (.92)	.01 (1.14)
R^2	.12	.24	.24
N	915	853	852

Note: t scores are in parentheses.

*$p < 0.10$, **$p < 0.05$, ***$p < 0.01$

Table 12.6. Regression Analyses of the Influence of Economic Orientations on Attitudes toward Peace in Israel, June 1996

	MODEL 1	MODEL 2	MODEL 3
Economic Orientations			
Socioeconomic issues are the central problems facing government	.41** (2.05)		.20 (1.26)
Evaluation of personal situation	.32*** (7.69)		.09** (2.53)
Government confidence		1.69*** (22.62)	1.15*** (14.34)
Control Variables			
Personal Security			−1.05*** (−12.14)
Political religious affiliation	−.69** (−2.17)	−.26 (−.99)	−.28 (−1.13)
Personal religiosity	−.92*** (10.19)	−.54*** (−6.96)	−.41*** (−5.62)
Education	.09*** (3.93)	.07*** (3.35)	.06*** (3.46)
Family expenditures (income proxy)	−.02 (−.27)	.03 (.65)	.06 (1.30)
Sex	.33** (2.40)	.12 (1.06)	.15 (1.42)
Age	.02*** (4.73)	.01 (1.87)	.00 (1.44)
R^2	.23	.46	.54
N	1,003	997	974

Note: t scores are in parentheses.

*$p < 0.10$, **$p < 0.05$, ***$p < 0.01$

the impact of economic orientations is conditional on aggregate economic circumstances deserves further study and would be an important finding if confirmed by future research.

The third and fourth hypotheses are addressed by including a measure of government confidence in the multivariate analyses. Model 2 in Tables 12.3, 12.5, and 12.6 shows the impact of government confidence on attitudes toward peace without economic variables included in the analysis. As anticipated in Hypothesis 3, citizens with greater confidence in their political leaders are more likely in all three cases to support negotiations and compromise. Furthermore, as shown in Model 3 in each table, this relationship remains robust when economic orientations are included in the analysis. It is notable that confidence in the government has explanatory power among both Israelis and Palestinians, despite the very different character of the regimes by which the two peoples are governed. It is also notable that the relationship holds among Palestinians in both 1999 and 2001. In the former year, the peace process was advancing, albeit slowly, and the economic situation was gradually improving. In the latter year, by contrast, there were violent confrontations between Israelis and Palestinians, and economic conditions had greatly deteriorated. Thus, taken together, Tables 12.3, 12.5, and 12.6 strongly suggest that Hypothesis 3 obtains across widely differing contexts and conditions.

An additional observation is that in Tables 12.5 and 12.6, but not in Table 12.3, government confidence accounts for a disproportionate share of the model's explanatory power. In the 1999 Palestinian analysis shown in Table 12.5, the R-square in Model 2 is twice the R-square in Model 1, going from .12 to .24. Similarly, the R-square in the Israeli case shown in Table 12.6 increased from .23 in Model 1 to .46 in Model 2. For the 2001 Palestinian case shown in Table 12.3, by contrast, the R-square in Model 2 is actually lower than the R-square in Model 1, raising the possibility that the explanatory power of government confidence varies in magnitude as a function of political circumstances. It may be that the influence of government confidence on attitudes toward peace, although remaining significant, is reduced when the prospects for conflict resolution are less favorable. A more specific hypothesis is that the influence of government confidence depends on the perceived intent of the other party to the conflict. With Israel carrying out military operations in the West Bank and Gaza in summer 2001, this interpretation fits the data and is deserving of further investigation.

The final hypothesis asks whether economic judgments influence citizen attitudes toward negotiations and peace indirectly by contributing to the level of confidence citizens have in government leaders. This is in contrast to the cost-benefit hypothesis, which represents a direct relationship between economic attitudes and those toward conflict resolution. The indirect ratio-nale anticipates that citizens who are discontent with economic conditions will have less confidence in their political leaders and thus be less likely to support the peace negotiations in which they are engaged. To test this pos-sibility, Model 3 in Tables 12.5 and 12.6 includes measures both of economic orientations and of government confidence. A comparison of Model 1 and Model 3 shows that the strength of the relationship between economic evalu-ations and attitudes toward peace is reduced substantially when confidence is added to the model. The coefficients and *t* scores of the economic variables are much lower in Model 3 than in Model 1 for both the Palestinian and Israeli analyses, although the effect appears to be greater in the Palestinian case. Moreover, the *R*-squares for Models 2 and 3 differ very little, indicating that the explanatory power of economic orientations and government con-fidence overlap. These findings suggest that individual dissatisfaction with economic circumstances influences attitudes toward peace largely by foster-ing or reinforcing distrust in political leaders.

This relationship holds in the Israeli case even after controlling for the effects of personal security. Model 3 in Table 12.6 shows that the effect of security is relatively strong. Respondents who feel that the peace process has reduced their sense of personal safety are more likely to support a hard-line approach to the Israeli-Palestinian conflict than are respondents who feel that the peace process has made them more secure. Despite the strength of this relationship, however, both personal economic evaluations and gov-ernment confidence remain significant. That evaluations of a respondent's personal situation retains significance after controlling for personal security increases the likelihood that the measure includes an economic dimension and is not limited to perceptions of physical safety and fear of terrorism. This final model thus provides a more rigorous test of Hypothesis 4 in the Israeli case, making it possible to suggest with more confidence that personal economic evaluations influence attitudes toward peace largely by affecting the level of trust in political leaders.

Several additional tests (not shown) were performed to probe the influ-ence of government confidence on attitudes toward peace among subsets of the Israeli population. As discussed earlier, some observers have argued that Israeli Jews of Afro-Asian origin may be less supportive of a compromise-oriented foreign policy because it is advocated by political leaders whom they distrust. Some also argue that the economic consequences of peace could be disproportionately disadvantageous for this group because of their lower socioeconomic status.[36] The same models presented in Table 12.6 were therefore completed including only Jews of Afro-Asian origin to determine whether a stronger or otherwise different pattern of variable relationships would emerge. This was not the case, however. The results for this group of respondents were almost identical to those for the entire sample. Similar analyses were performed using only respondents with low incomes and only those who reported having experienced discrimination in the past. Again, however, relationships differ very little from those shown in Table 12.6. Accordingly, the interaction between economic evaluations, government confidence, and attitudes toward peace does not appear to vary from one Israeli population category to another.

Measures of both government confidence and economic orientations are also included in the Palestinian 2001 analysis to test whether the direct and indirect relationships posited above are empirically distinct. Model 1 in Table 12.3 shows that Palestinian respondents who expect negative economic consequences from a peace agreement are less likely to support peace negotiations and reconciliation. This relationship provides support for the view that the influence of economic orientations works in terms of cost-benefit calculations and that citizens consider how a peace settlement will affect their economic well-being and then give or withhold their policy support based on these expectations.

This relationship should hold largely independent of citizens' evaluations of current government leaders. In the summer of 2001, few Palestinians saw the conclusion of a peace agreement, to say nothing of its implementation, as a near-term prospect. Therefore, the achievement of peace, if viewed as a possibility at all, was most likely judged to be sufficiently far in the future for leadership changes to have occurred, which suggests that confidence in present leaders should not affect cost-benefit assessments regarding the economic implications of peace. In addition, Palestinians are probably aware that the economic consequences of peace will depend on much more than domestic political leadership. Relevant considerations include the type and level of international aid, arrangements with Israel in such areas as borders and water resources, and the ability to attract investment capital from both domestic and foreign sources. For this reason, too, anticipated economic outcomes should influence attitudes toward peace independent of confidence in present-day leaders.

Table 12.3 provides some support for this logic. A comparison of Model 3 with Model 1 shows that the coefficients and t-scores change little when government confidence is added to the analysis. Moreover, the increase in R^2 from the second model to the third model indicates that the explanatory power of economic orientations and government confidence is largely separate. Thus, although more research is needed to explore the pathways linking economic orientations and attitudes toward peace, the findings presented in Tables 12.3 to 12.6 provide some evidence for the existence of both direct and indirection relationships.

Conclusion

Several general conclusions can be offered based on the findings presented in Tables 12.3 to 12.6. First, the analyses provide support for both of the theoretical perspectives presented earlier. One of these focuses on the direct link between economic orientations and attitudes toward foreign policy. It is based on the assumption that citizens make cost-benefit calculations when formulating political opinions. Applying this reasoning to the present study, it was anticipated that individuals would be more likely to support a negotiated resolution of the Israeli-Palestinian conflict to the extent that they expect the positive consequences of a settlement to outweigh any negative consequences. This rationale has been tested most directly and is supported most strongly by the analysis of the 2001 Palestinian and Israeli data. Respondents who believe that a peace settlement will worsen the condition of the national economy or their personal economic status (the personal pertaining only to the Palestinian case) are less likely than others to support peace negotiations and compromise.

Some evidence supporting this perspective also comes from analyses of the 1999 Palestinian and 1996 Israeli data. In both cases, perceptions of present-day national and personal evaluations exhibit a direct influence on attitudes toward the conflict. Specifically, citizens who are more dissatisfied with national or personal economic circumstances are less likely than others to support peace negotiations and reconciliation. This, too, implies that individuals who are dissatisfied with the economic situation tend to believe a compromise-oriented settlement will either perpetuate or worsen an already poor economic situation. This interpretation is advanced with some caution, given limitations of the available measures. It is nonetheless suggested by both the Israeli and Palestinian data, and it is therefore, at the very least, a plausible and potentially important finding that deserves further investigation.

Economic assessments also influence attitudes toward the conflict in an indirect way. This is the basis of the second perspective presented earlier, which argues that the link between economic evaluations and foreign policy attitudes is shaped by the level of confidence citizens have in their political leaders. The 1999 Palestinian and 1996 Israeli analyses provide support for this assertion. The multivariate findings show that government confidence is strongly related to support for peace negotiations and compromise. Also, and of even greater relevance, the analyses show that economic evaluations influence attitudes toward peace and reconciliation largely by helping to determine levels of trust in the government and its officials.

The importance of temporal considerations deserves to be mentioned when assessing these findings. The ups and downs of the peace process, to say nothing of the violence that began in mid-2000, the so-called al-Aqsa *Intifada,* raises the possibility that observations made at one point in time might not apply at another. One response is that replication is always helpful and usually necessary to increase confidence in research findings. In this regard, the limitations of the present study are similar to those of many empirical investigations. As in cross-sectional as well as longitudinal comparisons, replications that yield similar findings make it more likely that these findings are accurate and generalizable. Different findings may be an indication of error but, equally important, may reflect the influence of macro-level conditionalities that must be incorporated into any explanations that are advanced.

The present study does more than acknowledge the importance of replication, however. It also attempts to address temporal considerations by using data from several points in time following the 1993 Israel-PLO accord, including some before and some since the beginning of the al-Aqsa *Intifada.* Thus, although not all hypotheses are tested with data from different time periods, there is basis for advancing some tentative conclusions about generalizability and conditionalities. On the other hand, the explanatory power of economic orientations and government confidence has been shown to be significant both during periods of relative calm and during periods characterized by violent confrontations. As noted, this increases confidence in the generalizability of these relationships. On the other hand, the magnitude of some relationships appears to vary as a function of temporal conditions, and this finding has led to additional hypotheses that may be tested in future research.

In sum, economic considerations play an important role in shaping citizen views about the Palestinian-Israeli conflict. It is true, of course, that much of the variance in attitudes toward peace remains unexplained. Economic variables, even in combination with political, religious, and demographic variables, do not account for more than one-third of the variance in most of the models presented. Additional research is therefore necessary if the nature and determinants of attitudes toward conflict in the Middle East are to be fully understood. Nevertheless, the present study demonstrates that economic concerns and perceptions do play an important role in shaping views about the Israeli-Palestinian conflict. Economic orientations have a direct impact on attitudes toward negotiations and compromise, through what is most likely a series of cost-benefit calculations regarding the expected consequences of peace. The indirect influence of economic attitudes is also important. Individual judgments about economic conditions help to determine levels of confidence in political leaders, which in turn influence the way that citizens view the foreign policy positions advocated by these leaders.

CHAPTER 13

What Leads Some Ordinary Arab Men and Women to Approve of Terrorist Acts against the United States? Evidence from Survey Research in Algeria and Jordan (2007)

Mark Tessler and Michael D. H. Robbins

Rebel organizations seeking to upset the existing political order have long recognized the importance of obtaining the support of their constituent populations.[1] Organizations involved in civil wars require at least a passively supportive society in which to hide and from which to obtain the resources necessary for survival.[2] So, too, with organizations that use terrorism.[3] They need to obtain resources, hiding places, and infrastructure support, as well as to recruit fighters.[4] Societal support, whether implicit or explicit, is often a critical facilitator for terrorist organizations, allowing them to conduct operations more frequently and more easily.[5]

The importance of popular support for terrorist organizations is recognized not only by scholars but also by counterterrorism specialists.[6] Indeed, in a review of Homeland Security policies, Atran argues that the most important line of defense against terrorism may be finding ways to reduce popular support for terrorist organizations and activities.[7] The experience of Israel in forecasting and combating terrorism by Palestinian groups lends support to this assessment. According to Paz, organizations such as Hamas are highly responsive to the will of the Palestinian people.[8] Similarly, according to Ayalon, former head of Israel's security services, reductions in Palestinian terrorism between 1995 and 2000 were not a consequence of Israeli security policies but rather a response to Palestinian public opinion.[9] Because of the correlation between popular support and militant actions, Israel has been able to use public opinion surveys to forecast decreases and increases in Palestinian terrorism with substantial accuracy.

As the preceding suggests, an understanding of the determinants of popular support for terrorism has strategic as well as theoretical importance.

Success in combating terrorism will depend to a substantial degree on the extent to which terrorist organizations are deprived of such support.[10] But while the importance of popular attitudes toward terrorist organizations and activities is generally recognized, there is little agreement about the determinants of these attitudes. Against this background, the present study uses survey data from Algeria and Jordan to construct an empirical model that tests hypotheses about the determinants of support for terrorism among ordinary citizens. The focus is on international terrorism, especially that directed at the United States. The model includes independent variables associated with alternate explanations of the root causes of support for terrorism.

Explanations of Support for Terrorism among Ordinary Citizens

There has been little systematic research addressed to the question of why some ordinary citizens but not others support the activities of terrorist organizations that purport to struggle on their behalf. More common with respect to the Arab world are attempts to explain the strong anti-American sentiment that is pervasive in most Arab countries and research that focuses not on passive support for terrorism among Arab (and Muslim) publics but rather on the reasons why some groups and individuals actually carry out terrorist acts. The explanations offered by these analyses fall into two broad and competing categories, both of which suggest propositions that may also help to account for variance in popular attitudes toward terrorism. The first category focuses on religion and culture and includes assessments associated with the well-known Clash of Civilizations thesis. The second argues that explanatory power is to be found primarily in political and economic considerations.

Religious and Cultural Explanations

After the attacks of September 11, 2001, a University of Michigan survey found that 54 percent of a representative sample of Americans believed that the attackers had been motivated by a conflict between Christianity and Islam. This assertion, usually described as the Clash of Civilizations thesis, with emphasis placed on an alleged confrontation between Islam and the West, has been advanced by a number of prominent scholars to explain the anti-Western sentiment that is widespread in the Arab world.[11] It has been given particular currency by Samuel Huntington,[12] although the well-known scholar of the Middle East Bernard Lewis used the term earlier, and more recently.[13]

Writing in "The Roots of Muslim Rage," Lewis stated as early as 1990 that "it should now be clear that we [in the West] are facing a mood and a movement far transcending the level of issues and policies and the governments that pursue them. This is no less than a clash of civilizations—that perhaps irrational but surely historic reaction of an ancient rival against our Judeo-Christian heritage."[14] Linking this thesis to violent conflict, Huntington writes of "Islam's bloody borders," where Muslims and non-Muslims bump up against each other and conflict results.[15] He further asserts that an aggressive Muslim posture toward the West is rooted in the very nature of Islam and should not be understood as a product of Islamic fundamentalism or the militancy of a few Muslim extremists.

Although these assessments do not pertain directly to terrorism or even to passive support for terrorist activities, they offer an explanation of antipathy toward the West that is also found in some studies of terrorism. In accounts of Palestinian attacks against Israeli targets, for example, Moghaddam argues that perceived religious and value conflicts are key motivators for suicide terrorism;[16] and Paz contends in the same connection that many Palestinian militants perceive an "eternal struggle" between Judaism and Islam.[17]

Others, however, challenge explanations that emphasize religion and culture. On the one hand, a recent empirical study based on opinion surveys in five Arab countries "does not find evidence that a clash of cultures explains deteriorating relations with the West, generally, or with the U.S., specifically."[18] On the other, with respect to religion in particular, the proposed connection between Islam and terrorism has also been called into question. According to a major study by Esposito, the overwhelming majority of Muslims are appalled that violence is committed in the name of Islam.[19] It is therefore essential, he argues, not to conflate the religion of Islam with the actions of those who hijack Islamic discourse to justify acts of terrorism. Esposito's argument suggests that even if it can be established that Muslims who commit terrorist acts are themselves frequently influenced by religious ideas, it does not follow that deep religious involvement or conviction fosters a positive attitude toward terrorism among ordinary men and women.

Still other analyses place emphasis not on Islam as a system of religious values and beliefs but rather, more narrowly, on Islam as a political ideology and agenda. These analyses do not endorse the view that aggression toward the West is rooted in the fundamental character of Islam. They do consider it significant, however, that a substantial proportion of terrorist attacks, and suicide attacks in particular, are carried out by groups and individuals who are religiously motivated and claim inspiration from political Islam.[20] On the one hand, the conception of Islam as a political community, a community of believers, encourages militants to struggle against the real or perceived enemies of that community. On the other, beliefs about how God intends this community to be governed lend additional specificity to the group's platform and expose more fully those who, in the militants' view, are attempting to thwart its realization. According to this line of analysis, a political agenda attributed to Islam is central to the ideology and motivation of many terrorist groups.

Only a few empirical studies have sought to determine the degree to which political Islam does indeed shape the thinking of Muslim terrorists, and the results thus far are limited and inconclusive.[21] But regardless of the degree to which terrorists are themselves motivated by an Islamist political ideology, it is possible that an embrace of political Islam fosters popular support for those who carry out terrorist activities both generally and, more specifically, in the name of Islam. This is suggested by a study in Lebanon that found a correlation between support for political Islam and approval of terrorist acts carried out in the name of the religion.[22] By contrast, although militancy rather than support for terrorism is the dependent variable, findings from surveys in Palestine, Egypt, Jordan, Lebanon, and Kuwait found no significant relationship between support for political Islam and either an uncompromising attitude toward Israel or a refusal to seek a negotiated solution to the conflict.[23] This finding was repeated most recently in a poll conducted in the West Bank and Gaza following the victory of Hamas in the Palestinian legislative elections of January 2006.[24]

In addition to religious involvement and support for political Islam, cultural preferences and predispositions may help to explain why some men and women support terrorist acts against the United States or other Western countries. The Clash of Civilizations thesis asserts that anti-Western sentiment among Muslims is fueled by antipathy to Western cultural values, and similar assessments have more recently been offered to explain the widespread anti-Americanism in the Arab and Muslim world. In making this connection, Garfinkle refers to "cultural anti-Americanism," mentioning perceptions about America's presumed "vulgarity, disrespect for elders and teachers, and countless variations on puerile promiscuity."[25] Some observers attach particular importance to the status of women and gender relations in this context, alleging, for example, that "the liberation of women in Western societies and especially the U.S. is a part of modernity detested in the Arab-Islamic world."[26]

Cultural factors are also frequently emphasized in writings about Islamist movements, whether or not such movements are assumed to engage in terrorist activities. According to a recent analysis in the *Rand Review,* "[Muslim] fundamentalists reject democratic values and contemporary Western culture."[27] Similarly, according to Paz, Islamists believe in "a cultural clash of civilizations" and have sought with some success, especially among "intellectuals and highly educated Muslims," to foster the view that conflict with the West is part of "a war of cultures."[28]

As far as popular support for terrorism is concerned, the probable link, if there is one, is that distaste for Western cultural norms can produce antagonism toward the West—and perhaps even hatred if the United States and other Western societies are seen as imposing their culture and undermining the values and standards of the Arab and Muslim world, thereby creating sympathy for those who attack Western targets. A related consideration is that a dislike of Western culture may dehumanize the West in the eyes of some Arabs and Muslims. Several studies argue that dehumanization of the enemy is a vital cognitive link in the causal chain leading an individual to support terrorist actions.[29]

These possibilities about the explanatory power of attitudes and values relating to religion, political Islam, and Western culture, which the present study investigates with survey data from Algeria and Jordan, are summarized in the following propositions about determinants of support for terrorism against the United State among ordinary citizens in the Arab world.

> *Hypothesis 1.* Individuals who are more religious or have higher levels of religious involvement are more likely to approve of terrorist acts against U.S. targets.
>
> *Hypothesis 2.* Individuals who are more favorably disposed toward the platform of political Islam are more likely to approve of terrorist acts against U.S. targets.
>
> *Hypothesis 3.* Individuals who have a more negative view of Western culture, as reflected in opposition to interaction between women and men in the public sphere, are more likely to approve of terrorist acts against U.S. targets.
>
> *Hypothesis 4.* Individuals who believe Western culture is having an injurious effect on their society are more likely to approve of terrorist acts against U.S. targets.

Political Economy Explanations

Standing in opposition to analyses that attribute explanatory power to religion and culture are those that see political and economic considerations as much more important. Among these is the plausible view that terrorism is the product of socioeconomic deprivation. Public figures ranging from George W. Bush and Tony Blair to Shimon Peres and Elie Wiesel have claimed that poverty is the main cause of terrorism. Scholars and policy analysts have also sometimes argued that a reduction in poverty and economic deprivation is necessary to combat terrorism.[30] These assessments imply that support for terrorism, as well as terrorism itself, is fueled by economic distress.

This argument has been weakened by empirical evidence, however. On the one hand, studies of the characteristics of terrorists do not support the poverty and deprivation thesis. For example, Hassan conducted interviews with almost 250 members of organizations that use terrorism, including failed suicide terrorists and their families, and found that none reported significant economic deprivation.[31] Profiles of 129 Hizbollah militants killed in action[32] and of 335 deceased Palestinian terrorists[33] similarly found no association between poverty and the likelihood of becoming a terrorist. On the contrary, both studies found that terrorists tend to be relatively well off by the standards of their societies, a finding that is consistent with what is known about the Al Qaeda members involved in the 9/11 attacks.[34] Indeed, one study suggests that terrorist groups may actually reject would-be participants if they believe their motivation to be monetary rather than a commitment to the group's cause.[35]

Although personal poverty and deprivation appear to have limited explanatory power, support for terrorism may be fostered by perceptions about societal economic and political circumstances. This reflects a "socio-tropic" explanation; as reported in many political attitude studies, views are often shaped far less by one's personal situation than by an assessment of societal or national well-being. Research also demonstrates that although personal relative deprivation is not strongly related to inter-group attitudes and behavior, in-group or fraternal relative deprivation can prompt rebellious behavior, particularly when such deprivation can be attributed to foreign or out-group action.[36]

A number of observers advance sociotropic analyses to explain membership in terrorist organizations and the conduct of terrorist acts. Some analyses are general and broadly conceptual. Their authors argue that militancy and activism, including Islamic activism, are embedded in a political or economic context, or both, that shapes decisions and behavior.[37] Wiktorowicz observes, for example, that the actions of Palestinian Hamas have varied over time in accordance with changing conditions.[38] These include, as noted earlier, the degree to which there is public support for a campaign of armed struggle.[39] Other authors focus more specifically on terrorism and its relationship to societal conditions. Moghaddam and Saleh, both of whom examine the Palestinian case, emphasize the importance of collective distress and hopelessness in fostering terrorism, particularly when these are seen as linked to Israeli policies.[40]

Both economic and political considerations are relevant in this connection. With respect to the economy, poverty, corruption, and a growing gap between rich and poor may lead people to believe that the economic conditions of their country will worsen rather than improve in the years ahead. Thus, as a recent data-based study reports, expectations about future economic conditions contribute significantly to militancy in Palestinian attitudes toward Israel.[41] With respect to politics, deep anger is likely if people believe that their community's political rights have been denied. As Fathali Moghaddam notes, writing more generally, feelings of deprivation may express themselves as popular support for terrorism as well as an increase in terrorism itself. He contends that unrealized aspirations have produced a "groundswell of frustration and anger" and this has led to "greater [popular] sympathy for extremist 'anti-establishment' tactics."[42]

This situation is particularly likely to give rise to terrorism, and very probably to popular support for terrorist activities as well, when grievances are attributed to identifiable actors. With respect to terrorism itself, several analysts report that attacks against civilians are often seen as an appropriate and justified response to aggression by members of the targeted group.[43] Attitudes about terrorism appear to be influenced by a similar dynamic. Shikaki shows, for example, that support among West Bank and Gaza Palestinians for attacks against civilian Israeli targets varies in response to Israel's actions in these territories.[44]

The actors to whom grievances are attributed may include Western countries and the United States in particular. Complaints about U.S. actions in the Middle East, whether justified or not, may thus help to shape attitudes toward international affairs among Arab and Muslim publics. This is suggested by several data-based studies offering evidence that anti-Americanism among Arabs and Muslims is fostered primarily by negative assessments of U.S. foreign policy.[45] As Hamarneh observes in this connection, reporting on surveys carried out in five Arab countries in 2004, "Arabs disagree fundamentally with U.S. positions on issues such as the definition of terrorism, the Arab-Israeli conflict, and the war in Iraq."[46] Other analyses, however, dispute the proposed linkage between U.S. foreign policy and anti-Americanism,[47] which was the subject of considerable debate at a 2005 Carnegie Endowment roundtable.[48]

Domestic as well as foreign actors may be seen as responsible for an unsatisfactory status quo that fuels popular anger and associated acts of protest or rebellion. Research in Algeria and Jordan as well as other Arab countries offers evidence that support for antiestablishment Islamist movements is at least partly a response to the perception that national leaders are corrupt, authoritarian, and generally unconcerned about the welfare of ordinary citizens.[49] A study of Algeria, for example, described the political condition producing support for the Islamic Salvation Front as a "system of power, patronage and privilege that entrenched interests in the party, government and economy are unwilling to sacrifice in the name of some larger good."[50] The situation fueling public anger in Jordan has been described as "a system [where] cronyism is persuasive," with opportunities for enrichment channeled by insiders to "the same old faces, families and clans."[51] Under such circumstances, the government is "often resented, if not hated, [and] this produces one of two reactions: either complete apathy, or at least passivity, or alienation and activism in some anti-establishment medium."[52]

Although it is not self-evident that anger at domestic leaders would foster support for international terrorism, a connection is suggested by an insightful study carried out in Morocco during the war to liberate Kuwait following Saddam Hussein's invasion of that country in 1990. As in many other Arab countries, popular demonstrations erupted in Morocco against the U.S.-led coalition seeking to expel Iraq's army from Kuwait. This was puzzling to some observers, since Saddam had invaded a fellow Arab country and was known to be a brutal dictator. Yet it was the United States and its coalition partners, which included the government of Morocco and other Arab countries, that were viewed as the real enemy. Mounia Bennani-Chraibi, a Moroccan sociologist, investigated this apparent puzzle through interviews with young Moroccans and reported that "unshared wealth was the central theme of discourse." More specifically, U.S. and Arab leaders were seen as acting in concert to ensure the survival of a status quo that privileged the few while denying opportunity to the vast majority. Young Moroccans viewed the anti-Saddam coalition as a self-interested partnership in which American and Arab "enemies of the people" worked together to preserve a corrupt political and economic order.[53]

This discussion suggests several hypotheses about the impact of political and economic factors on attitudes toward terrorism against the United States in the Arab and perhaps broader Muslim world.

> *Hypothesis 5.* Individuals whose personal economic circumstances are disadvantageous are more likely to approve of terrorist acts against U.S. targets.
>
> *Hypothesis 6.* Individuals who believe that their country's economic situation is unfavorable are more likely to approve of terrorist acts against U.S. targets.
>
> *Hypothesis 7.* Individuals who hold more negative views about the foreign policy of the U.S. or other Western countries are more likely to approve of terrorist acts against U.S. targets.

Hypothesis 8. Individuals who hold more negative views about their own political leaders or government are more likely to approve of terrorist acts against U.S. targets.

Data and Methods

Data and Cases

Data with which to test the hypotheses listed above are provided by attitude surveys carried out in Algeria and Jordan in mid-2002. More broadly based surveys have also examined attitudes toward terrorism in the Arab and Muslim world, most notably those carried out by the Pew Research Center between 2002 and 2005. These surveys do not provide measures of many of the relevant independent variables, however. The surveys in Algeria and Jordan, by contrast, include questions about terrorism on interview schedules that probe much more deeply into attitudes relating to religion, culture, and issues of political economy.

The Algerian and Jordanian surveys both involved face-to-face interviews with representative national samples of adults over the age of eighteen. In Algeria the survey was conducted by a team of scholars at the University of Algiers as part of the World Values Survey (WVS),[54] with the country team adding questions pertaining to terrorism and world affairs to the standard WVS interview schedule. Stratified random sampling was used to select *communes,* the equivalent of counties in the United States. Quotas based on age and sex, informed by the 1998 national census, were employed to select respondents at the commune level. The survey was conducted in the late spring of 2002, and a total of 1,282 men and women were interviewed. The survey in Jordan, which was not affiliated with the WVS, was conducted in the early summer of 2002 by the Middle East Research group in Amman. Using a sampling frame provided by the government statistical office, a random sample of 1,000 respondents was selected and interviewed.

Although similar in some respects, Algeria and Jordan differ in important ways that are relevant to the present study. Accordingly, a comparison of the two countries involves features of a "most different systems" research design. Most important, perhaps, Algeria and Jordan differ with respect to their experience with terrorism. Algeria experienced prolonged civil conflict involving savage acts of domestic terrorism throughout the 1990s. On one side of this war were extremist Islamist groups, some of which were offshoots of legitimate political movements that had been suppressed by the government. On the other were not only the country's security forces but also militias and vigilante groups that were sometimes supported by the government.

Most accounts assert that there was brutality on all sides, with the number of Algerians killed usually estimated at 150,000 or more.[55] Some of the fighters were Algerians who had fought with Islamist forces against the Soviet Union in Afghanistan, thus reflecting a global dimension to the violence and terrorism that convulsed the country for almost a decade. Given Algeria's direct and intense experience with the horrors caused by terrorist acts, it is possible that passive support for international terrorism will be relatively low.

Jordan's experience with political violence and terrorism is quite different. The country has experienced much lower levels of domestic terrorism than Algeria, and there had been no recent terrorist attacks in the country at the time the survey was conducted. On the other hand, at least half of Jordan's population is of Palestinian origin, making the country's citizens particularly sensitive and presumably sympathetic to the goals of the al-Aqsa intifada and the associated armed struggle that had been taking place in the West Bank and Gaza for almost two years at the time the survey was conducted. Given this combination of low domestic terrorism and a strong connection to the Israeli-Palestinian conflict, Jordanians may very well have a perspective on terrorism that differs from that of Algerians and most likely one that is at least somewhat more supportive.

Another very important difference concerns the relationship between religion and the state. In Jordan, the monarch is a direct descendent of Prophet Muhammad, which provides the king with a measure of political legitimacy. The constitution recognizes Islam as the official state religion, and Islamic institutions, such as religious endowments and trusts (*awqaf*), exercise considerable political influence. In Algeria, although the constitution also recognizes Islam as the state religion, ruling elites have a predominantly secular orientation, and the influence of religious institutions is limited and circumscribed. This is reflected, for example, in the formation in 1991 of the *Comité national pour la sauveguarde de l'Algérie*, an alliance of parties, unions, women's groups, newspapers, and other associations committed to limiting the role of religion in political affairs.[56]

Algeria and Jordan have also had significantly different experiences with political Islam. In Algeria, the 1991 parliamentary elections were canceled following an Islamist victory in the first round of balloting. Indeed, the *Comité national pour la sauveguarde de l'Algérie* was formed largely to press for this cancellation to prevent the Islamic Salvation Front from coming to power. In Jordan, by contrast, the Islamic Action Front won the parliamentary elections of 1989 and became the dominant force in the governing coalition. The parliament subsequently enacted a number of laws reflecting the party's Islamist orientation, including several that increased sex segregation in public life.[57] Many of these laws were deeply unpopular, contributing—together with a change in electoral procedures and some manipulation by the palace—to the poor showing of the Islamic Action Front in subsequent parliamentary elections. Nevertheless, the Front remains a prominent and influential force in Jordanian political life.[58]

Still other differences between Algeria and Jordan include regime type, ideological orientation, colonial history, and foreign alliances. Algeria is a republic with a strong president and a tradition of state socialism and militant involvement in Third World causes. The country had a long and intense colonial experience under the French, and ties to France remain strong four decades after independence. Jordan, by contrast, is a conservative monarchy, has a more laissez-faire ideological orientation, and was closely aligned with the West during the cold war. The country did not experience the disruption of traditional life associated with intense colonial domination, and its most important external relationships outside the Middle East are with Britain and the United States.

Finally, there are important demographic and economic differences between the two countries. Algeria is one of the largest and most populous countries in the Arab world. Additionally, its population contains a large number of Berbers, and for some of them Arabic is not their first language. With respect to economic considerations, Algeria has excellent water resources, abundant arable land, and substantial reserves of oil and natural gas. As such, despite current economic problems, it has the potential to be one of the most economically developed countries in the Arab world. The situation in Jordan is very different. It is among the Arab countries with the smallest population, and there are almost no Jordanians for whom Arabic is not the first language. Landlocked, largely desert, and possessing few natural resources, Jordan is also one of the poorest countries in the Arab world.

All this suggests that a comparison of findings from Algeria and Jordan has the advantages and disadvantages of a research design involving dissimilar cases. There are, of course, some similarities between the two countries, such as the young age of their populations, high unemployment, and a rentier economic structure—based on petroleum exports in Algeria and remittances and aid in Jordan. But the differences are far more striking, and they involve factors that are particularly relevant for a study of passive support for terrorism among Muslim publics. Thus, as with other comparisons involving a most different systems research design, confidence in the generalizability of similar findings will increase, since they will have been found to apply under very different conditions. Alternatively, should the two countries yield dissimilar findings, it will not be possible to offer more than informed speculation about country-level factors that account for these differences.

The time period of the Algerian and Jordanian surveys also deserves mention. Both were carried out in the late spring and early summer of 2002, and this is probably fortuitous in at least some respects. The surveys followed the 9/11 terrorist attacks but not so closely as to reflect the shock of these events. Had the surveys been conducted closer to the 9/11 attacks, sympathy toward the United States may well have been inflated, and antipathy toward terrorist organizations and activities may have been artificially low. On the other hand, given that the surveys preceded the U.S. invasion of Iraq by almost a year, responses were probably not influenced by the heightened anger at the United States and the heightened sympathy for the Iraqi resistance that later became widespread in the Arab world.

No temporal setting is completely without conditioning effects, however, and at least some aspects of this period undoubtedly had an impact on attitudes toward terrorism against U.S. targets. The most important of these is probably the U.S.-led war in Afghanistan, which began in October 2001. Accordingly, as with any time-bounded study, the analysis must be replicated to determine whether observed relationships vary over time as well as space. And, if so, attributes of the time periods associated with particular findings should be treated as conditionalities and incorporated into the explanatory models being developed. The importance of replication notwithstanding, however, spring–early summer 2002 would seem to be an appropriate period during which to investigate the determinants of passive support for terrorism against the United States in the Arab and Muslim world and thereby establish a baseline with which to compare any causal relationships observed in future studies.

Variables and Measures

The Algerian and Jordanian surveys were conducted by different research teams using different interview schedules. As a result, although the two survey instruments asked many of the same questions, some attitudes and orientations pertinent to the present analysis are measured by items that are similar and comparable rather than identical.

The most important difference concerns the items used to measure attitudes toward terrorist acts against U.S. targets, the dependent variable in the analysis to follow. The measures not only possess face validity, however, they also appear to be conceptually equivalent, which is the critical consideration since determinants rather than levels of support for terrorism are being compared. In the Algerian survey, the dependent variable is measured by a single item that asked directly about the events of September 11. In the Jordanian case, two highly intercorrelated items ($r = .315$; $p \rightarrow .000$) have been combined to form an index measuring attitudes toward terrorist acts against U.S. targets. These items are given below:

> *Algeria.* As you know, a group of religious extremists hijacked four civilian airliners in September and crashed them into buildings

in New York and Washington, D.C., killing several thousand people. Do you strongly approve, approve, disapprove, or strongly disapprove of this action?

Jordan. As you may know, after the military campaign in Afghanistan began, some people called on all Muslims to join in armed jihad against the United States. Do you strongly support, somewhat support, somewhat oppose, or strongly oppose this call to armed jihad?

I shall now read you the names of some international figures. As I read each one, please tell me whether you believe he is very trustworthy, fairly trustworthy, not very trustworthy, or not at all trustworthy, or that you have not heard or read enough about him to offer an opinion.

—Al-Qaida leader Usama bin Laden

(Only one individual is listed here out of ten included in the survey. Among these ten, in addition to bin Laden, were UN Secretary General Kofi Annan, U.S. President George W. Bush, Saudi Arabian Crown Prince Abdullah, and Egyptian President Hosni Mubarak.)

Although different, the two measures are conceptually equivalent and operationalize the same normative orientation. And though neither uses the word "terrorism," the orientation measured in each instance is clearly approval-disapproval of terrorist acts directed at the United States. In the Algerian case, the item asks directly about a specific terrorist act—the attacks of September 11 on New York and Washington. In Jordan, although the questions do not ask about a specific act of international terrorism, the first item's inquiry about "armed jihad against the United States" references a type of activity of which the 9/11 events are the most dramatic and best-known example. Moreover, the second item adds a degree of specificity and thus contributes further to the equivalence of the Jordanian and Algerian measures. In calling for an assessment of Usama bin Laden, the item asks about the self-proclaimed architect of the 9/11 attacks, a man who publicly claimed responsibility for this and other attacks on U.S. targets and who was, in fact, being hunted by American forces in Afghanistan at the time the Jordanian survey was conducted.

In this case, as in the case of several independent variables, measurement procedures need not be identical; relationships observed in Algeria and Jordan can be instructively compared as long as the operational procedures measure the same concept. Should different variable relationships be found in the two countries, it is far more likely that this is the result of country-specific conditions rather than differences in measurement. At the same time, following the logic of replication and a most different systems research design, finding identical or highly similar patterns in the two countries will further increase confidence in both the accuracy and generalizability of these patterns.

The response distributions for these items, as shown in Table 13.1, demonstrate that the central tendency of the distributions is different in Algeria and Jordan. In Algeria, responses are skewed in the direction of opposition to terrorism. Specifically, 77 percent of the respondents disapprove of the 9/11 attacks and, of these, 58 percent disapprove strongly. On the other hand, 23 percent approve of these attacks, and 45 percent of these individuals approve strongly. In Jordan, responses are skewed in the opposite direction. Specifically, 56 percent express strong support for armed jihad against the United States, and another 15 percent express some support. Similarly, 45 percent of the Jordanian respondents judge Usama bin Laden to be very trustworthy, and another 21 percent judge him to be fairly trustworthy. This higher level of support for terrorist acts against the United States may partly be a result of the particular questions asked. It may also, as suggested earlier, reflect the fact that Jordan has experienced much less domestic political violence and, at the time of the survey, was more directly affected by the Palestinian intifada. These latter possibilities suggest what may be a promising avenue for future cross-national research. Nevertheless, the different levels of aggregate Algerian and Jordanian support for terrorism against the United States and the reasons for the difference do not affect the test of hypotheses specifying individual-level relationships.

In the multivariate analysis to follow, responses to the Algerian survey item have been divided into the categories of "approve" and "disapprove" of the events of September 11, thereby forming a dichotomized measure. In the Jordanian case, respondents have been divided according to whether they do or do not both express strong support for armed jihad against the United States and consider Usama bin Laden to be very trustworthy, thereby creating a dichotomous measure in this case as well. The distribution of ratings on this dichotomized two-item index is also presented in Table 13.1, which shows that 33 percent of the Jordanian respondents both express strong support for armed jihad against the United States and judge Usama bin Laden to be very trustworthy. This cutting point has been selected so that the variance to be explained in Jordan will be roughly comparable to that in Algeria.

Table 13.2 lists the items used in Algeria and Jordan to measure the independent variables in the eight hypotheses listed above. Four of these pertain to religion and culture: (1) religiosity or religious involvement; (2) attitudes toward political Islam; (3) attitudes toward Western cultural norms, indicated by views about gender relations; and (4) views about the societal effects of Western culture. The others pertain to economic and political

---

Algeria

As you know, a group of religious fundamentalists hijacked four civilian
airliners in September and crashed them into buildings in New York and
Washington, D.C., killing several thousand people. What is your opinion of
this action?

Strongly approve	10.1%
Approve	12.5%
Disapprove	32.9%
Strongly disapprove.	44.5%

Jordan

As you may know, after the military campaign in Afghanistan began, some
people called on all Muslims to join in armed jihad against the United States.
Do you strongly support, somewhat support, somewhat oppose, or strongly
oppose this call to armed jihad?

Strongly support	55.5%
Somewhat support	15.0%
Somewhat oppose	5.4%
Strongly oppose	24.1%

I would now like to read you the names of some international figures. As I read
each one, please tell me whether you believe he is very trustworthy, fairly trustworthy, not very trustworthy, or not at all trustworthy, or haven't you heard or
read enough about them to say?

Al-Qaida leader Usama bin Laden

Very trustworthy	45.2%
Fairly trustworthy	21.3%
Not very trustworthy	5.0%
Not at all trustworthy	13.8%
Haven't heard enough	14.8%

(In addition to bin Laden, the question called for evaluations of nine other
individuals, among them Secretary General Kofi Annan, U.S. President George
W. Bush, Saudi Arabian Crown Prince Abdullah, and Egyptian President Hosni
Mubarak.)

Index Based on Items Taken Together

Very high support for both Jihad and bin Laden	33.3%
Not very high support for both Jihad and bin Laden	66.7%

considerations: (5) personal economic circumstances; (6) assessments of the national economic situation; (7) views about U.S. foreign policy; and (8) assessments of domestic political institutions and leaders. Additionally, sex, age, and education are included in the model as control variables.

Most items possess face validity. Most also correlate strongly with one or more similar items on the interview schedule, which offers evidence of reliability and increases confidence in validity. To maximize comparability, however, and also to minimize missing data, only one similar item from the Algerian and Jordanian interview schedules is used to measure each independent variable. Assessment of domestic political institutions and leaders is the only independent variable measured by an index composed of two or more intercorrelated items. In the Jordanian case, no item asks directly about personal economic circumstances. An estimate is provided by questions that ask whether a respondent is employed (outside the home) and, if not, whether he or she is seeking employment. The interview schedules also require using somewhat different items to measure assessments of the national economic situation.

Findings

To test the hypotheses listed above, Table 13.3 presents regression analyses showing the relationship between the dependent variable and each independent variable for both Jordan and Algeria. The findings are strikingly similar for the two countries, which is all the more important given differences between the two countries in experience with terrorism; in political, economic, and demographic character; and in the questions used to measure a number of the variables. That findings are similar despite these many differences, any of which might have produced dissimilar variable relationships in Algeria and Jordan, increases confidence in both the accuracy and generalizability of the patterns observed.

One important similarity is the absence of support for hypotheses that attribute significant explanatory power to religious or cultural factors. With respect to Hypothesis 1, in neither Algeria nor Jordan are individuals with higher levels of religious involvement more likely to approve of terrorist acts against U.S. targets. Similarly, with respect to Hypothesis 3, in neither country are individuals with a more negative view of Western culture, as measured by attitudes toward interaction between women and men in public, more likely to approve of terrorist acts against U.S. targets. And again, with respect to Hypothesis 4, individuals who believe Western culture is having an injurious effect on their society are not more likely in either country to approve of terrorist acts against the United States.

The one very limited exception to the conclusion that religious and cultural factors have little explanatory power concerns Hypothesis 2, which

Table 13.2. Survey Items from Algeria and Jordan Used to
Measure Independent Variables

Religiosity and Religious Involvement (Hypothesis 1)

Algeria: How often do you attend religious services these days? More than
once a week, once a week, once a month, only on special holy days,
once a year, less often, practically never, never

Jordan: How often do you visit a mosque? Hardly ever, only during religious
holidays, only on Fridays and religious holidays, more than once a
week, at least once each day, five times each day

Attitude toward Political Islam (Hypothesis 2)

Algeria: Please tell me whether you strongly agree, agree, neither agree nor
disagree, disagree, or strongly disagree with the following statement:
Religious leaders should have no influence over the decisions of the
government.

Jordan: Please tell me which of the following contrasting statements is closest to your own view: (1) Political leaders in our country should be
selected solely by Islamic clerics. (2) Political leaders in our country
should be elected solely by the people.

Values Pertaining to Gender Relations (Hypothesis 3)

Algeria: Please indicate whether you strongly agree, agree, disagree, or
strongly disagree with the interpretation of Islam that is presented
in the following statement. It is a violation of Islam for male and
female university students to attend classes together.

Jordan: Please tell me whether you strongly agree, somewhat agree, somewhat disagree, or strongly disagree with the following statement:
Men and women should not be allowed to work in the same place.

Effects of Western Culture (Hypothesis 4)

Algeria: Please tell me whether you agree or disagree with the following
statement about the United States and other countries: Exposure to
the culture of the U.S. and other Western countries has a harmful
effect on our country.

Jordan: How much of a threat is posed to our culture by American popular
culture, such as music, television and films? Very serious threat,
serious threat, minor threat, no threat at all

Personal Economic Circumstances (Hypothesis 5)

Algeria: People sometimes describe themselves as belonging to the working class, the middle class, or the upper or lower class. Would you

Table 13.2. (continued)

| | describe yourself as belonging to the upper class, upper middle class, lower middle class, working class, or lower class? |
| Jordan: | Are you employed (outside the home)? If not, are you looking for employment? |

Country's Economic Situation (Hypothesis 6)

| Algeria: | Generally speaking, would you say that Algeria is run by a few big interests looking out for themselves or that it is run for the benefit of all the people? |
| Jordan: | Would you describe the current economic situation in Jordan as very good, fairly good, fairly bad, or very bad? |

Assessment of American Foreign Policy (Hypothesis 7)

| Algeria: | Please tell me which of the following statements about the United States best expresses your opinion. Almost all U.S policies toward other countries are good, some U.S policies toward other countries are good and some are bad, or almost all U.S. policies toward other countries are bad. |
| Jordan: | Do you strongly agree, somewhat agree, somewhat disagree, or strongly disagree that the U.S. often violates other people's human rights around the world? |

Evaluation of Domestic Political Institutions and Leaders (Hypothesis 8)

| Algeria: | I am going to name a number of Algerian organizations. For each one, please tell me how much confidence you have in that organization: a great deal of confidence, quite a lot of confidence, not very much confidence, or none at all: the government, the parliament, the military, the police. |
| Jordan: | I will now read a list of institutions in our country. As I read each one, please tell me how much confidence you have in each: a great deal of confidence, a fair amount of confidence, scant confidence, or no confidence at all: the government, the legal system, the police. |

proposes that persons who are more favorably disposed to the platform of political Islam are more likely to approve of terrorist acts against U.S. targets. There is no support for this hypothesis in Jordan. In Algeria the relationship is statistically significant, although not especially robust. More important, however, the direction of the relationship is the opposite of that proposed. In the Algerian case, men and women who are less favorably disposed to the

Table 13.3. Logistic Regression with Support for
Terrorism as Dependent Variable

VARIABLE	ALGERIA	JORDAN
Higher religious involvement	.056	.133
	(.042)	(.153)
Higher support for political Islam	−.193	.149
	(.085)*	(.123)
Oppose gender mixing in public	−.027	.179
	(.068)	(.104)
Western culture is harmful	.095	.092
	(.105)	(.085)
Personal economic situation unfavorable	.097	−.556
	(.095)	(.257)*
Country's economic situation unfavorable	−.090	.160
	(.134)	(.195)
Negative assessment of American foreign policy	.828	.221
	(.177)***	(.088)**
Negative evaluation of domestic political institutions and leaders	318	.286
	(.094)***	(.088)***
Female sex	−.134	.326
	(.209)	(.257)
Older age	−.289	−.021
	(.094)***	(.008)***
Higher education	−.063	−.019
	(.045)	(.068)

Note: Dependent variable is coded 0 = lesser support for terrorism, 1 = greater support for terrorism. Table presents logit coefficients ($\hat{\beta}$) with standard errors in parentheses.

*Statistically significant at .05 level.
**Statistically significant at .01 level.
***Statistically significant at .002 level.

platform of political Islam are more likely to approve of terrorist acts against U.S. targets.

A second similarity, equally or even more important, pertains to hypotheses that attribute significant explanatory power to political and economic factors. In neither Algeria nor Jordan do the data provide support for Hypothesis 6, which proposes that individuals who believe their country's economic situation is unfavorable are more likely to approve of terrorist acts against U.S. targets. By contrast, very strong support is provided by both the Algerian and Jordanian surveys for Hypotheses 7 and 8. The former proposes that individuals who hold more negative views about U.S. foreign policy are more likely to approve of terrorist acts against U.S. targets. The latter proposes that individuals who hold more negative views about their own government leaders and institutions are more likely to approve of terrorist acts against the United States. In both Algeria and Jordan, and for both hypotheses, the strength of the relationship is reflected in a p value approaching .000.

Only with respect to Hypothesis 5 is there a difference in the findings from Algeria and Jordan. This hypothesis proposes that individuals whose personal economic circumstances are disadvantageous are more likely to approve of terrorist acts against U.S. targets. Although the Algerian data provide no support for this hypothesis, a statistically significant relationship has been found in Jordan. As in the case of Hypothesis 2, however, the direction of this relationship is the opposite of that proposed. Jordanian men and women whose personal economic circumstances are more advantageous are more likely to approve of terrorist acts against U.S. targets.

A final similarity between the findings from Algeria and Jordan concerns the demographic variables included in the regression models. In both countries, there is no significant difference in attitudes relating to terrorism between men and women or between better-educated and less well-educated individuals. By contrast, again in both countries, younger individuals are much more likely than older individuals to express approval of terrorist acts against U.S. targets. The strength of this relationship is again reflected in a p value approaching .000 in both the Algerian and Jordanian cases.

Implications and Conclusion

Survey findings from Algeria and Jordan strongly suggest that religious and cultural orientations have little influence on individual attitudes toward terrorism against the United States, whereas considerations pertaining to politics—and perhaps to political economy more broadly—do possess substantial explanatory power. In neither the Algerian nor the Jordanian case is there support for hypotheses in which personal religious involvement, support for the platform of political Islam, opposition to Western values relating to gender relations, or a belief that Western cultural norms are injurious to one's society is an independent variable. These findings are in sharp contrast to what would be expected if, as claimed by the Clash of Civilizations thesis, Arab attitudes toward the United States are in substantial measure the product of a normative conflict between Islam and the West.

The data also indicate that factors with a specific economic focus have little explanatory power. In neither Algeria nor Jordan is support for terrorism against the United States more likely among individuals whose personal economic situation is disadvantageous. Indeed, some evidence, albeit limited, suggests that support is more likely among men and women in more advantageous economic circumstances. Similarly, men and women with a negative assessment of their country's economic situation are no more likely than others to express support for terrorism against the United States. Thus, the data strongly suggest that neither personal nor societal economic circumstances, by themselves, are important determinants of attitudes toward terrorism directed at the United States and perhaps toward international terrorism more generally.

The significance of these findings lies in the evidence they provide about factors that do not have explanatory power. These analyses based on survey data from Algeria and Jordan thus indicate the inadequacy of explanations that attribute popular support for terrorism either to Arab and Muslim religious and cultural values or to unsatisfactory economic conditions. Because both types of explanations are frequently advanced, the significance of these negative findings derives in part from the doubt they cast on the unidimensional, overly simplified, and sometimes ethnocentric assessments of Arab attitudes and behavior that are common in the United States and some other Western societies.

The contribution of the preceding analysis is not limited to negative findings, however, regardless of how useful these may be in raising doubts about explanations that have frequently been proposed to explain support for international terrorism in the Arab and Muslim world. Equally important, if not more so, are insights about the independent variables that do have explanatory power: level of confidence in domestic political institutions and assessments of U.S. foreign policy. More specifically, men and women with less confidence in domestic political institutions and with stronger disapproval of American foreign policy are more likely than others to express approval of terrorism against U.S. targets.

There would seem to be an important conceptual link between the two independent variables with significant explanatory power, one that sheds light on a political dynamic that may play a particularly important role in fostering support for terrorism against the United States and perhaps against Western targets more generally. As suggested in the discussion of political and economic factors, both domestic and international political actors may be seen as committed to the perpetuation of a status quo with which at least some ordinary citizens are highly dissatisfied. Indeed, those who are sufficiently discontent to approve of terrorist acts are likely to perceive a shared interest, and perhaps even an explicit partnership, between domestic and international actors devoted to preventing the kind of change that people believe would improve their life circumstances.

The data do not demonstrate that those who express support for terrorism against the United States have a conscious and fully articulated view along these lines. All that can be said with certainty is that negative assessments of both U.S. foreign policy and domestic political institutions are strongly associated with support for terrorist acts against U.S. targets. But the conclusion that such support is fostered primarily by antipathy toward powerful actors deemed responsible for the prevailing political and economic order, and that this is a consequence of antipathy toward both domestic and international political actors, constitutes a potentially important insight that is consistent with the evidence from two very dissimilar Arab countries. Accordingly, it offers an important line of inquiry for future empirical research.

The one important point to be added, which amplifies the preceding interpretation, is that younger men and women are significantly more likely than older individuals to express approval of terrorist acts against the United States and, if the preceding interpretation is correct, to have their views about terrorism shaped by anger at those believed to be responsible for the political and economic status quo. Given that personal economic circumstance is not related to attitudes toward terrorism, youth is probably not a proxy for economic uncertainty or distress. Indeed, in Jordan, support for terrorism against the United States is more likely among individuals, including young people, whose economic situation is relatively favorable. In any event, apparently, it is among younger persons that negative attitudes about those who exercise political power in the domestic and international arenas are most likely to produce approval of terrorist acts against U.S. targets.

The conclusion to be drawn from this interpretation is that support for terrorism against the United States does not flow directly from discontent with personal or even societal circumstances but rather from perceptions about who or what is responsible for the status quo and that this is especially the case among younger persons. As emphasized, this pattern has emerged with striking similarity in two Arab countries that differ greatly in character and experience, thus increasing confidence in its accuracy and generalizability. Accordingly, although the broader political dynamic attributed to findings from Algeria and Jordan has been inferred, not demonstrated, it follows plausibly from the variable relationships in both countries and points to a promising and potentially very important avenue for future research. Given recent terrorist attacks in several European countries, future research should also investigate whether the factors that account for variance in Arab attitudes toward terrorism against the United States are also determinants of attitudes toward terrorism against targets in other Western countries.

NOTES

INTRODUCTION

1. The first part of this discussion draws upon Mark Tessler and Amaney Jamal, "Political Attitude Research in the Arab World: Emerging Opportunities," *PS: Political Science & Politics* 39 *(July 2006): 1–5.*

2. The following volumes provide useful overviews of the status of survey research devoted to Arab political and social orientations in the early and mid-1980s: Monte Palmer, *Survey Research in the Arab World: An Analytical Index* (London: Menas, 1982); Tawfic Farah, ed., *Political Behavior in the Arab States* (Boulder, Colo.: Westview, 1983); Mark Tessler et al., eds., *The Evaluation and Application of Survey Research in the Arab World* (Boulder, Colo.: Westview, 1987).

3. I. William Zartman, "Political Science," in Leonard Binder, ed., *The Study of the Middle East: Research and Scholarship in the Humanities and Social Sciences* (New York: Wiley, 1976), 305. See also Gabriel Ben Dor, "Political Culture Approach to Middle East Politics," *International Journal of Middle East Studies* 8 (January 1977): 43–63.

4. Malcolm Kerr, "Foreword," in Farah, *Political Behavior in the Arab States*, xi.

5. Michael Hudson, "The Political Culture Approach to Arab Democratization: The Case for Bringing It Back In, Carefully," in Rex Brynen, Bahgat Korany, and Paul Noble, eds., *Political Liberalization and Democratization in the Arab World* (Boulder, Colo.: Lynne Reinner, 1995), 69.

6. William Quandt, "Hume and Quandt on Contemporary Algeria," *Middle East Policy* 6 (February 1999): 145.

7. Lisa Anderson, "Politics in the Middle East: Opportunities and Limits in the Quest for Theory," in Mark Tessler, ed., with Jodi Nachtwey and Anne Banda, *Area Studies and Social Science: Strategies for Understanding Middle East Politics* (Bloomington: Indiana University Press, 1999), 7.

8. This issue is discussed by a number of political scientists in Tessler, Nachtwey, and Banda, *Area Studies and Social Science.*

9. Iliya Harik, "Some Political and Cultural Considerations Bearing on Survey Research in the Arab World," in Tessler et al., *The Evaluation and Application of Survey Research in the Arab World,* 66–67.

10. Quoted in ibid., 68.

11. Mustapha Hamarneh. *Revisiting the Arab Street: Research from Within* (Amman, Jordan: Center for Strategic Studies, University of Jordan, 2005).

12. Details about the World Values Survey are available at http://www.world valuessurvey.org/ (accessed September 10, 2010).

13. Details about the Arab Barometer are available at http://www.arabbarometer. org/ (accessed September 10, 2010). The Arab Barometer was chosen by the American Political Science Association to receive the 2009 Lijphart/Przeworski/Verba Data Set Award, which is given annually for the best publicly available data set in the field of comparative politics.

14. Details about the Global Barometer are available at http://www.global barometer.net/ (accessed September 10, 2010).

15. The January 2008 issue of the *Journal of Democracy* contains articles based on research from many of the regional barometers, including the Arab Barometer. Many of these articles are reprinted in *How People View Democracy*, ed. Larry Diamond and Marc Platner (Baltimore, Md.: Johns Hopkins University Press, 2008). For an article that uses and integrates data from the various regional barometers, see Yun-han Chu et al., "Public Opinion and Democratic Legitimacy," *Journal of Democracy* 19 (April 2008): 74–87.

1. REGIME ORIENTATION AND PARTICIPANT CITIZENSHIP IN DEVELOPING COUNTRIES

1. Gabriel Almond and Sidney Verba, *The Civic Culture* (Princeton, N.J.: Princeton University Press, 1(63), 33.

2. Lucian Pye, "Introduction," in Lucian Pye and Sidney Verba, eds., *Political Culture and Political Development* (Princeton, N.J.: Princeton University Press, 1965), 13.

3. Gaetano Mosca, *The Ruling Class* (New York: McGraw-Hill, 1939); and Robert MacIver, *The Web of Government* (New York: Macmillan, 1947).

4. For example, Almond and Verba, *Civic Culture*; Gabriel Almond and G. Bingham Powell Jr., *Comparative Politics: A Developmental Approach* (Boston: Little, Brown, 1966); and Kenneth Sherill, "The Attitudes of Modernity," *Comparative Politics* 2 (1969): 184–210.

5. Leonard Binder, "National Integration and Political Development," *American Political Science Review* 58 (1964): 622–31; Dankwart Rustow and Robert E. Ward, "Introduction," in Rustow and Ward, eds., *Political Modernization in Japan and Turkey* (Princeton, N.J.: Princeton University Press, 1964); Alex Inkeles, "Participant Citizenship in Six Developing Countries," *American Political Science Review* 63 (1969): 1129–41; Samuel Huntington, "The Change to Change," in R. Macridis and B. Brown, eds., *Comparative Politics: Notes and Readings* (Homewood, Ill.: Dorsey, 1972); Samuel Huntington and Joan Nelson, *No Easy Choice: Political Participation in Developing Countries* (Cambridge, Mass.: Harvard University Press, 1976); and Gabriel Ben Dor, "Political Culture Approach to Middle East Politics," *International Journal of Middle East Studies* 8 (1977): 43–63.

6. See Daniel Lerner, *The Passing of Traditional Society* (New York: Free Press, 1958); Joseph Kahl, *The Measurement of Modernism* (Austin: University of Texas Press, 1968); Samuel Huntington, *Political Order in Changing Societies* (New Haven, Conn.: Yale University Press, 1968); Inkeles, "Participant Citizenship"; Norman Nie, G. Bingham Powell Jr., and Kenneth Prewitt, "Social Structure and Political Participation: Developmental Relationships," *American Political Science Review* 63 (1969): 361–78; Mark Tessler, "The Application of Western Theories and Measures of Political Participation to a Single-Party North African State," *Comparative Political Studies* 5 (1972): 175–91; and Fred Hayward, "Correlates of National Political Integration: The Case of Ghana," *Comparative Political Studies* 7 (1974): 165–92.

7. For example, Joseph Gusfield, "Tradition and Modernity: Misplaced Polarities in the Study of Social Change," *American Journal of Sociology* 72 (1965): 351–62.

8. For example, Lloyd Rudolph and Susanne Rudolph, *The Modernity of Tradition* (Chicago: University of Chicago Press, 1967).

9. For example, C. S. Whitaker Jr., *The Politics of Tradition: Continuity and Change in Northern Nigeria, 1964–1966* (Princeton, N.J.: Princeton University Press, 1970); S. N. Eisenstadt, *Post-Traditional Society* (New York: Norton, 1972); Mark Tessler, "Development, Oil, and Cultural Change in the Maghreb," in Naiern Sherbiny and Mark Tessler, eds., *Arab Oil: Impact of the Arab Countries and Global Implications* (New York: Praeger, 1976); and Mark Tessler and Linda Hawkins, Acculturation, Socioeconomic Status, and Attitude Change in Tunisia: Implications for Modernization Theory," *Journal of Modem African Studies* 17 (1979): 473–95.

10. For example, Charles Anderson, Fred von der Mehden, and Crawford Young, *Issues of Political Development* (Englewood Cliffs, N.J.: Prentice Hall, 1967); Robert Melson and Howard Wolpe, "Modernization and the Politics of Communalism: A Theoretical Perspective," *American Political Science Review* 64 (1970): 1112–30; and Ivo Feierabend, Rosalind Feierabend, and Betty Nesvold, "Social Change and Political Violence: Cross-National Patterns," in J. Finkle and R. Gable, eds., *Political Development and Social Change* (New York: Wiley, 1971).

11. For example, John Holm, *Dimensions of Mass Involvement in Botswana Politics: A Test of Alternative Theories,* Comparative Politics series (Beverly Hills, Calif.: Sage, 1974).

12. See Karl Deutsch, "Social Mobilization and Political Development," *American Political Science Review* 55 (1961): 493–511; and Melson and Wolpe, "Modernization and the Politics of Communalism."

13. Samuel Huntington, "Political Development and Political Decay," *World Politics* 17 (1965): 386–430; and Huntington, *Political Order in Changing Societies* (New Haven, Conn.: Yale University Press, 1968).

14. Alex Inkeles, "Making Men Modern: On the Causes and Consequences of Individual Change in Six Developing Countries," *American Journal of Sociology* 75 (1969): 208–25.

15. For example, Irene Tinker and Michele Bo Bramson, *Women and World Development* (Washington, D.C.: Overseas Development Council, 1976); Ester Boserup, *Women's Role in Economic Development* (London: Allyn and Unwin, 1970); and Jane Jaquette, *Women in Politics* (New York: Wiley, 1974).

16. For example, Robert LeVine, "Political Socialization and Culture Change," in Clifford Geertz, ed., *Old Societies and New States* (New York: Free Press, 1963); Kenneth Prewitt, "Political Socialization and Political Education in New Nations," in Roberta Sigel, ed., *Learning about Politics* (New York: Random House, 1970); and James A. Bill and Robert L. Hardgrave Jr., *Comparative Politics: The Quest for Theory* (Columbus, Ohio: Merrill, 1973), 115.

17. For example, David Apter, *The Politics of Modernization* (Chicago: University of Chicago Press, 1965), 22–28; William McCord, *In the Springtime of Freedom* (New York: Oxford University Press, 1965); and Joseph La Polombara and Myron Weiner, *Political Parties and Political Development* (Princeton, N.J.: Princeton University Press, 1966).

18. Paul E. Sigmund Jr., *The Ideologies of the Developing Nations* (New York: Praeger, 1967), 26.

19. For example, Donald Rothchild and Robert Curry Jr., *Scarcity, Choice, and Public Policy in Middle Africa* (Berkeley: University of California Press, 1978), 134.

20. Sigmund, *The Ideologies of the Developing Nations.*

21. James B. Mayfield, *Rural Politics in Nasser's Egypt* (Austin: University of Texas Press, 1971), 151.

22. Immanuel Wallerstein, "Introduction," in I. Wallerstein and P. Foster, eds., *Ghana and the Ivory Coast* (Chicago: University of Chicago Press, 1971).

23. Robert Denberger, "The Relevance of China's Development Experience for Other Developing Countries," *ITEMS* (SSRC) 31 (1977): 25–34.

24. Gunnar Myrdal, *Asian Drama: An Inquiry into the Poverty of Nations* (New York: Pantheon, 1968).

25. Francine Frankel, "Compulsion and Social Change: Is Authoritarianism the Solution to India's Economic Problems," *World Politics* 30 (1978): 215–40.

26. Immanuel Wallerstein, "The Decline of the Single-Party African State," in La Polambara and Weiner, *Political Parties and Political Development.*

27. For example, LeVine, "Political Socialization"; and Bill and Hardgrave, *Comparative Politics,* 110–13.

28. For example, Tessler, "The Application of Western Theories"; and Holm, *Dimensions of Mass Involvement in Botswana Politics.*

29. For example, Roberta Sigel, "Assumptions about the Learning of Political Values," *Annals* 361 (1965): 1–9.

30. Tawfic Farah and Faisal S. A. al-Salem, "Political Efficacy, Political Trust, and the Action Orientations of University Students in Kuwait," *International Journal of Middle East Studies* 8 (1977): 317–28.

31. For example, James Scott, "An Essay on the Political Functions of Corruption," *Asian Studies* 5 (1967): 501–23; and Maxwell Owusu, *Uses and Abuses of Political Power* (Chicago: University of Chicago Press, 1970).

32. Donald Campbell, "Degrees of Freedom and the Case Study," *Comparative Political Studies* 8 (1975): 178–93

33. For example, Charles Micaud, *Tunisia: The Politics of Modernization* (New York: Praeger, 1964); and "Leadership and Development: The Case of Tunisia," *Comparative Politics* 2 (1969): 463–84; Clement Henry Moore, *Tunisia Since Independence* (Berkeley: University of California Press, 1965; Lars Rudebeck, *Party and People: A Study of Political Change in Tunisia* (New York: Praeger, 1967); and Mark Tessler, William O'Barr, and David Spain, *Tradition and Identity in Changing Africa* (New York: Harper and Row, 1973).

34. Clement Henry Moore, "On Theory and Practice among Arabs," *World Politics* 24 (1971): 106–26.

35. Elbaki Hermassi, *Leadership and National Development in North Africa* (Berkeley: University of California Press, 1972); Abdelkader Zghal, "The Reactivation of Tradition in a Post-Traditional Society," in S. M. Eisenstadt, ed., *Post-Traditional Societies* (New York: Norton, 1972); John Entelis, "Ideological Change and an Emerging Counter-Culture in Tunisian Politics," *Journal of Modem African Studies* 12 (1974): 543–68; Mark Tessler, "Single-Party Rule in Tunisia," *Common Ground* (AUFS) 2 (1976): 55–64; and Tessler, "Women's Emancipation in Tunisia," in Lois Beck and Nikki Keddie, eds., *Women in the Muslim World* (Cambridge, Mass.: Harvard University Press, 1978).

36. Zghal, "The Reactivation of Tradition"; see also Mark Tessler, "Political Change and the Islamic Revival in Tunisia," *Maghreb Review* 5 (1980): 8–19.

37. Hermassi, *Leadership and National Development in North Africa,* 156.

38. Jean Fox O'Barr and Mark Tessler. "Gender and Participant Citizenship in Tunisia," in Tawfic Farah, ed., *Political Behavior in the Arab States* (Boulder, Colo.: Westview, 1983).

39. Donald Campbell and Julian Stanley, *Experimental and Quasi-Experimental Designs for Research* (Chicago: Rand-McNally, 1963).

40. Mark Tessler, "Problems of Measurement in Comparative Research: Perspectives from an African Survey," *Social Science Information* 12 (1973): 29–43

41. Tessler, "The Application of Western Theories."

42. Mark Tessler, "Response Set and Interviewer Bias," in William O'Barr, David Spain, and Mark Tessler, eds., *Survey Research in Africa: Its Applications and Limits* (Evanston, Ill.: Northwestern University Press, 1973).

43. For example, O'Barr, Spain, and Tessler, *Survey Research in Africa.*

44. Mark Tessler, "Cultural Modernity: Evidence from Tunisia," *Social Science Quarterly* 52 (1971): 290–308.

45. Holm, *Dimensions of Mass Involvement in Botswana Politics.*

2. THE ORIGINS OF POPULAR SUPPORT
FOR ISLAMIST MOVEMENTS

1. Youssef Ibrahim, "Militant Muslims Grow Stronger as Algeria's Economy Grows Weaker," *New York Times,* June 25, 1990.

2. Gary Abramson, "Rise of the Crescent," *Africa Report* (March–April 1992): 20.

3. *Quarterly Economic Review of Morocco* 1 (1987): 19.

4. Richard B. Parker, *North Africa: Regional Tensions and Strategic Concerns* (New York: Praeger, 1984), 17; Jon Marks, "Special Report on Morocco," *Middle East Economic Digest,* April 1, 1994, 33.

5. Marks, "Special Report on Morocco," 33.

6. Mounia Bennani-Chraibi, "Les représentations du monde des jeunes Marocains" [The view of the world of young Moroccans], Thèse de doctorat de l'Institut d'Etudes Politiques, Paris, 1993, 215, 241.

7. Mahfoud Bennoune, *The Making of Contemporary Algeria, 1830–1987: Colonial Upheavals and Post-independence Development* (Cambridge: Cambridge University Press, 1988), 227.

8. Willy Jansen, *Women Without Men* (Leiden: E. J. Brill, 1987), 18–20.

9. Djaafar Lesbet, "Effets de la crise du logement en Algérie: Des cités d'urgence à l'état d'exception," *Maghreb-Machrek: Monde Arabe—villes, pouvoirs et sociétés* (numéro spécial) 143 (January–March 1994): 220.

10. Georges Sabagh, "The Challenge of Population Growth in Morocco." *Middle East Report* (March–April 1993): 31.

11. Youssef Ibrahim, "In Algiers, Curfew and Threats of Worse," *New York Times,* June 7, 1991.

12. Mark Tessler, "The Alienation of Urban Youth," in I. William Zartman and Mark W. Habeeb, eds., *State and Society in Contemporary North Africa* (Boulder, Colo.: Westview, 1993).

13. Kenneth Brown, "Lost in Algiers," *Mediterraneans* 4 (summer 1993): 11.

14. "Etat, ville et mouvements sociaux au Maghreb et au Moyen Orient." *Maghreb-Machrek* 115 (1987): 59.

15. George D. Moffett, "North Africa's Disillusioned Youth," *Christian Science Monitor,* May 17, 1989.

16. Paul Digne, "Algérie: un navire à la dérive"; Albert Bourgi, "Etudiants: ou menera le désespoir?"; and François Soudan, "Tunisie: islamistes contre 'Albanais,'" all in *Jeune Afrique,* February 12, 1989.

17. Mark Tessler, "Explaining the 'Surprises' of King Hassan II: The Linkage between Domestic and Foreign Policy in Morocco; Part I: Tensions in North Africa in the Mid-1980s," *Universities Field Staff International Reports* 38 (1986).

18. James Paul, "States of Emergency: The Riots in Tunisia and Morocco," *MERIP Reports* 127 (October 1984).

19. Dirk Vandewalle, "Autopsy of a Revolt: The October Riots in Algeria" (Hanover, N.H.: Institute of Current World Affairs, 1988).

20. David Seddon, "The Politics of 'Adjustment' in Morocco," in Bonnie K. Campbell and John Loxley, eds. *Structural Adjustment in Africa* (New York: St. Martin's, 1989), 263.

21. Marks, "Special Report on Morocco," 33.

22. Dany Dufour, "L'Enseignement en Algérie," *Maghreb-Machrek* 80 (1978).

23. John Entelis, *Algeria: The Revolution Institutionalized* (Boulder, Colo.: Westview, 1986), 92.

24. Russell Stone, "Tunisia: A Single-Party System Holds Change in Abeyance," in I. William Zartman, *Political Elites in Arab North Africa: Morocco, Algeria, Tunisia, Libya, and Egypt* (New York: Longman, 1982), 164.

25. Willis Witter, "Moroccans See Good, Evil in Possible Economic Boom," *Washington Times,* September 22, 1993.

26. Azzedine Layachi, "Government, Legitimacy, and Democracy in Algeria," *Maghreb Report* (January–February 1992): 3.

27. Abla Amawi, "Democracy Dilemmas in Jordan," *Middle East Report* 174 (January/February 1992): 27.

28. Mark Tessler, "Anger and Governance in the Arab World: Lessons from the Maghrib and Implications for the West," *Jerusalem Journal of International Relations* 13 (1991): 11–12.

29. Tessler, "Anger and Governance in the Arab World," 13.

30. Omar Bendourou, "The Exercise of Political Freedoms in Morocco," *Review of the International Commission of Jurists* 40 (1988): 39–40.

31. Vandewalle, "Autopsy of a Revolt," 2.

32. John Entelis, "Algeria under Chadli: Liberalization without Democratization; or, Perestroika, Yes; Glasnost, No," *Middle East Insight* (fall 1988): 52–53.

33. Azzedine Layachi, and Abdel-kader Haireche, "National Development and Political Protest: Islamists in the Maghreb Countries," *Arab Studies Quarterly* 14 (spring–summer 1992): 75; see also John Entelis and Lisa Arone, "Algeria in Turmoil," *Middle East Policy* 1 (1992).

34. Tessler, "The Alienation of Urban Youth."

35. Michael W. Suleiman, "Attitudes, Values, and the Political Process in Morocco," in I. William Zartman, ed., *The Political Economy of Morocco* (New York: Praeger, 1987), 113.

36. Ibrahim Karawan, "Arab Dilemmas in the 1990s," unpublished paper, October 1993, 162.

37. Quoted in ibid.; also in Kevin Dwyer, *Arab Voices* (Berkeley: University of California Press, 1991), 20.

38. *La Guerre du Golfe et l'Avenir des Arabes: débats et réflexions* (Tunis: Cérès Productions, 1991); Abdelkader Zghal, "La guerre du Golfe et la recherche de la bonne distance," in *La Guerre du Golfe,* 161–62; David Pollock, *The "Arab Street"? Public Opinion in the Arab World,* Policy Paper No. 32 (Washington, D.C.: Washington Institute for Near East Policy, 1992), 31, 35.

39. Taher Labib, "L'intellectuel des sept mois," in *La Guerre du Golfe,* 195.

40. Alan Riding, "Tunisians, in Search of Roots, Turn toward Iraq," *New York Times,* October 10, 1990.

41. Fred Huxley, "Moroccan Public Backs PLO-Israel Peace Plan, Views U.S. Positively," USIA Opinion Research Memorandum, Washington, D.C., December 13, 1993.

42. *La Guerre du Golfe.*

43. Chadly Ayari, "Le monde arabe et l'enjeu économique du nouvel ordre mondial," in *La Guerre du Golfe,* 14.

44. Sami Yousif, "The Iraqi-U.S. War: A Conspiracy Theory," in Haim Bresheeth and Nira Yuval-Davis, eds., *The Gulf War and the New World Order* (London: Zed Books, 1991); Shibley Telhami, "Between Theory and Fact: Explaining American Behavior in the Gulf War," *Security Studies* (fall 1992); Karawan, "Arab Dilemmas in the 1990s."

45. Bennani-Chraibi, "Les Représentations du Monde des Jeunes Marocains," 392–436.

46. Ibid., 413.

47. Ibid., 417–18.

48. Jane Kokan, "Morocco: Riot Deaths as Hassan Faces Challenge," *London Times,* February 20, 1994.

49. "L'Islam contestataire en Tunisie," *Jeune Afrique,* March 14, 21, and 28, 1979.

50. Elbaki Hermassi, "La société tunisienne au miroir islamiste," *Maghreb-Machrek* 103 (1984).

51. Fouad Ajami, *The Arab Predicament: Arab Political Thought and Practice since 1967* (Cambridge: Cambridge University Press, 1981), 52.

52. Ibid., 55, 69.

53. Mark Tessler, "Political Change and the Islamic Revival in Tunisia," *Maghreb Review* 5 (1980): 13.

54. Susan Waltz, "The Islamist Appeal in Tunisia," *Middle East Journal* 40 (fall 1986); Dirk Vandewalle, "From the New State to the New Era: Toward a Second Republic in Tunisia." *Middle East Journal* 42 (1988); Souhayr Belhassen, "Nous oeuvrons pour que l'islam occupe sa place en Algérie." *Jeune Afrique,* February 12, 1989.

55. Vandewalle, "From the New State to the New Era," 617.

56. David Seddon, "The Politics of 'Adjustment' in Morocco," in Bonnie K. Campbell and John Loxley, eds. *Structural Adjustment in Africa* (New York: St. Martin's, 1989), 263.

57. Gary Abramson, "Rise of the Crescent," *Africa Report* (March–April, 1992): 20.

58. Layachi, and Haireche, "National Development and Political Protest," 76.

59. Rami G. Khouri, "The Arab Dream Won't Be Denied," *New York Times,* December 15, 1990.

60. Rami G. Khouri, "A Lesson in Middle East History and Humanity," *Jordan Times,* May 28, 1991.

61. Gundrun Krämer, "Liberalization and Democracy in the Arab World," *Middle East Report* 174 (January–February 1992): 23.

62. Jamal S. Al-Suwaidi, "Arab and Western Conceptions of Democracy: Evidence from a UAE Opinion Survey," in David Garnham and Mark Tessler, eds., *Democracy, War, and Peace in the Middle East* (Bloomington: Indiana University Press, 1995), 92.

63. Henry Munson, "Islamist Political Movements in North Africa," paper presented at the workshop "Politico-Religious Movements and Development in the Near East," Washington, D.C., June 1992, 19.

64. Al-Suwaidi, "Arab and Western Conceptions of Democracy," 93.

65. "L'Islam contestataire en Tunisie."; Mark Tessler, "Political Change and the Islamic Revival in Tunisia," *Maghreb Review* 5 (1980): 12.

66. Mark Tessler, "Regime Orientation and Participant Citizenship in Developing Countries: Hypotheses and a Test with Longitudinal Data from Tunisia," *Western Political Quarterly* 34 (December 1981).

67. Layachi and Haireche, "National Development and Political Protest," 76.

68. Youssef Ibrahim, "Jordan Feels Change within as Muslims Pursue Agenda," *New York Times,* December 26, 1992.

69. Ibrahim A. Karawan, "'ReIslamization Movements' according to Kepel: On Striking Back and Striking Out," *Contention* 2 (fall 1992): 172.

70. Layachi and Haireche, "National Development and Political Protest," 78.

71. Youssef Ibrahim, "In Algiers, Curfew and Threats of Worse," *New York Times,* June 7, 1991; Layachi and Haireche, "National Development and Political Protest," 79.

72. Layachi and Haireche, "National Development and Political Protest," 76.

73. François Burgat and William Dowell, *The Islamic Movement in North Africa* (Austin: University of Texas Press, 1993), 281.

74. Youssef Ibrahim, "Militant Muslims Grow Stronger as Algeria's Economy Grows Weaker," *New York Times,* June 25, 1990.

75. Youssef Ibrahim, "PLO Is Facing Growing Discontent," *New York Times,* April 5, 1992.

76. Dirk Vandewalle, "Ben Ali's New Tunisia," *Universities Field Staff International Reports* 8 (1989–90): 5.

3. ISLAM AND DEMOCRACY IN THE MIDDLE EAST

1. Lisa Anderson, "Politics in the Middle East: Opportunities and Limits in the Quest for Theory," in Mark Tessler, with Jodi Nachtwey and Anne Banda, eds., *Area Studies and Social Science: Strategies for Understanding Middle East Politics* (Bloomington: Indiana University Press, 1999), 6.

2. Hilal Khashan, "History's Legacy," *Middle East Quarterly* 5 (March 1998): 43–44.

3. Rami Khouri, "A View from the Arab World," *Jordan Times,* July 5, 2000.

4. Miral Fahmy, "Mubarak to Put Economy before Politics," *Reuters Global Newsbank,* September 27, 1999.

5. Samuel Huntington, "Democracy's Third Wave," in Larry Diamond and Marc Plattner, eds., *The Global Resurgence of Democracy* (Baltimore, Md.: Johns Hopkins University Press, 1993), 13–15.

6. Scott Mainwaring, "Democratic Survivability in Latin America," in Howard Handelman and Mark Tessler, eds., *Democracy and Its Limits: Lessons from Asia, Latin*

America, and the Middle East (Notre Dame, Ind.: University of Notre Dame Press, 1999), 45.

7. Yun-han Chu, Larry Diamond, and Doh Chull Shin, "Growth and Equivocation in Support for Democracy: Taiwan and Korea in Comparative Perspective," paper presented at the Annual Meeting of the American Political Science Association, Washington, D.C., August 31–September 3, 2000, 2.

8. Ronald Inglehart, "Culture and Democracy," in Lawrence E. Harrison and Samuel Huntington, eds., *Culture Matters: How Values Shape Human Progress* (New York: Basic Books, 2000), 96.

9. Iliya Harik, "Pluralism in the Arab World, *Journal of Democracy* 5 (July 1994): 56.

10. Richard Rose, William Mishler, and Christian Haerpfer, *Democracy and Its Alternatives: Understanding Post-Communist Societies* (Baltimore, Md.: Johns Hopkins University Press, 1998), 98.

11. James Gibson, "The Resilience of Mass Support for Democratic Institutions and Processes in the Nascent Russian and Ukrainian Democracies," in V. Tismaneanu, ed., *Political Culture and Civil Society in Russia and the New States of Eurasia* (New York: M. E. Sharpe, 1995), 55.

12. Khalil Shikaki, "The Transition to Democracy in Palestine," *Journal of Palestine Studies* 98 (1996): 2–14; Isabelle Daneels, *Palestine's Interim Agreement with Democracy* (Jerusalem: Jerusalem Media and Communication Centre, 1998).

13. Hilal Khashan, *Arab Attitudes toward Israel and Peace* (Washington D.C.: Washington Institute for Near East Policy, 2000).

14. Nevine Khalil, "Listening to the Masses" [in Arabic], *Al-Ahram Weekly,* October 1–7, 1998.

15. *Jordanian Opinion Survey regarding Jordanian-Palestinian Relations* [in Arabic] (Amman: Jordan University Center for Strategic Studies, 1995); Maher Massis, "Jordan: A Study of Attitudes toward Democratic Changes," *Arab Studies Quarterly* 20 (summer 1998): 37–63.

16. Anderson, "Politics in the Middle East," 7; Michael Hudson, "The Political Culture Approach to Arab Democratization: The Case for Bringing It Back In, Carefully," in Rex Brynen, Bahgat Korany, and Paul Noble, eds., *Political Liberalization and Democratization in the Arab World* (Boulder, Colo.: Lynne Reinner, 1995).

17. Mehran Kamrava, *Democracy in the Balance: Culture and Society in the Middle East* (New York: Chatham House, 1998), 201, 223.

18. Ibrahim A. Karawan, *Islamist Impasse* (London: International Institute for Strategic Studies. 1997); Dale Eickelman and James Piscatori, *Muslim Politics* (Princeton, N.J.: Princeton University Press, 1996).

19. Galal Amin, *Egypt's Economic Predicament* (Leiden: Brill, 1995); Mark Tessler, "The Origins of Popular Support for Islamist Movements: A Political Economy Analysis," in John Entelis, ed., *Islam, Democracy, and the State in North Africa* (Bloomington: Indiana University Press, 1997).

20. Youssef Choueiri, "The Political Discourse of Contemporary Islamist Movements," in Abdel Salem Sidahmed and Anoushiravam Ehteshami, eds., *Islamic Fundamentalism* (Boulder, Colo.: Westview, 1996); Bernard Lewis, *The Shaping of the Modern Middle East* (New York: Oxford University Press, 1994), 54–56.

21. Elie Kedourie, *Democracy and Arab Political Culture* (London: Frank Cass, 1994), 5–6; also Samuel Huntington, "Will More Countries Become Democratic?" *Political Science Quarterly* 99 (summer 1984): 208.

22. Fred Halliday, *Islam and the Myth of Confrontation: Religion and Politics in the Middle East* (London: I. B. Tauris, 1995), 116; John Esposito and James Piscatori, "Democratization and Islam," *Middle East Journal* 45 (1991): 424–40.

23. Shukri Abed, "Islam and Democracy," in David Garnham and Mark Tessler, eds., *Democracy, War, and Peace in the Middle East* (Bloomington: Indiana University Press, 1995), 127–28.

24. John Esposito and John Voll, *Islam and Democracy* (Oxford: Oxford University Press, 1996); Mohamed Elhachmi Hamdi, "Islam and Democracy: The Limits of the Western Model," *Journal of Democracy* 7 (April 1996): 81–85; Fatima Mernissi, *Islam and Democracy: Fear of the Modern World* (Reading, Mass.: Addison-Wesley, 1992).

25. *Muslim Democrat* 2 (November 2000): 3, 4, 8.

26. Jamal Al-Suwaidi, "Arab and Western Conceptions of Democracy," in Garnham and Tessler, *Democracy, War, and Peace in the Middle East,* 87–88.

27. Ted G. Jelen, "Religion and Public Opinion in the 1990s: An Empirical Overview," in Barbara Norrander and Clyde Wilcox, eds., *Understanding Public Opinion* (Washington D.C.: Congressional Quarterly Press, 1996); Bernadette Hayes, "The Impact of Religious Identification on Political Attitudes: An International Comparison," *Sociology of Religion* 56 (1995): 177–94; Jelen, *The Political Mobilization of Religious Beliefs* (New York: Praeger, 1991).

28. James L. Guth and John C. Green, "Salience: The Core Concept?" in David C. Leege and Lyman A. Kellstedt, eds., *Rediscovering the Religious Factor in American Politics* (Armonk: M. E. Sharpe, 1993).

29. Ted G. Jelen, "Religion and Foreign Policy Attitudes: Exploring the Effects of Denomination and Doctrine," *American Politics Quarterly* 22 (1994): 382–400.

30. Martha Abele MacIver, "Religious Politicization among Western European Mass Publics," in William H. Swatos Jr., ed., *Religious Politics in Global and Comparative Perspective* (New York: Greenwood, 1989).

31. Ted G. Jelen, "Swords, Plowshares, and Philistines: A Comparative Analysis of Religion and Attitudes toward Security Policy," paper presented at the Annual Meeting of the American Political Science Association, San Francisco, August 29–September 1, 1996.

32. Ted G. Jelen, Sue Thomas, and Clyde Wilcox, "The Gender Gap in Comparative Perspective: Gender Differences in Abstract Ideology and Concrete Issues in Western Europe," *European Journal of Politics* 25 (February 1994): 1171–86.

33. Shikaki, "The Transition to Democracy in Palestine"; Mark Tessler and Jodi Nachtwey, "Palestinian Political Attitudes: An Analysis of Survey Data from the West Bank and Gaza," *Israel Studies* 4 (spring 1999): 22–43.

34. Georges Sabagh, Jodi Nachtwey, and Mark Tessler, "Islam, Gender, and the Demographic Challenge in North Africa," paper presented at the Annual Meeting of the Middle East Studies Association, Chicago, 1998; Tessler, "The Contribution of Public Opinion Research to an Understanding of the Information Revolution and Its Impact in North Africa," in Jamal S. Al-Suwaidi, ed., *The Impact of the Information and Communication Revolution on Society and State in the Arab World* (London: I. B. Tauris, 1998); Tessler, "Morocco's Next Political Generation," *Journal of North African Studies* 5, no. 1 (2000): 1–26.

35. Mark Tessler and Jamal Sanad. "Will the Arab Public Accept Peace with Israel: Evidence from Surveys in Three Arab Societies," in Gregory Mahler and Efraim Karsh, eds., *Israel at the Crossroads* (London: I. B. Tauris, 1994); Tessler, "The Origins of Popular Support for Islamist Movements."

4. POLITICAL GENERATIONS IN DEVELOPING COUNTRIES

1. Karl Mannheim, "The Problem of Generations," in Paul Kecskemeti, ed., *Essays on the Sociology of Knowledge* (London: Routledge and Kegan Paul, 1952 [1928]), 276–320.; Theodore M. Newcomb, "Some Patterned Consequences of Membership in a College Community," in Theodore M. Newcomb et al., eds., *Readings in Social Psychology* (New York: Henry Holt, 1947), 345–57; Theodore M. Newcomb et al. *Persistence and Change* (New York: Wiley, 1967); Norman B. Ryder, "The Cohort as a Concept in the Study of Social Change," *American Sociological Review* 30 (1965): 843–61.

2. See David C. Rubin, Tamara A. Rahhal, and Leonard W. Poon, "Things Learned in Early Adulthood Are Remembered Best," *Memory & Cognition* 26, no. 1 (1998): 3–19; Howard Schuman, and Amy D. Corning. "Collective Knowledge of Public Events: The Soviet Era from the Great Purge to Glasnost," *American Journal of Sociology* 105, no. 4 (2000): 913–55; Howard Schuman, and Cheryl Rieger, "Collective Memory and Collective Memories," in Rubin, H. Spinnler and W. Wagenaar, eds., *Theoretical Perspectives on Autobiographical Memory* (Dordrecht, Netherlands: Kluwer, 1992), 323–36.; Howard Schuman and Cheryl Rieger. "Historical Analogies, Generational Effects, and Attitudes toward War," *American Sociological Review* 57 (1992): 315–26; Howard Schuman et al., "Generations and Collective Memories in Lithuania," in N. Schwarz and S. Sudman, eds., *Autobiographical Memory and the Validity of Retrospective Reports* (New York: Springer-Verlag, 1994), 313–33; Howard Schuman and Jacqueline Scott, "Generations and Collective Memories," *American Sociological Review* 54, no. 3 (1989): 351–81.

3. Paul DiMaggio, "Culture and Cognition," *Annual Review of Sociology* 23 (1997): 263–87; Ronald Inglehart, *The Silent Revolution: Changing Values and Political Styles in Advanced Industrial Society* (Princeton, N.J.: Princeton University Press, 1977); Ronald Inglehart and Wayne E. Baker, "Modernization, Cultural Change, and the Persistence of Traditional Values," *American Sociological Review* 65, no. 1 (2000.): 19–51.

4. Duane F. Alwin, "Attitude Factors in Adulthood: The Role of Generational and Life-Cycle Factors," in Dagmar Krebs and Peter Schmidt, eds., *New Directions in Attitude Measurement* (Berlin: De Gruyter, 1993); Duane F. Alwin, "Aging, Personality, and Social Change: The Stability of Individual Differences over the Adult Life Span," in D. L. Featherman, R. M. Lerner, and M. Perlmutter, eds., *Life-Span Development and Behavior,* Vol. 12 (Hillsdale, N.J.: Erlbaum, 1994); Duane F. Alwin, Ronald L. Cohen, and Theodore M. Newcomb, *Political Attitudes over the Life Span: The Bennington Women after Fifty Years* (Madison: University of Wisconsin Press, 1991); Jon A. Krosnick and Ronald L. Alwin, "Aging and Susceptibility to Attitude Change," *Journal of Personality and Social Psychology* 57 (September 1989): 416–25; David O. Sears, "On the Persistence of Early Political Dispositions: The Roles of Attitude Object and Life Stage," in L. Wheeler, ed., *Review of Personality and Social Psychology,* Vol. 4 (Beverly Hills, Calif.: Sage, 1983), 79–116.

5. See Donald O. Sears, "Life-Stage Effects on Attitude Change, Especially among the Elderly," in S. B. Kiesler, J. N. Morgan, and V. K. Oppenheimer, eds., *Aging: Social Change,* (New York: Academic Press, 1981), 183–204.

6. Kent M. Jennings, "Political Knowledge over Time and across Generations," *Public Opinion Quarterly* 60 (1996): 228–52.

7. Rubin, Rahhal, and Poon, "Things Learned in Early Adulthood Are Remembered Best"; Schuman, Howard, and Scott, "Generations and Collective Memories."

8. See Paul B. Baltes, Ursula M. Staudinger, and Ulman Lindenberger, "Lifespan Psychology: Theory and Application to Intellectual Functioning," *Annual Review of Psychology* 50 (1999): 471–507; Kent M. Jennings and Richard G. Niemi, *Generations and Politics: A Panel Study of Young Adults and Their Parents* (Princeton, N.J.: Princeton University Press, 1981); David O. Sears and Nicholas A. Valentino, "Politics Matters: Political Events as Catalysts for Preadult Socialization," *American Political Science Review* 91 (1997): 45–63.

9. See Michael J. Shanahan, "Pathways to Adulthood in Changing Societies: Variability and Mechanisms in Life Course Perspective," *Annual Review of Sociology* 26 (2000): 667–92.

10. Catherine R. Cooper and Jill Denner, "Theories Linking Culture and Psychology: Universal and Community-Specific Processes," *Annual Review of Psychology* 49 (1998): 559–84; Richard A. Settersten Jr. and Karl Ulrich Mayer, "The Measurement of Age, Age Structuring, and Life Course," *Annual Review of Sociology* 23 (1997): 233–61; Michael J. Shanahan, "Pathways to Adulthood in Changing Societies."

11. See Paul B. Baltes, H. W. Reese, and J. R. Nesselroad, *Life-Span Developmental Psychology: Introduction to Research Methods.* Hillsdale, N.J.: Erlbaum, 1988 [1977]); Baltes, Staudinger, and Lindenberger, "Lifespan Psychology"; D. Magnusson, L. R. Bergman, and G. Rudinger, eds., *Problems and Methods in Longitudinal Research: Stability and Change* (Cambridge: Cambridge University Press, 1991).

12. See Jennings, "Residues of a Movement: The Aging of the American Protest Generation," *American Political Science Review* 81, no. 2 (1987): 367–82; Mannheim, "The Problem of Generations"; Sears and Valentino, "Politics Matters."

13. Schuman, Howard, and Scott, "Generations and Collective Memories"; Sears and Valentino, "Politics Matters."

14. Paul DiMaggio, "Culture and Cognition," *Annual Review of Sociology* 23 (1997): 263–87; Kristen Renwick Monroe, James Hankin, and Renée Bukovchik Van Vecten. "The Psychological Foundations of Identity Politics," *Annual Review of Political Science* 3 (2000): 419–47; S. Moscovici, "Notes toward a Description of Social Representations," *European Journal of Social Psychology* 18 (1988): 211–50.

15. Jennings, "Residues of a Movement."

16. Sears and Valentino. "Politics Matters."

17. See J. H. Holland et al., *Induction: Processes of Inference, Learning, and Discovery* (Cambridge, Mass.: MIT Press, 1986).

18. See Harry C. Triandis and Eunkook M. Suh, "Cultural Influences on Personality," *Annual Review of Psychology* 53 (2002): 133–60.

19. Schuman, Howard, and Scott, "Generations and Collective Memories," 359.

20. Schuman, Howard, and Corning, "Collective Knowledge of Public Events"; Schuman, Howard, and Scott. "Generations and Collective Memories."

21. Inglehart and Baker, "Modernization, Cultural Change, and the Persistence of Traditional Values."

22. John Entelis, "Religion and Politics in Algeria: Conflict or Consensus?" *Islam and Christian-Muslim Relations* 12 (2001): 417.

23. James Ciment, *Algeria: The Fundamentalist Challenge* (New York: Facts on File, 1997); Alistair Horne, *A Savage War of Peace: Algeria 1954–1962* (New York: Penguin Books, 1979).

24. Matthew Connelly, *A Diplomatic Revolution: Algeria's Fight for Independence and the Origins of the Post–Cold War Era* (New York: Oxford University Press, 2002).

25. John Ruedy, *Modern Algeria: The Origins and Development of a Nation* (Bloomington: Indiana University Press, 1992), 207–30.

26. Mahfoud Bennoune, *The Making of Contemporary Algeria, 1830–1987: Colonial Upheavals and Post Independence* (Cambridge: Cambridge University Press, 1989), 121–22; Robert Malley, *The Call for Algeria: Third Worldism, Revolution, and the Turn to Islam* (Berkeley: University of California Press, 1996).

27. Ruedy, *Modern Algeria*, 231–37.

28. William Quandt, *Between Ballots and Bullets: Algeria's Transition from Authoritarianism* (Washington, D.C.: The Brookings Institution, 1998), 5.

29. Luis Martinez, *La Guèrre Civile en Algérie, 1990–1998* (Paris: Karthala, 1998).

30. See Ronald L. Alwin and Jon A. Krosnick," Aging, Cohorts, and the Stability of Sociopolitical Orientations over the Life Span," *American Journal of Sociology* 97, no. 1 (1991): 169–95; Sears and Valentino, "Politics Matters."

31. Quandt, *Between Ballots and Bullets,* 31; Mark Tessler, "The Origins of Popular Support for Islamist Movements: A Political Economy Analysis," in John P. Entelis, ed., *Islam, Democracy, and the State in North Africa* (Bloomington: Indiana University Press, 1997), 102; Dirk Vandewalle, *Autopsy of a Revolt: The October Riots in Algeria* (Hanover, N.H.: Institute of Current World Affairs, 1988), 2.

32. Mark Tessler, "Democratic Concern and Islamic Resurgence: Converging Dimensions of the Arab World's Political Agenda," in Handelman and Tessler, *Democracy and Its Limits.*

33. Inglehart and Baker, "Modernization, Cultural Change, and the Persistence of Traditional Values."

34. Using the American Association for Public Opinion Research's [2000] standard definition RR5, the response rate for the combined first two waves of the study is 95.7 percent.

35. Mark Tessler, "The Contribution of Public Opinion Research to an Understanding of the Information Revolution and Its Impact in North Africa," in J. S. Al-Suwaidi, ed., *The Impact of the Information and Communication Revolution on Society and State in the Arab World* (London: I. B. Tauris, 1998), 73–91; Tessler, "Morocco's Next Political Generation," *Journal of North African Studies* 5, no. 1 (2000): 1–26; Tessler, "Islam and Democracy in the Middle East: The Impact of Religious Orientations on Attitudes toward Democracy in Four Arab Countries," *Comparative Politics* 34 (April 2002): 337–54.

36. See Alwin and Krosnick, "Aging, Cohorts, and the Stability of Sociopolitical Orientations over the Life Span"; Sears and Valentino, "Politics Matters."

37. This orientation, measured in a similar fashion, has also been explored in previous research. See Inglehart and Baker, "Modernization, Cultural Change, and the Persistence of Traditional Values."

38. Ronald Inglehart, *Culture Shift in Advanced Industrial Society* (Princeton, N.J.: Princeton University Press, 1990); Inglehart and Baker, "Modernization, Cultural

Change, and the Persistence of Traditional Values"; Tessler, "Morocco's Next Political Generation."

39. Settersten and Mayer, "The Measurement of Age, Age Structuring, and Life Course," 239.

40. Rubin, Rahhal, and Poon, "Things Learned in Early Adulthood Are Remembered Best."

41. Sears and Valentino, "Politics Matters."

42. Mannheim, "The Problem of Generations"; Schuman, Howard, and Rieger, "Collective Memory and Collective Memories"; Schuman et al., "Generations and Collective Memories in Lithuania"; Schuman, Howard, and Scott, "Generations and Collective Memories."

43. Jennings, "Residues of a Movement."

44. Settersten and Mayer, "The Measurement of Age, Age Structuring, and Life Course."

45. We also carried out an empirical test of our decision regarding the definition of "formative years." We sequentially ran regressions with cohort membership defined by nine different eight-year age spans during the years associated with each of the five historical periods discussed above. These began with 10–17 years of age and then proceeded to 11–18, 12–19, and so on through 18–25. The results of this analysis, which are not presented, can be easily summarized: although generally similar across all older age spans, the models in which cohort effects stand out most clearly and consistently are those in which the 18–25 age span was employed. This lends additional validity to our operational definition of "formative years."

46. A follow-up regression analysis was carried out in the case of these three statistically significant relationships. Dummies for all five cohorts were included in the analysis, followed by a Wald test of the difference between the cohort related to the dependent variable and each of the other four cohorts. This was done in order to be sure that the orientations of the cohort in question differed not only from those of all other cohorts taken together but from those of each other individual cohort as well. It may also be noted that we considered an alternative to defining political generations on the basis of historical context, using instead an *ahistorical*, age-based definition that resembles the method employed by Schumann and Scott ("Generations and Collective Memories"). To assess the explanatory utility of "context free" cohort categories, we divided respondents into seven ascending eight-year age categories, beginning with those who were 18 to 25 years old at the time the survey was conducted, followed by those who were 26 to 33, and so on through those respondents who were 66 to 73 at the time of the 1995 survey. An indicator variable representing each age group was included in a single regression for each dependent variable. Schumann and Scott describe this approach as "working backwards," such that "cohorts defined initially in arbitrary age terms [are then] redefined generationally by . . . qualitatively distinct events and changes" (ibid., 360). This method did not show distinguishable effects for most age groups and most dependent variables; the only exceptions were instances where membership in an age group overlapped with membership in a cohort defined in terms of historical era.

47. Quandt, *Between Ballots and Bullets*, 3.

5. THE DEMOCRACY BAROMETERS

1. *Arab Human Development Report* (New York: United Nations Development Programme [UNDP], 2002), chap. 7, available at http://www.arab-hdr.org/ (accessed September 10, 2010).

2. *Arab Human Development Report* (New York: UNDP, 2003), introduction, available at http://www.arab-hdr.org/ (accessed September 10, 2010).

3. Marina Ottaway and Thomas Carothers, "Middle East Democracy," *Foreign Policy* (November–December 2004): 22–28. See also Marcia Posusney and Michelle Angrist, eds., *Authoritarianism in the Middle East* (Boulder, Colo.: Lynne Rienner, 2005).

4. See, for example, Mark Tessler and Eleanor Gao, "Gauging Arab Support for Democracy," *Journal of Democracy* 16 (July 2005): 83–97; Mark Tessler, "Do Islamic Orientations Influence Attitudes Toward Democracy in the Arab World? Evidence from Egypt, Jordan, Morocco, and Algeria," *International Journal of Comparative Sociology* 2 (spring 2003): 229–49; Mark Tessler, Mansoor Moaddel, and Ronald Inglehart, "Getting to Arab Democracy: What Do Iraqis Want?" *Journal of Democracy* 17 (January 2006): 38–50.

5. Ronald Inglehart et al., eds., *Human Beliefs and Values: A Cross-cultural Sourcebook Based on the 1999–2002 Values Surveys* (Mexico City: Siglo XXI, 2004).

6. The Arab Barometer team consists of partners in five Arab countries: Fares Braizat of the Center for Strategic Studies, Jordan; Khalil Shikaki of the Center for Policy and Survey Research, Palestine; Ghanim al-Najjar of Kuwait University, Kuwait; Mhammed Abderebbi of Hassan II University–Mohammadia, Morocco; and Abdallah Bedaida of the University of Algiers, Algeria. The first wave of the Arab Barometer project was funded by the Middle East Partnership Initiative (MEPI) of the U.S. Department of State.

7. Additional surveys in the first wave of the Arab Barometer are scheduled to be carried out in Yemen and Lebanon in early 2008.

8. The characteristics attributed to democracy were assessed by the following item: "People often differ in their views on the characteristics that are essential to democracy. If you have to choose only one thing, what would you choose as the most important characteristic, and what would be the second most important?" The response code listed the four attributes discussed in the text and also gave respondents the option of specifying another characteristic. Almost 99 percent of the respondents selected one of the four listed characteristics.

9. For excellent discussions of the compatibility of Islam and democracy, see Khaled Abou Fadl, *Islam and the Challenge of Democracy* (Princeton, N.J.: Princeton University Press, 2004); John Esposito and John Voll, *Islam and Democracy* (New York: Oxford University Press, 1996); José Casanova, "Civil Society and Religion: Retrospective Reflections on Catholicism and Prospective Reflections on Islam," *Social Research* 68 (winter 2001): 1041–80; and Vali Nasr, "The Rise of 'Muslim Democracy'?" *Journal of Democracy* 16 (April 2005): 13–27. For a data-based examination of why support for Islam in politics is compatible with support for democracy, see Amaney Jamal, "Reassessing Support for Democracy and Islam in the Arab World: Evidence from Egypt and Jordan," *World Affairs* 169 (fall 2006): 51–63.

10. Samuel P. Huntington, *The Clash of Civilizations and the Remaking of the World Order* (New York: Simon and Schuster, 1996), 135–39. See also his article "Will

More Countries Become Democratic?" *Political Science Quarterly* 99 (summer 1984): 193–218.

11. Francis Fukuyama, *The End of History and the Last Man* (New York: Avon, 1992), 45–46.

12. See, for example, Daniel Pipes, "Debate: Islam and Democracy," PBS *"Wide Angle,"* July 15, 2003, available at http://www.danielpipes.org/article/1167 (accessed September 10, 2010). See also Bernard Lewis, *The Shaping of the Modern Middle East* (New York: Oxford University Press, 1994); and Elie Keddourie, *Democracy and Arab Political Culture* (Washington, D.C.: Washington Institute for Near East Policy, 1992).

13. We used factor analysis to assess the consistency among a number of survey items designed to measure judgments pertaining to political Islam. Many of these items loaded highly on a common factor, offering evidence of reliability and increasing confidence in validity. The item asking whether men of religion should have influence over government decisions was the best single indicator of this dimension, and for purposes of clarity and parsimony it is used in the present analysis as a measure of support for political Islam.

14. Our regression tables are available at http://www.journalofdemocracy.org/articles/gratis/TesslerGraphics-19-1.pdf (accessed September 10, 2010).

6. POLITICAL CULTURE IN TURKEY

1. Scott Mainwaring, "Democratic Survivability in Latin America," in Handelman and Tessler, *Democracy and Its Limits*, 45.

2. Yun-han Chu, Larry Diamond, and Doh Chull Shin, "Halting Progress in Korea and Taiwan," *Journal of Democracy* 12, no. 1 (2001): 122.

3. Juan J. Linz and Alfred Stepan, "Toward Consolidated Democracies," *Journal of Democracy* 7, no. 2 (1996): 16.

4. Adam Przeworski, *Democracy and the Market: Political and Economic Reforms in Eastern Europe and Latin America* (Cambridge: Cambridge University Press, 1991), 26

5. Yılmaz Esmer, *Devrim, evrim, statüko: Türkiye'de sosyal, siyasal, ekonomik değerler* [Revolution, evolution and status-quo: Social, political, and economic values in Turkey] (Istanbul: TESEV Yayınları, 1999), 28–29.

6. Metin Heper and Aylin Güney, "The Military and the Consolidation of Democracy: The Recent Turkish Experience," *Armed Forces and Society* 26, no. 4 (2000): 637.

7. Ali Çarkoğlu, "Religiosity and Public Policy Evaluations in Turkey," unpublished manuscript (2001), 2.

8. Ibid., 4.

9. Heper and Güney, "The Military and the Consolidation of Democracy," 639.

10. Çarkoğlu, "Religiosity and Public Policy Evaluations in Turkey," 4.

11. Paul Kubicek, "The Earthquake, Europe, and Prospects for Political Change in Turkey," *Middle East Review of International Affairs* 5, no. 2 (2001), available at meria.idc.ac.il/news/2001/01news7 (accessed September 10, 2010).

12. Larry Diamond, "Is the Third Wave Over," *Journal of Democracy* 7, no. 3 (1996): 20–37.

13. Ergün Özbudun, *Contemporary Turkish Politics: Challenges to Democratic Consolidation* (Boulder, Colo.: Lynne Rienner, 2000), 151–54

14. Heper and Güney, "The Military and the Consolidation of Democracy," 650.

15. Ronald Inglehart, "Culture and Democracy," in Lawrence E. Harrison and Samuel Huntington, eds., *Culture Matters: How Values Shape Human Progress* (New York: Basic Books, 2000), 96.

16. Richard Rose, William Mishler, and Christian Haerpfer, *Democracy and Its Alternatives: Understanding Post-Communist Societies* (Baltimore, Md.: Johns Hopkins University Press, 1998), 96.

17. Linz and Stepan, "Toward Consolidated Democracies," 14–15.

18. Jeremy Salt, "Turkey's Military 'Democracy,'" *Current History* 98, no. 625 (1999): 72.

19. Heper and Güney, "The Military and the Consolidation of Democracy," 636–7; Frank Tachau and Metin Heper, "The State, Politics, and the Military in Turkey," *Comparative Politics* 16, no. 1 (1983): 17–33.

20. Esmer, *Devrim, Evrim, Statüko*, 43.

21. Elie Kedourie, *Democracy and Arab Political Culture* (London: Frank Cass, 1994), 5–6; also Bernard Lewis, *The Shaping of the Modern Middle East* (New York: Oxford University Press, 1994), 54–6; Y. Choueiri, "The Political Discourse of Contemporary Islamist Movements," in Abdel Salem Sidahmed and Anoushiravam Ehteshami, eds., *Islamic Fundamentalism* (Boulder, Colo.: Westview, 1996).

22. Fred Halliday, *Islam and the Myth of Confrontation: Religion and Politics in the Middle East* (London: I. B. Tauris, 1995), 116; John Esposito and James Piscatori, "Democratization and Islam," *Middle East Journal* 45, no.3 (1991): 427–40.

23. John Esposito and John Voll, *Islam and Democracy* (Oxford: Oxford University Press, 1996); Mohamed Elhachmi Hamdi, "Islam and Democracy: The Limits of the Western Model," *Journal of Democracy* 7, no. 2 (1996): 81–85; Fatima Mernissi, *Islam and Democracy: Fear of the Modern World* (Reading, Mass.: Addison-Wesley, 1992).

24. Shukri Abed, "Islam and Democracy," in David Garnham and Mark Tessler, eds., *Democracy, War, and Peace in the Middle East* (Bloomington: Indiana University Press, 1995), 128–29.

25. Ergün, Özbudun, "Turkey: How Far from Consolidation?," *Journal of Democracy* 7, no. 3 (1996): 134; Heper and Güney, p. 639.

26. Çarkoğlu, "Religiosity and Public Policy Evaluations in Turkey," 4; Ali Çarkoğlu and Binnaz Toprak, *Türkiye'de din, toplum ve siyaset* [Religion, society, and politics in Turkey] (Istanbul: TESEV Yayınları, 2000).

27. Özbudun, "Turkey," 134.

28. Rose, Mishler and Haerpfer, *Democracy and Its Alternatives*, 98.

29. James Gibson, "The Resilience of Mass Support for Democratic Institutions and Processes in the Nascent Russian and Ukrainian Democracies," in Vladimir Tismaneanu, ed., *Political Culture and Civil Society in Russia and the New States of Eurasia* (New York: M. E. Sharpe, 1995), 55.

30. Esmer, *Devrim, Evrim, Statüko*, 85.

31. Ibid., 79.

32. Rose, Mishler and Haerpfer, *Democracy and Its Alternatives*, 98.

33. Alberto Marradi, "Factor Analysis as an Aid in the Formulation and Refinement of Empirically Useful Concepts," in Edgar F. Borgatta and David J. Jackson, eds., *Factor Analysis and Measurement in Sociological Research* (London: Sage, 1981), 17–18.

34. Rose, Mishler and Haerpfer, *Democracy and Its Alternatives*, 98.

35. Robert Rohrschneider, "Explaining Citizen's Views about Civil Liberties across the Globe: The Micro- and Macro-Level Sources of Political Intolerance," paper presented at the Annual Meeting of the American Political Science Association, San Francisco, 2001.

36. Mark Tessler, "Do Islamic Orientations Influence Attitudes toward Democracy in the Arab World: Evidence from the World Values Survey in Egypt, Jordan, Morocco, and Algeria," *International Journal of Comparative Sociology* 2 (spring 2003): 229–49.

37. Mark Tessler, "Islam and Democracy in the Middle East: The Impact of Religious Orientations on Attitudes toward Democracy in Four Arab Countries," *Comparative Politics* 34, no. 3 (2002): 337–54; Chu, Diamond, and Shin, "Halting Progress in Korea and Taiwan," 122–36; Pamela Waldron-Moore, "Eastern Europe at the Crossroads of Democratic Transition," *Comparative Political Studies* 32, no.1 (1999): 32–62; Robert Mattes and Hermann Thiel, "Consolidation and Public Opinion in South Africa," *Journal of Democracy* 9, no. 1 (1998): 95–110; Rose, Mishler, and Haerpfer, *Democracy and Its Alternatives;* Dan Ottemoeller, "Popular Perceptions of Democracy: Elections and Attitudes in Uganda," *Comparative Political Studies* 31, no. 1 (1998): 98–124; Doh Chull Shin and Huoyan Shyu, "Political Ambivalence in South Korea and Taiwan," *Journal of Democracy* 8, no. 3 (1997): 109–24; Marta Lagos, "Latin America's Smiling Mask," *Journal of Democracy* 8, no. 3 (1997): 125–34.

38. Esmer, *Devrim, Evrim, Statüko,* 86.

39. Tessler, "Islam and Democracy"; idem, "Do Islamic Orientations Influence Attitudes."

40. Özbudun, "Turkey," 123; also Clement Henry Dodd, *The Crisis of Turkish Democracy* (Hull: Eothen, 1983), 1.

41. Tessler, "Islam and Democracy"; idem, "Do Islamic Orientations Influence Attitudes."

7. ASSESSING THE INFLUENCE OF RELIGIOUS PREDISPOSITIONS ON CITIZEN ORIENTATIONS RELATED TO GOVERNANCE AND DEMOCRACY

1. Samuel Huntington, "Democracy's Third Wave," in Larry Diamond and Marc Plattner, eds., *The Global Resurgence of Democracy* (Baltimore, Md.: Johns Hopkins University Press, 1993), 13.

2. Robert Ross, "Where Are Postcommunist Countries Going?" *Journal of Democracy* 8, no. 2 (1997): 92–108; and Philippe Schmitter and Terry Lynn Karl, "What Democracy Is . . . and Is Not," in Diamond and Plattner, *The Global Resurgence of Democracy,* 47.

3. Gabriel Almond and Sidney Verba, *The Civic Culture: Political Attitudes and Democracy in Five Nations* (Boston: Little, Brown, 1963), 3; and Gabriel Almond and Sidney Verba, *The Civic Culture Revisited* (Boston: Little, Brown, 1963), 27.

4. Ronald Inglehart, "Culture and Democracy," in Lawrence E. Harrison and Samuel Huntington, eds., *Culture Matters: How Values Shape Human Progress* (New York: Basic Book, 2000), 96.

5. Elie Kedourie, *Democracy and Arab Political Cultures* (London: Frank Cass, 1994), 5–6; Bernard Lewis, *The Shaping of the Modern Middle East* (New York: Oxford University Press, 1994), 54–56; and Samuel Huntington, *The Third Wave* (Norman: University of Oklahoma Press, 1991), chap. 6.

6. Mark Tessler, "Islam and Democracy in the Middle East: The Impact of Religious Orientations on Attitudes toward Democracy in Four Arab Countries," *Comparative Politics* 34, no. 3 (2002): 337–54; Mark Tessler, "Do Islamic Orientation Influence Attitudes toward Democracy in the Arab World: Evidence from Egypt, Jordan, Morocco, and Algeria," *International Journal of Comparative Sociology* 2, no. 1 (2003): 229–49; and Saiful Mujani, "Religious Democrats: Democratic Culture and Muslim Participation in Post-Suharto Indonesia," Ph.D. diss., Ohio State University, 2004.

7. Mark Tessler, Carrie Konold, and Megan Reif, "Political Generations in Developing Countries: Evidence and Insights from Algeria," *Public Opinion Quarterly* 68, no. 2 (2004): 184–216.

8. DEMOCRACY AND THE POLITICAL CULTURE ORIENTATIONS OF ORDINARY CITIZENS

1. Samuel Huntington, "Democracy's Third Wave," in Larry Diamond and Marc Plattner, eds., *The Global Resurgence of Democracy* (Baltimore, Md.: Johns Hopkins University Press, 1993), 13.

2. Richard Rose, "Where Are Post-Communist Countries Going?" *Journal of Democracy* 8, no. 3 (1997): 98; Philippe Schmitter and Terry Lynn Karl, "What Democracy Is . . . and Is Not," in Diamond and Plattner, *The Global Resurgence of Democracy,* p. 47.

3. Gabriel Almond and Sidney Verba, *The Civic Culture: Political Attitudes and Democracy in Five Nations* (Boston: Little, Brown, 1963); Almond and Verba, *The Civic Culture Revisited* (Boston: Little, Brown, 1980).

4. Ronald Inglehart, "Culture and Democracy," in Lawrence E. Harrison and Samuel Huntington, eds., *Culture Matters: How Values Shape Human Progress* (New York: Basic Books, 2000), 96.

5. Richard Rose, William Mishler, and Christian Haerpfer, "Democracy and Its Alternatives: Understanding Postcommunist Societies" (Cambridge: Polity, 1998), 98.

6. James L. Gibson, Raymond M. Duch, and Kent L. Tedin, "Democratic Values and the Transformation of the Soviet Union," *Journal of Politics* 54, no. 2 (1992): 329–71; Andrew Nathan and Tianjia Shi, "Cultural Requisites for Democracy in China: Findings from a Survey," *Daedalus* 122, no. 2 (1993): 95–123; Tom Rice and Jan L. Feldman, "Civic Culture and Democracy from Europe to America," *Journal of Politics* 39, no. 4 (1997): 1143–72; John A. Booth and Patricia Bayer Richard, "Civil Society, Political Capital, and Democratization in Central America," *Journal of Politics* 60, no. 3 (1998): 780–800; Russell Dalton, "Citizen Attitudes and Political Behavior," *Comparative Political Studies* 33, no. 6–7 (2000): 912–40; Carlos Garcia-Rivero, Hennie Kotze, and Pierre Du Toit, "Political Culture and Democracy: The South African Case," *Politikon* 29, no. 2 (2002): 163–81; Ronald Inglehart and Christian Welzel, "Political Culture and Democracy: Analyzing Cross-Level Linkages," *Comparative Politics* 36, no. 1 (2003): 61–79.

7. United Nations Development Programme, *Arab Human Development Report (4): The Rise of Women in the Arab World* (New York: United Nations Development Programme [UNDP], 2006).

8. Ronald Inglehart and Pippa Norris, "The True Clash of Civilizations," *Foreign Policy* 135 (March–April 2003): 63–70.

9. Steven Fish, "Islam and Authoritarianism," *World Politics* 55, no. 1 (2002): 4–37.

10. James L. Gibson, "The Resilience of Mass Support for Democratic Institutions and Processes in the Nascent Russian and Ukrainian Democracies," in Vladimir Tismaneanu, ed., *Political Culture and Civil Society in Russia and the New States of Eurasia* (New York: M. E. Sharpe, 1995); Gibson, "The Paradoxes of Political Tolerance in Processes of Democratization," *Politikon: South African Journal of Political Science* 23, no. 2 (1996): 5–21; Gibson, "A Sober Second Thought: An Experiment in Persuading Russians to Tolerate," *American Journal of Political Science* 42, no. 3 (1998): 819–50.

11. Garcia-Rivero, Kotze, and Du Toit, "Political Culture and Democracy."

12. Rose, Mishler, and Haerpfer, "Democracy and Its Alternatives."

13. Robert Putnam, *Making Democracy Work: Civic Traditions in Modern Italy* (Princeton, N.J.: Princeton University Press, 1992).

14. Larry Diamond, *Developing Democracy: toward Consolidation* (Baltimore, Md.: Johns Hopkins University Press, 1999).

15. Sidney Verba, Kay L. Schlozman, and Henry Brady, "Beyond SES: A Resource Model of Political Participation," *American Political Science Review* 89, no. 2 (1995): 271–94.

16. Ibid.

17. Michael Delli Carpini, "In Search of the Informed Citizen: What Americans Know about Politics and Why It Matters," *Communication Review,* 41, no. 1 (2000): 129–64.

18. Michael Delli Carpini and Scott Keeter, *What Americans Know about Politics and Why It Matters* (New Haven, Conn.: Yale University Press, 1996).

19. As shown in the appendix to this chapter, one of the two items pertaining to tolerance was different in Algeria than in Jordan and Palestine. This item pertains to the rights of non-Muslim citizens.

9. GENDER, FEMINISM, AND ATTITUDES TOWARD INTERNATIONAL CONFLICT

1. For discussions of the connection between gender and international studies from a variety of perspectives, see V. Spike Peterson and Anne Sisson Runyan, *Global Gender Issues* (Boulder, Colo.: Westview, 1993); Rebecca Grant and Kathleen Newland, eds., *Gender and International Relations* (Bloomington: Indiana University Press, 1991); J. Ann Tickner, *Gender in International Relations* (Ithaca, N.Y.: Cornell University Press, 1992); Hilary Charlesworthy, Christine Chinkin, and Shelley Wright, "Feminist Approaches to International Law," *American Journal of International Law* 85 (October 1991): 613–45; Sue Ellen M. Charlton, Jana Everett, and Kathleen Staudt, eds., *Women, the State, and Development* (Albany: State University of New York Press, 1989); Christine Sylvester, "Empathetic Cooperation: A Feminist Method for IR," *Millenium* 23 (1994); and Yolande Cohen, ed., *Women and Counter-Power* (New York: Black Rose Books, 1989).

2. Palestine here refers to the West Bank and Gaza. The public opinion data from Palestine employed in the present study are from a survey of the Palestinian population of these Israeli-occupied territories.

3. Lisa Brandes, "The Gender Gap and Attitudes toward War," paper presented at the Annual Meeting of the Midwest Political Science Association, Chicago, 1992;

Robert Y. Shapiro and Harpreet Mahajan, "Gender Differences in Policy Preferences: A Summary of Trends from the 1960's to the 1980's," *Public Opinion Quarterly* 50 (1986): 42–61; and Tom W. Smith, "Gender and Attitudes toward Violence," *Public Opinion Quarterly* 48 (1984): 384–96.

4. Pamela Johnston Conover and Virginia Shapiro, "Gender, Feminist Consciousness, and War," *American Journal of Political Science* 37 (November 1993): 1079–99.

5. Ibid., 1095.

6. Carol Gilligan, *In a Different Voice* (Cambridge, Mass.: Harvard University Press, 1982).

7. Dorothy G. McGuigan, ed., *The Role of Women in Conflict and Peace* (Ann Arbor: University of Michigan Press, 1977).

8. For example, see Sara Ruddick, *Maternal Thinking: Toward a Politics of Peace* (New York: Ballentine, 1989); Jean Bethke Elshtain, "Reflections on War and Political Discourse," *Political Theory* 13, no. 1 (1985): 39–57; Mary G. Dietz, "Citizenship with a Feminist Face: The Problem with Maternal Thinking," *Political Theory* 13, no. 1 (1985): 19–37; and Patricia Ward Scaltsas, "Do Feminist Ethics Counter Feminist Aims?" in Eve Browning Cole and Susan Coultrap-McQuin, eds., *Explorations in Feminist Ethics* (Bloomington: Indiana University Press, 1992).

9. See Marysia Zalewski, "The Women/'Women' Question in International Relations," *Millenium* 23, no. 2 (1994): 407–23.

10. See Alison M. Jaggar, "Feminist Ethics: Projects, Problems, Prospects," in Claudia Card, ed., *Feminist Ethics* (Lawrence: University of Kansas Press, 1991); Elshtain, "Reflections on War and Political Discourse."

11. Ruddick, *Maternal Thinking: Toward a Politics of Peace;* Dietz, "Citizenship with a Feminist Face."

12. Elshtain, "Reflections on War and Political Discourse."

13. Jaggar, "Feminist Ethics."

14. See Kumari Jayawardena, *Feminism and Nationalism in the Third World* (London: Zed Books, 1986); Cynthia Enloe, *Does Khaki Become You? The Militarization of Women's Lives* (London: Pluto, 1983); Julie Marie Peteet, *Gender in Crisis: Women and the Palestinian Resistance Movement* (New York: Columbia University Press, 1991); Chandra Talpade Mohanty, Anne Russo, and Lourdes Torres, eds., *Third World Women and the Politics of Feminism* (Bloomington: Indiana University Press, 1991); Deniz Kandiyoti, "Introduction," in Kandiyoti, ed., *Women, Islam, and the State* (Philadelphia: Temple University Press, 1991); Roberta Hamilton and Michele Barrett, eds., *The Politics of Diversity: Feminism, Marxism, and Nationalism* (London: Verso, 1986); Fred Halliday, "Hidden from International Relations: Women and the International Arena," in Grant and Newland, *Gender and International Relations;* and Mary E. Hawkesworth, *Beyond Oppression: Feminist Theory and Political Strategy* (New York: Continuum, 1990).

15. Jayawardena, *Feminism and Nationalism in the Third World.*

16. Valentine M. Moghadam, "Introduction," in Moghadam, ed., *Identity Politics and Women: Cultural Reassertions and Feminisms in International Perspective* (Boulder, Colo.: Westview, 1994).

17. Elshtain, "Reflections on War and Political Discourse"; Hanna Papanek, "The Ideal Woman and the Ideal Society: Control and Autonomy and the Construction of Identity," in Moghadam, *Identity Politics and Women.*

18. See Maxine Molyneux, "Women's Rights and the International Context: Some Reflections on the Post-Communist States," *Millenium* 23, no. 2 (1994): 287–313.

19. See Peteet, *Gender in Crisis;* Salim Tamari, "The Palestinian Movement in Transition: Historical Reversals and the Uprising," in Rex Brynen, ed., *Echoes of the Intifada: Regional Repercussions of the Palestinian-Israeli Conflict* (Boulder, Colo.: Westview, 1991); and Raymonda Tawil, *My Home, My Prison* (London: Zed Books, 1983).

20. See Catherine Hoskyns, "Gender Issues in International Relations," *Review of International Studies* 20 (October 1994): 225–39.

21. Enloe, *Does Khaki Become You?*

22. Adam Przeworski and Henry Teune, *The Logic of Comparative Social Inquiry* (New York: Wiley, 1970).

23. Dafna N. Izraeli and Ephriam Taboury, "The Political Context of Feminist Attitudes in Israel," in Yael Azmon and Dafna N. Izraeli, eds., *Women in Israel* (New Brunswick, N.J.: Transaction, 1993); and Natalie Rein, *Daughters of Rachel: Women in Israel* (New York: Penguin Books, 1980).

24. See Naomi Chazan, "Israeli Women and Peace Activism," in Barbara Swirski and Marilyn Safir, eds., *Calling the Equality Bluff* (New York: Pergamon, 1991); Simona Sharoni, "Is Feminism a Threat to National Security?" *Ms. Magazine,* January–February 1993; Nurit Gillath, "Women Against War: Parents Against Silence," in Swirski and Safir, *Calling the Equality Bluff;* Roberta Micallef, "Israeli and Palestinian Women's Peace Movements," in Elizabeth Warnock Fernea and Mary Evelyn Hocking, eds., *The Struggle for Peace* (Austin: University of Texas Press, 1992).

25. See Barbara Swirski, "Israeli Feminism: New and Old," in Swirski and Safir, *Calling the Equality Bluff;* Nahla Abdo, "Women of the Intifada: Gender, Class, and National Liberation," *Race and Class* 32, no. 4 (1991); and Simona Sharoni, *Gender and the Israeli-Palestinian Conflict* (Syracuse, N.Y.: Syracuse University Press, 1994).

26. Madeleine Tress, "Halacha, Zionism, and Gender: The Case of Gush Emunim," in Moghadam, *Identity Politics and Women.*

27. See Afaf Lutfi al-Sayyid Marsot, "The Revolutionary Gentlewoman in Egypt," in Lois Beck and Nikki Keddie, eds., *Women in the Muslim World* (Cambridge, Mass.: Harvard University Press, 1978); and Thomas Philipp, "Feminism in Nationalist Politics in Egypt," in Beck and Keddie, *Women in the Muslim World.*

28. See Margot Badran, "Independent Women: More than a Century of Feminism in Egypt," in Judith Tucker, ed., *Arab Women* (Bloomington: Indiana University Press, 1993).

29. Valentine M. Moghadam, *Modernizing Women* (Boulder, Colo.: Lynne Rienner, 1993), 157.

30. Mark Tessler and Jolene Jesse, "Gender and Support for Islamist Movements: Evidence from Egypt, Kuwait, and Palestine," *Muslim World* 84 (April 1996): 194–222.

31. Elizabeth W. Fernea, "The Veiled Revolution," in Donna Lee Bowen and Evelyn A. Early, eds., *Everyday Life in the Muslim Middle East* (Bloomington: Indiana University Press, 1993); Moghadam, "Introduction"; Kandiyoti, "Introduction."

32. Moghadam, "Introduction"; Badran, "Independent Women."

33. Souad Dajani, "Palestinian Women under Israeli Occupation," in Tucker, *Arab Women.*

34. Mervat Hatem, "Post-Islamist and Post-Nationalist Feminist Discourses," in Tucker, *Arab Women.*

35. Tessler and Jesse, "Gender and Support for Islamist Movements."

36. Philippa Strum, *The Women Are Marching: The Second Sex and the Palestinian Revolution* (New York: Lawrence Hill, 1992).

37. Abdo, "Women of the Intifada." See also Dajani, "Palestinian Women under Israeli Occupation"; and Tawil, *My Home, My Prison.*

38. Nuha Abu Daleb, "Palestinian Women and their Role in the Revolution," *Peuples Mediterraneens* 5 (October–December 1978): 26–49; Soraya Antonius, "Fighting on Two Fronts: Conversations with Palestinian Women," *Journal of Palestine Studies* 8 (spring 1979): 26–45.

39. Abdo, "Women of the Intifada."

40. Ibid.; Micallef, "Israeli and Palestinian Women's Peace Movements"; Sharoni, "Is Feminism a Threat to National Security?"

41. See Suad M. Al-Sabah, *Development Planning in an Oil Economy and the Role of Women: The Case of Kuwait* (London: East Lords, 1983); Shamlan Y. Al-Essa, *The Manpower Problem in Kuwait* (London: Routledge and Kegan Paul International, 1981); and Kamla Nath, "Education and Employment among Kuwaiti Women," in Beck and Keddie, *Women in the Muslim World.*

42. Farida Allaghi and Aisha Almana, "Survey of Research on Women in the Arab Gulf Region," in F. Pinter, ed., *Social Science Research and Women in the Arab World* (Paris: UNESCO, 1984).

43. Jamal Sanad and Mark Tessler, "Women and Religion in a Modern Islamic Society: The Case of Kuwait," in Emile Sahliyeh, ed., *The Politics of Religious Resurgence in the Contemporary World* (Albany: State University of New York Press, 1990).

44. Hatem, "Post-Islamist and Post-Nationalist Feminist Discourses," 35; David Ottoway, "Feminists Seek Voice in Kuwaiti Politics," *Washington Post,* April 14, 1984.

45. Hatem, "Post-Islamist and Post-Nationalist Feminist Discourses," 37.

46. For additional methodological information and discussion of this project, see Mark Tessler and Jamal Sanad, "Will the Arab Public Accept Peace with Israel: Evidence from Surveys in Three Arab Societies," in Gregory Mahler and Efriam Karsh, eds., *Israel at the Crossroads* (London: I. B. Tauris, 1994).

47. Ibid. See also Mark Tessler, "The Origins of Popular Support for Islamist Movements: A Political Economy Analysis," in John Entelis, ed., *Islam, Democracy, and the State of North Africa* (Bloomington: Indiana University Press, 1997).

48. Khalil Shikaki, *Results of a Public Opinion Poll: The West Bank and Gaza Strip, September 29–30 and October 1, 1994* (Nablus: Center for Palestine Research and Studies, 1994).

49. Charlotte Bunch, *Passionate Politics* (New York: St. Martin's, 1987), 303.

50. For an interesting study that advances a similar conclusion, see Eileen F. Babbitt and Tamra Pearson D'estrée, "An Israeli-Palestinian Women's Workshop: Application of an Interactive Problem-Solving Approach," in Chester A. Crocket, Fen Olser Hampson, and Pamela Aall, eds., *Managing Global Chaos: Sources and Responses to International Conflict* (Washington, D.C.: United States Institute of Peace, 1995). The authors conducted a workshop involving Israeli and Palestinian women in December 1992. They report that participants did see themselves as having an important role to play in the pursuit of peace but not one that is more important than, or even qualitatively different from, that to be played by men.

10. ISLAM AND ATTITUDES
TOWARD INTERNATIONAL CONFLICT

1. Judith Goldstein and Robert O. Keohane, *Ideas and Foreign Policy: Beliefs, Institutions, and Political Change* (Ithaca, N.Y.: Cornell University Press, 1993), 16.

2. David C. Leege, "Religion and Politics in Theoretical Perspective," in David C. Leege and Lyman A. Kellstedt, eds., *Rediscovering the Religious Factor in American Politics* (Armonk, N.Y.: M. E. Sharpe, 1993), 10.

3. K. Wald, *Religion and Politics in the United States* (Washington, D.C.: Congressional Quarterly Press, 1992); Leege, "Religion and Politics in Theoretical Perspective," 3–25.

4. Leege, "Religion and Politics in Theoretical Perspective"; Peter L. Berger, *The Sacred Canopy: Elements of a Sociological Theory of Religion* (Garden City, N.Y.: Doubleday, 1969).

5. Ted G. Jelen, "Swords, Plowshares, and Philistines: A Comparative Analysis of Religion and Attitudes toward Security Policy," paper presented at the Annual Meeting of the American Political Association, San Francisco, August 29–September 1, 1996.

6. Leege, "Religion and Politics in Theoretical Perspective."

7. Jose Casavona, *Public Religions in the Modern World* (Chicago: University of Chicago Press, 1994), 16–17.

8. Bernadette C. Hayes, "The Impact of Religious Identification on Political Attitudes: An International Comparison," *Sociology of Religion* 56 (1995): 177–94; Ted. G. Jelen, *The Political Mobilization of Religious Beliefs* (New York: Praeger, 1991); Jelen, "Religion and Public Opinion in the 1990s: An Empirical Overview," in Barbara Norrander and Clyde Wilcox, eds., *Understanding Public Opinion* (Washington, D.C.: Congressional Quarterly Press, 1996), 55–68.

9. Peter L. Benson and Dorothy Williams, *Religion on Capitol Hill: Myths and Realities* (San Francisco: Harper and Row, 1982).

10. David C. Leege and Lyman A. Kellstedt, "Religious Worldviews and Political Philosophies: Capturing Theory in the Grand Manner through Empirical Data," in Leege and Kellstedt, *Rediscovering the Religious Factor in American Politics*, 216–31.

11. Monte Palmer, Madhia El Safty, and Earl Sullivan, "The Relationship between Economic and Religious Attitudes in Egypt," paper presented at the Annual Meeting of the Middle East Studies Association, Providence, R.I., November 1996.

12. Mark Tessler, "The Origins of Popular Support for Islamist Movements: A Political Economy Analysis," in John Entelis, ed., *Islam, Democracy, and the State in North Africa* (Bloomington: Indiana University Press, 1997), 93–126.

13. Judith Palmer Harik, "Between Islam and the System: Sources and Implication of Popular Support for Lebanon's Hizbollah," *Journal of Conflict Resolution* 40 (1996): 57.

14. James L. Guth and John C. Green, "Salience: The Core Concept?" in Leege and Kellstedt, *Rediscovering the Religious Factor in American Politics*, 157–74.

15. Martha A. MacIver, "Religious Politicization among Western European Mass Publics," in William H. Swatos Jr., ed., *Religious Politics in Global and Comparative Perspective* (New York: Greenwood, 1989), 111–30.

16. Ted G. Jelen, "Religion and Foreign Policy Attitudes: Exploring the Effects of Denomination and Doctrine," *American Politics Quarterly,* 22 (1994): 382–400.

17. Jelen, "Swords, Plowshares, and Philistines."

18. Benson and Williams, *Religion on Capitol Hill.*

19. Jamal Al-Suwaidi, "Arab and Western Conceptions of Democracy: Evidence from a UAE Opinion Survey," in David Garnham and Mark Tessler, eds., *Democracy, War, and Peace in the Middle East* (Bloomington: Indiana University Press, 1995), 87.

20. Hassan Hanafi, "The Relevance of the Islamic Alternative in Egypt," *Arab Studies Quarterly* 4 (spring 1982): 65.

21. Johannes Jansen, *The Neglected Duty: The Creed of Sadat's Assassins and Islamic Resurgence in the Middle East* (London: Macmillan 1986), 44; Derek Hopwood, *Egypt: Politics and Society, 1945–1981* (London: Allen & Unwin, 1982), 119.

22. Dale Eickelman, "Muslim Politics: The Prospects for Democracy in North Africa and the Middle East," in Entelis, *Islam, Democracy, and the State in North Africa,* 17–42; Mark Tessler and Jolene Jesse, "Gender and Support for Islamist Movements: Evidence from Egypt, Kuwait, and Palestine," *Muslim World* 86 (1996): 194–222.

23. John Waterbury, "Democracy Without Democrats? The Potential for Political Liberalization in the Middle East," in Ghassan Salamé, ed., *Democracy Without Democrats? The Renewal of Politics in the Muslim World* (New York: I. B. Tauris, 1994), 23–47.

24. Tessler, "The Origins of Popular Support for Islamist Movements."

25. Ibrahim A. Kawaran, "'ReIslamization Movements' According to Kepel: On Striking Back and Striking Out," *Contention* 2 (fall 1992): 172.

26. Mark Tessler and Ina Warriner "Gender, Feminism, and Attitudes toward International Conflict: Exploring Relationships with Survey Data from the Middle East," *World Politics* 49 (1997): 250–81; Tessler, "The Origins of Popular Support for Islamist Movements"; Khalil Shikaki, "The Transition to Democracy in Palestine," *Journal of Palestine Studies* 98 (winter 1996): 2–14.

27. James Stevens, *Applied Multivariate Statistics for the Social Sciences* (Mahwah, N.J.: Erlbaum, 1996), 365.

28. Palmer, El Safty and Sullivan, "The Relationship between Economic and Religious Attitudes in Egypt.."

29. Benson and Williams, *Religion on Capitol Hill.*

30. Tessler and Marilyn Grobschmidt, "Democracy in the Arab World and the Arab-Israeli Conflict," in Garnham and Tessler, *Democracy, War, and Peace in the Middle East,* 157–60.

31. Arthur Lowrie, *Islam, Democracy, the State, and the West: A Roundtable with Dr. Hassan Al-Turabi* (Tampa, Fla.: World and Islam Studies Enterprise, 1993); Shukri Abed, "Islam and Democracy," in Garnham and Tessler, *Democracy, War, and Peace in the Middle East,* 116–32.

32. Samuel Huntington, *The Clash of Civilizations and the Remaking of World Order* (New York: Simon and Schuster, 1997).

33. Garnham and Tessler, *Democracy, War and Peace in the Middle East.*

34. V. Spike Peterson and Anne Sisson Runyan, *Global Gender Issues* (Boulder, Colo.: Westview, 1993), 81–82; Jean Bethke Elshtain, "Reflections on War and Political Discourse," *Political Theory* 13 (1985): 39–57.

35. Tessler and Warriner, "Gender, Feminism, and Attitudes toward International Conflict."

36. Brad Lockerbie, "Economic Dissatisfaction and Political Alienation in Western Europe," *European Journal of Political Research* 23 (1993): 281–93; Carolyn Funk and

Patricia García-Monet, "The Relationship between Personal and National Concerns in Public Perceptions about the Economy," *Political Research Quarterly* 50, no. 2 (1997): 317–42.

37. Mark Tessler and Jodi Nachtwey, "Economic Influences on Attitudes toward International Conflict: Hypotheses and a Test with Survey Data from the Arab World and Israel," paper presented at the Annual Meeting of the International Studies Association, Minneapolis, Minn., March 1998.

11. FURTHER TESTS OF THE
WOMEN AND PEACE HYPOTHESIS

1. Mark Tessler and Ina Warriner, "Gender, Feminism, and Attitudes toward International Conflict: Exploring Relationships with Survey Data from the Middle East," *World Politics* 49 (1997): 250–81.

2. V. Spike Peterson and Ann Sisson Runyan, *Global Gender Issues* (Boulder, Colo.: Westview, 1993), 81–82; see also Jean Bethke Elshtain, "Reflections on War and Political Discourse," *Political Theory* 13 (1985): 39–57.

3. Elshtain, "Reflections on War and Political Discourse"; Patricia Ward Scaltsas, "Do Feminist Ethics Counter Feminist Aims?" in Eve Browning Cole and Susan Coultrap-McQuin, eds., *Explorations in Feminist Ethics* (Bloomington: Indiana University Press, 1992), 15–26. .

4. Mary G. Dietz, "Citizenship with a Feminist Face: The Problem with Maternal Thinking," *Political Theory* 13 (1985): 19–38; Sara Ruddick, *Maternal Thinking: Toward a Politics of Peace* (Boston: Beacon, 1989).

5. J. Ann Tickner, "Hans Morgenthau's Principles of Political Realism: A Feminist Reformulation," in Rebecca Grant and Kathleen Newland, eds., *Gender and International Relations* (Bloomington: Indiana University Press, 1991), 33; see also Jane S. Jacquette, "Power as Ideology: A Feminist Analysis," in J. H. Stiehm, ed., *Women's Views of the Political World of Men* (Dobbs Ferry, N.Y.: Transnational, 1984), 9–29.

6. Peterson and Runyan, *Global Gender Issues,* 81.

7. Pamela J. Conover and Virginia Sapiro, "Gender, Feminist Consciousness, and War," *American Journal of Political Science* 37 (November 1993): 1079–-99.

8. David Fite, Marc Genest, and Clyde Wilcox, "Gender Differences in Foreign Policy Attitudes: A Longitudinal Analysis," *American Politics Quarterly* 18 (1990): 492–512; Alison M. Jaggar, "Feminist Ethics: Projects, Problems, Prospects," in Claudia Card, ed., *Feminist Ethics* (Lawrence: University of Kansas Press, 1991); Ted G. Jelen, Sue Thomas, and Clyde Wilcox, "The Gender Gap in Comparative Perspective," *European Journal of Political Research* 25 (1994): 171–86; Mary E. Bendya et al., "Gender Differences in Public Attitudes toward the Gulf War: A Test of Competing Hypotheses," *Social Science Journal* 335 (1996): 1–22; Clyde Wilcox, Lara Hewitt, and Dee Allsop, "The Gender Gap in Attitudes Toward the Gulf War: A Cross-National Perspective," *Journal of Peace Research* 33 (1996): 67–82.

9. Jaggar, "Feminist Ethics "; Marysia Zalewski, "The Women/'Women' Question in International Relations." *Millennium* 23 (1994): 407–23.

10. Zalewski, "The Women/'Women' Question in International Relations."

11. Jaggar, "Feminist Ethics."

12. Tickner, "Hans Morgenthau's Principles of Political Realism," 32; see also Nancy C. M. Hartsock, *Money, Sex, and Power: Toward a Feminist Historical Materialism* (Boston: Northeastern University Press, 1983), 210.

13. Fite, Genest, and Wilcox. "Gender Differences in Foreign Policy Attitudes."

14. Tom W. Smith, "Gender and Attitudes toward Violence," *Public Opinion Quarterly* 48 (1984): 384–96; Robert Y. Shapiro and Harpeet Mahajan, "Gender Differences in Policy Preferences: A Summary of Trends from the 1960s to the 1980s," *Public Opinion Quarterly* 50 (1986): 42–61; Lisa Brandes, "The Gender Gap and Attitudes Toward War," paper presented at the Annual Meeting of the Midwest Political Science Association, Chicago, 1992.

15. Conover and Sapiro, "Gender, Feminist Consciousness, and War."

16. Ibid., 1905.

17. Bendya et al., "Gender Differences in Public Attitudes toward the Gulf War."

18. Wilcox, Hewitt, and Allsop, "The Gender Gap in Attitudes toward the Gulf War."

19. Lisa Togeby, "The Gender Gap in Foreign Policy Attitudes," *Journal of Peace Research* 31 (1994): 375–92.

20. Jelen, Thomas, and Wilcox, "The Gender Gap in Comparative Perspective."

21. Wilcox, Hewitt, and Allsop, "The Gender Gap in Attitudes toward the Gulf War."

22. Adam Przeworski and Henry Teune, *The Logic of Comparative Social Inquiry* (New York: Wiley, 1970).

23. David Garnham, "Explaining Middle Eastern Alignments during the Gulf War," *Jerusalem Journal of International Relations* 13 (1991): 63–83.

24. Kenneth J. Meier, "The Value of Replicating Social Science Research," *Chronicle of Higher Education,* February 7, 1997.

25. Mark Tessler, "Toward Scientific Cumulativeness: Operational Needs and Strategies," in Mark Tessler, ed., *The Evaluation and Application of Survey Research in the Arab World* (Boulder, Colo.: Westview, 1987).

26. Mark Tessler, and Jamal Sanad, "Will the Arab Public Accept Peace with Israel: Evidence from Surveys in Three Arab Societies," in Gregory Mahler and Efraim Karsh, eds., *Israel at the Crossroads* (London: British Academic Press, 1994); Khalil Shikaki, "The Transition to Democracy in Palestine," *Journal of Palestine Studies* 98 (1996); Mark Tessler, "The Origins of Popular Support for Islamist Movements: A Political Economy Analysis," in John Entelis, ed., *Islam, Democracy, and the State in North Africa* (Bloomington: Indiana University Press, 1997); Mark Tessler and Jodi Nachtwey, "Islam and Attitudes toward International Conflict: Evidence from Survey Research in the Arab World," *Journal of Conflict Resolution* 42 (1998).

27. Tessler and Nachtwey, "Islam and Attitudes Toward International Conflict "; Mark Tessler and Jamal Nachtwey, "Economic Influences on Attitudes toward International Conflict: Hypotheses and a Test with Survey Data from the Arab World and Israel," paper presented at the Annual Meeting of the International Studies Association, Minneapolis, 1998.

28. Conover, and Sapiro, "Gender, Feminist Consciousness, and War," 1095.

29. Dafna N. Izraeli and Ephraim Taboury, "The Political Context of Feminist Attitudes in Israel," in Yael Azmon and Dafna N. Izraeli, eds., *Women in Israel* (New Brunswick, N.J.: Transaction, 1993).

30. Togeby, "The Gender Gap in Foreign Policy Attitudes"; Wilcox, Hewitt, and Allsop, "The Gender Gap in Attitudes toward the Gulf War."

31. Valerie Morgan, "Women and the Peace Process in Northern Ireland," Global Forum Occasional Papers series, Duke University Center for International Studies, Durham, N.C., 1996, 6.

12. THE POLITICAL ECONOMY OF ATTITUDES TOWARD PEACE AMONG PALESTINIANS AND ISRAELIS

1. Mark Tessler and Jodi Nachtwey, "Islam and Attitudes toward International Conflict: Evidence from Survey Research in Five Middle Eastern Countries," *Journal of Conflict Resolution* 42, no. 5 (1998): 619–36.

2. Mark Tessler, Jodi Nachtwey, and Audra Grant, "Further Tests of The Women and Peace Hypothesis: Evidence from Cross-National Survey," *International Studies Quarterly* 43 (1999): 519–31.

3. Jeffrey W. Knopf, "How Rational Is 'The Rational Public'? Evidence from U.S. Public Opinion on Military Spending," *Journal of Conflict Resolution* 42, no. 5 (1998): 544–71.

4. Virginia. A. Chanley, "U.S. Public Views of International Involvement from 1964 to 1993: Time-Series Analyses of General and Militant Internationalism," *Journal of Conflict Resolution* 43, no. 1 (1999): 23–44.

5. Jeffrey A. Frieden and David A. Lake, *International Political Economy: Perspectives on Global Power and Wealth,* 2nd ed. (New York: St. Martin's, 1991); Robert Gilpin, *The Political Economy of International Relations* (Princeton, N.J.: Princeton University Press, 1987).

6. Donald R. Kinder and D. Roderick Kiewiet, "Economic Discontent and Political Behavior: The Role of Personal Grievances and Collective Economic Judgments in Congressional Voting," *American Journal of Political Science* 23 (1979): 495–526; Michael S. Lewis-Beck, *Economics and Elections: The Major Western Democracies* (Ann Arbor: University of Michigan Press, 1988); Alexander Pacek and Benjamin Radcliff, "The Political Economy of Competitive Elections in the Developing World," *American Journal of Political Science* 39, no. 3 (1995): 745–59; Alfred G. Cuzán and Charles M. Bundrick, "Presidential Popularity in Central America: Parallels with the United States," *Political Research Quarterly* 50, no. 4 (1997): 833–49; Matthew Gabel and Guy D. Whitten, "Economic Conditions, Economic Perceptions, and Public Support for European Integration," *Political Behavior* 19, no. 1 (1997): 81–96; Kurt Weyland, "Peasants or Bankers in Venezuela? Presidential Popularity and Economic Reform Approval, 1989–1993," *Political Research Quarterly* 51, no. 2 (1998): 341–62.

7. Allan Kornberg and Harold Clarke, *Citizens And Community: Political Support in a Representative Democracy* (Cambridge: Cambridge University Press, 1992); M. Stephen Weatherford, "Political Economy and Political Legitimacy: The Link between Economic Policy and Political Trust," in Harold D. Clarke, Marianne C. Stewart, and Gary Zuk, eds., *Economic Decline and Political Change: Canada, Great Britain, the United States* (Pittsburg: Pittsburgh University Press, 1992); Brad Lockerbie, "Economic Dissatisfaction and Political Alienation in Western Europe," *European Journal of Political Research* 23 (1993): 281–93; C. J. Anderson and C. A. Guillory, "Political Institutions and Satisfaction with Democracy: A Cross-National Analysis of Consensus and Majoritarian Systems," *American Political Science Review* 91, no. 1 (1997): 66–81.

8. Harold D. Clarke, Nitish Dutt, and Allen Kornberg, "The Political Economy of Attitudes toward Policy and Society in Western and European Democracies," *Journal of Politics* 55 (1993): 998–1021.

9. Weatherford, "Political Economy."

10. Majid Al-Haj, Elihu Katz, and Samuel Shye, "Arab and Jewish Attitudes: Toward a Palestinian State," *Journal of Conflict Resolution* 37, no. 4 (1993): 619–32.

11. Palestinian Central Bureau of Statistics (PCBS) Online, "Poverty in Palestine" (updated March 2, 2000), available at http://www.pcbs.org/english/househol/poverty .htm (accessed January 15, 2001); PCBS Online, "Labour Force—Current Main Indicators: Basic Changes in the Labour Force Indicators in Palestinian Territory during 1995–2000" (2000), available at http://www.pcbs.org/english/labor/lab_curr .htm (accessed January 15, 2001). For more recent information, see http://www.pcbs .gov.ps/Default.aspx?tabID=1&lang=en (accessed September 10, 2010).

12. Shaul Mishal, Ranan D. Kuperman, and David Boaz, *Investment in Peace: The Politics of Economic Cooperation between Israel, Jordan, and the Palestinian Authority* (Brighton, UK: Sussex Academic Press, 2001), chap. 3.

13. PCBS Online, "Labour Force"; *The World Factbook 2000* (Washington, D.C.: Central Intelligence Agency, 2000), available at https://www.cia.gov/library/ publications/the-world-factbook/ (accessed September 10, 2010).

14. *The World Factbook 2000.*

15. Jacob Shamir and Khalil Shikaki. "Between Conflict and Reconciliation: Determinants of Reconciliation and Compromise among Israelis and Palestinians," *Journal of Peace Research* 30 (March 2002): 185–202.

16. Hilal Khashan, *Policy Focus: Arab Attitudes toward Israel and Peace* (Washington, DC: Washington Institute for Near East Policy, 2000), 34–35.

17. Mishal, Kuperman, and Boaz, *Investment in Peace,* chap. 4.

18. United Nations Conference on Trade and Development (UNCTAD), *Report on UNCTAD's Assistance to the Palestinian People* (Geneva: United Nations, 1999).

19. Mark Tessler, "Israel at Peace with the Arab World," Occasional Paper, Emirates Center for Strategic Studies and Research, Abu Dhabi, 1995.

20. Mishal, Kuperman, and Boaz, *Investment in Peace,* chap. 2.

21. Ibid., chap. 4.

22. PCBS Online, "Press Report on Labour Force Survey Results: October– December 2000" (2001), available at http://www.pcbs.org/english/press_4/prs_la19 .htm (accessed January 15, 2001). For more recent information, see http://www.pcbs .gov.ps/Default.aspx?tabID=1&lang=en (accessed September 10, 2010).

23. *The World Factbook 2000;* UNCTAD, *Report on UNCTAD's Assistance to the Palestinian People.*

24. Center for Palestine Research and Studies (CPRS), "Results of Poll #48" (Nablus, Palestine: Center for Palestine Research and Studies, 2000); CPRS, "Results of Poll #47" (Nablus, Palestine: Center for Palestine Research and Studies, 2000).

25. Freedom House, "Israel-Administered Territories and Palestinian Authority– Administered Territories," November 2, 2000, available at http://www.freedomhouse. org/template.cfm?page=180 (accessed September 10, 2010).

26. Amnesty International, "Palestinian Authority Silencing Dissent," September 5, 2000, available at http://web.amnesty.org/ai.nsf/Index/MDE210162000 ?OpenDocument&of=COUNTRIES\PALESTINIAN+AUTHORITY; Amnesty International, "Palestinian Authority," 2000, available at http://www.amnesty.org/en/ region/palestinian-authority (accessed September 10, 2010).

27. CPRS, "Results of Poll #47."

28. Eisenstadt, S. N., *Israeli Society* (New York: Basic Books, 1967), 142; Mark Tessler, *A History of the Israeli-Palestinian Conflict* (Bloomington: Indiana University Press, 1994), 370.

29. Peter Grose, *A Changing Israel* (New York: Vintage, 1985), 86.

30. Nissim Rejwan, "The Two Israels: A Study in Europocentrism." *Judaism* 16 (winter 1967): 108.

31. Alan Dowty, *The Jewish State a Century Later* (Berkeley: University of California Press, 2000), 118.

32. Sammy Smooha, *Israel: Pluralism and Conflict* (Berkeley: University of California Press, 1978); Tessler, *A History of the Israeli-Palestinian Conflict,* 503–504.

33. State of Israel, "State of the Economy: 1999–2000" (Tel Aviv: Israeli Ministry of Finance, International Division, 1999), available at http://www.finance.gov.il/ hachnasot/bud99/budget_e4.htm (accessed September 10, 2010); International Labour Office (ILO), *Yearbook of Labour Statistics* (Geneva: International Labour Office, 2000).

34. Sammy Smooha, "The Implications of the Transition to Peace for Israeli Society," *Annals of the American Academy of Political and Social Science* 555 (1998): 39–41.

35. Tessler and Nachtwey, "Islam and Attitudes."

36. Smooha, "The Implications of the Transition to Peace for Israeli Society."

13. WHAT LEADS SOME ORDINARY ARAB MEN AND WOMEN TO APPROVE OF TERRORIST ACTS AGAINST THE UNITED STATES?

1. Nelson Kasfir, "Dilemmas of Popular Support in Guerilla War: The National Resistance Army in Uganda, 1981–86," *Journal of Modern African Studies* 43 (2002): 271–96; Paul Collier and Anke Hoeffler, "Greed and Grievance in Civil War," World Bank Policy Research Paper 2355, World Bank, Washington, D.C. (2000).

2. Jeremy Weinstein, "Resources and the Information Problem in Rebel Recruitment," *Journal of Conflict Resolution* 49 (2005): 598–624.

3. There is no standard and consistently employed definition of terrorism. See William O'Neill, *Beyond the Slogans: How Can the UN Respond to Terrorism?* (New York: International Peace Academy, United Nations, 2002); also Jacob Shamir and Khalil Shikaki, "Self-serving Perceptions of Terrorism among Israelis and Palestinians," *Political Psychology* 23 (2002): 537–57). Further complicating matters, the term has strong political and normative connotations. For purposes of the present study, "terrorism" refers to politically motivated violence against noncombatant members of an "enemy" community—that is, action or threatened action that seeks to kill or injure civilians with the goal of altering the policies or behavior of the community to which the civilians belong.

4. Harvey Kushner, "Suicide Bombers: Business as Usual" *Studies in Conflict and Terrorism* 19 (1996): 329–38.

5. Jeffrey Ross, "Structural Causes of Oppositional Political Terrorism: Towards a Causal Model," *Journal of Peace Research* 30 (1993): 317–29.

6. Scott Atran, "Genesis of Suicide Terrorism," *Science* 299, no. 5612 (2003): 1534–39; Martha Crenshaw, "The Psychology of Terrorism: An Agenda for the 21st Century," *Political Psychology* 21 (2000): 405–20; Jerrold Post, "Rewarding Fire with Fire: Effects of Retaliation on Terrorist Group-Dynamics," *Terrorism* 10 (1987): 23–35.

7. Scott Atran, "Who Wants to Be a Martyr?" *New York Times,* May 7, 2003.

8. Reuven Paz, *Is Hamas Reevaluating the Use of Terrorism?* (Herzliya, Israel: Institute for Counter-Terrorism, 1998), available at http://www.ict.org.il/Articles/ tabid/66/currentpage/1/Default.aspx (accessed September 10, 2010).

9. Ami Ayalon, "Fighting Terrorism: Lessons from the Front Line," in R. B. Satloff, ed., *War on Terror: The Middle East Dimension* (Washington, D.C.: Washington Institute for Near East Policy, 2002), 3–7.

10. Hoffman, *Al Qaeda, Trends in Terrorism and Future Potentialities: An Assessment* (Santa Monica, Calif.: RAND, 2003), available at http://www.rand.org/publications/P/ P8078/P8078.pdf (accessed September 10, 2010).

11. Pew Research Center, "Global Opinion: The Spread of Anti-Americanism," Pew Research Center, Trends 2005, available at http://pewresearch.org/assets/files/ trends2005-global.pdf (accessed September 10, 2010).

12. Samuel Huntington, "The Clash of Civilizations?" *Foreign Affairs* 72 (summer 1993): 22–49; and Huntington, *The Clash of Civilizations and the Remaking of World Order* (New York: Simon and Schuster, 1996).

13. Bernard Lewis, "The Roots of Muslim Rage: Why So Many Muslims Deeply Resent the West and Why Their Bitterness Will Not Be Easily Mollified," *Atlantic Monthly* 266 (September 1990): 47–60; and Lewis, *What Went Wrong: Western Impact and Middle Eastern Response* (New York: Oxford University Press, 2002).

14. Lewis, "The Roots of Muslim Rage," 60; see also Lewis, *What Went Wrong*.

15. Huntington, "The Clash of Civilizations?" 210, 217.

16. Assaf Moghaddam, "Palestinian Suicide Terrorism in the Second Intifada: Motivations and Organizational Aspects," *Studies in Conflict and Terrorism,* 26 (2003): 65–92.

17. Reuven Paz, *Radical Islamist Terrorism* (Herzliya, Israel: Institute for Counter-Terrorism, 2001), available at http://www.ict.org.il/Articles/tabid/66/currentpage/1/ Default.aspx (accessed September 10, 2010).

18. Mustafa Hamarneh, *Revisiting the Arab Street: Research from Within* (Amman, Jordan: Center for Strategic Studies, University of Jordan, 2005).

19. John Esposito, *Unholy War: Terror in the Name of Islam* (New York: Oxford University Press, 2002).

20. Scott Atran, *In Gods We Trust: The Evolutionary Landscape of Religion,* Evolution and Cognition series (New York: Oxford University Press, 2002); Sheri Berman, "Islamism, Revolution, and Civil Society," *PS: Political Science and Politics* 1 (2003): 257–72.

21. Ariel Merari, "Deterring Fear: Government Responses to Terrorist Attacks," *Harvard International Review* 23 (2002): 26–31; Merari, "Deterring Terrorism: States, Organizations, Individuals," *Justice* 31 (2002): 3–6; Brian Barber, *Heart and Stones: Palestinian Youth from the Intifada* (New York: St. Martin's, 2003).

22. Simon Haddad and Hilal Khashan, "Islam and Terrorism: Lebanese Muslim Views on September 11," *Journal of Conflict Resolution* 46 (2002): 812–28; Judith Palmer Harik, "Between Islam and the System: Sources and Implications of Popular Support for Lebanon's Hizballah," *Journal of Conflict Resolution* 40 (1996): 41–67.

23. Mark Tessler and Jodi Nachtwey, "Islam and Attitudes toward International Conflict: Evidence from Survey Research in the Arab World," *Journal of Conflict Resolution* 42 (1998): 619–36; Mark Tessler, "The Nature and Determinants of Arab Attitudes toward Israel," in D. Penslar and J. Stein, eds., *Contemporary Antisemitism: Canada and the World* (Toronto: University of Toronto Press, 2004), 96–119.

24. Khalil Shikaki, "Ramallah: Palestinian Center for Policy and Survey Research, PSR Poll 19, March 16–18, 2006, available at http://www.pcpsr.org/survey/polls/2006/ p19e.html (accessed September 10, 2010).

25. Adam Garfinkle, "Anti-Americanism, U.S. Foreign Policy, and the War on Terrorism," in A. Garfinkle, ed., *A Practical Guide to Winning the War on Terrorism*

(Palo Alto, Calif.: Hoover Books Online, 2004), 203, available at http://www.hoover .org/publications/books/3009071.html (accessed September 10, 2010).

26. Jamie Glazov, "Hating America," *FrontPageMagazine.com* (August 12, 2004), available at http://www.frontpagemag.com/Articles/ReadArticle.asp?ID=14624 (accessed September 10, 2010).

27. Cheryl Bernard, "Five Pillars of Democracy: How the West Can Promote an Islamic Reformation," *Rand Review* (spring 2004), available at http://www.rand.org/ publications/randreview/issues/spring2004/pillars.html (accessed September 10, 2010).

28. Rueven Paz, "Islamists and Anti-Americanism," *Middle East Review of International Affairs* 7 (2003): 53.

29. Ehud Sprinzak, "The Psychopolitical Formation of Extreme Left Terrorism in a Democracy: The Case of the Weathermen," in W. Reich, ed., *Origins of Terrorism* (New York: Cambridge University Press, 1990), 65–86; Albert Bandura, "Mechanisms of Moral Disengagement," in W. Reich and W. Laqueur, eds., *Origins of Terrorism* (Washington, D.C.: Woodrow Wilson Center, 1990), 161–91.

30. O'Neill, *Beyond the Slogans;* Claude Berribi, "Evidence about the Link between Education, Poverty and Terrorism among Palestinians," Princeton University Industrial Relations Section Working Paper no. 477 (September 2003), available at http://papers.ssrn.com/sol3/papers.cfm?abstract_id=487467 (accessed September 10, 2010).

31. Nasra Hassan, "An Arsenal of Believers," *New Yorker,* November 19, 2001.

32. Alan Krueger and Jitka Maleckova, "Does Poverty Cause Terrorism? The Economics and the Education of Suicide Bombers," *New Republic,* June 24, 2002.

33. Berribi, "Evidence about the Link between Education, Poverty and Terrorism among Palestinians."

34. Jodi Wilgoren, "After the Attacks: The Hijackers; A Terrorist Profile That Confounds the Experts," *New York Times,* September 15, 2001.

35. Ami Pedahzur, Arie Perliger, and Leonard Weinberg, "Altruism and Fatalism: The Characteristics of Palestinian Suicide Terrorists," *Deviant Behavior* 24 (2003): 405–23.

36. Peter Grant and Rupert Brown, "From Ethnocentrism to Collective Protest: Responses to Relative Deprivation and Threats to Social Identity," *Social Psychology Quarterly* 58 (1995): 195–212; Serge Guimond and Lise Dube-Simard, "Relative Deprivation Theory and the Quebec Nationalist Movement. The Cognition-Emotion Distinction and the Personal-Group Deprivation Issue," *Journal of Personality and Social Psychology* 44 (1983): 526–35.

37. Lisa Anderson, "Fulfilling Prophecies: State Policy and Islamist Radicalism," in J. Esposito, ed., *Political Islam: Revolution, Radicalism, or Reform?* (Boulder, Colo.: Lynne Reiner, 1997), 17–31; Christopher Alexander, "Opportunities, Organizations, and Ideas: Islamists and Ideas in Tunisia and Algeria," *International Journal of Middle East Studies* 32 (2000): 465–90; Salwa Ismail, "The Paradox of Islamist Politics," *Middle East Report* 221 (2001): 34–39.

38. Quintan Wiktorowicz, "Introduction," in Q. Wiktorowicz, ed., *Islamic Activism: A Social Movement Theory Approach* (Bloomington: Indiana University Press, 2004), 14–15.

39. Shaul Mishal and Avraham Sela, *The Palestinian Hamas: Vision, Violence, and Coexistence* (New York: Columbia University Press, 2000).

40. Moghaddam, "Palestinian Suicide"; Basel Saleh, "Economic Conditions and Resistance to Occupation in the West Bank and Gaza Strip: There Is a Causal Connection," paper presented at the Graduate Student Forum, Kansas State University, April 4, 2003.

41. Jodi Nachtwey and Mark Tessler, "The Political Economy of Attitudes toward Peace among Palestinians and Israelis," *Journal of Conflict Resolution* 46 (2002): 260–85.

42. Fathali Moghaddam, "The Staircase to Terrorism: A Psychological Exploration," *American Psychologist* 60 (2005): 161–69.

43. Daniel Munoz-Rojas, "Violations of International Humanitarian Law: Their Psycho-Sociological Causes and Prevention," Armed Groups Project, International Committee of the Red Cross, Geneva, Switzerland, 2003, available at http://www.armedgroups.org/images/stories/pdfs/munoz_paper_3.pdf (accessed September 10, 2010); Jeremy Ginges and Ariel Merari, "When Do People Decide to Kill for a Cause? Testing a Social Identity Explanation of Variance in the Extremism of Political Behavior within an Aggrieved Population," unpublished paper, New School for Social Research, New York/Tel Aviv University, 2003.

44. Khalil Shikaki, "Palestinians Divided," *Foreign Affairs* 81 (January/February 2002): 89–105.

45. Shibley Telhami, *Reflections of Hearts and Minds: Media, Opinion, and Identity in the Arab World* (Washington, D.C.: Brookings Institution, 2006); Mark Tessler, "Arab and Muslim Political Attitudes: Stereotypes and Evidence from Survey Research," *International Studies Perspectives* 4 (2003): 175–80.

46. Hamarneh, *Revisiting the Arab Street,* 17.

47. Barry Rubin, "The Real Roots of Arab Anti-Americanism," *Foreign Affairs* 81 (November/December 2002): 73–85.

48. Tod Lindberg, "Does Anti-Americanism Matter to American Foreign Policy?" opening remarks, Carnegie Endowment for International Peace and Central European University Conference, Washington, D.C., November 3, 2005; "Anti-Americanism—Due to What the U.S. Is or What the U.S. Does?" Special Policy Forum Report of the Washington Institute for Near East Policy, December 2, 2003.

49. Mark Tessler, "The Origins of Popular Support for Islamist Movements: A Political Economy Analysis," in John Entelis, ed., *Islam, Democracy, and the State in North Africa* (Bloomington: Indiana University Press, 1997), 93–126; Jodi Nachtwey and Mark Tessler, "Explaining Women's Support for Political Islam: Contributions from Feminist Theory," in Mark Tessler, Jodi Nachtwey, and Anne Banda, eds., *Area Studies and Social Science: Strategies for Understanding Middle East Politics* (Bloomington: Indiana University Press, 1999), 102–20.

50. John Entelis, "Algeria under Chadli: Liberalization without Democratization; or, Perestroika, Yes; Glasnost, No!" *Middle East Insight* (fall 1988): 52–53.

51. Abla Amawi, "Democracy Dilemmas in Jordan," *Middle East Report* 174 (1992): 27.

52. Michael Suleiman, "Attitudes, Values, and the Political Process in Morocco," in I. W. Zartman, ed., *The Political Economy of Morocco* (New York: Praeger, 1987), 113.

53. Mounia Bennani-Chraibi, "Les représentations du monde des jeunes Marocains" [The view of the world of young Moroccans], Ph.D. diss., l'Institut d'Etudes Politiques, Paris, 1993, 392–436.

54. See the World Values Survey (WVS), available at http://worldvaluessurvey.org (accessed September 10, 2010).

55. Luis Martinez, "Why the Violence in Algeria?" in Michael Bonner, Megan Reif, and Mark Tessler, *Islam, Democracy, and the State in Algeria: Lessons for the Western Mediterranean and Beyond* (London: Routledge, 2005), 14–27; Mohammed Hafez, "From Marginalization to Massacres: A Political Process Explanation of GIA Violence in Algeria," in Quintan Wiktorowicz, ed., *Islamic Activism: A Social Movement Theory Approach* (Bloomington: Indiana University Press, 2004), 37–60; Mark Tessler, "The View from the Street: The Attitudes and Values of Ordinary Algerians," in Bonner, Reif, and Tessler, *Islam, Democracy, and the State,* 184–201.

56. Stathis Kalyvas, "Commitment Problems in Emerging Democracies: The Case of Religious Parties," *Comparative Politics* 32 (200): 386.

57. Laurie Brand, "Arab Women and Political Liberalization: Challenges and Opportunities," in Handelman and Tessler, *Democratization and Its Limits,* 242–61.

58. Emile Sahliyeh, "The State and the Islamic Movement In Jordan," *Journal of Church and State* 47 (2005): 109–31.

REFERENCES

Abdo, Nahla. "Women of the Intifada: Gender, Class, and National Liberation." *Race and Class* 32, no. 4 (1991): 19–34.

Abed, Shukri. "Islam and Democracy." In *Democracy, War, and Peace in the Middle East,* ed. David Garnham and Mark Tessler. Bloomington: Indiana University Press, 1995.

Abou Fadl, Khaled. *Islam and the Challenge of Democracy.* Princeton, N.J.: Princeton University Press, 2004.

Abramson, Gary. "Rise of the Crescent." *Africa Report,* March–April 1992.

Adoni, Lamis. "King Hussein Leads Jordan into a New Era." *Middle East International,* November 17, 1989.

Ajami, Fouad. *The Arab Predicament: Arab Political Thought and Practice since 1967.* Cambridge: Cambridge University Press, 1981.

Al-Essa, Shamlan Y. *The Manpower Problem in Kuwait.* London: Routledge, Kegan Paul International, 1981.

Alexander, C. "Opportunities, Organizations, and Ideas: Islamists and Ideas in Tunisia and Algeria." *International Journal of Middle East Studies* 32 (2000): 465–90.

Al-Haj, Majid, Elihu Katz, and Samuel Shye. "Arab and Jewish Attitudes: Toward a Palestinian State." *Journal of Conflict Resolution* 37, no. 4 (1993):619–32.

Al-Khalil, Samir. "In the Middle East, Does Democracy Have a Chance?" *New York Times Magazine,* October 14, 1990.

Allaghi, Farida, and Aisha Almana. "Survey of Research on Women in the Arab Gulf Region." In *Social Science Research and Women in the Arab World.* Paris: UNESCO, 1984.

Almond, Gabriel, and G. Bingham Powell Jr. *Comparative Politics: A Developmental Approach.* Boston: Little, Brown, 1966.

Almond, Gabriel, and Sidney Verba. *The Civic Culture: Political Attitudes and Democracy in Five Nations.* Princeton, N.J.: Princeton University Press, 1963.

———. *The Civic Culture Revisited.* Boston: Little, Brown, 1980.

Al-Sabah, Suad M. *Development Planning in an Oil Economy and the Role of Women: The Case of Kuwait.* London: East Lords, 1983.

Al-Suwaidi, Jamal. "Arab and Western Conceptions of Democracy: Evidence from a UAE Opinion Survey." In *Democracy, War, and Peace in the Middle East,* ed. David Garnham and Mark Tessler. Bloomington: Indiana University Press, 1995.

Alwin, Duane F. "Aging, Personality, and Social Change: The Stability of Individual Differences over the Adult Life Span." In *Life-Span Development and Behavior,* Vol. 12, ed. D. L. Featherman, R. M. Lerner, and M. Perlmutter. Hillsdale, N.J.: Erlbaum, 1994.

———. "Attitude Factors in Adulthood: The Role of Generational and Life-Cycle Factors." In *New Directions in Attitude Measurement,* ed. Dagmar Krebs and Peter Schmidt. Berlin: De Gruyter, 1993.

Alwin, Duane F., Ronald L. Cohen, and Theodore M. Newcomb. *Political Attitudes over the Life Span: The Bennington Women after Fifty Years.* Madison: University of Wisconsin Press, 1991.

Alwin, Duane F., and Jon A. Krosnick. "Aging, Cohorts, and the Stability of Sociopolitical Orientations over the Life Span." *American Journal of Sociology* 97, no. 1 (1991): 169–95.

Amawi, Abla. "Democracy Dilemmas in Jordan." *Middle East Report* 174 (January/ February 1992): 26–29.

American Association for Public Opinion Research (AAPOR). *Standard Definitions: Final Dispositions of Case Code and Outcome Rates for Surveys.* Lenexa, Kans.: AAPOR, 2000.

Amin, Galal. *Egypt's Economic Predicament.* Leiden: Brill, 1995.

Amnesty International Online. "Palestinian Authority." Amnesty International Report, 2000. Available at http://www.amnesty.org/en/region/palestinian-authority (accessed September 10, 2010).

———. "Palestinian Authority Silencing Dissent." Amnesty International Report, September 5, 2000. Available at http://www.amnesty.org/en/region/palestinian-authority (accessed September 10, 2010).

Amos, D. "Iraq's Arab Neighbors: Anti-Americanism Runs High." *All Things Considered.* National Public Radio, October 22, 2004.

Anderson, Christopher J., and Christine A. Guillory. "Political Institutions and Satisfaction with Democracy: A Cross-National Analysis of Consensus and Majoritarian Systems." *American Political Science Review* 91, no. 1 (1997.): 66–81.

Anderson, Charles, Fred Von der Mehden and Crawford Young. *Issues of Political Development.* Englewood Cliffs, N.J.: Prentice Hall, 1967.

Anderson, Lisa. "Fulfilling Prophecies: State Policy and Islamist Radicalism." In *Political Islam: Revolution, Radicalism, or Reform?* ed. John Esposito. Boulder, Colo.: Lynne Reinner, 1997.

———. "Politics in the Middle East: Opportunities and Limits in the Quest for Theory." In *Area Studies and Social Science: Strategies for Understanding Middle East Politics,* ed. Mark Tessler, with Jodi Nachtwey and Anne Banda. Bloomington: Indiana University Press, 1999.

Antonius, Soraya. "Fighting on Two Fronts: Conversations with Palestinian Women." *Journal of Palestine Studies* 8 (spring 1979).

Apter, David. *The Politics of Modernization.* Chicago: University of Chicago Press, 1965.

Arab Human Development Report. New York: UNDP, 2002. Available at http://www.arab-hdr.org/ (accessed September 10, 2010).

———. New York: UNDP, 2003. Available at http://www.arab-hdr.org/ (accessed September 10, 2010).

Arab Human Development Report (4): The Rise of Women in the Arab World. New York: United Nations Development Programme (UNDP), 2006.

Atran, Scott. "Genesis of Suicide Terrorism." *Science* 299, no. 5612 (2003): 1534–39.

———. "Individual Factors in Suicide Terrorism." *Science* 304, no. 5667 (2004): 1534–39.

———. *In Gods We Trust: The Evolutionary Landscape of Religion.* Evolution and Cognition series. New York: Oxford University Press, 2002.

———. "The Strategic Threat from Suicide Terrorism." Related Publication 03-33. AEI-Brookings Joint Center for Regulatory Studies, December 2003.

———. "Who Wants to Be a Martyr?" *New York Times,* May 7, 2003).

Ayalon, Ami. "Fighting Terrorism: Lessons from the Front Line." In *War on Terror: The Middle East Dimension,* ed. Robert B. Satloff. Washington D.C.: Washington Institute for Near East Policy, 2002.

Ayari, Chadly. "Le monde arabe et l'enjeu économique du nouvel ordre mondial." In *La Guerre du Golfe et l'Avenir des Arabes: débats et réflexions.* Tunis: Cérès Productions, 1991.

Babbitt, Eileen F., and Tamra Pearson D'estrée. "An Israeli-Palestinian Women's Workshop: Application of an Interactive Problem-Solving Approach." In *Managing Global Chaos: Sources and Responses to International Conflict,* ed. Chester A. Crocket, Fen Olser Hampson, and Pamela Aall. Washington, D.C.: United States Institute of Peace, 1995.

Badran, Margot. "Independent Women: More Than a Century of Feminism in Egypt." In *Arab Women,* ed. Judith Tucker. Bloomington: Indiana University Press, 1993.

Baltes, Paul B., Hayne W. Reese, and John R. Nesselroad. *Life-Span Developmental Psychology: Introduction to Research Methods.* Hillsdale, N.J.: Erlbaum, 1988 [1977].

Baltes, Paul B., Ursula M. Staudinger, and Ulman Lindenberger. "Lifespan Psychology: Theory and Application to Intellectual Functioning." *Annual Review of Psychology* 50 (1999): 471–507.

Bandura, Albert. "Mechanisms of Moral Disengagement." In *Origins of Terrorism,* ed. Walter Reich and W. Laqueur. Washington, D.C.: Woodrow Wilson Center Press, 1998.

Barber, Brian. *Heart and Stones: Palestinian Youth from the Intifada.* New York: St. Martin's, 2003.

Belhassen, Souhayr. "Nous oeuvrons pour que l'islam occupe sa place en Algerie." *Jeune Afrique* 1519 (February 12, 1989): 52–55.

Ben Dor, Gabriel. "Political Culture Approach to Middle East Politics." *International Journal of Middle East Studies* 8 (1977): 43–63.

Bendourou, Omar. "The Exercise of Political Freedoms in Morocco." *Review of the International Commission of Jurists* 40 (1988): 31–41.

Bendyna, Mary E., Tamara Finucane, Lynn Kirby, John P. O'Donnell, and Clyde Wilcox. "Gender Differences in Public Attitudes toward the Gulf War: A Test of Competing Hypotheses." *Social Science Journal* 35 (1996): 1–22.

Bennani-Chraibi, Mounia. *Les Représentations du Monde des Jeunes Marocains.* Paris: Thèse de doctorat de l'Institut d'Etudes Politiques, 1993.

Bennoune, Mahfoud. *The Making of Contemporary Algeria, 1830–1987: Colonial Upheavals and Post-Independence Development.* Cambridge: Cambridge University Press, 1988.

Benson, Peter L., and Dorothy Williams. *Religion on Capitol Hill: Myths and Realities.* San Francisco: Harper and Row, 1982.

Berger, Peter L. *The Sacred Canopy: Elements of a Sociological Theory of Religion.* Garden City, N.Y.: Doubleday, 1969.

Berman, Sheri. "Islamism, Revolution, and Civil Society." *PS: Political Science and Politics* 1 (2003): 257–72.

Bernard, Cheryl. "Five Pillars of Democracy: How the West Can Promote an Islamic Reformation." *Rand Review* (spring 2004). Available at http://www.rand.org/publications/randreview/issues/spring2004/pillars.html (accessed September 10, 2010).

Berribi, Claude. "Evidence about the Link between Education, Poverty, and Terrorism among Palestinians." Social Science Research Network, 2003. Available at http://papers.ssrn.com/sol3/papers.cfm?abstract_id=487467 (accessed September 10, 2010).

Bill, James A., and Robert L. Hardgrave Jr. *Comparative Politics: The Quest for Theory.* Columbus, Ohio: Merrill, 1973.

Binder, Leonard. "National Integration and Political Development." *American Political Science Review* 58 (1964): 622–31.

Booth, John A., and Patricia B. Richard. "Civil Society, Political Capital, and Democratization in Central America." *Journal of Politics* 60, no. 3 (1998): 780–800.

Boserup, Ester. *Women's Role in Economic Development.* London: Allyn and Unwin, 1970.

Bourgi, Albert. "Etudiants: ou menera le desespoir?" *Jeune Afrique* 1519 (February 12, 1989): 38–42.

Brand, Laurie. "Arab Women and Political Liberalization: Challenges and Opportunities." In *Democratization and Its Limits: Lessons from Asia, Latin America, and the Middle East,* ed. Howard Handelman and Mark Tessler. South Bend, Ind.: Notre Dame University Press, 1999.

Brandes, Lisa. "The Gender Gap and Attitudes toward War." Paper presented at the Annual Meeting of the Midwest Political Science Association, Chicago, 1992.

Brown, Kenneth. "Lost in Algiers." *Mediterraneans* 4 (summer 1993): 8–18.

Bunch, Charlotte. *Passionate Politics.* New York: St. Martin's, 1987.

Burgat, François, and William Dowell. *The Islamic Movement in North Africa.* Austin: University of Texas Press, 1993.

Campbell, Donald. "Degrees of Freedom and the Case Study." *Comparative Political Studies* 8 (1975): 178–93.

Campbell, Donald, and Julien Stanley. *Experimental and Quasi-Experimental Designs for Research.* Chicago: Rand-McNally, 1963.

Cantori, Louis. "The Transition to Democracy in Egypt: From What to Where?" Paper presented at the Annual Meeting of the Middle East Studies Association, 1989.

Çarkoğlu, Ali. "Religiosity and Public Policy Evaluations in Turkey." Unpublished manuscript, 2001.

Çarkoğlu, Ali, and Binnaz Toprak. *Türkiye'de din, toplum ve siyaset* [Religion, society, and politics in Turkey]. Istanbul: Tesev Yayınları, 2000.

Casanova, José. "Civil Society and Religion: Retrospective Reflections on Catholicism and Prospective Reflections on Islam." *Social Research* 68 (winter 2001): 1041–80.

———. *Public Religions in the Modern World.* Chicago: University of Chicago Press, 1994.

Center for Palestine Research and Studies (CPRS). "Results of Poll #47." Nablus, Palestine: Center for Palestine Research and Studies, 2000.

———. "Results of Poll #48." Nablus, Palestine: Center for Palestine Research and Studies, 2000.

Central Intelligence Agency. *The World Factbook 2000.* Washington, D.C.: Central Intelligence Agency, 2000. Available at https://www.cia.gov/library/publications/the-world-factbook/ (accessed September 10, 2010).

Chanley, Virginia A. "U.S. Public Views of International Involvement from 1964 to 1993: Time-Series Analyses of General and Militant International-ism." *Journal of Conflict Resolution* 43, no. 1 (1999): 23–44.

Charef, Abed. *Algerie: Octobre 1988.* Algiers: Editions Laphomic, 1990.

Charlesworthy, Hilary, Christine Chinkin, and Shelley Wright. "Feminist Approaches to International Law." *American Journal of International Law* 85 (October 1991).

Charlton, Sue Ellen M., Jana Everett, and Kathleen Staudt, eds. *Women, the State, and Development.* Albany: State University of New York Press, 1989.

Chazan, Naomi. "Israeli Women and Peace Activism." In *Calling the Equality Bluff,* ed. Barbara Swirski and Marilyn Safir. New York: Pergamon, 1991.

Choueiri, Youssef. "The Political Discourse of Contemporary Islamist Movements." In *Islamic Fundamentalism,* ed. Abdel Salem Sidahmed and Anoushiravam Ehteshami. Boulder, Colo.: Westview, 1996.

Chu, Yun-han, Michael Bratton, Marta Lagos, Sandeep Shastri, and Mark Tessler. "Public Opinion and Democratic Legitimacy." *Journal of Democracy* 19 (April 2008): 74–87.

Chu, Yun-han, Larry Diamond, and Doh Chull Shin, "Growth and Equivocation in Support for Democracy: Taiwan and Korea in Comparative Perspective." Paper presented at the Annual Meeting of the American Political Science Association, Washington, D.C., August 31–September 3, 2000.

———. "Halting Progress in Korea and Taiwan." *Journal of Democracy* 12 (January 2001): 122–36.

Ciment, James. *Algeria: The Fundamentalist Challenge.* New York: Facts on File, 1997.

Clarke, Harold D., Nitish Dutt, and Allen Kornberg. "The Political Economy of Attitudes toward Policy and Society in Western and European Democracies." *Journal of Politics* 55 (1993): 998–1021.

Cohen, Yolande, ed., *Women and Counter-Power.* New York: Black Rose Books, 1989.

Collier, Paul, and Anka Hoeffler. "Greed and Grievance in Civil War." *World Bank Policy Research Paper 2355.* Washington, D.C.: World Bank, 2000.

Connelly, Matthew. *A Diplomatic Revolution: Algeria's Fight for Independence and the Origins of the Post–Cold War Era.* New York: Oxford University Press, 2002.

Conover, Pamela Johnston, and Virginia Shapiro, "Gender, Feminist Consciousness, and War." *American Journal of Political Science* 37 (November 1993): 1079–99.

Cooper, Catherine R., and Jill Denner. "Theories Linking Culture and Psychology: Universal and Community-Specific Processes." *Annual Review of Psychology* 49 (1998): 559–84.

Crenshaw, M. "The Psychology of Terrorism: An Agenda for the 21st Century." *Political Psychology* 21 (2000): 405–420.

Cuzán, Alfred G., and Charles M. Bundrick. "Presidential Popularity in Central America: Parallels with the United States." *Political Research Quarterly* 50, no. 4 (1997): 833–49.

Dajani, Souad. "Palestinian Women under Israeli Occupation." In *Arab Women: Old Boundaries, New Frontiers,* ed. Judith Tucker. Bloomington: Indiana University Press, 1993.

Daleb, Nuha Abu. "Palestinian Women and Their Role in the Revolution." *Peuples Mediterraneens* 5 (October–December 1978).

Dalton, R. "Citizen Attitudes and Political Behavior." *Comparative Political Studies* 33, no. 6/7 (2000): 912–40.

Daneels, Isabelle. *Palestine's Interim Agreement with Democracy.* Jerusalem: Jerusalem Media and Communication Centre, 1998.

Delli Carpini, Michael. "In Search of the Informed Citizen: What Americans Know about Politics and Why It Matters." *Communication Review* 41, no. 1 (2000): 129–64.

Delli Carpini, Michael, and Scott Keeter. *What Americans Know about Politics and Why It Matters.* New Haven, Conn.: Yale University Press, 1996.

Denberger, Robert. "The Relevance of China's Development Experience for Other Developing Countries." *ITEMS (SSRC)* 31 (1977): 25–34.

Deutsch, Karl. "Social Mobilization and Political Development." *American Political Science Review* 55 (1961): 493–511.

Diamond, Larry. *Developing Democracy: Toward Consolidation.* Baltimore, Md.: Johns Hopkins University Press, 1999.

———. "Is the Third Wave Over." *Journal of Democracy* 7 (October, 1996): 20–37.

Dietz, Mary G. "Citizenship with a Feminist Face: The Problem with Maternal Thinking." *Political Theory* 13, no. 1 (1985): 19–38.

Digne, Paul. "Algerie: un navire a la derive." *Jeune Afrique* 1519 (February 12, 1989): 38–42.

DiMaggio, Paul. "Culture and Cognition." *Annual Review of Sociology* 23 (1997): 263–87.

Dodd, Clement Henry. *The Crisis of Turkish Democracy.* Hull, England: Eothen, 1983.

Dowty, A. *The Jewish State a Century Later.* Berkeley: University of California Press, 2000.

Dufour, Dany. "L'Enseignement en Algérie." *Maghreb-Machrek* 80 (1978): 33–53.

Dwyer, Kevin. *Arab Voices.* Berkeley: University of California Press, 1991.

Eickelman, Dale. "Muslim Politics: The Prospects for Democracy in North Africa and the Middle East." In *Islam, Democracy, and the State in North Africa,* ed. John Entelis. Bloomington: Indiana University Press, 1997.

———. "Religion in Polity and Society." In *The Political Economy of Morocco,* ed. I. William Zartman. New York: Praeger, 1987.

Eickelman, Dale, and James Piscatori. *Muslim Politics.* Princeton, N.J.: Princeton University Press, 1996.

Eisenstadt, S. N. *Israeli Society.* New York: Basic Books, 1967.

———. *Post-Traditional Society.* New York: Norton, 1972.

El-Mossadeq, Rkia. "Political Parties and Power-Sharing." In *The Political Economy of Morocco,* ed. I. William Zartman. New York: Praeger, 1987.

Elshtain, Jean Bethke. "Reflections on War and Political Discourse." *Political Theory* 13, no. 1 (1985): 39–57.

Enloe, Cynthia. *Does Khaki Become You? The Militarization of Women's Lives.* London: Pluto, 1983.

Entelis, John. "Algeria under Chadli: Liberalization without Democratization; or, Perestroika, Yes; Glasnost, No." *Middle East Insight* (fall 1988): 47–64.

———. *Algeria: The Revolution Institutionalized.* Boulder, Colo.: Westview, 1986.

———. "Ideological Change and an Emerging Counter-Culture in Tunisian Politics." *Journal of Modem African Studies* 12 (1974): 543–68.

———. "Religion and Politics in Algeria: Conflict or Consensus?" *Islam and Christian-Muslim Relations* 12 (2001): 417–34

Entelis, John, and Lisa Arone. "Algeria in Turmoil." *Middle East Policy* 1 (1992): 23–35.

Esmer, Yılmaz. *Devrim, evrim, statüko: Türkiye'de sosyal, siyasal, ekonomik değerler* [Revolution, evolution, and status-quo: Social, political, and economic values in Turkey]. Istanbul: TESEV Yayınları, 1999.

Esposito, John. *Unholy War: Terror in the Name of Islam.* New York: Oxford University Press, 2002.

Esposito, John, and James Piscatori, "Democratization and Islam." *Middle East Journal* 45 (1991): 424–40.

Esposito, John, and John Voll. *Islam and Democracy.* Oxford: Oxford University Press, 1996.

"Etat, ville et mouvements sociaux au Maghreb et au Moyen Orient." *Maghreb-Machrek* 115 (1987): 53–69.

Fahmy, Miral. "Mubarak to Put Economy before Politics." *Reuters Global Newsbank* (September 27, 1999).

Farah, Tawfic, ed. *Political Behavior in the Arab States.* Boulder, Colo.: Westview, 1983.

Farah, Tawfic, and Faisal S. A. Al-Salem. "Political Efficacy, Political Trust, and the Action Orientations of University Students in Kuwait." *International Journal of Middle East Studies* 8 (1977): 317–28.

Feierabend, Ivo, Rosalind Feierabend, and Betty Nesvold. "Social Change and Political Violence: Cross-National Patterns." In *Political Development and Social Change,* ed. J. Finkle and R. Gable. New York: Wiley, 1971.

Fernea, Elizabeth W. "The Veiled Revolution." In *Everyday Life in the Muslim Middle East,* ed. Donna Lee Bowen and Evelyn A. Early. Bloomington: Indiana University Press, 1993.

Fish, M. Steven. "Islam and Authoritarianism." *World Politics* 55 (October, 2002): 4–37

Fite, David, Marc Genest, and Clyde Wilcox. "Gender Differences in Foreign Policy Attitudes: A Longitudinal Analysis." *American Politics Quarterly* 18 (1990): 492–513.

Frankel, Francine. "Compulsion and Social Change: Is Authoritarianism the Solution to India's Economic Problems." *World Politics* 30 (1978): 215–40.

Freedom House Online. "Israel-Administered Territories and Palestinian Authority–Administered Territories." Report of November 2, 2000. Available at http://www.freedomhouse.org/template.cfm?page=180 (accessed September 10, 2010).

Frieden, Jeffrey A., and David A. Lake. *International Political Economy: Perspectives on Global Power and Wealth.* 2nd ed. New York: St. Martin's, 1991.

Fukuyama, Francis. *The End of History and the Last Man.* New York: Avon, 1992.

Funk, Carolyn L., and Patricia A. García-Monet. "The Relationship between Personal and National Concerns in Public Perceptions about the Economy." *Political Research Quarterly* 50, no. 2 (1997): 317–42.

Gabel, Matthew, and Guy D. Whitten. "Economic Conditions, Economic Perceptions, and Public Support for European Integration." *Political Behavior* 19, no. 1 (1997): 81–96.

Garcia-Rivero, Carlos, Hennie Kotze, and Pierre Du Toit. "Political Culture and Democracy: The South African case." *Politikon* 29, no. 2 (2002): 163–81.

Garfinkle, Adam. "Anti-Americanism, U.S. Foreign Policy, and the War on Terrorism." In *A Practical Guide to Winning the War on Terrorism,* ed. A. Garfinkle, 197–218. Palo Alto: Hoover Books Online, 2004. Available at http://www.hoover.org/publications/books/3009071.html (accessed September 10, 2010).

Garnham, David. "Explaining Middle Eastern Alignments during the Gulf War." *Jerusalem Journal of International Relations* 13 (1991): 63–83.

Garnham, David, and Mark Tessler, eds. *Democracy, War, and Peace in the Middle East.* Bloomington: Indiana University Press, 1995.

Gibson, James L. "The Paradoxes of Political Tolerance in Processes of Democratization." *Politikon: South African Journal of Political Science* 23, no. 2 (1996): 5–21.

———. "The Resilience of Mass Support for Democratic Institutions and Processes in the Nascent Russian and Ukrainian Democracies." In *Political Culture and Civil Society in Russia and the New States of Eurasia,* ed. V. Tismaneanu. Armonk, N.Y.: M. E. Sharpe, 1995.

———. "A Sober Second Thought: An Experiment in Persuading Russians to Tolerate." *American Journal of Political Science* 42, no. 3 (1998): 819–50.

Gibson, James L., Raymond M. Duch, and Kent L. Tedin. "Democratic Values and the Transformation of the Soviet Union." *Journal of Politics* 54, no. 2 (1992): 329–71.

Gillath, Nurit. "Women Against War: Parents Against Silence." In *Calling the Equality Bluff,* ed. Barbara Swirski and Marilyn Safir. New York: Pergamon, 1991.

Gilligan, Carol. *In a Different Voice.* Cambridge, Mass.: Harvard University Press, 1982.

Gilpin, R. *The Political Economy of International Relations.* Princeton, N.J.: Princeton University Press, 1987.

Ginges, Jeremy. "Deterring the Terrorist: A Psychological Evaluation of Different Strategies for Deterring Terrorism." *Terrorism and Political Violence* 9 (1997): 170–85.

Ginges, Jeremy, and Ariel Merari. "When Do People Decide to Kill for a Cause? Testing a Social Identity Explanation of Variance in the Extremism of Political Behavior within an Aggrieved Population." Unpublished paper, 2003.

Glazov, Jamie. "Hating America." FrontPageMagazine.com, August 12, 2004. Available at http://www.frontpagemag.com/Articles/ReadArticle .asp?ID=14624 (accessed September 10, 2010).

Goldstein, Judith, and Robert O. Keohane. *Ideas and Foreign Policy: Beliefs, Institutions, and Political Change.* Ithaca, N.Y.: Cornell University Press, 1993.

Grant, Peter R., and Rupert Brown. "From Ethnocentrism to Collective Protest: Responses to Relative Deprivation and Threats to Social Identity." *Social Psychology Quarterly* 58 (1995): 195–212.

Grant, Rebecca, and Kathleen Newland, eds., *Gender and International Relations.* Bloomington: Indiana University Press, 1991.

Grose, Peter. *A Changing Israel.* New York: Vintage, 1985.

Guimond, Serge, and Lise Dube-Simard. "Relative Deprivation Theory and the Quebec Nationalist Movement: The Cognition-Emotion Distinction and the Personal-Group Deprivation Issue." *Journal of Personality and Social Psychology* 44 (1983): 526–35.

Gusfield, Joseph. "Tradition and Modernity: Misplaced Polarities in the Study of Social Change." *American Journal of Sociology* 72 (1965): 351–62.

Guth, James L., and John C. Green. "Salience: The Core Concept?" In *Rediscovering the Religious Factor in American Politics,* ed. David C. Leege and Lyman A. Kellstedt. Armonk, N.Y.: M. E. Sharpe, 1993.

Haddad, Simon, and Hilal Khashan. "Islam and Terrorism: Lebanese Muslim Views on September 11." *Journal of Conflict Resolution* 46 (2002): 812–28.

Hafez, Mohammed. "From Marginalization to Massacres: A Political Process Explanation of GIA Violence in Algeria." In *Islamic Activism: A Social Movement Theory Approach,* ed. Quintan Wiktorowicz, 37–60. Bloomington: Indiana University Press, 2004.

Halasa, Serene. "Arab Scholars Call for New Order Based on Democracy, Urge End to Iraq Sanctions." *Jordan Times,* May 30–31, 1991.

Halliday, Fred. "Hidden from International Relations: Women and the International Arena." In *Gender and International Relations,* ed. R. Grant and K. Newland. Bloomington: Indiana University Press, 1991.

———. *Islam and the Myth of Confrontation: Religion and Politics in the Middle East.* London: I. B. Tauris, 1995.

Hamarneh, Mustapha. *Revisiting the Arab Street: Research from Within.* Amman: Center for Strategic Studies, University of Jordan, 2005. Available at http://www.jcss.org/SubDefault.aspx?PageId=56&PubId=61&PubType=1 (accessed September 10, 2010).

Hamdi, Mohamed Elhachmi. "Islam and Democracy: The Limits of the Western Model." *Journal of Democracy* 7 (April 1996): 81–85.

Hamilton, Roberta, and Michele Barrett, eds. *The Politics of Diversity: Feminism, Marxism, and Nationalism.* London: Verso, 1986.

Hanafi, Hasna. "The Relevance of the Islamic Alternative in Egypt." *Arab Studies Quarterly* 4 (spring 1982): 54–74.

Harik, Iliya. "Pluralism in the Arab World." *Journal of Democracy* 5 (July 1994): 56.

———. "Some Political and Cultural Considerations Bearing on Survey Research in the Arab World." In *The Evaluation and Application of Survey Research in the Arab World,* ed. Mark Tessler, Monte Palmer, Tawfic E. Farah, and Barbara Lethem Ibrahim. Boulder, Colo.: Westview, 1987.

Harik, Judith P. "Between Islam and the System: Sources and Implications of Popular Support for Lebanon's Hizballah." *Journal of Conflict Resolution* 40 (1996): 41–67.

Hartsock, Nancy C. M. *Money, Sex, and Power: Toward a Feminist Historical Materialism.* Boston: Northeastern University Press, 1983.

Hassan, Nasra. "An Arsenal of Believers." *New Yorker,* November 19, 2001.

Hatem, Mervat. "Post-Islamist and Post-Nationalist Feminist Discourses." In *Arab Women,* ed. Judith Tucker. Bloomington: Indiana University Press, 1993.

Hawkesworth, Mary E. *Beyond Oppression: Feminist Theory and Political Strategy.* New York: Continuum, 1990.

Hayes, Bernadette. "The Impact of Religious Identification on Political Attitudes: An International Comparison." *Sociology of Religion,* 56 (1995):177–94.

Hayward, Fred. "Correlates of National Political Integration: The Case of Ghana." *Comparative Political Studies* 7 (1974): 165–92.

Heper, Metin, and Aylin Güney. "The Military and the Consolidation of Democracy: The Recent Turkish Experience." *Armed Forces and Society* 26, no. 4 (2000), 635–57.

Hermassi, Elbaki. "La société tunisienne au miroir islamiste." *Maghreb-Machrek* 103 (1984): 39–56.

———. *Leadership and National Development in North Africa.* Berkeley: University of California Press, 1972.

Hoffman, Bruce. *Al Qaeda, Trends in Terrorism and Future Potentialities: An Assessment.* Santa Monica: RAND, 2003. Available at http://www.rand.org/publications/P/P8078/P8078.pdf (accessed September 10, 2010).

Holland, John H., Keith J. Holyoak, Richard E. Nisbett, and Paul Thagard. *Induction: Processes of Inference, Learning, and Discovery.* Cambridge, Mass.: MIT Press, 1986.

Holm, John. *Dimensions of Mass Involvement in Botswana Politics: A Test of Alternative Theories.* Comparative Politics series. Beverly Hills, Calif.: Sage, 1974.

Hopwood, Derek. *Egypt: Politics and Society, 1945–1981.* London: Allen & Unwin, 1982.

Horne, Alistair. *A Savage War of Peace: Algeria 1954–1962.* New York: Penguin Books, 1979.

Hoskyns, Catherine. "Gender Issues in International Relations." *Review of International Studies* 20 (October 1994).

Hudson, Michael. "Democratization and the Problem of Legitimacy in Middle East Politics." *Middle East Studies Association Bulletin* 22 (1988): 157–72.

———. "The Democratization Process in the Arab World: An Assessment." Paper presented at the Annual Meeting of the American Political Science Association, 1990.

———. "The Political Culture Approach to Arab Democratization: The Case for Bringing It Back In, Carefully." In *Political Liberalization and Democratization in the Arab World,* ed. Rex Brynen, Bahgat Korany, and Paul Noble. Boulder: Lynne Reinner, 1995.

Huntington, Samuel. "The Change to Change." In *Comparative Politics: Notes and Readings,* ed. Roy Macridis and B. Brown. Homewood, Ill.: Dorsey, 1972.

———. "The Clash of Civilizations?" *Foreign Affairs* 72 (summer 1993): 22–49.

———. *The Clash of Civilizations and the Remaking of the World Order.* New York: Simon and Schuster, 1996.

———. "Democracy's Third Wave." In *The Global Resurgence of Democracy,* ed. Larry Diamond and Marc Plattner. Baltimore, Md.: Johns Hopkins University Press, 1993.

———. "Political Development and Political Decay." *World Politics* 17 (1965): 386–430.

———. *Political Order in Changing Societies.* New Haven, Conn.: Yale University Press, 1968.

———. *The Third Wave.* Norman: University of Oklahoma Press, 1991.

———. "Will More Countries Become Democratic?" *Political Science Quarterly* 99 (summer 1984): 193–218.

Huntington, Samuel, and Joan Nelson. *No Easy Choice: Political Participation in Developing Countries.* Cambridge, Mass.: Harvard University Press, 1976.

Huxley, Fred. "Moroccan Public Backs PLO-Israel Peace Plan, Views U.S. Positively." Washington, D.C.: USIA Opinion Research Memorandum, December 13, 1993.

Ibrahim, Youssef. "In Algiers, Curfew and Threats of Worse." *New York Times,* June 7, 1991.

———. "Jordan Feels Change within as Muslims Pursue Agenda." *New York Times,* December 26, 1992.

———. "Militant Muslims Grow Stronger as Algeria's Economy Grows Weaker." *New York Times,* June 25, 1990.

———. "PLO Is Facing Growing Discontent." *New York Times.* April 5, 1992.

Inglehart, Ronald. "Culture and Democracy." In *Culture Matters: How Values Shape Human Progress,* ed. Lawrence E. Harrison and Samuel Huntington. New York: Basic Books, 2000.

———. *Culture Shift in Advanced Industrial Society.* Princeton, N.J.: Princeton University Press, 1990.

———. *The Silent Revolution: Changing Values and Political Styles in Advanced Industrial Society.* Princeton, N.J.: Princeton University Press, 1977.

Inglehart, Ronald, and Wayne E. Baker. "Modernization, Cultural Change, and the Persistence of Traditional Values." *American Sociological Review* 65, no. 1 (2000): 19–51.

Inglehart, Ronald, Miguel Basanez, Jaime Deiz-Medrano, Loek Halman, and Ruud Luijkx. *Human Beliefs and Values: A Cross-cultural Sourcebook Based on the 1999–2002 Values Surveys.* Mexico City: Siglo XXI, 2004.

Inglehart, Ronald, and Pippa Norris. "The True Clash of Civilizations." *Foreign Affairs,* 135 (March–April 2003), 63–70.

Inglehart, Ronald, and Christian Welzel. "Political Culture and Democracy: Analyzing Cross-Level Linkages." *Comparative Politics* 36, no. 1 (2003): 61–79.

Inkeles, Alex. "Making Men Modern: On the Causes and Consequences of Individual Change in Six Developing Countries." *American Journal of Sociology* 75 (1969): 208–225.

———. "Participant Citizenship in Six Developing Countries." *American Political Science Review* 63 (1969): 1129–41.

International Labour Office (ILO). *Yearbook of Labour Statistics.* Geneva: International Labour Office, 2000.

Ismail, Salwa. "The Paradox of Islamist Politics." *Middle East Report* 221 (2001): 34–39.

Izraeli, Dafna N., and Ephriam Taboury, "The Political Context of Feminist Attitudes in Israel." In *Women in Israel,* ed. Yael Azmon and Dafna N. Izraeli. New Brunswick, N.J.: Transaction, 1993.

Jacqueite, Jane S. "Power as Ideology: A Feminist Analysis." In *Women's Views of the Political World of Men,* ed. J. H. Stiehm, 9–29. Dobbs Ferry, N.Y.: Transnational, 1984.

Jaggar, Alison M. "Feminist Ethics: Projects, Problems, Prospects." In *Feminist Ethics,* ed. Claudia Card. Lawrence: University of Kansas Press, 1991.

Jamal, Amaney. "Reassessing Support for Democracy and Islam in the Arab World: Evidence from Egypt and Jordan." *World Affairs* 169 (fall 2006): 51–63.

Jansen, Johannes J. G. *The Neglected Duty: The Creed of Sadat's Assassins and Islamic Resurgence in the Middle East.* London: Macmillan, 1986.

Jansen, Willy. *Women Without Men.* Leiden: E. J. Brill, 1987.

Jaquette, Jane. *Women in Politics.* New York: Wiley, 1974.

Jayawardena, Kumari. *Feminism and Nationalism in the Third World.* London: Zed Books, 1986.

Jelen, Ted G. *The Political Mobilization of Religious Beliefs.* New York: Praeger, 1991.

———. "Religion and Foreign Policy Attitudes: Exploring the Effects of Denomination and Doctrine." *American Politics Quarterly* 22 (1994): 382–400.

———. "Religion and Public Opinion in the 1990s: An Empirical Overview." In *Understanding Public Opinion,* ed. Barbara Norrander and Clyde Wilcox. Washington D.C.: Congressional Quarterly Press, 1996.

———. "Swords, Plowshares, and Philistines: A Comparative Analysis of Religion and Attitudes toward Security Policy." Paper presented at the Annual Meeting of the American Political Science Association, San Francisco, August 29–September 1, 1996.

Jelen, Ted G., Sue Thomas, and Clyde Wilcox, "The Gender Gap in Comparative Perspective: Gender Differences in Abstract Ideology and Concrete Issues in Western Europe." *European Journal of Politics* 25 (February 1994): 171–86.

Jennings, Kent M. "Political Knowledge over Time and across Generations." *Public Opinion Quarterly* 60 (1996): 228–52.

———. "Residues of a Movement: The Aging of the American Protest Generation." *American Political Science Review* 81, no. 2 (1987): 367–82.

Jennings, Kent M., and Richard G. Niemi. *Generations and Politics: A Panel Study of Young Adults and Their Parents.* Princeton, N.J.: Princeton University Press, 1981.

Jordanian Opinion Survey regarding Jordanian-Palestinian Relations [in Arabic]. Amman: Jordan University Center for Strategic Studies, 1995.

Kahl, Joseph. *The Measurement of Modernism.* Austin: University of Texas Press, 1968.

Kalyvas, Stathis. "Commitment Problems in Emerging Democracies: The Case of Religious Parties." *Comparative Politics* 32 (2000): 379–98.

Kamrava, Mehran. *Democracy in the Balance: Culture and Society in the Middle East.* New York: Chatham House, 1998.

Kandiyoti, Deniz, "Introduction." In *Women, Islam, and the State,* ed. Deniz Kandiyoti. Philadelphia: Temple University Press, 1991.

Karawan, Ibrahim A. "Arab Dilemmas in the 1990s." Unpublished paper, October 1993.

———. *Islamist Impasse.* London: International Institute for Strategic Studies, 1997.

———. "'ReIslamization Movements' According to Kepel: On Striking Back and Striking Out." *Contention* 2 (fall 1992): 161–79.

Kasfir, Nelson. "Dilemmas of Popular Support in Guerilla War: The National Resistance Army in Uganda, 1981–86." *Journal of Modern African Studies* 43 (2002): 271–96.

Keddourie, Elie. *Democracy and Arab Political Culture.* Washington, D.C.: Washington Institute for Near East Policy, 1992.

Kerr, Malcolm. "Foreword." In *Political Behavior in the Arab States,* ed. Tawfic Farah. Boulder, Colo.: Westview, 1983.

Khalil, Nevine. "Listening to the Masses" [in Arabic], *Al-Ahram Weekly,* October 1–7, 1998.

Khashan, Hilal. *Arab Attitudes toward Israel and Peace.* Washington D.C.: Washington Institute for Near East Policy, 2000.

———. "History's Legacy." *Middle East Quarterly,* 5 (March 1998): 43–44.

Khouri, Rami G. "The Arab Dream Won't Be Denied." *New York Times,* December 15, 1991.

———. "A Lesson in Middle East History and Humanity." *Jordan Times,* May 28, 1991.

———. "A View from the Arab World." *Jordan Times,* July 5, 2000.

Kinder, Donald R., and D. Roderick Kiewiet. "Economic Discontent and Political Behavior: The Role of Personal Grievances and Collective Economic Judgments in Congressional Voting." *American Journal of Political Science* 23 (1979): 495–526.

Knopf, Jeffrey W. "How Rational Is 'The Rational Public'? Evidence from U.S. Public Opinion on Military Spending." *Journal of Conflict Resolution* 42, no. 5 (1998): 544–71.

Kokan, Jane. "Morocco: Riot Deaths as Hassan Faces Challenge." *London Times,* February 20, 1994.

Kornberg, Allen, and Harold Clarke. *Citizens and Community: Political Support in a Representative Democracy.* Cambridge: Cambridge University Press. 1992.

Ko'war, Samira. "Fundamentalists Gain Strength." *Christian Science Monitor,* November 10, 1989.

Kramer, Gundrun. "Liberalization and Democracy in the Arab World." *Middle East Report* 174 (January–February 1992): 22–25.

Krosnick, Jon A., and Duane F. Alwin. "Aging and Susceptibility to Attitude Change." *Journal of Personality and Social Psychology* 57 (September 1989): 416–25.

Krueger, Alan B., and Jitka Maleckova. "Does Poverty Cause Terrorism? The Economics and the Education of Suicide Bombers." *New Republic,* June 24, 2002.

———. "Seeking the Roots of Terror." *Chronicle of Higher Education,* June, 6, 2003. Available at http://chronicle.com/free/v49/i39/39b01001.htm.

Kubicek, Paul. "The Earthquake, Europe, and Prospects for Political Change in Turkey." *Middle East Review of International Affairs* 5 (June, 2001).

Kushner, Harvey. "Suicide Bombers: Business as Usual." *Studies in Conflict and Terrorism* 19 (1996): 329–38.

La Guerre du Golfe et l'Avenir des Arabes: débats et réflexions. Tunis: Cérès Productions, 1991.

La Polombara, Joseph, and Myron Weiner. *Political Parties and Political Development.* Princeton, N.J.: Princeton University Press, 1966.

Labib, Taher. "L'intellectuel des sept mois." In *La Guerre du Golfe et l'Avenir des Arabes: débats et réflexions.* Tunis: Cérès Productions, 1991.

Lagos, Marta. "Latin America's Smiling Mask." *Journal of Democracy* 8 (July, 1997): 125–34.

Layachi, Azzedine. "Government, Legitimacy, and Democracy in Algeria." *Maghreb Report.* January–February, 1992.

Layachi, Azzedine, and Abdel-kader Haireche. "National Development and Political Protest: Islamists in the Maghreb Countries." *Arab Studies Quarterly* 14 (spring–summer 1992): 69–92.

Leege, David C. "Religion and Politics in Theoretical Perspective." In *Rediscovering the Religious Factor in American Politics,* ed. D. C. Leege and L. A. Kellstedt, 3–25. Armonk, N.Y.: M. E. Sharpe, 1993.

Leege, David C., and Lyman A. Kellstedt. "Religious Worldviews and Political Philosophies: Capturing Theory in the Grand Manner through Empirical Data." In *Rediscovering the Religious Factor in American Politics,* ed. D. C. Leege and L. A. Kellstedt, 216–31. Armonk, N.Y.: M. E. Sharpe, 1993.

Lerner, Daniel. *The Passing of Traditional Society.* New York: Free Press, 1958.

Lesbet, Djaafar. "Effets de la crise du logement en Algérie: Des cités d'urgence à l'état d'exception." *Maghreb-Machrek: Monde Arabe—villes, pouvoirs et sociétés (numéro spécial)* 143 (January–March 1994): 212–24.

Lesch, Ann. "Democracy in Doses: Mubarak Launches His Second Term as President." *Arab Studies Quarterly* 11 (1989): 87–108.

LeVine, Robert. "Political Socialization and Culture Change." In *Old Societies and New States,* ed. Clifford Geertz. New York: Free Press, 1963.

Lewis, Bernard. "The Roots of Muslim Rage: Why So Many Muslim Deeply Resent the West and Why Their Bitterness Will Not Be Easily Mollified." *Atlantic Monthly* 266 (September, 1990): 47–60.

———. *The Shaping of the Modern Middle East.* New York: Oxford University Press, 1994.

———. *What Went Wrong: Western Impact and Middle Eastern Response.* New York: Oxford University Press, 2002.

Lewis-Beck, Michael S. *Economics and Elections: The Major Western Democracies.* Ann Arbor: University of Michigan Press, 1988.

Lindberg, Tod. Opening Remarks. Carnegie Endowment for International Peace and Central European University Conference "Does Anti-Americanism Matter to American Foreign Policy?" Washington, D.C., November 3, 2005.

Linz, Juan J., and Alfred Stephan. "Toward Consolidated Democracies." *Journal of Democracy* 7 (April 1996): 14–33.

"L'Islam contestataire en Tunisie." *Jeune Afrique,* March 14, 21 and 28, 1979.

Lockerbie, Brad. "Economic Dissatisfaction and Political Alienation in Western Europe." *European Journal of Political Research* 23 (1993): 281–93.

Lowrie, Arthur. *Islam, Democracy, the State, and the West: A Roundtable with Dr. Hassan Al-Turabi.* Tampa, Fla.: World and Islam Studies Enterprise, 1993.

MacIver, Martha Abele. "Religious Politicization among Western European Mass Publics." In *Religious Politics in Global and Comparative Perspective,* ed. William H. Swatos Jr. New York: Greenwood, 1989.

MacIver, Robert. *The Web of Government.* New York: Macmillan, 1947.

Magnusson, David, Lars R. Bergman, and Georg Rudinger, eds. *Problems and Methods in Longitudinal Research: Stability and Change.* Cambridge: Cambridge University Press, 1991.

Mainwaring, Scott. "Democratic Survivability in Latin America." In *Democracy and Its Limits: Lessons from Asia, Latin America, and the Middle East,* ed. Howard Handelman and Mark Tessler. Notre Dame, Ind.: University of Notre Dame Press, 1999.

Makram-Ebeid, Mona. "Political Opposition in Egypt: Democratic Myth or Reality." *Middle East Journal* 43 (1989): 423–36.

Malley, Robert. *The Call for Algeria: Third Worldism, Revolution, and the Turn to Islam.* Berkeley: University of California Press, 1996.

Mannheim, Karl. "The Problem of Generations." In *Essays on the Sociology of Knowledge,* ed. Paul Kecskemeti, 276–320. London: Routledge and Kegan Paul, 1952 [1928].

Marks, Jon. "Special Report on Morocco." *Middle East Economic Digest,* April 1, 1994.

Marradi, Alberto. "Factor Analysis as an Aid in the Formulation and Refinement of Empirically Useful Concepts." In *Factor Analysis and Measurement in Sociological Research,* ed. Edgar F. Borgatta and David J. Jackson. London: Sage, 1981.

Marsot, Afaf Lutfi al-Sayyid. "The Revolutionary Gentlewoman in Egypt." In Women in the Muslim World, ed. Lois Beck and Nikki Keddie. Cambridge, Mass.: Harvard University Press, 1978.

Martinez, Luis. La Guèrre Civile en Algerie, 1990–1998. Paris: Karthala, 1998.

———. "Why the Violence in Algeria?" In Islam, Democracy and the State in Algeria: Lessons for the Western Mediterranean and Beyond, ed. M. Bonner, M. Reif, and M. Tessler, 14–27. London: Routledge, 2005.

Massis, Maher. "Jordan: A Study of Attitudes toward Democratic Changes." Arab Studies Quarterly 20 (summer 1998), 37–63.

Mattes, Robert, and Hermann Thiel. "Consolidation and Public Opinion in South Africa." Journal of Democracy 9 (January, 1998): 95–110.

Mayfield, James B. Rural Politics in Nasser's Egypt. Austin: University of Texas Press, 1971.

McCord, William. In the Springtime of Freedom. New York: Oxford University Press, 1965.

McGuigan, Dorothy G., ed. The Role of Women in Conflict and Peace. Ann Arbor: University of Michigan Press, 1977.

Meier, Kenneth. "The Value of Replicating Social Science Research." Chronicle of Higher Education, February 7, 1997.

Melson, Robert, and Howard Wolpe. "Modernization and the Politics of Communalism: A Theoretical Perspective." American Political Science Review 64 (1970): 1112–30.

Merari, Ariel. "Deterring Fear: Government Responses to Terrorist Attacks." Harvard International Review 23 (2002): 26–31.

———. "Deterring Terrorism: States, Organizations, Individuals." Justice 31 (2002): 3–6.

———. "Social, Organization, and Psychological Factors in Suicide Terrorism." In Root Causes of Suicide Terrorism, ed. T. Bjørgo, 70–86. London: Routledge, 2005.

Mernissi, Fatima. Islam and Democracy: Fear of the Modern World Reading, Mass.: Addison-Wesley, 1992.

Micallef, Roberta. "Israeli and Palestinian Women's Peace Movements." In The Struggle for Peace, ed. Elizabeth Warnock Fernea and Mary Evelyn Hocking. Austin: University of Texas Press, 1992.

Micaud, Charles. "Leadership and Development: The Case of Tunisia." Comparative Politics 2 (1969): 463–84.

———. Tunisia: The Politics of Modernization. New York: Praeger, 1964.

Mishal, Shaul, Ranan D. Kuperman, and David Boaz. Investment in Peace: The Politics of Economic Cooperation between Israel, Jordan, and the Palestinian Authority. Brighton, U.K.: Sussex Academic Press, 2001.

Mishal, Shaul, and Avraham Sela. The Palestinian Hamas: Vision, Violence, and Coexistence. New York: Columbia University Press, 2000.

Moffett, George D. "North Africa's Disillusioned Youth." *Christian Science Monitor,* May 17, 1989.

Moghadam, Assaf. "Palestinian Suicide Terrorism in the Second Intifada: Motivations and Organizational Aspects." *Studies in Conflict and Terrorism* 26 (2003): 65–92.

Moghadam, Valentine M. "Introduction." In *Identity Politics and Women: Cultural Reassertions and Feminisms in International Perspective,* ed. V. Moghadam. Boulder, Colo.: Westview, 1994.

———. *Modernizing Women.* Boulder, Colo.: Lynne Rienner, 1993.

Mohanty, Chandra Talpade, Anne Russo, and Lourdes Torres, eds., *Third World Women and the Politics of Feminism.* Bloomington: Indiana University Press, 1991.

Molyneux, Maxine. "Women's Rights and the International Context: Some Reflections on the Post-Communist States." *Millenium* 23, no. 2 (1994).

Monroe, Kristen Renwick, James Hankin, and Renée Bukovchik Van Vechten. "The Psychological Foundations of Identity Politics." *Annual Review of Political Science* 3 (2000): 419–47.

Moore, Clement Henry. "On Theory and Practice among Arabs." *World Politics* 24 (1971): 106–26.

———. *Tunisia since Independence.* Berkeley: University of California Press, 1965

Morgan, Valerie. "Women and the Peace Process in Northern Ireland." Global Forum Occasional Papers series. Duke University Center for International Studies, Durham, N.C., 1996.

Mosca, Gaetano. *The Ruling Class.* New York: McGraw Hill, 1939.

Moscovici, Serge. "Notes toward a Description of Social Representations." *European Journal of Social Psychology* 18 (1988): 211–50.

Mujani, Saiful. "Religious Democrats: Democratic Culture and Muslim Participation in Post-Suharto Indonesia." Ph.D. diss., Ohio State University, 2004.

Munoz-Rojas, Daniel. "Violations of International Humanitarian Law: Their Psycho-sociological Causes and Prevention." Armed Groups Project, 2003. Available at http://www.armedgroups.org/images/stories/pdfs/munoz_paper_3.pdf (accessed September 10, 2010).

Munson, Henry, "Islamist Political Movements in North Africa." Paper presented at a workshop on "Politico-Religious Movements and Development in the Near East," Washington, D.C., June 1992.

Muslim Democrat 2 (November 2000): 3, 4, 8.

Myrdal, Gunnar. *Asian Drama: An Inquiry into the Poverty of Nations.* New York: Pantheon, 1968.

Nachtwey, Jodi, and Mark Tessler. " Explaining Women's Support for Political Islam: Contributions from Feminist Theory." In *Area Studies and Social Science: Strategies for Understanding Middle East Politics,* ed. M. Tessler, with J. Nachtwey and A. Banda. Bloomington: Indiana University Press, 1999.

———. "The Political Economy of Attitudes toward Peace among Palestinians and Israelis." *Journal of Conflict Resolution* 46 (2002): 260–85.

Nasr, Vali. "The Rise of 'Muslim Democracy.'" *Journal of Democracy* 16 (April 2005): 13–27.

Nath, Kamla. "Education and Employment among Kuwaiti Women." In *Women in the Muslim World,* ed. Lois Beck and Nikki Keddie. Cambridge, Mass.: Harvard University Press, 1978.

Nathan, Andrew, and Tianjian Shi. "Cultural Requisites for Democracy in China: Findings from a Survey." *Daedalus* 122, no. 2 (1993): 95–123.

Newcomb, Theodore M. "Some Patterned Consequences of Membership in a College Community." In *Readings in Social Psychology,* ed. Theodore M. Newcomb et al., 345–57. New York: Holt, 1947.

Newcomb, Theodore M., Kathryn E. Koenig, Richard Flacks, and Donald P. Warwick. *Persistence and Change.* New York: Wiley, 1967.

Nie, Norman, G. Bingham Powell Jr., and Kenneth Prewitt. "Social Structure and Political Participation: Developmental Relationships." *American Political Science Review* 63 (1969): 361–78.

O'Barr, Jean Fox, and Mark Tessler. "Gender and Participant Citizenship: Evidence from Tunisia." n.d.

O'Neill, William. "Beyond the Slogans: How Can the UN Respond to Terrorism?" New York: International Peace Academy, United Nations, 2002.

Ottaway, Marina, and Thomas Carothers. "Middle East Democracy." *Foreign Policy,* November–December 2004, 22–28.

Ottemoeller, Dan. "Popular Perceptions of Democracy: Elections and Attitudes in Uganda." *Comparative Political Studies* (February 1998): 98–124.

Ottoway, David, "Feminists Seek Voice in Kuwaiti Politics." *Washington Post,* April 14, 1984.

Owusu, Maxwell. *Uses and Abuses of Political Power.* Chicago: University of Chicago Press, 1970.

Özbudun, Ergun. *Contemporary Turkish Politics: Challenges to Democratic Consolidation.* London: Lynne Rienner, 2000.

———. "Turkey: How Far from Consolidation?" *Journal of Democracy* 7 (October, 1996): 123–38.

Pacek, Alexander, and Benjamin Radcliff. "The Political Economy of Competitive Elections in the Developing World." *American Journal of Political Science* 39, no. 3(1995): 745–59.

Palestinian Central Bureau of Statistics (PCBS) Online. "Labour Force-Current Main Indicators: Basic Changes in the Labour Force Indicators in Palestinian Territory during 1995–2000." 2000. Available at http://www.pcbs.org/english/labor/lab_curr.htm (accessed January 15, 2001).

———. "Poverty in Palestine." Updated March 2, 2000. Available at http://www.pcbs.org/english/househol/poverty.htm (accessed January 15, 2001).

———. "Press Report on Labour Force Survey Results: October–December, 2000." 2001. Available at http://www.pcbs.org/english/press_4/prs_la19.htm (accessed January 15, 2001).

Palmer, Monte. *Survey Research in the Arab World: An Analytical Index.* London: Menas, 1982.

Palmer, Monte, Madiha El Safty, and Earl Sullivan. "The Relationship between Economic and Religious Attitudes in Egypt." Paper presented at the Annual Meeting of the Middle East Studies Association, Providence, R.I., November, 1996.

Papanek, Hanna. "The Ideal Woman and the Ideal Society: Control and Autonomy and the Construction of Identity." In *Identity Politics and Women: Cultural Reassertions and Feminisms in International Perspective,* ed. V. M. Moghadam. Boulder, Colo.: Westview, 1994.

Parker, Richard B. *North Africa: Regional Tensions and Strategic Concerns.* New York: Praeger, 1984.

Paul, James. "States of Emergency: The Riots in Tunisia and Morocco." *MERIP Reports* 127 (October 1984).

Paz, Reuven. "Is Hamas Reevaluating the Use of Terrorism?" 1998. Available at http://www.ict.org.il/Articles/tabid/66/currentpage/1/Default.aspx (accessed September 10, 2010).

———. "Islamists and Anti-Americanism." *Middle East Review of International Affairs* 7 (2003): 53–61.

———. "Radical Islamist Terrorism." 2001. Available at http://www.ict.org.il/Articles/tabid/66/currentpage/1/Default.aspx (accessed September 10, 2010).

Pedahzur, Ami, Arie Perliger, and Leonard Weinberg. "Altruism and Fatalism: The Characteristics of Palestinian Suicide Terrorists." *Deviant Behavior* 24 (2003): 405–23.

Peteet, Julie Marie. *Gender in Crisis: Women and the Palestinian Resistance Movement.* New York: Columbia University Press, 1991.

Peterson, V. Spike, and Anne Sisson Runyan, *Global Gender Issues.* Boulder, Colo.: Westview, 1993.

Pew 2005. "Global Opinion: The Spread of Anti-Americanism." Pew Research Center, Trends 2005. Available at http://pewresearch.org/assets/files/trends2005-global.pdf (accessed September 10, 2010).

Philipp, Thomas. "Feminism in Nationalist Politics in Egypt." In *Women in the Muslim World,* ed. L. Beck and N. Keddie. Cambridge, Mass.: Harvard University Press, 1978.

Pipes, Daniel. "Debate: Islam and Democracy." PBS "Wide Angle." July 15, 2003. Available at http://www.danielpipes.org/article/1167 (accessed September 10, 2010).

Pollock, David. "The 'Arab Street'? Public Opinion in the Arab World." Policy Paper No. 32. Washington, D.C.: Washington Institute for Near East Policy, 1992.

Post, Jerrold M. "Rewarding Fire with Fire: Effects of Retaliation on Terrorist Group Dynamics." *Terrorism* 10 (1987): 23–35.

Posusney, Marcia, and Michelle Angrist, eds. *Authoritarianism in the Middle East.* Boulder, Colo.: Lynne Rienner, 2005.

Prewitt, Kenneth. "Political Socialization and Political Education in New Nations." In *Learning about Politics,* ed. Roberta Sigel. New York: Random House, 1970.

Przeworski, Adam. *Democracy and the Market: Political and Economic Reforms in Eastern Europe and Latin America.* Cambridge: Cambridge University Press, 1991.

Przeworski, Adam, and Henry Teune. *The Logic of Comparative Social Inquiry.* New York: Wiley, 1970.

Putnam, Robert D. *Making Democracy Work: Civic Traditions in Modern Italy.* Princeton, N.J.: Princeton University Press, 1992.

Pye, Lucian. "Introduction." In *Political Culture and Political Development,* ed. Lucian Pye and Sidney Verba. Princeton, N.J.: Princeton University Press, 1965.

Quandt, William. *Between Ballots and Bullets: Algeria's Transition from Authoritarianism.* Washington, D.C.: Brookings Institution, 1998.

———. "Hume and Quandt on Contemporary Algeria." *Middle East Policy* 6 (February 1999): 141–49.

Quarterly Economic Review of Morocco, no. 1 (1987).

Randall, Jonathan. "In Tunisia, a Fight against Theocracy." *International Herald Tribune,* June 7, 1991.

Rein, Natalie. *Daughters of Rachel: Women in Israel.* New York: Penguin Books, 1980.

Rejwan, Nissim. "The Two Israels: A Study in Europocentrism." *Judaism* 16 (winter, 1967): 97–108.

Rice, T. W., and J. L. Feldman. "Civic Culture and Democracy from Europe to America." *Journal of Politics* 39, no. 4 (1997): 1143–72.

Riding, Alan. "Tunisians, in Search of Roots, Turn toward Iraq." *New York Times,* October 10, 1990.

Rohrschneider, Robert. "Explaining Citizen's Views about Civil Liberties across the Globe: The Micro and Macro-Level Sources of Political Intolerance." Paper presented at the Annual Meeting of the American Political Science Association, San Francisco, Calif., 2001.

Rose, Richard. "Where Are Postcommunist Countries Going?" *Journal of Democracy* 8 (July 1997): 92–108.

Rose, Richard, William Mishler, and Christian Haerpfer. *Democracy and Its Alternatives: Understanding Post-Communist Societies.* Baltimore, Md.: Johns Hopkins University Press, 1998.

Ross, Jeffrey I. 1993. "Structural Causes of Oppositional Political Terrorism: Towards a Causal Model." *Journal of Peace Research* 30:317–29.

Rothchild, Donald, and Robert Curry Jr. *Scarcity, Choice, and Public Policy in Middle Africa.* Berkeley: University of California Press, 1978.

Rubin, Barry. "The Real Roots of Arab Anti-Americanism." *Foreign Affairs* 81 (November/December 2004): 73–85.

Rubin, David C., Tamara A. Rahhal, and Leonard W. Poon. "Things Learned in Early Adulthood Are Remembered Best." *Memory & Cognition* 26, no. 1 (1998): 3–19.

Ruddick, Sara. *Maternal Thinking: Toward a Politics of Peace.* New York: Ballantine Books, 1989.

Rudebeck, Lars. *Party and People: A Study of Political Change in Tunisia.* New York: Praeger, 1967.

Rudolph, Lloyd, and Susanne Rudolph. *The Modernity of Tradition.* Chicago: University of Chicago Press, 1967.

Ruedy, John. *Modern Algeria: The Origins and Development of a Nation.* Bloomington: Indiana University Press, 1992.

Rustow, Dankwart, and Robert E. Ward. "Introduction." In *Political Modernization in Japan and Turkey,* ed. Dankwart Rustow and Robert E. Ward. Princeton, N.J.: Princeton University Press, 1964.

Ryder, Norman B. "The Cohort as a Concept in the Study of Social Change." *American Sociological Review* 30 (1965): 843–61.

Sabagh, Georges. "The Challenge of Population Growth in Morocco." *Middle East Report* (March–April 1993): 30–35.

Sabagh, Georges, Jodi Nachtwey, and Mark Tessler. "Islam, Gender, and the Demographic Challenge in North Africa." Paper presented at the Annual Meeting of the Middle East Studies Association, Chicago, 1998.

Sahliyeh, Emile. "The State and the Islamic Movement in Jordan." *Journal of Church and State* 47 (2005): 109–31.

Sahliyeh, Emile, and Mark Tessler. "Experimentation with Democracy: The Cases of Jordan and Tunisia." Paper presented at the Annual Meeting of the American Political Science Association, 1990.

Saleh, Basel. "Economic Conditions and Resistance to Occupation in the West Bank and Gaza Strip: There Is a Causal Connection." Paper presented to the Graduate Student Forum, Kansas State University, April 4, 2003.

Salt, Jeremy. "Turkey's Military Democracy." *Current History* 98 (February 1999): 72–78.

Sanad, Jamal, and Mark Tessler, "Women and Religion in a Modern Islamic Society: The Case of Kuwait." In *The Politics of Religious Resurgence in the Contemporary World,* ed. Emile Sahliyeh. Albany: State University of New York Press, 1990.

Scaltsas, Patricia Ward. "Do Feminist Ethics Counter Feminist Aims?" In *Explorations in Feminist Ethics,* ed. Eve Browning Cole and Susan Coultrap-McQuin. Bloomington: Indiana University Press, 1992.

Schmitter, Philippe, and Terry Lynn Karl. "What Democracy Is . . . and Is Not." In *The Global Resurgence of Democracy,* ed. Larry Diamond and Marc Plattner. Baltimore, Md.: Johns Hopkins University Press, 1993.

Schuman, Howard, and Amy D. Corning. "Collective Knowledge of Public Events: The Soviet Era from the Great Purge to Glasnost." *American Journal of Sociology* 105, no. 4 (2000): 913–55.

Schuman, Howard, and Cheryl Rieger. "Collective Memory and Collective Memories." In *Theoretical Perspectives on Autobiographical Memory,* ed. D. C. Rubin, H. Spinnler, and W. Wagenaar, 323–36. Dordrecht, Netherlands: Kluwer, 1992.

————. "Historical Analogies, Generational Effects, and Attitudes toward War." *American Sociological Review* 57 (1992): 315–26.

Schuman, Howard, Cheryl Rieger, and V. Guidys. "Generations and Collective Memories in Lithuania." In *Autobiographical Memory and the Validity of Retrospective Reports,* ed. N. Schwarz and S. Sudman, 313–33. New York: Springer-Verlag, 1994.

Schuman, Howard, and Jacqueline Scott. "Generations and Collective Memories." *American Sociological Review* 54, no. 3 (1989): 351–81.

Scott, James. "An Essay on the Political Functions of Corruption." *Asian Studies* 5 (1967): 501–23.

Sears, David O. "Life-Stage Effects on Attitude Change, Especially among the Elderly." In *Aging: Social Change,* ed. S. B. Kiesler, J. N. Morgan, and V. K. Oppenheimer, 183–204. New York: Academic Press, 1981.

————. "On the Persistence of Early Political Dispositions: The Roles of Attitude Object and Life Stage." In *Review of Personality and Social Psychology,* Vol. 4, ed. L. Wheeler, 79–116. Beverly Hills, Calif.: Sage, 1983.

Sears, David O., and Nicholas A. Valentino. "Politics Matters: Political Events as Catalysts for Preadult Socialization." *American Political Science Review* 91 (1997): 45–63.

Seddon, David. "The Politics of 'Adjustment' in Morocco." In *Structural Adjustment in Africa,* ed. Bonnie K. Campbell and John Loxley. New York: St. Martin's, 1989.

Settersten, Richard A., Jr., and Karl Ulrich Mayer. "The Measurement of Age, Age Structuring, and Life Course." *Annual Review of Sociology* 23 (1997): 233–61.

Shamir, Jacob, and Khalil Shikaki. "Between Conflict and Reconciliation: Determinants of Reconciliation and Compromise among Israelis and Palestinians." *Journal of Peace Research* 30 (March 2002): 185–202.

Shanahan, Michael J. "Pathways to Adulthood in Changing Societies: Variability and Mechanisms in Life Course Perspective." *Annual Review of Sociology* 26 (2000): 667–92.

Shapiro, Robert Y., and Harpreet Mahajan, "Gender Differences in Policy Preferences: A Summary of Trends from the 1960's to the 1980's." *Public Opinion Quarterly* 50 (1986): 42–61.

Sharoni, Simona. *Gender and the Israeli-Palestinian Conflict.* Syracuse, N.Y.: Syracuse University Press, 1994.

————. "Is Feminism a Threat to National Security." *Ms. Magazine,* January– February 1993.

Sherill, Kenneth. "The Attitudes of Modernity." *Comparative Politics* 2 (1969): 184–210.

Shikaki, Khalil. "Palestinians Divided." *Foreign Affairs* 81 (January/February 2002): 89–105.

————. PSR Poll 19, March 16–18. Ramalleh: Palestinian Center for Policy and Survey Research, 2006. Available at http://www.pcpsr.org/survey/polls/2006/p19e.html (accessed September 10, 2010).

————. *Results of a Public Opinion Poll: The West Bank and Gaza Strip, September 29–30 and October 1, 1994.* Nablus: Center for Palestine Research and Studies, 1994.

————. "The Transition to Democracy in Palestine." *Journal of Palestine Studies* 98 (winter 1996): 2–14.

Shin, Doh Chull, and Huoyan Shyu. "Political Ambivalence in South Korea and Taiwan." *Journal of Democracy* 8 (July 1997): 109–24.

Sigel, Roberta. "Assumptions about the Learning of Political Values." *Annals* 361 (1965): 1–9.

Sigmund, Paul E., Jr. *The Ideologies of the Developing Nations.* New York: Praeger, 1967.

Smith, Tom W. "Gender and Attitudes toward Violence." *Public Opinion Quarterly* 48 (1984): 384–96.

Smooha, Sammy. "The Implications of the Transition to Peace for Israeli Society." *Annals of the American Academy of Political and Social Science* 555 (1998): 26–45.

————. *Israel: Pluralism and Conflict.* Berkeley: University of California Press, 1978.

Soudan, François. "Tunisie: islamistes contre 'albanais.'" *Jeune Afrique,* February 12, 1989.

Sprinzak, E. "The Psychopolitical Formation of Extreme Left Terrorism in a Democracy: The Case of the Weathermen." In *Origins of Terrorism,* ed. W. Reich, 65–86. New York: Cambridge University Press. 1990.

State of Israel. "State of the Economy: 1999–2000." Tel Aviv: Israeli Ministry of Finance, International Division, 1999. Available at http://www.finance.gov.il/ hachnasot/bud99/budget_e4.htm (accessed September 10, 2010).

Stevens, J. *Applied Multivariate Statistics for the Social Sciences.* Mahwah, N.J.: Erlbaum, 1996.

Stone, Russell. "Tunisia: A Single-Party System Holds Change in Abeyance." In *Political Elites in Arab North Africa,* ed. I. William Zartman et al. New York: Longman, 1982.

Strum, Philippa. *The Women Are Marching: The Second Sex and the Palestinian Revolution.* New York: Lawrence Hill, 1992.

Suleiman, Michael W. "Attitudes, Values, and the Political Process in Morocco." In *The Political Economy of Morocco,* ed. I. William Zartman. New York: Praeger, 1987.

"A Survey of the Arab World." *The Economist,* May 12, 1990.

Swirski, Barbara. "Israeli Feminism: New and Old." In *Calling the Equality Bluff,* ed. Barbara Swirski and Marilyn Safir. New York: Pergamon, 1991.

Sylvester, Christine. "Empathetic Cooperation: A Feminist Method for IR." *Millenium* 23 (1994).

Tachau, Frank, and Metin Heper. "The State, Politics, and the Military in Turkey." *Comparative Politics* 16 (October 1983): 17–33.

Tamari, Salim. "The Palestinian Movement in Transition: Historical Reversals and the Uprising." In *Echoes of the Intifada: Regional Repercussions of the Palestinian-Israeli Conflict*, ed. Rex Brynen. Boulder, Colo.: Westview, 1991.

Tawil, Raymonda. *My Home, My Prison*. London: Zed Books, 1983.

Telhami, Shibley. "Between Theory and Fact: Explaining American Behavior in the Gulf War." *Security Studies* (fall 1992).

———. *Reflections of Hearts and Minds: Media, Opinion, and Identity in the Arab World*. Washington, D.C.: Brookings Institution, 2006.

Telhami, Shibley, and Barry Rubin. "Anti Americanism—Due to What the U.S. Is or What the U.S. Does?" Policy Watch #811. Washington Institute for Near East Policy, December 2, 2003. Available at http://www.washingtoninstitute.org/templateC05.php?CID=1689 (accessed September 10, 2010).

Tessler, Mark. "Alienation of Urban Youth." In *Polity and Society in Contemporary North Africa*, ed. I. William Zartman and Mark W. Habeeb. Boulder, Colo.: Westview, 1993.

———. "Anger and Governance in the Arab World: Lessons from the Maghrib and Implications for the West." *Jerusalem Journal of International Relations* 13 (1991): 7–33.

———. "The Application of Western Theories and Measures of Political Participation to a Single-Party North African State." *Comparative Political Studies* 5 (1972): 175–91.

———. "Arab and Muslim Political Attitudes: Stereotypes and Evidence from Survey Research." *International Studies Perspectives* 4 (2003): 175–80.

———. "The Contribution of Public Opinion Research to an Understanding of the Information Revolution and Its Impact in North Africa." In *The Impact of the Information and Communication Revolution on Society and State in the Arab World*, ed. Jamal S. Al-Suwaidi. London: I. B. Tauris, 1998.

———. "Cultural Modernity: Evidence from Tunisia." *Social Science Quarterly* 52 (1971): 290–308.

———. "Democratic Concern and Islamic Resurgence: Converging Dimensions of the Arab World's Political Agenda." In *Democracy and Its Limits: Lessons from Latin America, Asia, and the Middle East*, ed. Howard Handelman and Mark Tessler. Notre Dame, Ind.: Notre Dame University Press, 1999.

———. "Development, Oil, and Cultural Change in the Maghreb." In *Arab Oil: Impact of the Arab Countries and Global Implications*, ed. Naiem Sherbiny and Mark Tessler. New York: Praeger, 1976.

———. "Do Islamic Orientations Influence Attitudes toward Democracy in the Arab World: Evidence from Egypt, Jordan, Morocco, and Algeria." *International Journal of Comparative Sociology* 2 (spring 2003): 229–49.

———. "Explaining the 'Surprises' of King Hassan II: The Linkage between Domestic and Foreign Policy in Morocco; Part I: Tensions in North Africa in the Mid-1980s." *Universities Field Staff International Reports*, no. 38 (1986).

———. "Image and Reality in Moroccan Political Economy." In *The Political Economy of Morocco*, ed. I. William Zartman. New York: Praeger, 1987.

————. "Islam and Democracy in the Middle East: The Impact of Religious Orientations on Attitudes toward Democracy in Four Arab Countries." *Comparative Politics* 34, no. 3 (2002): 337–54.

————. "Morocco: Institutional Pluralism and Monarchical Dominance." In *Political Elites in Arab North Africa,* ed. I. William Zartman et. al. New York: Longman, 1982.

————. "Morocco's Next Political Generation." *Journal of North African Studies* 5, no. 1 (2000): 1–26.

————. "The Nature and Determinants of Arab Attitudes toward Israel." In *Contemporary Antisemitism: Canada and the World,* ed. D. Penslar and J. Stein, 96–119. Toronto: University of Toronto Press, 2004.

————. "The Origins of Popular Support for Islamist Movements: A Political Economy Analysis." In *Islam, Democracy, and the State in North Africa,* ed. J. Entelis, 93–126. Bloomington: Indiana University Press, 1997.

————. "Political Change and the Islamic Revival in Tunisia." *Maghreb Review* 5 (1980): 8–19.

————. "Problems of Measurement in Comparative Research: Perspectives from an African Survey." *Social Science Information* 12 (1973): 29–43

————. "Regime Orientation and Participant Citizenship in Developing Countries: Hypotheses and a Test with Longitudinal Data from Tunisia." *Western Political Quarterly* 34 (December 1981): 479–98.

————. "Response Set and Interviewer Bias." In *Survey Research in Africa: Its Applications and Limits,* ed. William O'Barr, David Spain, and Mark Tessler. Evanston, Ill.: Northwestern University Press, 1973.

————. "Single-Party Rule in Tunisia." *Common Ground (AUFS)* 2 (1976): 55–64.

————. "Toward Scientific Cumulativeness: Operational Needs and Strategies." In *The Evaluation and Application of Survey Research in the Arab World,* ed. Mark Tessler, Monte Palmer, Tawfic E. Farah, and Barbara Lethem Ibrahim. Boulder, Colo.: Westview, 1987.

————. "Tunisia's New Beginning." *Current History* (April 1990): 169–84.

————. "The View from the Street: The Attitudes and Values of Ordinary Algerians." In *Islam, Democracy, and the State in Algeria: Lessons for the Western Mediterranean and Beyond,* ed. M. Bonner, M. Reif, and M. Tessler. London: Routledge, 2005.

————. "Women's Emancipation in Tunisia." In *Women in the Muslim World,* ed. Lois Beck and Nikki Keddie. Cambridge, Mass.: Harvard University Press, 1978.

Tessler, Mark, and Eleanor Gao. "Gauging Arab Support for Democracy." *Journal of Democracy* 16 (July 2005): 83–97.

Tessler, Mark, and Marilyn Grobschmidt. "The Relationship between Democracy in the Arab World and the Arab-Israeli Conflict." In *Democracy, War, and Peace in the Middle East,* ed. David Garnham and Mark Tessler. Bloomington: Indiana University Press, 1995.

Tessler, Mark, and Linda Hawkins. "Acculturation, Socioeconomic Status, and Attitude Change in Tunisia: Implications for Modernization Theory." *Journal of Modern African Studies* 17 (1979): 473–95.

Tessler, Mark, and Amaney Jamal. "Political Attitude Research in the Arab World: Emerging Opportunities." *PS: Political Science & Politics* 39 (July 2006): 1–5.

Tessler, Mark, and Jolene Jesse. "Gender and Support for Islamist Movements: Evidence from Egypt, Kuwait, and Palestine." *Muslim World* 86 (April 1996): 194–222.

Tessler, Mark, Carrie Konold, and Megan Reif, "Political Generations in Developing Countries: Evidence and Insights from Algeria." *Public Opinion Quarterly* 68, no. 2 (2004): 184–216.

Tessler, Mark, Mansoor Moaddel, and Ronald Inglehart. "Getting to Arab Democracy: What Do Iraqis Want?" *Journal of Democracy* 17 (January 2006): 38–50.

Tessler, Mark, and Jodi Nachtwey. "Economic Influences on Attitudes toward International Conflict: Hypotheses and a Test with Survey Data from the Arab World and Israel." Paper presented at the Annual Meeting of the International Studies Association, Minneapolis, March, 1998.

———. "Islam and Attitudes toward International Conflict: Evidence from Survey Research in the Arab World." *Journal of Conflict Resolution* 42 (1998): 619–36.

———. "Palestinian Political Attitudes: An Analysis of Survey Data from the West Bank and Gaza." *Israel Studies* 4 (spring 1999): 22–43.

———. "Partisan Preferences and Attitudes toward Peace among Palestinians in West Bank and Gaza Strip." Paper presented at the Annual Meeting of the American Political Science Association, August 1997.

Tessler, Mark, William O'Barr, and David Spain. *Tradition and Identity in Changing Africa.* New York: Harper and Row, 1973.

Tessler, Mark, Monte Palmer, Tawfic E. Farah, and Barbara Lethem Ibrahim. *The Evaluation and Application of Survey Research in the Arab World.* Boulder, Colo.: Westview, 1987.

Tessler, Mark, and Jamal Sanad, "Will the Arab Public Accept Peace with Israel: Evidence from Surveys in Three Arab Societies." In *Israel at the Crossroads,* ed. Gregory Mahler and Efriam Karsh. London: I. B. Tauris, 1994.

Tessler, Mark, and Ina Warriner. "Gender, Feminism, and Attitudes toward International Conflict: Exploring Relationships with Survey Data from the Middle East." *World Politics* 49 (1997): 250–81.

Tickner, J. Ann. *Gender in International Relations.* Ithaca, N.Y: Cornell University Press, 1992.

———. "Hans Morgenthau's Principles of Political Realism: A Feminist Reformulation." In *Gender and International Relations,* ed. R. Grant and K. Newland, 27–40. Bloomington: Indiana University Press, 1991.

Tinker, Irene, and Michele Bo Bramson. *Women and World Development.* Washington, D.C.: Overseas Development Council, 1976.

Togeby, Lise. "The Gender Gap in Foreign Policy Attitudes." *Journal of Peace Research* 31 (1994): 375–92.

Tress, Madeleine. "Halacha, Zionism, and Gender: The Case of Gush Emunim." In *Identity Politics and Women: Cultural Reassertions and Feminisms in International Perspective,* ed. V. M. Moghadam. Boulder, Colo.: Westview, 1994.

Triandis, Harry C., and Eunkook M. Suh. "Cultural Influences on Personality." *Annual Review of Psychology* 53 (2002): 133–60.

Tyler, Tom R., and Regina A. Schuller. "Aging and Attitude Change." *Journal of Personality and Social Psychology* 53 (1991): 133–60.

United Nations Conference on Trade and Development (UNCTAD). "Report on UNCTAD's Assistance to the Palestinian People." Geneva: United Nations, 1999.

Vandewalle, Dirk. *Autopsy of a revolt: The October Riots in Algeria.* Hanover, NH: Institute of Current World Affairs, 1988.

———. "Ben Ali's New Tunisia." Universities Field Staff International Reports, no. 8 (1989–90): 4.

———. "From the New State to the New Era: Toward a Second Republic in Tunisia." *Middle East Journal* 42 (1988): 602–20.

Verba, Sidney, Kay L. Schlozman, and Henry E. Brady. "Beyond SES: A Resources Model of Political Participation." *American Political Science Review* 89, no. 2 (1995): 271–94.

Wald, Kenneth. *Religion and Politics in the United States.* Washington D.C.: Congressional Quarterly Press, 1992.

Waldron-Moore, Pamela. "Eastern Europe at the Crossroads of Democratic Transition." *Comparative Political Studies* 32 (February 1999): 32–62.

Wallerstein, Immanuel. "The Decline of the Single-Party African State." In *Political Parties and Political Development,* ed. J. LaPalombara and M. Weiner. Princeton, N.J.: Princeton University Press, 1966.

———. "Introduction." In *Ghana and the Ivory Coast,* ed. I. Wallerstein and P. Foster. Chicago: University of Chicago Press, 1971.

Waltz, Susan. "Human Rights and Practical Ideology in North Africa, with Particular Attention to the Case of Morocco." Paper presented at the Annual Meeting of the Middle East Studies Association, San Antonio, Texas, 1990.

———. "The Islamist Appeal in Tunisia." *Middle East Journal* 40 (fall 1986): 651–71.

Ware, Louis B. "Ben Ali's Constitutional Coup in Tunisia." *Middle East Journal* 42 (fall 1988): 587–601.

Washington Institute for Near East Policy. "Anti-Americanism—Due to What the U.S. Is or What the U.S. Does?" Special Policy Forum Report of the Washington Institute for Near East Policy, December 2, 2003.

Waterbury, John. "Democracy without Democrats? The Potential for Political Liberalization in the Middle East." In *Democracy without Democrats? The Renewal of Politics in the Muslim World,* ed. G. Salamé, 23–47. New York: I. B. Tauris, 1994.

Weatherford, M. Stephen. "Political Economy and Political Legitimacy: The Link between Economic Policy and Political Trust." In *Economic Decline and*

Political Change: Canada, Great Britain, the United States, ed. Harold D. Clarke, Marianne C. Stewart, and Gary Zuk. Pittsburg, Pa.: Pittsburgh University Press, 1992.

Weinstein, Jeremy. "Resources and the Information Problem in Rebel Recruitment." *Journal of Conflict Resolution* 49 (2005): 598–624.

Weyland, Kurt. "Peasants or Bankers in Venezuela? Presidential Popularity and Economic Reform Approval, 1989–1993." *Political Research Quarterly* 51, no. 2 (1998): 341–62.

Whitaker, C. S., Jr. *The Politics of Tradition: Continuity and Change in Northern Nigeria 1964–1966.* Princeton, N.J.: Princeton University Press, 1970.

Wiktorowicz, Quintan. "Introduction." In *Islamic Activism: A Social Movement Theory Approach,* ed. Q. Wiktorowicz, 1–33. Bloomington: Indiana University Press, 2004.

———. *The Management of Islamic Activism: Salafis, the Muslim Brotherhood, and State Power in Jordan.* Albany: State University of New York Press, 2001.

Wilcox, Clyde, Joseph Ferrar, and Dee Allsop. "Group Differences in Early Support for Military Action in the Gulf." *American Politics Quarterly* 21 (1993): 343–59.

Wilcox, Clyde, Lara Hewitt, and Dee Allsop. "The Gender Gap in Attitudes toward the Gulf War: A Cross-National Perspective." *Journal of Peace Research* 33 (1996): 67–82.

Wilgoren, Jodi. "The Hijackers: A Terrorist Profile That Confounds the Experts." *New York Times,* September 15, 2001.

Witter, Willis. "Moroccans See Good, Evil in Possible Economic Boom." *Washington Times,* September 22, 1993.

Yousif, Sami. "The Iraqi-U.S. War. A Conspiracy Theory." In *The Gulf War and the New World Order,* ed. Haim Bresheeth and Nira Yuval-Davis. London: Zed Books, 1991.

Zalewski, Marysia. "The Women/'Women' Question in International Relations." *Millenium* 23, no. 2 (1994): 407–23.

Zartman, I. William. "Political Science." In *The Study of the Middle East: Research and Scholarship in the Humanities and Social Sciences,* ed. Leonard Binder. New York: Wiley, 1976.

———. "Tunisia: Transition to Democracy." Paper presented at the Tunisia Country Day Program of the School of Advanced International Studies, Washington, D.C., April 4–15, 1989.

Zghal, Abdelkader. "La guerre du Golfe et la recherche de la bonne distance." In *La Guerre du Golfe et l'Avenir des Arabes: débats et réflexions.* Tunis: Cérès Productions, 1991.

———. "The Reactivation of Tradition in a Post-Traditional Society." In *Post-Traditional Societies,* ed. S. M. Eisenstadt. New York: Norton, 1972.

INDEX

Italicized page numbers refer to tables.

MARK TESSLER is Samuel J. Eldersveld Collegiate Professor of Political Science at the University of Michigan, where he also serves as Vice Provost for International Affairs. He is the author, coauthor, or editor of thirteen books, including *A History of the Israeli-Palestinian Conflict* (IUP, 2009) and *Area Studies and Social Science: Strategies for Understanding Middle East Politics* (IUP, 1999). He has also published more than sixty scholarly articles based on public opinion research in the Middle East.